Essays on Culture, Religion and Rights

ECPR Press

ECPR Press is an imprint of the European Consortium for Political Research in partnership with Rowman & Littlefield International. It publishes original research from leading political scientists and the best among early career researchers in the discipline. Its scope extends to all fields of political science, international relations and political thought, without restriction in either approach or regional focus. It is also open to interdisciplinary work with a predominant political dimension.

ECPR Press Editors

Essays on Culture, Religion and Rights

Peter Jones

ecpr PRESS

ROWMAN & LITTLEFIELD
London • New York

Published by Rowman & Littlefield International, Ltd.
6 Tinworth Street, London, SE11 5AL
www.rowman.com

In partnership with the European Consortium for Political Research, Harbour House, 6-8 Hythe Quay, Colchester, CO2 8JF, United Kingdom

British Library Cataloguing in Publication Data
A catalogue record for this book is available from the British Library

ISBN: HB 978-1-78661-567-1

Library of Congress Cataloging-in-Publication Data

Names: Jones, Peter, 1945 December 19 - author.
Title: Essays on culture, religion and rights / Peter Jones.
Description: London ; New York : ECPR Press, [2020] | Includes bibliographical references and index. | Summary: "A rigorous examination of the issues raised by cultural and religious pluralism"—Provided by publisher.
Identifiers: LCCN 2020024785 (print) | LCCN 2020024786 (ebook) | ISBN 9781786615671 (cloth) | ISBN 9781786615695 (epub)
Subjects: LCSH: Cultural pluralism. | Religious pluralism. | Civil rights.
Classification: LCC HM1271 .J6565 2020 (print) | LCC HM1271 (ebook) | DDC 305.8—dc23
LC record available at https://lccn.loc.gov/2020024785
LC ebook record available at https://lccn.loc.gov/2020024786

To Emily, Franklyn and Ruben

Contents

Acknowledgments   ix

Preface   xi

Introduction   xiii

1   Political Theory and Cultural Diversity   1

2   Human Rights and Diverse Cultures: Continuity or Discontinuity?   31

3   Collective and Group-Specific: Can the Rights of Ethno-Cultural Minorities Be Human Rights?   53

4   Equality, Recognition and Difference   83

5   Bearing the Consequences of Belief   109

6   Belief, Autonomy and Responsibility: The Case of Indirect Religious Discrimination   129

7   Liberty, Equality and Accommodation   151

8   Religious Exemption and Distributive Justice   175

9   Conscientious Claims, Ill-Founded Belief and Religious Exemption   205

10   Blasphemy, Offensiveness and Law   229

11   Respecting Beliefs and Rebuking Rushdie   253

12   Religious Belief and Freedom of Expression: Is Offensiveness Really the Issue?   279

Index   297

Index of Legal Cases   303

Index of Statutes and International Instruments 305

Acknowledgments

The following chapters have appeared in earlier publications, as indicated below.

Chapter 1. Political Theory and Cultural Diversity
Critical Review of International, Social and Political Philosophy, vol. 1, no. 1 (1998), 28–62.

Chapter 2. Human Rights and Diverse Cultures: Continuity or Discontinuity?
Critical Review of International, Social and Political Philosophy, vol. 3, no. 1 (2000), 27–50.

Chapter 3. Collective and Group-Specific: Can the Rights of Ethno-Cultural Minorities Be Human Rights?
In *Ethno-Cultural Diversity and Human Rights: Challenges and Critiques*, ed. Gaetano Pentassuglia, 27–58. Leiden: Brill Nijhoff, 2018.

Chapter 4. Equality, Recognition and Difference
Critical Review of International, Social and Political Philosophy, vol. 9, no. 1 (2006), 23–46.

Chapter 5. Bearing the Consequences of Belief
Journal of Political Philosophy, vol. 2, no. 1 (1994), 24–43.

Chapter 6. Belief, Autonomy and Responsibility: The Case of Indirect Religious Discrimination
In *Authenticity, Autonomy and Multiculturalism*, ed. Geoffrey Brahm Levey, 66–85. London: Routledge, 2015.

Chapter 7. Liberty, Equality and Accommodation
In *Multiculturalism Rethought: Interpretations, Dilemmas and New Direc-tions*, ed. Tariq Modood and Varun Uberoi, 126–56. Edinburgh: Edinburgh University Press, 2015.

Chapter 8. Religious Exemption and Distributive Justice
This essay is published in full for the first time here. An abbreviated version was published in *Religion in Liberal Political Philosophy*, eds Cécile La-borde and Aurélia Bardon, 163–76. Oxford: Oxford University Press, 2017.

Chapter 9. Conscientious Claims, Ill-Founded Belief, and Religious Exemp-tion
In *Religious Beliefs and Conscientious Exemptions in a Liberal State*, ed. John Adenitire, 31–50. Oxford: Hart Publishing, 2019.

Chapter 10. Blasphemy, Offensiveness and Law
British Journal of Political Science, vol. 10, no. 2 (1980), 129–48.

Chapter 11. Respecting Beliefs and Rebuking Rushdie
British Journal of Political Science, vol. 20, no. 4 (1990), 415–37.

Chapter 12. Religious Belief and Freedom of Expression: Is Offensiveness Really the Issue?
Res Publica, vol. 17, no. 1 (2011), 75–90.

Preface

This collection of essays is a companion to my *Essays on Toleration* (London: ECPR Press/Rowman & Littlefield, 2018). The subject of this volume is broader than that of the previous collection. We tolerate only insofar as we object; if we do not object, we have no occasion to tolerate. Hence toleration, as a value and a practice, relates to cases in which people take exception to one another's differences. But people can hold different beliefs, belong to different cultures, pursue different ways of life, possess different preferences and exhibit many other sorts of differentiating characteristics whilst also taking no exception to one another's differences. Differences are not always therefore occasions for toleration. Yet, even when they are not, they can still give rise to difficult and contentious questions: What constitutes fair or reasonable arrangements for a society whose citizens associate themselves with different cultures or adhere to different faiths, including no faith? How far should a society go, if it should go any distance at all, in making special efforts to accommodate the different cultural or religious commitments of its citizens? And what should citizens who are committed to a particular culture or religious faith be able to demand of others who do not share their commitments? Those are some of the more basic questions this collection addresses. Ultimately, however, the various issues addressed in the two essay collections reduce to a single question: how should contemporary societies, particularly liberal democratic societies, respond to the diversities of belief, value and culture that now characterise their populations?

Each essay in this volume was originally published as a self-contained journal article or contribution to an edited collection and, since I have opted to republish each with as little textual revision as possible, the essays sometimes overlap in the issues they tackle and the arguments they make. I have left those overlaps in place so that each chapter will continue to make sense as a stand-alone essay.

I want to record my thanks to the participants in the workshop on 'The Role of the State in a Multi-Faith Society' that I ran with Stuart White of Jesus College, Oxford, some years ago as part of the AHRC/ESRC's joint research programme on Religion and Society, led by Linda Woodhead of Lancaster University. The workshop brought together political philosophers, academic and practising lawyers, and representatives of faith communities and was the most rewarding interdisciplinary meeting of minds that I have experienced during my career. The seeds of several of the essays republished here were sown during that workshop.

I am grateful to Ian O'Flynn and Albert Weale for encouraging me to compile this collection and for the stimulation and support they have provided for my work over many years. I am also indebted to Ian for his detailed comments on the content of this volume. I thank, too, Rebecca Anastasi, Madeleine Hatfield and Dhara Snowden of the ECPR Press and Rowman & Littlefield International partnership for their good-humoured assistance in preparing the volume for publication. Last, and certainly not least, I am indebted to my wife, Pat, for her support and encouragement and for tolerating my spending so much of my nominal retirement closeted in my study. She has provided the illustration for the book's cover, as she did for my *Essays on Toleration*. I dedicate this book to our three lovely grandchildren.

Introduction

How should contemporary societies, particularly those commonly described as 'liberal democratic', provide for the cultural and religious differences that characterise their populations? Many of those differences are not new. Most Western societies have long histories of religious division, which have sometimes been sources of bitter conflict, especially during the post-Reformation era. Many also exhibit long-standing differences of culture, such as differences of national identity or language, whose origins antedate the states within whose jurisdictions they now fall. But, during recent decades, immigration has markedly increased the cultural and religious plurality of Western societies. That relatively new source of difference has yielded societies that are not only more diverse but also more deeply diverse. For example, societies whose most salient religious differences once lay in different forms of Christianity now often possess large numbers of citizens who adhere to other faiths, such as Islam, Hinduism and Sikhism; they have become multi-faith rather than merely multi-denominational. Migrants coming from continents such as Asia and Africa have greatly increased the diversity of cultures now represented in European societies, as have movements of populations within Europe itself. Some liberal democratic societies, such as the United States, Canada, Australia and New Zealand, have majority populations who historically have themselves been the migrants or 'settlers'. Those populations have become no less multicultural than those of Europe, but their societies also encompass indigenous peoples, such as Native Americans, Aborigines and Maori, who present other, deep and comprehensive forms of cultural difference.

How should societies deal with those differences? Solutions have sometimes been found in self-government. Cultural differences have sometimes fuelled claims to political independence so that a cultural group can determine its own rules and arrangements. It is rarer for religious differences alone to ground claims to political independence, although they can contribute powerfully to them. The model, in such cases, is a pre-existing political unit which, rather than providing for cultural and religious differences, dissolves into separate units so that differences cease to exist within each unit. In other cases, different groups remain within the jurisdiction of a single state but possess a measure of self-government or 'autonomy' over their internal affairs. Indigenous peoples are often afforded arrangements of that sort, as are some minorities whose national or regional identities differ significantly from those of their wider society's population.

For the multiplicity of cultural and religious differences that now characterise Western societies, however, these sorts of arrangement are exceptions. Minority groups are too great in number and their memberships too dispersed for regimes of self-government to be feasible and, even if they were feasible, majority populations would resist the balkanisation that minority self-government would entail. Moreover, in general, cultural and religious minorities do not seek that sort of political separation and would be unhappy to swap the rules and arrangements they share with other citizens for subordination to a group-authority. Even in societies that devolve a measure of autonomy to indigenous peoples or minority groups, some rules and arrangements remain to which all citizens are subject, and the model I sketched above, in which the boundaries of political units map perfectly onto differences of culture and religion, is no more than a fantasy. With the possible exception of Iceland (which separated fully from Denmark in 1944), the populations of Western states do not exhibit the homogeneities which that model presupposes.

The members of culturally and religiously diverse societies need, therefore, to find a way of living together with their diversity. At least they do if they are to live together on terms that all of them can accept as reasonable and legitimate. A majority or a dominant group may, of course, impose its culture or its favoured religion on the rest of a society and be heedless of other cultural or religious allegiances, but we can reasonably insist that a response to diversity should be grounded in more than an assertion of power.

The idea of toleration has been extremely important for the development of ways of dealing with religious differences that move beyond outright conflict or repression (Jones 2018). Liberal democratic societies conceive themselves as committed to religious toleration, but they are also guided by an idea of equal toleration. In the past, regimes of toleration were frequently one-sided affairs. A ruling political power endorsed and upheld a particular denomination of a particular faith and, insofar as it extended toleration to other religions, it did so as a matter of grace and assigned them an inferior status and a less generous liberty than was enjoyed by the regime's favoured religion. Several contemporary states, such as Iran and Saudi Arabia, have regimes that still fit that description. However, liberal democratic regimes now subscribe to the idea that religious freedom is a right to which all are entitled and all should enjoy equally. They also accept that it is no part of the proper task of a liberal democratic state either to favour or to penalise any particular religion *qua* religion. They subscribe, in other words, to an even-handed conception of religious toleration. That conception can be nested in the larger idea that people have the right to live whatever form of life they choose, including a life guided by a religious faith, provided they do so in a manner that is consistent with others enjoying the same right.

These ideas are, of course, ideals, and not every liberal democratic state instantiates them perfectly. Some states, such as Denmark, England and Scotland, still have established churches, although nowadays their establishment does not take a form that impedes the practice of other religions. More importantly, the ideas of religious freedom and its equal possession do not interpret themselves. For example, freedom of belief may be absolute, but freedom to act never is. Where, then, should we set the limits of what may be done in the name of religion, and do we have greater reason to tolerate an objectionable practice if and because the practice is religious? Even if a religious practice is intrinsically unobjectionable, it may still come into conflict with a state's laws. A religion's dress code, for example, may be at odds with laws designed to protect citizens' health and safety, and ritual slaughter may take forms that conflict with a state's animal welfare legislation. What should happen in such cases? We can require that a state, in enacting laws and pursuing policies, should do so only for genuinely non-religious reasons but hold that, provided it meets that test, it should remain 'blind' to religious differences. It should, that is, require the religious, like others, to bear whatever burdens (or benefits) the law happens to bring their way. After all, equality before the law requires that all citizens should be subject to the same laws. Or we might hold that the state should be 'sensitive' to its citizens' religious convictions and do its best to accommodate them, so that, as far as possible, no group of citizens is disadvantaged relative to others for reasons of religion. That sensitivity would not require the state routinely to yield to the demands of people's religious convictions, but would require it to take account of ways in which its laws or policies affected religious groups adversely and, if the balance of considerations permitted, do something to avoid or mitigate that adverse effect.

Equivalent issues arise for cultural difference. We can include in the equal freedom of citizens to live the form of life they choose their freedom to live in conformity with their inherited culture if they so wish, subject to the usual qualification that they do so in ways that are consistent with the rights of others. But then, as before, we face questions about the proper scope of that freedom and about whether treating people fairly in respect of their cultures requires a state to be blind or sensitive to cultural differences. However, because the range of beliefs and practices encompassed by the term 'cultural' is so sprawling and inclusive, it is often difficult to know what constitutes equal or fair treatment of cultural differences. For example, we often cope with religious differences by assigning them to the private rather than the public sphere (where 'private' means neither 'behind closed doors' nor 'unshared with others' but only not subject to resolution through a society's political processes). But it can be more difficult to provide for cultural differences by operationalizing the public/private distinction and not feasible to insist that a state, in the conduct of its affairs, should be as bereft of cultural particularities as it should be of religious commitments. Public affairs have to be conducted in either a single language or a limited number of languages, for example, and legislators will sometimes have to resolve conflicts of belief and value which are also conflicts of culture. Moreover, factors such as the relative size of a group, its history in relation to the society in which it now exists, and its geographical concentration or dispersion within that society—factors that would normally be considered irrelevant to the religious freedom a group should enjoy—can bear significantly on the demands a cultural group can reasonably make of a society.

These issues arise internationally and globally as well as in the domestic governance of societies. The UN's Universal Declaration of Human Rights (UDHR), for instance, makes people's religious and cultural allegiances matters of human rights, as do its International Covenant on Civil and Political Rights and its International Covenant on Economic, Social and Cultural Rights, along with many of the more specific human rights declarations and conventions that the UDHR has spawned. Typically, those documents formulate their rights in highly general terms, which enable them to win easy endorsement. But when those rights are bent to earth and made to address the complicated realities of social life—as they are frequently, for example, by the European Court of Human Rights—what exactly they are entitlements to is often both far from clear and hotly contested.

What the terms 'culture' and 'religion' describe is easier to recognise than to define. Culture is particularly difficult to pin down because it is so comprehensive. It may reasonably be said to include everything that belongs to the social milieu in which a person exists and that contributes to that person's conception of the world and the form of life he or she leads. In discussions of cultural diversity, however, 'culture' is often used more narrowly to describe a way of life someone inherits from their forebears, although that inherited way of life can change as it passes across generations. We normally think of culture as a collective phenomenon—something that people share with others rather than an aura unique to each individual. That thought can easily lead to another: the patchwork conception of cultures, in which humanity is divided neatly into separate cultures, with each person belonging to a single culture and each culture having a content that demarcates it clearly from its neigh-

bours. Everyone agrees that the patchwork conception is a misleading carica-
ture. However we individuate cultures, we shall find they are internally diverse and share significant features with other cultures. Moreover, cultures
influence and interpenetrate one another, probably now more than ever, so
that our world is intercultural rather than simply culturally diverse.

Yet, however untidy and interwoven the reality of culture, we can still
intelligibly describe people as possessing different cultures and characterise
both humanity as a whole and particular societies as 'multicultural'. At least,
that is sufficiently the case for people frequently to identify a particular
culture as theirs, to assert claims in respect of it, and to worry about its being
subordinated to, or displaced by, other cultures. The exposure of cultures to
one another can result in a blending and blunting of their differences, but it
may also yield a heightened awareness and more jealous guarding of their
distinctive features.

Religion is a more tractable phenomenon than culture, and religions are
generally easier to individuate than cultures. Yet coming up with a formal
definition of religion that encompasses all and only the beliefs and practices
that we commonly identify as 'religious' is also notoriously difficult. I shall
not wrestle with that difficulty here. The religions that raise the issues I
examine in this volume are paradigm instances of 'religion' and would be so
regarded by legislatures and courts. There can, however, be contentious
cases, and legally much can hang on whether a body of belief is deemed
religious.[1] European jurisdictions often sidestep those difficulties by protecting 'religion or belief', a formula they have adopted from the European
Convention on Human Rights (ECHR), which the ECHR itself took from the
UN's UDHR whose rights include the freedom to manifest one's 'religion or
belief in teaching, practice, worship and observance' (Article 18). The formula 'religion or belief' can obviate the need for a precise definition of
religion since, if a belief has an uncertain claim to be religious, it can still
qualify for protection as a 'belief'. In truth, however, the formula merely
relocates the issue of definition, since courts and others have then to wrestle
with what counts as a 'belief' within its meaning.

The formula 'religion or belief' indicates that claims made for religions
need not be unique to them. If, for example, a society should go to special
lengths to accommodate the normative imperatives of its citizens' religions,
should it not be similarly accommodating of its citizens' non-religious conscientious convictions? The ECHR, in giving everyone the right to freedom
of conscience as well as religion (Article 9), implies that it should. Other
jurisdictions are less generous, at least formally. The US Constitution, for
example, protects the free exercise of religion but makes no similar provision
for cognate non-religious belief. The US Supreme Court has, even so, sometimes stretched the scope of the 'free exercise' clause to encompass non-
religious conscientious belief.[2]

Chapters 1 to 4 focus primarily on the claims of culture and the remaining chapters on those of religion. However, that division can be one of emphasis only; in the literature on diversity, issues that some characterise as religious others describe as cultural. Clearly, the two phenomena can be closely associated. A culture often encompasses a religion and a religion often stands at the centre of a culture and lends it coherence and normativity. Moreover, to present their relationship as one between separate phenomena can be to misrepresent it. Frequently the religious and the cultural are one and the same, so that a belief, practice or institution is describable as either. Nor is it easy to give one of them primacy. A religion can shape or radically change a culture, but religions are themselves significantly cultural in that so much in their traditions, institutions and practices goes beyond anything that can be found in a religious text. Cultures and the religions are not, of course, coextensive. Religions, such as Christianity, Islam and Buddhism, have been embraced by populations in different parts of the world whose cultures have remained significantly different. Conversely, the members of a population may embrace different faiths as well as different variants of the same faith and yet share a largely common culture in the conduct of their non-religious lives. The two are nevertheless frequently if unevenly associated.

CULTURES, RIGHTS, AND RECOGNITION

How, then, should we provide for cultural diversity? 'Culture' is frequently twinned with 'relativism'. Can we find in relativism reason to provide for the diverse cultures of humanity in an even-handed fashion? Cultural relativism holds that all of human life is cocooned within cultures, including our understandings of the world and the values we embrace. Hence, there is no non-relative territory upon which we can stand in order to determine what is right *simpliciter*, including how we might properly provide for cultural diversity. One culture may take a benign and respectful view of others; another may reckon that others are inferior to itself and undeserving of any form of respect. For the relativist, there can be no non-relative way of deciding between these conflicting perspectives. Relativism is therefore of little help to us.

A quite different approach suggests that humanity should regard its different cultures as a shared good. We should recognize that cultures are highly valuable human creations, from which we have much to learn and in which there is much to value. That is why we should cherish cultural diversity rather than view it as a problem to be solved or an inconvenience to be overcome. Much can be said in defence of this positive conception of cultural difference,[3] but we cannot be wholly content with it for two reasons. First, cultures conflict as well as differ. They often manifest conflicting conceptions of what is good or right and therefore cannot view one another with unqualified approval. Secondly, whatever merit we may find in one another's cultures, the shared good approach overlooks the special significance that a particular culture has for its bearers, and it is that significance that is typically to the fore in well-disposed efforts to provide for cultural diversity.

In Chapter 1, I propose a third approach which is driven by the idea of providing for cultural diversity fairly. On this approach, the ultimate objects of our concern should be not cultures but the people who bear them. Respecting cultures is really a matter of respecting and treating fairly those whose cultures they are. That, in turn, demands a perspective external to any particular culture so that we can deal with people's cultural differences in a neutral or impartial fashion. It is that perspective that the relativist dismisses as impossible, but there is nothing mysterious or extravagant about it. It requires only that we appreciate that others' cultures matter to them as ours does to us and that we respond to that appreciation by seeking to treat one another as bearers of different cultures, in an even-handed way.

I reject therefore the view that an impartial approach, which is separate from the diversity for which it seeks to provide, is implausible merely because the diversity at stake is cultural. More particularly, an 'external' perspective seems indispensible if the notion of dealing with cultural diversity fairly (or unfairly) is to make sense. The mere notion that there can be such a perspective, however, still leaves much to be settled. One issue concerns the proper scope of 'culture' itself. For the 'culturalist', culture is all-consuming, but others have reason to take a different view. People who take their religious beliefs seriously as beliefs, for example, have reason to deny that their beliefs are mere figments of culture, artefacts of nothing more than custom and tradition. Another issue is what should count as even-handedness: if people should have equal opportunities to live according to their cultures, what should count as *equal* opportunities? And does that equality suffice, or should cultures also be entitled to equal recognition (an issue I take up in Chapter 4)? A third issue concerns amongst whom we should seek to be fair. Cultures are group phenomena. Should our objects of concern therefore be groups rather than individuals and, if it should, how are we to individuate cultural groups and decide whose voice is to count as the authentic or authoritative voice of a group?

A fourth issue is whether fair provision for cultural diversity in a society need be a condition of equality for all cultures present in that society. Since I say little about that issue in Chapter 1 or elsewhere in this volume, I comment on it briefly here. Very often practicalities stand in the way of securing a condition of precise equality amongst the bearers of different cultures. A society can do much to ensure that its citizens are free to live in accordance with their inherited cultures insofar as they wish to, and it can use measures, such as discrimination law, to minimise the extent to which cultural alle-

giances become obstacles to the enjoyment of equal opportunity in education, employment and access to goods and services. But it can be difficult for
a society to represent the different cultures of its citizens equally in all
aspects of its public life, such as its system of law or the language or languages that it recognises as usable for public purposes. Thus, even in societies that are committed to multiculturalism, it is common to find that the
society's historical culture, or the culture of its 'host' population, has a pre-
eminence not enjoyed by the cultures of its migrant minorities.

The issue here is not one of practicalities only however. Suppose that a
minority of Greeks migrate to Poland and a minority of Poles migrate to
Greece. Practicalities aside, would we think it incumbent on each society to
reinvent itself so that it becomes Greek and Polish in equal measure? If not,
we must think that some asymmetry between the culture of the host society
and those of its migrant minorities is acceptable rather than merely unavoidable. Will Kymlicka, for example, has argued that, in opting to migrate,
people voluntarily relinquish the rights they possessed as members of their
original national culture. They do not forfeit all cultural rights and their new
society should offer them fair terms of integration, but they have no right to a
separate 'societal culture' (Kymlicka 1995: 94–100; 2001: 152–76). In addition, indigenous peoples, such as the Inuit in Canada and Aborigines in
Australia whose minority status is not of their own choosing, and national
minorities, who have become minorities through accidents of history such as
shifting state borders, are often thought to have stronger claims in respect of
their cultures than migrant minorities.[4] Note, however, that these asymme-
tries are justified by the way in which the bearers of different cultures in a
society are differently circumstanced. They do not reflect different evaluations of the cultures themselves or of their bearers, and to that extent they
remain consistent with the idea of dealing with cultural diversity impartially.

Cultural diversity is often thought to be especially problematic for the
idea of human rights. That idea ascribes rights to humanity at large, and the
cultural diversity exhibited by humanity as a whole far exceeds that to be
found within any society. But the challenge for human rights presented by
cultural diversity is more than merely circumstantial. Human rights thinking
is by its very nature universalist, and that can seem to place it fundamentally
at odds with cultures and their differences. If there is that conflict, human
rights theorists will have a hard time turning their doctrine into a global
reality. They will also confront powerful objections to the theory itself. Why
should the idea of human rights enjoy a privileged status? Why, given the
many different beliefs, values and ways of life to be found amongst humanity, should they be subordinated to and displaced by that idea?

How then might we reconcile human rights thinking with the fact of
cultural difference? I propose in Chapter 2 a way of conceiving human rights
that draws on the approach to cultural diversity set out in Chapter 1. I preface

that account with a distinction between two strategies we might pursue in seeking to reconcile human rights with cultural diversity: the 'continuous' and the 'discontinuous' (Dworkin 1990: 16–22).

A continuous strategy would aim to establish a continuity of content between human rights and the many different cultures to which human beings adhere. It would seek to uncover a core of value common to all cultures and use that core to supply the content of human rights. I catalogue a number of objections to that strategy, including the probability that a common core, if there is one to be found, would be too meagre to do the job and that, rather than seeking to provide for diversity, the continuous strategy seeks to avoid it.

A discontinuous strategy would aim for a separation—a 'discontinuity'— between human rights and the diversity of cultures for which they aim to provide. The job of human rights is not to eradicate or supplant cultural diversity, nor to compete with the many cultures that contribute to it. Its concern is with the people who possess cultures rather than the cultures they possess, and its purpose is to regulate the way in which people relate to one another as the bearers of different cultures. Human rights ascribe to human beings both an equal moral status and a right of equal freedom to pursue whatever culture they embrace. In ascribing that status and that right equally to all, human rights provide for human beings impartially and, more particularly, without reference to whatever cultures they hold. Thus, we can think of the diversity of cultures and belief as existing at a 'first level' and the regulation of that diversity by human rights as operating at a distinct 'second level'. It is by functioning at that different level that human rights aim to provide for, rather than to compete with, the cultures whose pursuit they regulate.

That division of labour will not, of course, remove every conflict between human rights and cultural difference. Insofar as the former ascribes equal moral status and equal rights to people, it must seek to override cultures insofar as they reject those equalities. The idea of human rights is also not the only candidate for a second-level role. A decision procedure which was unconstrained by rights and sought to deal with diversity purely procedurally, for example by use of a majoritarian decision rule, might also claim impartiality *qua* procedure. Or we might treat groups rather than individuals as the ultimate bearers of cultural rights. I do not pretend therefore that a discontinuous conception of human rights can be without controversy or that it can avoid every sort of conflict. I claim only that a discontinuous approach enables us to make sense of a world in which there can be both diverse cultures and rights common to humanity.

The question of the compatibility of human rights and cultural difference arises with reference to a more particular issue. Human rights theories and human rights declarations and conventions sometimes ascribe rights to ethno-cultural minorities. That is unremarkable insofar as they insist only that individuals belonging to minorities should enjoy the same fundamental rights as individuals belonging to majorities. Some of the rights ascribed to ethno-cultural minorities are, however, at odds with human rights as commonly conceived. First, cultures, nationalities, languages and the like are collective phenomena, and rights ascribed to ethno-cultural groups are sometimes assigned to them as groups rather than individually. Yet human rights are generally thought of as rights held by humans individually. Secondly, some rights ascribed to ethno-cultural minorities are 'group-specific'; they are special to minorities rather than general to mankind. But human rights are generally supposed to be universal to humanity, so can rights held only by some qualify as human rights?

Chapter 3 confronts those questions. It argues that whether group rights can be human rights depends on whether those rights are 'corporate' or 'collective' in conception. Traditionally, group rights have been understood corporately as rights possessed by groups as unitary entities which possess moral standing as those entities, a standing not reducible to that of their individual members. So understood, group rights cannot be human rights because the entities that hold them are not human beings. Conceived collectively, a group right is a right held jointly by the several members of the group, and the moral standing that underwrites their collective right is that of the several individuals who make up the right-holding group. So understood, a right's being a group right is no barrier to its being a human right. If people have human rights in respect of their culture, language or religion, for example, they may hold some of those rights individually and others collectively with those who share their culture, language or religion.

The proposition that rights can be simultaneously human and group-specific may encounter greater resistance. Some rights assigned to minorities are not truly group-specific. The UN's International Covenant on Civil and Political Rights, for example, provides that minorities shall not be denied the right 'to enjoy their own culture, to profess and practise their own religion, or to use their own language' (Article 27). It makes no mention of the equivalent rights of majorities, but that is only because majorities, since they are majorities, are unlikely to be denied rights to their culture, religion and language. Other human rights documents do, however, announce rights, such as language rights, that are genuinely different for majorities and minorities and also different for different minorities. Nor are ethno-cultural minorities unique in that respect. Some human rights are ascribed uniquely, for example, to women and to children. Can we make sense of that? We can, I argue, if what makes a right 'human' is the status in virtue of which it is held, rather than its being possessed indiscriminately by all. Of course, most of the rights we hold in virtue of being human will be possessed by all. But the rights people hold in virtue of their human status can vary according to their condition (e.g. childhood or indigeneity) or their circumstances (e.g. historical or social context). That is why the rights held by ethno-cultural minorities can sometimes be simultaneously human and group-specific.

The rights approach to cultural difference generally seeks to secure conditions in which people are free to live according to their cultures, insofar as they do not infringe the rights of others and do not suffer disadvantage for so doing. But is that enough? Demands for 'recognition' have become increasingly common in recent decades, including demands for the recognition of cultures. What exactly is the recognition that people now demand?

The term 'recognition' has several meanings. The most relevant here is recognition that positively affirms what it acknowledges. Recognition is something for which people are said to 'struggle', and they will struggle only for what they deem a gain. The political demand for recognition is also commonly a demand for equal recognition. Thus Charles Taylor observes that the politics of recognition demands that we recognise 'the equal value of different ways of being. It is this acknowledgement of equal value that a politics of identity-recognition requires' (Taylor 1992: 51). Hence, recognition requires us to acknowledge 'the equal value of different cultures; that we not only let them survive, but acknowledge their *worth*' (Taylor 1994: 64, emphasis in the original).

People have frequently struggled to be accorded a status already enjoyed by others; they have sought to be recognised, for example, as persons or citizens or human beings with rights. But more recently people have begun to demand recognition for what distinguishes them rather than for what they share with others. They demand recognition for their difference rather than their sameness, and the recognition they demand is merit recognition rather than status recognition. Thus, as Taylor indicates, the demand for equal cultural recognition has become a demand that we should recognise not merely people's equal status as the bearers of cultures but also the equal merit of their cultures. It is that demand that I question in Chapter 4.

Why should I accord recognition to your particular identity—because that recognition matters to you or because it matters to me? The obvious answer is because it matters to you. In that case, there must be a reason why what matters to you should matter to me because it matters to you. You must have moral significance for me in advance of and independently of your having a particular identity that you wish me to recognise. That moral significance will derive from my having reason to recognise you as a person or a human being or a fellow citizen or as someone with a similarly general and morally salient identity. Hence, it will be my recognising you as a person, for example, that gives me reason to recognise your particular identity. But, in that case, the notion that we should substitute recognition of people's particular identities for more general forms of recognition will be wrong-headed. My recognition of your particular identity must proceed by way of—must be mediated by—my recognising you under a more general identity, such as 'person'.

What is being recognised here? The answer is status rather than merit. When I recognise you as a person, I recognise you as having moral status. It is your having that status that gives me reason to take seriously what matters to you, including your particular identity, because it matters to you. Moreover, since people as persons have equal moral status, the status I recognise you to possess is a status you have equally with others. What recognition, then, am I according to your particular identity? Answer: I recognise it (only) as the identity of someone who possesses a morally significant status and a status equal with that of others. I also, by implication, recognise that your particular identity should receive whatever respect is due to the identities of people of equal status because they possess that status.

That recognition falls a long way short of merit recognition. But can we coherently demand merit recognition as a matter of right? Consider the demand for equal merit recognition of cultures. We can recognise a culture to be of merit only if we genuinely discover it to be so, and we can recognise all cultures to be equally meritorious only if we genuinely discover them to be so. Otherwise, our merit recognition can be only, as Taylor concedes, a disingenuous pretence. Moreover, as we have already noticed, cultures conflict as well as differ, and people cannot therefore subscribe to their own culture, including its beliefs and values, while simultaneously recognising the equal merit of others.

RELIGION, ACCOMMODATION, AND EXEMPTION

The subjects of Chapters 1 through 4 are broad-ranging. Those of Chapters 5 through 9 are more specific. Each relates to religion in particular, rather than culture in general, and each focuses on the issue of religious accommodation. 'Accommodation' here describes measures a society takes, or might take, in order to provide for the diverse commitments and ways of life of its citizens. Such measures are not new. Policies of religious toleration, for example, sought to deal with religious differences by giving citizens the freedom to pursue their different faiths. As noted earlier, those policies were often far from even-handed. There was, even so, a significant difference between societies that accommodated religious diversity through toleration, however unevenly, and those that sought to eliminate it through repression.

Nowadays policies of accommodation are pursued in a far more positive spirit. They are frequently associated with minorities of recent migrant heritage. That is because migrants often bring with them cultures and religions that are new to societies, at least as significant presences, and societies need to adjust their rules and arrangements to make room for them. Much accommodation is of a modest sort; it does little other than include new minorities in a society's existing arrangements. For example, the staffing of hospital and prison chaplaincies may be adjusted to provide for new religions. Efforts can be made to secure the representation of new minorities in a society's governing institutions, such as its legal system and police. Educational curricula may be amended. Health care may be delivered with a new sensitivity to cultural difference, and so on. Although I describe these sorts of accommodation as 'modest', they can involve large-scale and long-term policies of great significance both for minorities and society at large. They can also be controversial. How far, for example, should a society revise its educational curricula in order to suit new minorities, and how far should it expect those new minorities to adjust to its existing educational provision? These instances of accommodation are modest only in that they aim to include new minorities in the arrangements a society has already made for its population at large. They do not treat minorities differently from other members of the population.

There are, however, forms of accommodation that accord special treatment to particular groups, and it is the issues raised by that sort of accommodation that Chapters 5 through 9 examine. This sort of accommodation is often described as 'exemption' since its paradigm case is one in which the demands of a law conflict with the practice of a group, and legislators remove the difficulty in which that places the group by exempting them from the law. For example, in the UK during the 1970s, legislation was introduced requiring motorcyclists to wear safety helmets. That created a problem for Sikh motorcyclists who believed they should not remove their turbans. After a protest campaign, the government amended the law so that turban-wearing Sikhs were no longer required to wear a safety helmet. Some years later, the carrying of knives in public was legally prohibited. That too was potentially a source of difficulty for devout Sikhs who believed that they should comply with their religion's five Ks, one of which requires the carrying of a *kirpan* (a dagger or small sword). This time, however, a clause was written into the legislation exempting those who carry knives for religious reasons. Another example is the legal exemption granted to Jews and Muslims from UK animal welfare legislation so that they can slaughter animals according to the rites of their religions, which preclude the use of stunning. Exemptions of this sort are common in liberal democratic societies, although the picture is far from uniform. For example, Germany and the Netherlands, like the UK, currently make provision for unstunned ritual slaughter, while Denmark, France and Norway have banned the practice.

I have indicated that policies of accommodation can be targeted as features of a group's culture other than its religion. Religious exemptions are also sometimes described as 'cultural'. Those who prefer that description may believe that exemptions are more significant as accommodations of culture than of religion. I take the opposite view. It is no accident that almost all of the exemptions that might be described as cultural turn out to be religious, since their being religious is central to the case for their being exemptions, a claim I defend in Chapter 7.

I have associated accommodation with new migrant minorities, but that association can be misleading. Religious exemptions can also be directed towards 'old' minorities, such as religious Jews in Europe. Societies with a largely Christian heritage may, in spite of that heritage, include Christian groups who have reason to seek and who often receive exemptions. The Amish and the Hutterites of North America are notable examples. Exemption may also be an issue for more mainstream Christians, such as those who seek legal protection from employers' demands that they work on Sundays, or that they officiate at ceremonies for same-sex marriages or civil partnerships, or that they refrain from wearing religious symbols visibly in the workplace.

Another significant class of exemptions are those catering for conscientious but non-religious convictions. Exemption from military service on grounds of conscientious objection is one of the oldest and most widespread examples of exemption, and it is usually granted nowadays on grounds of non-religious as well as religious conscience. British law governing abortion exempts doctors and nurses from the obligation to participate in abortions if they conscientiously object to doing so, no matter whether their objection is religious or non-religious in foundation.

The issue of exemption therefore arises, actually or potentially, in a wide spectrum of cases. The paradigm instance of exemption is, as I noted above, statutory exemption, but in many societies exemptions are sourced in two additional ways.

A declaration of citizens' fundamental rights, including the right to freedom of religion, is a common feature of most liberal democratic states, and exemptions are sometimes grounded in those rights. The US Constitution provides that Congress shall make no law prohibiting the 'free exercise' of religion. The Canadian Charter of Rights and Freedoms recognises freedom of conscience and religion. The European Convention on Human Rights states that everyone has the right to freedom of thought, conscience and religion. Documents of that sort typically leave unspecified or vague what precisely the rights they announce are rights to. The task of specifying their precise content usually falls to judges, for whom it becomes inescapable when they are required to adjudicate disputed claims that a right has been violated or interfered with. Sometimes those claims arise because a society, or one of its institutions, has a rule that cuts across and impedes or 'burdens' the practice of a religion. The rule may well be religiously neutral in purpose and its disadvantageous impact unintended. Even so, its conflicting with a religious practice raises the question whether, in so doing, it infringes the right to religious freedom of those whose practice it burdens. In deciding such cases, courts are in effect deciding whether the religious claimant is entitled to be exempt from the rule. Some of the most celebrated issues of exemption, such as those represented by the *Sherbert* and *Smith* cases in the United States,[5] have arisen in that way.

A second important arena for exemption is law on indirect discrimination. Indirect discrimination arises when someone (e.g. an employer) has a rule or practice whose effect, though not usually its intention, is to disadvantage people of a particular identity relative to those of other identities and to do so in a way that is deemed unjustified. In Britain, the Equality Act 2010 provides comprehensively for discrimination in employment and in the provision of goods and services. It protects a number of characteristics from discrimination, including 'religion or belief'. The Act prohibits direct religious discrimination; for example, an employer's refusing to employ people because they are Muslim or because they are not Muslim. It also prohibits indirect religious discrimination. A person, A, discriminates indirectly against another person, B, if A has a 'provision, criterion or practice' (a PCP) that disadvantages B relative to those of other religions or none, and which A cannot show to be a 'proportionate means of achieving a legitimate aim'. If, for example, an employer has a dress code that disadvantages Sikhs relative to others because it conflicts with their religion's dress code, the employer is guilty of indirect discrimination unless she can show that her PCP (her dress code) is a proportionate means of achieving a legitimate aim. If she fails to meet that test, she need not abandon her dress code, but she must exempt her Sikh employees from it. British discrimination law on religion or belief has its origins in an EU directive of 2000[6] and is therefore European rather than peculiarly British in character. Indirect discrimination is prohibited in many non-European countries, including the United States.

In Chapter 5, I examine whether people's religious beliefs should entitle them to exemptions. Should not people take responsibility for, and so bear the consequences of, their beliefs? Consider the case of Mr Ahmad which provides my point of departure in that chapter. He was a schoolteacher and a Muslim who believed he should attend Friday prayers. His doing so meant that he was unavailable for part of the teaching day on Fridays, and other teachers had to cover for his absence. Eventually he was told that, if he continued to absent himself, he would have to transfer to a part-time contract. In response Mr Ahmad resigned and claimed constructive dismissal; his claim was rejected at every stage of the appeal process that followed, including his petition to the European Court of Human Rights. Was Mr Ahmad treated fairly? Should the school have accommodated his continued absence out of respect for his beliefs, or was he rightly required to bear the costs of his beliefs rather than offload them onto the school and its staff?

It seems reasonable to require religious believers to take responsibility for whatever beliefs they embrace and to bear whatever burdens their beliefs bring their way, but why? Unlike given features of ourselves, such as our race, sex or genetic endowment, beliefs are frequently said to be chosen, which is why it should fall to believers to meet whatever demands their beliefs make. Whether we can really be said to 'choose' our beliefs turns out, however, to be a contentious matter for both epistemological and sociological reasons. We might turn instead to the idea of freedom of belief, understood as the freedom both to hold a belief and to live according to its dictates. If we each have that freedom, it is reasonable that we should each meet the costs of the use we make of it rather than require others to pick up the bill.

That, however, does not conclude the matter since the consequence that Mr Ahmad encountered was not uniquely a consequence of his belief. It was a consequence of his belief combined with the fact that Friday is for the most part a working day in Britain. If Friday were to replace Sunday as Britain's non-working day, it would be Christians rather than Muslims who would confront Mr Ahmad's difficulty. How then should we take account of the dual origin of Mr Ahmad's predicament? I suggest that, in some cases, such as the construction of places of worship, the acquisition of religious artefacts or the conduct of pilgrimages, believers should bear the costs that their beliefs bring their way, even though those costs arise not from their beliefs alone but also from others' charging for labour and materials at going market rates. In other cases—cases that arise not from a society's standing background arrangements but from more particular measures, such as rules relating to safety helmets or the carrying of knives—it is reasonable to weigh the claims of religious believers against the considerations with which they compete and to exempt believers if the scales come down on their side.

In Chapter 6, I revisit (originally after a twenty-year interval) the issue of consequences and who should bear them, but in a different context: law governing indirect religious discrimination (IRD). Had that law existed at the time of Mr Ahmad's case, he may have fared better, although a court may still have ruled that a school's requiring all of its full-time staff to be available for the full working week was a 'proportionate means for achieving a legitimate aim'. The exemptions required by IRD law are unlike statutory exemptions in that the parties required to exempt are members of civil society—employers and providers of goods and services—rather than the state (although discrimination law applies to governments and government agencies in their roles as employers and providers). That again raises the question of where the costs of belief should fall. It does so particularly acutely when the costs, if they are shifted from the believer, fall upon individuals rather than large impersonal organisations such as commercial corporations or local authorities. That is illustrated by the sample case I use in Chapter 6, in which an employment tribunal required the owner of a small hairdressing salon to set aside the practice of requiring her stylists to show their hair in the style of the salon—a practice common in hairdressing salons and one that, as the tribunal acknowledged, was of particular importance for this salon—because a prospective Muslim employee would not remove her hijab while working there.

Here, as before, I argue that we can reasonably hold people responsible for the religious beliefs they embrace and for meeting the demands of their beliefs. But, as before, that can be only half the story since the consequences at issue arise not from a belief alone but from its intersection with an employer's or provider's PCP. How are we to make sense of the issue of consequences in the context of IRD law? I suggest that the assumption behind IRD law is that normal organisations (including religious organisations) should be able to pursue their normal aims through appropriate means without being impeded by the religious beliefs of others. That is why an employer's or a provider's using 'proportionate means to achieve a legitimate aim' is a defence against IRD. The 'proportionality' of a means should be understood in terms of its efficacy and indispensability for achieving an aim, assuming the aim to be 'legitimate'. An employer or provider is required to accommodate a religious believer only when the cost of her doing so is not significant, where 'significant' indicates that it would impede her use of proportionate means. Thus, up to the threshold set by 'significance' so understood, she must, if her PCP conflicts with a belief, exempt the believer. Beyond that threshold, her obligation to exempt ceases. That interpretation is, however, at variance with judicial practice which has adopted an understanding of proportionality that is more indiscriminately utilitarian than the understanding I propose.

While Chapters 5 and 6 address the issue of whether and when religious exemptions should be granted, they do not consider what justifies exemptions if they are justified. People can object to rules and arrangements, or to their incidental consequences, for all sorts of reason. Why, because an objection is driven by religious belief, should it count for more than objections of other sorts, including those that express people's 'ordinary' likes and dislikes? Why should religious preferences count for more than other sorts of preference?

Two distinguished contributors to debates on multiculturalism, Bhikhu Parekh and Brian Barry, have grappled with that question. Both couch the issue of exemption in the language of culture, although all of their leading examples are religious, and both take the idea of equal opportunity to be central to the justifiability of exemptions. Parekh (2006) argues that securing equality of opportunity in multicultural circumstances requires accommodation and exemption. He also argues that opportunity is a 'subject-dependent' concept in that the opportunities really available to people are limited by their cultural attachments: 'a facility, a resource, or a course of action is only a mute and passive possibility and not an opportunity for an individual if she lacks the capacity, the cultural disposition or the necessary cultural knowledge to take advantage of it' (2006: 241). Thus, an opportunity that requires a Sikh to remove his turban, or an Orthodox Jew to remove his yarmulke, or a Muslim woman to wear a knee-length skirt, is really no opportunity at all.

In response, Barry (2001) insists that people's opportunities are the choice sets objectively available to them. Individuals may have preferences that lead them to turn away from some opportunities, but those forsaken opportunities remain real opportunities. Thus, for Barry, equality of opportunity provides no reason why we should depart from general rules in order to accommodate people's cultural or faith-based wishes. On the contrary, such departures would treat people unequally and unfairly.

In Chapter 7, I challenge both authors' assumption that equality is the driving value behind exemption. I also side with Parekh in his debate with Barry over the nature of opportunity. As Parekh argues, opportunity does have a 'subject-dependent' dimension, but he misfires in characterising that dimension in terms of capacity, disposition and knowledge. The relevant consideration is rather that religions (or 'cultures' if that is how we choose to style them) incorporate obligations or other normative imperatives to which their bearers believe themselves subject. People are religiously or culturally 'unfree' to take up some opportunities, not because others prevent them or because they lack the relevant know-how, but because doing so would require them to set aside dress codes, dietary requirements, ritual practices and the like with which they believe they are obligated to comply. It is this which distinguishes, for example, the turban-wearing Sikh's unwillingness to wear a safety helmet from the thrill seeker's desire to ride a motorcycle bareheaded. It is also the prescriptive nature of religious beliefs that explains why they in particular, rather than cultures indiscriminately, are candidates for exemption. Of course, if it is not religious beliefs merely as such but their prescriptive nature which explains why they, but not 'ordinary preferences', should be candidates for exemption, we have reason to accept that people's non-religious conscientious convictions are also candidates for exemption; but that is surely as it should be.

Parekh and Barry are not alone in believing that the justifiability of religious exemptions turns primarily on the demands of equality. Equality is advanced more frequently than any other value by academic defenders of exemption. The belief that exemptees enjoy special privileges is, they argue, mistaken. A justified religious exemption merely prevents a minority's suffering a disadvantage that others would not. Properly conceived, exemptions are instruments of distributive justice.

In Chapter 8, I question whether distributive justice is the foremost issue presented by exemptions. I do not claim that exemptions are distributively unjust, nor that distributive justice has no bearing on them. Rather I claim that, for most exemptions, the principal issue lies elsewhere. Two distinctions are fundamental to the case I make. One is that between a distribution and its distribuend (what the distribution distributes). The other is between two types of distribuend: (a) the freedom to embrace, pursue and practise a religion and (b) the opportunity to enjoy non-religious goods, an opportunity that has the potential to be diminished for some because they subscribe to a particular religion. In Britain and many other European countries, the difference between these distribuends is reproduced in the difference between two bodies of law. Human rights law aims to protect people's freedom of religion. Law on indirect religious discrimination does not. It aims to protect people's opportunities in employment and in their access to goods and services from being diminished because of their 'religion or belief'. I leave for the moment the question of which distribuend is uppermost in statutory religious exemptions.

Exemptions granted by way of IRD law are, I concede, efforts to secure equality of opportunity, although I indicate in Chapters 6 and 7 how limited is the equality that IRD law aims to secure. Exemptions granted by way of human rights law are a different matter. Of course, all individuals have human rights equally (subject to the argument presented in Chapter 3 which we can overlook here). But, when a court confronts a claim that the right to religious liberty has been interfered with, the issue it faces concerns not the liberty's distribution; it is simply a given that all are entitled to the same religious liberty. Rather, it is the constitution of the religious freedom to which there is a human right: just how much does that freedom encompass; how far does it extend? In other words, the issue concerns the make-up of the distribuend rather than its distribution.

When we turn to statutory religious exemptions, some of those evidently aim, like human rights exemptions, to provide for religious or conscientious liberty; for example, exemptions from obligations to perform military service or to participate in abortions. Others are more plausibly conceived as exemptions that aim to preserve non-religious goods for the exemptees, such as those enabling Sikhs to ride motorcycles and to work on construction sites without wearing safety helmets. With many statutory exemptions, however, it is impossible to discern which distribuend has primacy. But even if we suppose it is a non-religious good, it is implausible to conceive the exemption as an exercise in distributive justice. Statutory exemptions are altogether too particular, occasional and contingent to be conceivable as constituents of an overarching scheme of distributive justice. They are more plausibly understood as exercises in adhockery, albeit adhockery for which there can be a good, all-things-considered, reason.

When law sets out to protect religious belief, which religious beliefs should it protect? Should they be whatever beliefs individuals hold, irrespective of how justifiably or unjustifiably they hold them? Or should beliefs be legally protected only if they meet an objective test, such as their being demonstrably grounded in the religious faith to which a claimant subscribes?

The prevailing orthodoxy amongst both Western judiciaries and liberal political theorists is that courts should use the first, 'subjective', approach. Provided courts are satisfied that a claimant's belief is sincerely held, they should not subject it to any objective test of validity, plausibility or reasonableness.

That orthodoxy can escape controversy so long as the claimant's freedom of belief demands no more from others than their non-interference. But suppose a claimant goes on to insist that her belief entitles her to an exemption. Exemptions are dispensations from rules with which others have to comply and often impose costs and inconvenience on others. Should we insist, even so, that nothing about the belief matters beyond the sincerity with which it is held? Suppose a claimant believes incorrectly that her faith requires her to do *y* and to refrain from doing *z*; should her error make no difference to her entitlement to an exemption?

In Chapter 9, I cite several cases that have raised that question. Not all went on to be tested in law, but some did and exposed divisions between judges and tribunal members on what the answer should be. Two justifications are commonly given for the subjectivist position, which differ in kind as well as content. One is a principled claim about the religious freedom to which there is a right. That right belongs to believers rather than to belief and therefore protects whatever believers happen sincerely to believe. A court which subjected a belief to an objective test of merit would violate that right.[7] The other justification is pragmatic. Judges are not equipped to rule on abstruse and contested issues of theology and should therefore abstain from any attempt to assess the merits of a claimant's belief.

The principled justification does not, I argue, withstand scrutiny. The pragmatic claim is less easily dismissed. It is not obviously true; courts often confront complex financial or medical cases, and judges do not wash their hands of such cases merely because they themselves lack financial or medical expertise. On the other hand, disputes concerning religious beliefs possess special features which make it understandable that judges should wish to avoid entanglement with them. We may conclude therefore that courts should adhere to the subjective orthodoxy but, if we do, we are accepting that pragmatism will sometimes justify an exemption to which, in principle, the exemptee has no right.

RELIGION, FREEDOM OF EXPRESSION, AND RESPECTING BELIEFS

The accommodation of religion seeks to remove obstacles or burdens that would otherwise hinder its practice. Controversies concerning religion and free expression have, in recent years, assumed a different shape. Rather than focusing on how we might safeguard religious practice, they have focused on whether the beliefs of the religious might justifiably limit other people's freedom of expression. The claims of religion and those of free expression need not be at odds. Historically, battles for freedom of expression have been in significant measure struggles to cast off the shackles imposed upon it by the dogmas and institutions of religion; but the growth of religious freedom has also gone hand in hand with the development of free expression. The freedoms to declare and defend a religious belief, to scrutinise and reject the beliefs of others, and to argue against religious belief of any kind are essential components of freedom of religion. To that extent, the two freedoms have gone together.

The degree to which societies in our world value and uphold those freedoms still varies greatly. As in previous chapters, I am concerned in Chapters 10 through 12 with religiously plural societies whose pluralism is accepted by those societies. More particularly, I take for granted that those societies embrace religious freedom and hold that each of their citizens is equally entitled to it. Yet, even if we assume that background, issues relating to religion and the proper scope of free expression remain. In Chapter 8, I argue that the principal issue raised by religious exemption is not whether freedom is distributed equally, but what should be the make-up of the freedom that is distributed equally. The same applies to freedom of expression. However generously or ungenerously we define the scope of free expression, we can still distribute it equally; so positing an equal right to freedom of expression does not tell us how extensive or limited that freedom should be.

What kind of limit upon free expression could then be accepted by a society committed to equal liberty in general and to freedom of religion in particular? Clearly it cannot be a limit grounded in a particular religion's claim to be uniquely true, accompanied by the claim that, since 'error has no rights', the propagation of beliefs at odds with itself should not be tolerated. If limiting speech is to be consistent with equal religious liberty, a limit must be justified by something other than the merit a particular religion claims for itself.

A justification which passes that test is curbing speech in order to prevent incitement to violence. That justification is widely accepted, and accordingly incitement to violence is commonly legally proscribed. Many broadly liberal societies also now have hate-speech laws prohibiting speech that either expresses hatred or that aims to incite hatred in others. Laws prohibiting religious hate speech have an obvious rationale. They protect religious adherents from treatment they should not have to suffer and safeguard a society against efforts to create disharmony and conflict amongst its members (Modood 2019; Waldron 2012). But they are not without problem, since so much turns on what 'hate' is reckoned to include. Those who adhere to a religion have an incentive to interpret 'hate' generously so that it includes negative comment on their faith. The elision of criticism with hatred is an especial danger in an era of identity politics when, by incorporating their faith into their identity, religious adherents are able to represent negative comments on their faith as assaults upon themselves.

I mention hate speech here primarily to distinguish it from the kind of expressions upon which I focus in Chapters 10 through 12: expressions that treat religious subjects in a coarse, ridiculing, mocking, obscene, scatological or otherwise offensive or disrespectful fashion. For the religious, expressions of that sort amount to desecrations of figures, symbols and texts central to their faith. Those expressions may be caught up with expressions of hatred, but they need not be and were not, for the most part, in the real-life cases to which I refer in Chapters 10 through 12.

Chapter 10 was prompted by the prosecution of *Gay News* and its editor, Denis Lemon, in 1979 for blasphemous libel. The English common law offence of blasphemy had existed for centuries but was, by the 1970s, generally thought moribund. That did not deter the campaigner, Mary Whitehouse, who successfully brought a private prosecution for blasphemy against *Gay News* for publishing a poem by James Kirkup recounting the homosexual fantasies of a Roman centurion as he removed the body of Christ from the cross. The case raised the question of whether, in a modern, plural and largely secular society, blasphemy should still be a legal offence. The law was eventually abolished, although not until 2008, by which time the introduction of a law prohibiting incitement to religious hatred had smoothed the path to its abolition. The case raised more general questions concerning whether people's most cherished religious beliefs should be open to obscene, scatological, mocking or other forms of negative treatment and, if they should not, on what grounds and to what extent they should be protected. Rather than disappearing, those questions have grown in prominence during the decades that have followed the *Gay News* case, particularly for those Western societies which, during that time, have become significantly multifaith.

A law prohibiting blasphemy as a religious wrong would obviously be problematic for a liberal democratic society but, by the end of the nineteenth century, the common law of blasphemy had been recast so that that was not its purpose. Judges ruled that even the fundamentals of Christianity could be attacked consistently with the law, provided the 'decencies of controversy' were observed. What the law prohibited were attacks that were 'calculated and intended to insult the feelings and the deepest religious convictions of the great majority of persons amongst whom we live'.[8] The law, in other words, sought to protect Christian believers rather than Christian belief, and it sought to protect them not from every sort of challenge but only from attacks that were deliberately offensive. That people should not be subjected to offensive treatment has become a common enough proposition in our own age. Moreover, once our purpose becomes protecting people from what they find offensive, we can, without inconsistency, extend that protection to all religious adherents whatever their faith.

Should we, then, protect the religious from offensive treatments of their beliefs? In Chapter 10, I give a sympathetic hearing to the case for taking offence seriously. I also notice the central place that the sacred has in most religions, which renders their adherents, especially and intelligibly, susceptible to offence. On the other hand, objections to the offensive have to compete with the many considerations that argue in favour of freedom of expression. If we are to prohibit the offensive, we have to find some non-arbitrary way of keeping our prohibition within bounds. I examine a number of possible criteria. None is problem-free and that, I conclude, provides reason to fight shy of using law to protect religious sensibilities.

The *Gay News* case was no more than a local curiosity compared with the global firestorm ignited by publication of Salman Rushdie's *Satanic Verses* in 1988. The book was widely and angrily condemned by Muslims for its insulting and blasphemous treatment of Muhammad and other figures sacred to Islam. Many non-Muslims, including leading representatives of Christianity and Judaism, expressed sympathy for the outraged reaction of Muslims. Calls were made for the book to be banned, and it was banned in several countries, including some in which Islam was not the majority religion. Fuel was added to the flames by a *fatwa* issued by the Supreme Leader of Iran, Ayatollah Khomeini, sentencing Rushdie to death and calling upon 'all zealous Muslims' to ensure that the sentence was carried out. Rushdie went into hiding for many years and survived without suffering physical harm. Some associated with his book were less fortunate, including its Japanese translator, who was stabbed to death by an objector.

Although the episode that came to be known as the 'Rushdie Affair' dwarfed in scale and duration the controversy that had surrounded the *Gay News* case, it raised similar issues; in particular, should a society require its members to defer to beliefs which they themselves do not share and, if it should, how far should that deference extend? In considering that question in Chapter 11, I turn away from offensiveness to a different idea: 'respect for beliefs'. That idea is an extension of the widely shared principle that we should respect one another's freedom to hold and to live in accordance with whatever religious beliefs we embrace; the respect we owe one another as believers should include not attacking one another's beliefs. Although I use the expression 'respect for beliefs', the respect the principle demands is really respect for people as the bearers of beliefs and only derivatively for the beliefs that they bear.

'Respect for beliefs' does not presuppose that the beliefs at issue are true. It can function therefore, like a requirement to refrain from offensiveness, as a principle that can be shared by the members of a plural society even though they differ fundamentally in their beliefs. In other ways, however, it differs from the idea of offensiveness. Respect for beliefs is a more objective requirement; it does not focus on people's mental states, and its demands do not vary according to the different subjective experiences that people undergo. The two ideas also have different ethical underpinnings. The notion that experiencing offence is 'bad' is essentially utilitarian in inspiration; the idea that people owe respect to others as believers is more deontological in character and foundation.

How demanding, then, is respect for beliefs? In a strong form, it could forbid challenges and criticisms that threaten to undermine people's beliefs. So interpreted, it would come up against the most imposing arguments for free expression, particularly J. S. Mill's argument that freedom of thought and discussion is indispensable if we are to appraise the truth of beliefs. Truth, it might be alleged, is irrelevant to religious faith, but no serious religious believer could accept that proposition. Thus, if the principle of respect for beliefs is to be plausible, it must be more modest in its demands. That takes us back to the 'decencies of controversy'. The most promising interpretation of those decencies turns on a distinction between 'manner' and 'matter': respecting others' beliefs should not limit the matter (the substance) of what we say but only the manner in which we say it. That distinction offers an attractive solution, since it limits free expression in an apparently unobjectionable way: if we are free to state the substance of a view, we can hardly object to being unfree to state it in an unnecessarily abusive fashion. The reality of disentangling manner from matter is however more difficult than the distinction's simplicity suggests. Nor does 'manner' capture all that objectors typically find objectionable. In the *Gay News* case, it was clearly the matter, rather than the manner, of James Kirkup's poem that resulted in a successful prosecution. Equally, it was *what* Rushdie was understood to have suggested about Muhammad and the Koran, rather than merely *how* he did so, that upset his Muslim objectors.

Recourse to the idea of respect for beliefs does not therefore provide us with a simple solution to the Rushdie Affair or to the many similar cases which have arisen since that episode, such as the controversies prompted by the Danish cartoons of Muhammad and the representation of Jesus Christ in *Jerry Springer: The Opera*. Why then substitute it for the idea of offence, particularly since people reach so readily for the language of offence in cases of this sort? In the years between writing Chapters 10 and 12, I became increasingly perturbed by the readiness with which people resorted to the language of offence and by the unreflective confidence with which they supposed that, in taking offence, they gained a knock-down objection to whatever they were offended by. In Chapter 12, I present a sceptical appraisal of that unreflective supposition.

To be offended is to undergo a negative experience. It is 'negative' in that it is unpleasant, disagreeable or 'disutile' in some other way. It is an 'experience' in that it describes a mental state. We may speak as though offensiveness is an objective property of what we find offensive, as when we say '*x* is offensive' rather than '*x* offends me', but, on inspection, offensiveness always refers to a mental state which *x* induces in a subject, such as a particular person or the typical person.

In some cases, we may be able to say little to justify our offence beyond insisting that it is the reaction we experience. That is often true of unmediated sensory offence: some sights are revolting, some tastes disgusting, and some odours foul. It is not true, however, of 'belief-based offence', in which an offended reaction depends on a belief about the wrongness of what has occasioned the offence. In such cases, our offended reaction indicates our negative appraisal of what offends us, and our objection properly resides in that negative appraisal rather than in any offence we experience.

Consider the analogous case in which we complain that someone's objectionable conduct makes us angry. Typically in such cases, our complaint is not that we are caused to experience anger. Rather, our anger is a response to the wrongfulness of the conduct, and it is the wrongfulness of the conduct about which we mean to complain. Similarly, if we complain that another's conduct is offensive, our real complaint is unlikely to be that we are caused to experience offence. Rather, it is the conduct itself to which we take exception. That point is evaluative as well as empirical in its significance. If someone uses the language of offence to complain about another's conduct, we should ask them *why* they find the conduct offensive, and it is the reasonableness and gravity of their objection that should determine the seriousness with which we take their complaint. If they can say no more than 'I just don't like it' or 'It offends me', they give us little reason to curb another's freedom.

In cases of belief-based offence, then, the claim to be offended should *eo ipso* count for very little. We should turn instead to the principle of respect for beliefs, which I outline in Chapter 11. That principle does not require us to assimilate objections to disagreeable experiences. It avoids difficult appraisals of the authenticity or intensity of the negative experience people claim to undergo, and it provides no reason to be more indulgent of the sensitive and the intemperate than of the resilient and the stoical. It is also closer in concern to what really matters to those who object to derogatory treatment of their beliefs.

I have indicated that, while the idea of respect for beliefs should weigh with us, we cannot rely upon it to determine in any simple or precise fashion where the boundary between the acceptable and the unacceptable should fall. Much will depend on context and circumstance and, even then, scope for reasonable disagreement is likely to remain. For those reasons, along with the strong case for free expression on religious matters, my conclusion re-

mains constant across Chapters 10, 11 and 12. We should not turn to legislatures and courts to prescribe where and when others' beliefs should limit our
freedom of expression; but our conduct should not be governed by law only.
It may be right, all things considered, that we should remain legally free to
say whatsoever we wish about people's religious beliefs and also howsoever
we wish; but we can still have good non-legal reason to curb the use we make
of that legal freedom.

The issues examined in these essays have several dimensions, some of
which—e.g. anthropological, sociological, theological—I leave largely un-
touched, partly because of the limits of my own competence. The essays are
primarily exercises in analytical political philosophy. The adjective 'analytical' indicates little more than their being efforts to deal with issues as clearly,
rigorously and accessibly as I can manage. Like most current work in political philosophy, the essays are often simultaneously exercises in moral philosophy. Perhaps less commonly, I make frequent reference to law. I do so
partly because the question 'what should law be?' is one that political philosophy ought obviously to address, and partly because legal cases frequently
reveal, as well as illustrate, significant aspects of that question. But I also
believe that political philosophers have much to learn from the reasoning,
concepts and distinctions that judges have developed in interpreting and
applying law. Finally, the essays are efforts to move between general moral
principles and practical issues of policy, and much of their content lies at the
applied end of the subject. Before long, the specific cases that provide their
causes célèbres will be overtaken by others but, as long as humanity continues to be culturally and religiously diverse, the larger questions raised by
those cases will persist.

NOTES

1. On which see Ahdar and Leigh 2013: 139–55, and Greenawalt 2006: 124–56.
2. E.g. *United States v. Seeger*, 380 U.S. 163 (1965); *Welsh v. United States*, 398 U.S. 333
(1970).
3. See Parekh (2006) for a particularly cogent statement of this defence.
4. For a qualified defence of this thought, see Patten 2014: 269–97.
5. *Sherbert v. Verner*, 374 U.S. 398 (1963); *Employment Division v. Smith*, 494 U.S. 872
(1990). The primary issue in *Sherbert* was whether a Seventh-Day Adventist, who lost her job
because she refused to work on Saturdays (her religion's Sabbath) and could not find another
job for the same reason, should nevertheless be entitled to state unemployment benefits. In
Smith, it was whether the members of a Native American church, whose religious practice
included smoking an hallucinogenic substance, peyote, should be free to smoke peyote even
though state drug laws banned its use. The two cases were celebrated, however, not for those
immediate issues but for the larger question they presented: how far should the Constitution's
'free exercise' clause entitle religious believers to be exempt from laws that were otherwise
constitutional?

6. EU: Council Directive 2000/78/EC, 27 November 2000. Law prohibiting religious discrimination was first introduced into Britain in 2003 for employment and in 2006 for the provision of goods and services. Both bodies of law were incorporated in the Equality Act 2010. Law prohibiting discrimination on grounds of religion and political opinion has existed in Northern Ireland since 1976.

7. I point out in Chapter 9 that courts do screen belief-based practices for their moral acceptability. A court will not, for example, protect a religious practice that violates a human right. However, moral acceptability and theological soundness are different matters.

8. The words are those of Lord Coleridge in *R. v. Ramsey and Foote* (1883), 15 Cox C. C. 231 at 238.

REFERENCES

Ahdar, Rex, and Ian Leigh. 2013. *Religious Freedom in the Liberal State*, second edition. Oxford: Oxford University Press.

Barry, Brian. 2001. *Culture and Equality: An Egalitarian Critique of Multiculturalism*. Cambridge: Polity.

Dworkin, Ronald. 1990. 'Foundations of Liberal Equality'. In *The Tanner Lectures on Human Values, XI, 1990*, ed. G. B Peterson, 1–119. Salt Lake City: University of Utah Press.

Greenawalt, Kent. 2006. *Religion and the Constitution, Vol. I, Free Exercise and Fairness*. Princeton, NJ: Princeton University Press.

Jones, Peter. 2018. *Essays on Toleration*. London: ECPR Press/Rowman & Littlefield.

Kymlicka, Will. 1995. *Multicultural Citizenship: A Liberal Theory of Minority Rights*. Oxford: Clarendon Press.

Modood, Tariq. 2019. 'Maintaining Civility and the Feelings of the Hated'. In his *Essays on Secularism and Multiculturalism*, 61–74. London: ECPR Press/Rowman & Littlefield.

Parekh, Bhikhu. 2006. *Rethinking Multiculturalism: Cultural Diversity and Political Theory*, second edition. Basingstoke: Palgrave Macmillan.

Rushdie, Salman. 1988. *The Satanic Verses*. London: Viking.

Taylor, Charles. 1992. *The Ethics of Authenticity*. Cambridge, MA: Harvard University Press.

Taylor, Charles. 1994. 'The Politics of Recognition'. In *Multiculturalism: Examining the Politics of Recognition*, ed. Amy Gutmann. Princeton, NJ: Princeton University Press.

Waldron, Jeremy. 2012. *The Harm in Hate Speech*. Cambridge, MA: Harvard University Press.

Chapter One

Political Theory and Cultural Diversity

In this chapter I examine some of the issues raised for political theory by cultural diversity. I shall suggest that how we should respond to social diversity depends, in some measure, upon how we characterise it and that characterising a diversity as 'cultural' steers us towards some strategies and away from others. I shall use a working assumption throughout that cultural diversity is something that we should be predisposed to accommodate and provide for rather than simply eradicate. Clearly there may be limits to how complete that accommodation either can be or should be, but there remains an obvious difference between attempting to provide for cultural diversity and seeking to destroy it. I shall argue that taking cultural diversity seriously entails providing for it fairly, and that providing for it fairly requires an impartial or neutral approach, the very sort of approach that is frequently dismissed as impossible by those who stress the significance of cultural difference.

Social diversity and the response it should receive have been major preoccupations of recent political theory. It has bulked large in liberal political theory, as one would expect given the concerns that underlie both past and present liberal thinking. But it has also preoccupied many political theorists who would not describe themselves as liberals and some who reject liberalism on the very ground that it fails adequately to provide for social diversity. 'Social diversity' is a phrase that encompasses many different types of diversity: differences in religious belief, in sexual conduct, in career aspiration, in family life, and so on. Why pick on cultural diversity? The answer might appear to be that it is a prominent form of social diversity and one that is particularly challenging for those who worry about how we can accommodate diversity, but that answer would be inadequate. Cultural diversity is not—like differences in religious faith or in aesthetic taste—just one more diversity that we can set alongside others. Cultures pretend to be all-embracing so that cultural diversity encompasses every kind of diversity that people exhibit in their lives. It therefore presents us with an interpretation of the totality of human diversity.

What are the fundamental features of what we think of, paradigmatically, as a culture? First, a culture is conceived as embodying a comprehensive form of life. It encompasses the whole range of human living: beliefs, values, aspirations, diet, clothing, music, economic forms and anything else that forms part of how we live. Nothing that makes up human living falls beyond the reach of culture. Second, a culture has a significant measure of internal integration and coherence. Rather than being a mere conglomeration of unrelated fragments of living, it consists of a coherent pattern of life typically held together by a common system of belief. There may be differences within a culture, but those differences are contained within a larger commonality. Third, cultures envelop their members. Each of us lives within a culture, and none of us is capable of being without a culture any more than we can stand outside our physical selves.

Fourth, cultures are humanly constructed. They are not naturally given features of the world like the physical constitution of the human body; they are humanly invented modes of life. But, fifth, cultures are not consciously constructed; they are not the self-conscious creations of those who bear them at any particular moment. Typically cultures are evolved and inherited so that human beings bear a culture they themselves have not created. In that respect cultures are like languages, which is unsurprising since languages are themselves constituents of cultures. People may, of course, alter and develop the culture they inherit, but that too is less a matter of conscious design than a consequence of unplanned shifts in circumstance and of myriad separate decisions. Finally, and following from the other features of culture, people are the creations of their culture. We do not determine, but are determined by, our culture. If we believe our lives to have been self-created, we suffer from an illusion or, at least, whatever authorship we might claim for ourselves has been achieved on terms, and within limits, set by our culture. Cultures may be human creations, but they are creations that rule their creators.

I do not make these statements as my own claims about the way the world is. Rather I present them as features of what, paradigmatically, we understand a culture to be and of how humanity appears when it is conceived as so many bearers of culture. For ease of reference, I shall describe this conception of the human condition as 'culturalism'. It is recognisable as a way in which many people talk about the world for much of the time. It is also a conception of the world that is open to challenge. For example, what we recognise as cultural differences in the real world are often more partial, fractured and impure than those suggested by the culturalist's model.[1] I shall myself point to other ways in which we may cast doubt upon culturalism.

However, for the most part, I shall simply take the world as the culturalist conceives it and consider how we might provide satisfactorily for its diversity. Even if our world is less neat and tidy than the culturalist's paradigm, we may still learn something about how we ought to deal with it by working from that paradigm.

In developing my argument, I shall make much use of the pronoun 'we'. This 'we', real or imagined, refers to ourselves conceived variously as political theorists or state officials or citizens of multicultural societies or members of a culturally diverse world. The common feature that 'we' possess is simply our confronting a diversity of cultures and having to decide what we should do, or what should be done, to provide for that diversity.

CULTURES AND RELATIVISM

Two features of culturalism explain why it is so often associated with relativism. First, if beliefs are constituents of cultures and if cultures are human constructions, then beliefs must also be human constructions. If we continue to describe beliefs as 'true' or 'false', they will be true or false only with reference to the culture to which they belong. They cannot be true or false merely as such. Second, culturalism seems to cancel the possibility of any non-cultural terrain on which we might stand in order to form a view of the world unmediated by a particular culture. Stepping outside our cultures seems no more possible than stepping outside our selves.

Culturalism therefore seems to ensnare us within relativism. But perhaps that does not matter. Perhaps relativism itself implies a prescription of how we should deal with cultural diversity.

Claims of cultural relativism come in different forms. The simplest of these is merely empirical: that, as a matter of fact, what people believe, value, and so on is peculiar to, and determined by, the culture to which they belong. That alleged fact is something we may have to take into account in structuring human arrangements but, of itself, it does not inform us what those arrangements ought to be.

A second form of relativism, and one that is prescriptive, holds that good or right conduct consists in each person's conforming to the norms of his or her culture. The French should follow the norms of French culture, Iranians should follow the norms of Iranian culture, the Inuit should conform to the norms of Inuit culture, and so on.

A relativism of this sort attracts some communitarians, but it has some puzzling features. Why should we wish to hold that it is right for individuals or groups to conform to the norms of their culture, and wrong for them to depart from those norms, independently of any estimate we make of the content of a culture? An answer might be found in the overriding value we should place upon sustaining community life but, if that is our answer, we have shifted to a form of universalism and asserted a value that pretends to be external to any particular culture. This relativist position also supposes that we can readily identify the norms of each culture, whereas, in reality, telling a Frenchman to conform to French culture and an Iranian to conform to Iranian culture will often leave them uncertain of just what they should do.

However, the merits or demerits of this sort of cultural relativism are not my immediate concern. I want to ask only whether it gives us a clear and common direction on how we should deal with cultural diversity. The answer, fairly obviously, is that it does not. All it requires is that we each conform to our culture. Thus, if our culture provides us with reason for tolerating or respecting the cultures of others, that is what we should do; if our culture demands no such respect—if, on the contrary, our culture demands that we spread it far and wide at the expense of other cultures—that is what we should do.

In the history of humanity, the second of these injunctions has been far from rare. That is, people have very often thought that others' cultures are *not* as good as their own and that they should strive to supplant others' cultures with their own. There is good reason for that. If cultures encompass people's beliefs about what is true and right, those within a particular culture must believe that the conflicting beliefs of a different culture are false and wrong. Thus, it is quite intelligible that people have frequently thought that they are justified, and perhaps duty-bound, to replace the cultures of others with their own 'better' culture.

A third form of relativism is content to assert only that there are no standards that we can apply across all cultures to assess their value. Values are themselves cocooned within cultures, and there can be no values above or outside cultures that can serve as external standards of assessment. We can therefore judge no culture better than any other. That claim is sometimes associated with the assertion that all cultures are of *equal* value, but an assertion of equal value implies a cross-cultural judgement of the very sort that this relativism excludes. If cultures are incommensurable, there can be no estimate of their relative value, including no claim that they are of equal value or that none is better than another. All that incommensurability implies is that no culture can be *reckoned* better than another.

This negative claim takes us some way towards a case for accommodating cultural diversity in that it eliminates one argument that might be brought against that accommodation: that some cultures, because of their superiority, ought to prevail over others. But that alone is not enough to make a case for promoting or protecting or tolerating cultural diversity, for it does not establish that there is anything wrong or regrettable about one culture's displacing another. It removes one possible justification that might be given for that displacement, but it provides no reason why we should hold that it is positively wrong or undesirable that one culture should prevail over or displace another.

So, unsurprisingly, cultural relativism provides us with no clear indication of how we should respond to cultural diversity. More particularly, if we are searching for a reason for tolerating or respecting or cherishing that diversity, we shall not find it in cultural relativism. Relativism provides us with little more than a shrug of the shoulders.

If we are to find any reason for giving value to cultural diversity and if we are to develop a strategy for providing for that diversity, we have to achieve two related things. First, we have to find normative significance in something's being *a* culture rather than only in the things that make up our *own* culture. Second, we have to climb out of the perspective of any particular culture and address the world of cultures, as it were, 'from the outside'. Now, as I have already observed, culturalism in one of its voices denies that that second move is possible. Yet it is a move that culturalism has itself already made. Culturalism does not present itself as the expression of a particular culture. It presents itself as a true description of the cultural make-up of the world, a description that presupposes that we can view that world from the outside. All of the general claims about cultures that make up what I have called 'culturalism' presuppose that external perspective. Culturalism therefore belies any claim it might itself make about the impossibility of viewing the world independently of any particular culture.

In going on to examine the issues posed by cultural diversity, I want to distinguish two perspectives from which that diversity might be viewed. The first is what I have just described as the 'external perspective' and is exemplified by culturalism itself. It is the perspective of someone who looks upon the world of cultures as if he were positioned outside or above that world and is therefore able to view it as an external observer. I shall contrast that with the 'internal perspective'—a perspective internal to a particular culture. When people view cultural diversity from that perspective, they look out upon the world from inside their particular culture.

CULTURAL DIVERSITY AS A COLLECTIVE GOOD

With that distinction in place, let me now turn to the question of how we might find normative significance in diverse cultures rather than only in a specific culture. Various sorts of answers might be given to that question. I shall distinguish two and focus on the second.

The first type of answer proposes that cultures are valuable not only or primarily for those whose cultures they are; rather they are valuable at least potentially for everyone. Cultures, it is sometimes said, are highly valuable human creations; they add to the valuable things present in the world, and we should seek to sustain them for that reason. We all stand to benefit from the different modes of life, forms of understanding, aesthetic products, culinary traditions and so on that cultural diversity places before us. If a culture disappears, our world is poorer for it.[2]

This form of valuing implies a fundamentally non-distributive approach to cultural diversity. The multiplicity of cultures is conceived as a good common to all humanity. Of course, if we adopt this view, we must still confront questions about how we should manage the competing or conflicting features of cultures within a single society or among humanity at large. But, fundamentally, those questions will not be questions about how we can fairly distribute goods amongst people with different and competing cultural interests; rather they will be about how we can best maintain and promote cultural diversity as a good in which we all share.

There is a great deal that recommends this view. The world is certainly richer for the diverse forms of music, literature, art and so on that emanate from different cultures. But there are reasons why we are unlikely to find the collective good approach an adequate response to the phenomenon of cultural diversity from either an external or an internal perspective. If we approach cultural diversity from an external perspective, we can endorse that diversity as good only if we bring some notion of the good to that judgement. That is not necessarily problematic, but it is worth noticing that claims about the good of cultural diversity are typically made in a form that implies the external perspective and that relies upon a notion of the good that is grounded independently of the diversity that they value. In addition, it is unlikely that any such notion of the good would be indiscriminate in according value to diverse cultures, though again that feature of this approach need not rank as a failing.

Something that is more obviously a failing is that the collective good approach, on its own, takes no account of the special value that each person's culture has for that person. Even if everyone can find something of value in everyone else's culture, we surely suppose that each culture has a value special to those whose culture it is. It is wholly inadequate to give significance to a culture only insofar as it has value for humanity at large. An adequate response to cultural diversity must recognise the special significance that each culture has for its bearers.

If we shift to an internal perspective, it is certainly possible that the members of one culture will find things of value in the cultures of others. For example, the literatures and musical forms of others' cultures may resonate with those of our own and have value for us in spite of their origins in another's world. But things become more problematic when cultural diversity exhibits conflict—conflicting beliefs and conflicting values. Can we really be happy to regard the world as better for the existence of diverse beliefs many of which we reckon to be false, diverse values many of which we regard as mistaken, and diverse practices many of which we believe to be bad? Although I pose this question in a semi-rhetorical fashion, the answer does not have to be an unqualified 'no'. If we accept that there is reasonable doubt about which beliefs are false and which values mistaken, including the beliefs and values that we ourselves hold, we may welcome a diversity which keeps a number of possibilities open and alive for humanity. In still more generous mood, we might reflect, after the manner of John Stuart Mill, that, even if we are certain that our own beliefs are true, there is merit in their continuing to be challenged and questioned.

Yet, although we may sometimes find compensating merit in what we reckon to be the error of others, that is clearly a hazardous foundation upon which to rest the good of cultural diversity. The internal perspective is much more likely to result in a selective appreciation of cultural diversity: when we look out upon the world from our own cultures, we will endorse those aspects of others' cultures that, from our own internal perspective, appear to be good and reject those that seem bad. That, in turn, is likely to result in different and conflicting conclusions about what sort of cultural diversity there should be. The sort of cultural diversity that an Iranian Shi'ite Muslim might be persuaded to accept may well differ from that endorsed by a French republican atheist. In other words, conceptions of the collective good of cultural diversity may themselves be diverse in a culturally related fashion. If that is so, appeals to the good of cultural diversity will evoke responses that reproduce that diversity rather than secure a consensus on what sort of diversity there should be.

DEALING FAIRLY WITH CULTURAL DIVERSITY

While there is much to be said in defence of the collective good argument, we cannot expect it to provide comprehensively for cultural diversity. We need an approach that recognises that each culture has special value for its bearers and that aims to deal fairly with cultural differences, rather than one that insists only that those differences provide a good that is equally and identically a good for everyone. We need to take seriously the 'diversity' in cultural diversity and to consider how we might provide for it fairly.

Once we move to a distributive notion such as fairness, we have to decide who or what it is that we should be fair amongst. The answer suggested by the phrase 'cultural diversity' is 'cultures', but that cannot be right since cultures are not themselves moral entities to which we can intelligibly owe obligations of fairness. Insisting that we should be fair to cultures merely as cultures is like insisting that we should be fair to paintings or to languages or to musical compositions. These things may have value, but they do not have moral standing. We might speak of 'wronging a culture' or of 'treating a culture unfairly', but that is only because we sometimes use 'culture' as a shorthand expression for a group of people distinguished by a culture. So, if we seek to deal fairly with cultural diversity, it is not cultures that will be the ultimate objects of our concern, but the people who bear them. Respecting cultural diversity becomes a matter of respecting the people who exhibit that diversity.

This approach to cultural diversity goes most readily with an external perspective, and I shall begin by examining the issues it raises from that perspective. I shall assume that, from this perspective, we wish to deal fairly with cultural differences because we believe people should be treated with equal concern and respect. That assumption leaves open the question of whether, in dealing with cultures, the ultimate objects of our concern and respect should be the groups who bear cultures or the individuals who make up those groups; I postpone consideration of that issue for the moment. (I use 'people' in a way that is deliberately ambiguous between these two possibilities.) It also leaves unanswered why concern and respect for people should entail concern and respect for their cultures. It is not implausible to deny that there must be a link here: if I believe that someone is imprisoned in a stultifying and oppressive culture, my concern and respect for them might reasonably issue in an effort to emancipate them from their cultural bonds. But, insofar as we suppose that respecting people requires respecting their cultures, we are likely to do so for two sorts of reason.

One reason focuses upon identity, upon who people are. If people are absorbed by a culture to the extent that culturalism suggests, who they are cannot be divorced from the culture to which they belong. We cannot both respect people and dismiss their cultures, for their very identities are tied inextricably to their cultures. Thus, Kantian thoughts about respecting people, either as individuals or as groups, must extend to respecting their cultural identities.

A second reason focuses upon well-being. If people's lives are lived within a culture, if everything that gives structure and meaning to their lives is derived from their culture, their well-being will be inextricably caught up with their culture. Anything that damages or diminishes their culture must damage or diminish their well-being. What makes for human well-being is, of course, highly controversial. But, if we accept that people's lives are as completely and as inextricably caught up with their cultures as culturalism suggests, we can agree that their well-being is tied to their culture even though we might otherwise disagree about what makes for human well-being. Thus, if our concern is to protect and promote people's well-being, that must also take in a concern for their cultures.

These two reasons need be at no great distance from each other. Indeed, while some may insist that identity has an independent moral significance, others will hold that identities matter only for what they contribute to people's well-being. I shall express no view on the merits of the two well-known philosophical positions represented by these two reasons and none on whether one might satisfactorily subsume the other. If we are convinced by either or both, we have strong reason for translating our concern and respect for people into a concern and respect for their cultural particularities. If, in addition, we are committed to treating people with *equal* concern and respect, we must deal with their cultural particularities in an even-handed or fair way.

Dealing with cultural differences fairly, against this background, requires that we deal with them neutrally or impartially.[3] By a 'neutral' or 'impartial' strategy, I mean one that is not drawn from any particular culture; that does not seek to privilege any particular culture; and that, as far as possible, allows or enables people to live according to their own cultures and refrains from imposing alternative modes of life upon them. The last of these three elements of impartiality is necessary if we are to show concern and respect for people's cultural identities, and the first two are required if we are to show that concern and respect equally.

There are various tests we might use to help us think through this strategy, such as a Rawlsian original position in which the veil of ignorance hangs between people and their cultural identities, or a Scanlon/Barry test of reasonable rejection (Barry 1995; Rawls 1971, 1993b; Scanlon 1982). I do not wish to be distracted by the question of which philosophical technique better models impartiality of the sort I intend here. However, the approach I am describing is clearly inspired by a distinction between the right and the good of a sort that is fundamental to theorists such as John Rawls and Brian Barry. They seek not to arbitrate on which of many diverse conceptions of the good is the best or the most truthful conception. Rather, they withdraw from that issue and move to a different plane of argument, one which considers how we might provide justly and impartially for individuals who possess different conceptions of the good. Similarly, the approach I am describing here refrains from ranking cultures in an order of merit and seeks only to provide impartially for people who possess different cultures. The split between the principles that are to regulate cultural diversity and the cultures that they regulate parallels that between the right and the good. Of course, some of what is contained within cultures may be more naturally described as 'principles of right' than as 'conceptions of the good'. But that does not matter. We can still distinguish principles contained within diverse cultures from principles designed to provide fairly for diverse cultures.

Political theories that claim impartiality or neutrality are frequently dismissed as naive and bogus, and the claim that we can deal with cultural diversity impartially is especially likely to attract these charges (e.g. Young 1990: 96–116). But it is difficult to understand why this claim should be found so extravagant or implausible. Recall that, strictly, we are aiming to be fair not amongst cultures but amongst the people who bear them. We are not therefore required to gain an even and comprehensive insight into the detail of every particular culture. Nor need there be any attempt to assess the relative merits of different cultures as a prelude to trading off their competing claims. The task is simply to deal with people committed to their cultures in an even-handed manner.

Moreover, many of those who complain about the fraudulence of impartiality are unwilling to give up their claims that we should respond to people's differences 'equally' or 'fairly' or 'justly'. But any of those responses must surely incorporate some notion of impartiality. It is also surprising to find reproachful accusations of 'bias' set alongside assertions of the impossibility of impartiality. If we dispense with any notion of impartiality, how can we condemn, or even identify, bias? People may, of course, hold that different cultures ought not to be treated impartially, though, as I shall explain in a moment, that is often because they reckon that something more than 'culture' is at stake. However, among those who do insist that cultural diversity should be dealt with fairly or justly, I want to claim that the real issue is not whether we should be impartial but what form that impartiality should take. In particular, although impartialist or neutralist approaches are commonly associated with liberalism, the impartiality at issue here need not take a liberal form.

Before developing that claim, I want to switch to the internal perspective and consider whether any idea of dealing fairly with cultural diversity might emerge from that perspective and, if so, how. At first sight, the prospects may seem bleak. If we each look out upon the world from our cultural bunkers, we may seem incapable of having any thought about the outside world except that it is strangely unlike our own and perhaps that it ought to be more like our own. We may also seem unlikely to have aspirations that relate to the outside world except possibly to refashion it in the image of our own. But that prognosis is unjustifiably pessimistic. What I want to suggest is that people can readily move from an internal to an external perspective.

If I, from my culture, look out at you in your culture and you, in your culture, look back at me in my culture, we can see one another as each situated in a culture and as each committed to that culture. We can see that we are symmetrically situated and symmetrically committed. I can see that your culture matters to you as mine does to me, and you can see that my culture matters to me as yours does to you. We can therefore begin to conceive what it is to be someone possessed of a culture, why in general terms cultures matter, why I cannot reasonably expect you to be less concerned about your culture than I am about mine, and why you cannot reasonably expect me to be less concerned about my culture than you are about yours. In other words, we can begin to see ourselves as just one culture-bearing group in a world of many culture-bearing groups and to think about what might be a reasonable arrangement for that world taken as a whole, rather than thinking only within the confines of our own culture. We can begin to conceive of ourselves and our situation as these appear from the 'outside', to see ourselves as others see us and as we see them. We are then in a position to think impartially about cultural diversity even though we are ourselves part of that diversity.

Achieving an external perspective of this sort does not require that we somehow shed all our cultural particularities and mutate into decultured ciphers. It requires only that we come to see our cultural particularities as particularities, to place them in a context of many particularities, and to appreciate that others' particularities matter to them as ours do to us. An external perspective is not, therefore, something that displaces and replaces our internal perspectives; rather it is something we can add to our internal perspectives.[4]

Of course there can be no guarantee that people's thoughts will in fact take this direction. I am concerned only to rebut the belief that there is something about *cultural* diversity that makes an impartial response either impossible or peculiarly difficult. In fact, there is one respect in which regarding diversity as cultural makes an 'impartial' and 'fair' response peculiarly appropriate and acceptable. Consider, by way of contrast, a diversity of belief about what is true or morally right, where 'true' and 'morally right' are understood in full-blooded senses such that everyone involved accepts that only one set of beliefs can be correct. Here there is real conflict among people and, given that they are at odds over a single truth or a single right, it is not obvious that the appropriate response to their conflict is a distributive one invoking an idea of fairness. We might, for example, say that all of the individuals involved have the same overriding interest in lighting upon the single correct belief, rather than any special interest associated with their particular belief merely because that happens to be the belief they currently hold. If my beliefs are true, I have an interest in their prevailing, but only because they are true; if they are false I, along with everyone else, have an interest in their rejection.[5] If people's beliefs become detached from their interests in this way, it is not at all clear that we should respond to a diversity of belief as though we were confronting a set of competing interests that needs to be brokered in a fair way.

Consider how the picture changes if everyone is willing to subsume their beliefs and values within the concept of culture. In that case, they will no longer conceive themselves as in dispute over a single truth or a single right. Rather, they will see themselves as separated only by their different inherited modes of life and ways of thinking and by the investment each of them has in a particular mode of life and a particular way of thinking. They differ rather than disagree: they are not really engaged in a 'conflict' at all, in the sense of a tussle over what is uniquely true or right. They simply exhibit different traditions, different humanly constructed ways of thinking and forms of life, that result in different and possibly competing demands that need to be regulated in a fair way. Thus, if we are willing to think of our differences as cultural, we are peculiarly well-placed to think of them as *merely* differences and to acknowledge that they ought to be dealt with in an even-handed fashion.

Indeed, the real difficulty with which the internal perspective presents cultural diversity is not that it rules out any prospect of people coming to think in terms of a fair way of dealing with that diversity. Rather, it lies in whether people are willing to regard their differences as merely 'cultural'. If they are, then, as I have just explained, that should facilitate rather than impede their acceptance of one another's differences and their readiness to see them dealt with in an impartial fashion. But people may well reject the proposition that their differences are properly or adequately described as 'cultural'. For example, neither party in the dispute between evolutionary theory and creationism is likely to accept that their dispute is adequately or properly characterised as a clash of cultures. Rather it is a dispute about what really is true about the origins of mankind and other species. Likewise, while academic theologians may perform all sorts of tricks that claim somehow to reconcile religion with relativism, most ordinary people who have serious religious beliefs hold those beliefs as truth-claims about the existence of a deity, about what that deity requires of them, and so on. They could not accept that religious beliefs were merely cultural constructs without undermining the very beliefs that they hold. The real problem, then, is not that there is an incompatibility between cultural diversity and an impartial handling of that diversity. It is that the culturalist's description of the world is not the only possible description of the world nor one that stands in a neutral, second-order relation to other possible descriptions of the world. It is a controversial description that many people are likely to reject.

If that is so, we have to cope not merely with a social diversity all of whose features are objectively given, but with a diversity of conceptions of that diversity. The culturalist's conception of the world becomes itself part of the diversity with which we have to deal. That takes us on to the larger question of whether it is possible to conceptualise diversity in a form that is both comprehensive and unskewed towards any particular way of seeing the world. That is too large and difficult a question to pursue here. Having noticed that conceiving diversity as 'cultural' is itself contestable, I shall simply leave unanswered the question of how we should handle that contest. Instead, I want to return to the question of what is involved in dealing fairly and impartially with a diversity that we are content to regard as cultural.

WHAT SORT OF IMPARTIALITY?

Being impartial amongst cultures must mean responding to them equally. But what form should that equal response take? We can answer that question differently, and the idea of impartiality alone seems unable to tell us which answer is right. Consider, by way of example, two different views on this issue.

The first view endorses what we might describe as cultural *laissez-faire*. Each culture must take its chances in the world as we find it. If some cultures fare better than others, so be it. We must allow people to live according to the cultures with which they align themselves, but we have no obligation to intervene to even up the circumstances of cultures or to take special steps to assist cultural groups whose continued viability is threatened by their failure to retain a critical mass of adherents. Chandran Kukathas's approach to cultural diversity falls within this view (Kukathas 1992a, 1993; see also Gray 1993: especially 264–68).

A second view holds that we should try to secure conditions in which each group is equally able to enjoy its culture. If the culture of one group is in danger of being overwhelmed by that of a larger group, we should take steps to ensure that the minority can enjoy its culture on terms roughly equal with those of the majority. Will Kymlicka, for example, argues that a culture, as a context of choice, is a Rawlsian primary good and that we should try to create conditions in which everyone can enjoy that primary good roughly equally. If an indigenous minority finds its culture threatened by that of the larger society in which it exists, it may need to receive special rights that will help protect its culture. These 'group-differentiated' or 'community-specific' rights do not violate impartiality; they simply correct for the unequal circumstances of cultural groups and secure a more genuine equality (Kymlicka, 1989, 1992, 1995).[6]

These two views illustrate the difference between negative and positive forms of impartiality.[7] The first, negative, view embargoes any measure designed to advantage or disadvantage particular cultures but recognises no obligation positively to equalise their circumstances. Its neutrality is of the 'hands-off' variety. The second, positive, view seeks to deal impartially with cultures by correcting (some if not all of) their unequal circumstances. Its neutrality is regulative and requires that we equalise the background conditions of cultures rather than leave them undisturbed.[8] There may be reasons for favouring one of these views over the other, but those, I suggest, cannot be reasons of impartiality, for both views can claim to respond impartially to cultural diversity: neither draws on a particular culture or aims to privilege a particular culture or seeks to supplant a culture with an alternative form of life.

Consider a third view, one that requires a still more positive approach. It demands 'equal recognition' for cultures, where 'recognition' requires that we acknowledge not only the importance that each culture has for its bearers but also the 'good' of each culture. If we refuse to endorse the worth of a culture, we fail to treat it equally. On this view, it is not enough that we allow, or provide for, each group to live according to its culture while ourselves taking either no view or an adverse view of the intrinsic value of that culture. We are required to recognise both the worth and the equal worth of each culture.

Although my primary concern here is to cite rather than to evaluate different impartialist approaches to cultural diversity, I shall pause to say a little more about this third view since the demands of 'equal recognition' are significant and problematic in a number of ways. If cultural diversity presents us with a number of different and conflicting conceptions of what is good, and if our task is to find a way of accommodating that conflictual diversity, it seems odd to begin by insisting that everyone recognise that all cultures are equally good. That simply ignores the nature of the diversity that we confront. Equal recognition also requires us to bring a common standard of value to all cultures and to believe that, whatever the appropriate standard is, all cultures will perform equally when judged against it. That seems plainly incredible. Unlike the collective good approach which asks us to believe only that there is *something* of value in each culture, equal recognition insists that we find precisely *equal* value in each culture.

Equal recognition, then, seems to demand more from us than it is reasonable to require. So why might it be insisted upon? The answer, as Charles Taylor suggests, lies in the conjunction of culture and identity (Taylor 1994). If we must show equal respect for people, and if people's identities are embedded in their cultures, it becomes difficult to respect their identities equally while valuing their cultures unequally. That is perhaps why Taylor himself—even though he catalogues the many problems that attend the assertion of equal worth, including the absurdity of insisting that we must, as a matter of moral obligation, find the judgement of equal worth to be true—still proposes that we should operate with a 'presumption' of the equal worth of all cultures (1994: 63–73).[9] Axel Honneth, too, sees the 'struggle for recognition' as one that will not be complete until it has secured mutual approval and endorsement amongst people for their different particularities and ways of life (Honneth 1995: especially 121–39).

The fundamental problem with the demand for recognition in this strong form is the contradictory commitments it asks people to accept. People are allowed to believe in the worth of their own culture, including the beliefs and values that it embodies, yet they are also required to believe that others' cultures, embodying different and conflicting beliefs and values, are of no less worth. How can we expect people to embrace that absurdity? The problem eases considerably if people are prepared to adopt the perspective of culturalism. If they are willing to regard all beliefs and values, including their own, as no more than cultural constructs, then, as I explained earlier, it will be very much easier for them to find one another's cultures acceptable. A diversity of belief and value will become little different in character from a diversity in mode of dress or form of etiquette. A judgement of equal worth will also be less problematic, though still not unproblematic. As before then, one critical matter here is whether people are prepared to accept the culturalist's description of themselves. They may very well not be but, even if they are, it is not clear why they should go on to discover that all cultures are of equal value. What culturalism is more likely to yield is a merely negative belief: the belief that cultures are incommensurable so that there is no foundation for judging one culture better than another. Still, if what drives the demand for equal recognition is an anxiety about achieving equal respect for people's cultural identities, that merely negative belief may be enough to remove any epistemic or evaluative obstacle to securing that respect.

'Equal recognition', as I have described it here, involves a judgement about the 'good' of cultures and may therefore seem improperly described as an impartialist view. It certainly differs from approaches which seek impartiality by abstaining from any assessment of the relative merit of cultures. But the impartiality at issue here is not, in the first instance, neutrality on any matter concerning the relative value of cultures; it is impartiality amongst people who bear cultures. It is hard to see how equal recognition would not qualify as impartial in that second respect.

We might still, of course, regard this sort of equal recognition as a mistaken or misguided form of impartiality, but that is part of my point. Impartiality alone is not enough. We have to decide upon the sort of impartiality we should bring to cultural diversity. It might be alleged that, in making that decision, we must be drawing upon a particular culture and so forfeiting any claim to impartiality just as some critics allege that, as soon as we give substance to principles of right, we must be drawing upon a conception of the good. But that is entirely unconvincing. Different forms of even-handedness can be identified quite separately from the cultures to which they might be applied. Thus disputes about the response appropriate to cultural diversity and dismissals of certain forms of response that claim impartiality need not be evidence that an impartial approach is either bogus or unsustainable. All it may indicate is that people are at odds over the *kind* of impartial response that we should make to cultural diversity and therefore over what constitutes a fair or just response to that diversity.

IMPARTIALITY AMONGST WHOM?

Another dimension of this issue, and one that has often led people to mistake different forms of impartiality for different expressions of partiality, concerns the identity of those amongst whom we should be impartial. If we are to be fair in our handling of cultural diversity, amongst whom should we be fair? To whom is our obligation of respect owed? Who or what should be the ultimate object of our moral concern?

Immediately, there seem to be two possibilities: individuals and groups. In fact, that simple division is too simple since, if we opt for groups, we have to confront a further question: which groups? But, for the moment, let me work with a simple distinction between individuals and groups.

Must that distinction be practically significant? It may not be. If a culture is the focus of a perfect consensus, responding to the cultural interests of a group and responding to cultural interests of its individual members will require the same things. But cultures are rarely entirely homogeneous; there are usually degrees of difference and dissent within them. In a multicultural society and, indeed, in a multicultural world (a world in which there is increasing interaction between different cultural groups) this sort of division and dissension is likely to be exacerbated, since the interpenetration of cultures often promotes heterogeneity and tension within populations that had previously experienced greater uniformity. Whether we adopt an external or an internal perspective, therefore, we are likely to confront conflicting claims about who constitutes a cultural entity, about what a particular culture requires, about who can speak authoritatively for a culture, and about the respects in which people's lives should or should not be subject to a particular culture. We then have to decide to which voices we should respond. In the first instance, this issue is one of moral standing: to whom should we accord ultimate standing, to individuals or to groups?[10] It is easy to mistake what that choice entails. If we suppose that it simply reproduces the tired and imprecise distinction between individualism and collectivism or the somewhat clearer distinction between liberalism and communitarianism, we shall be misled. If we attribute moral standing only to individuals, we can still allow that individuals have shared interests in collective goods and that the interests they share with others are no less significant than those they possess on their own. Indeed, as Joseph Raz has effectively shown, one can even ascribe rights to groups while ascribing moral standing only to their individual members (Raz 1986: 207–8). A number of individuals may share an interest in a good, and their joint interest in that good may be of sufficient moment to justify their having a right to that good and others having the duties that that right entails; yet, if we were to consider only the interest of a single member of that group, that would not suffice to ground the relevant right. Thus individuals can hold a right jointly (a 'group right') that none of them holds individually.

Consider, for example, the specific case of cultural rights. Suppose we have a body of people who form a cultural minority and who, for all the usual reasons, have an interest in the continuance of their culture, but who find their culture in danger of being overwhelmed by that of the majority society. The interest of any single member of the minority in the maintenance of his culture is unlikely to be adequate to justify imposing duties upon the majority society to institute measures to protect and sustain the culture of the minority. But the joint interest of all the individuals who make up the cultural minority in the maintenance of their culture may well suffice, so that the members of the cultural minority will possess a right jointly that none of them possesses individually. In that way, we can ascribe a right to a group of individuals *qua* group even though we invest the group with no moral standing that is not reducible to the independent moral standing of its individual members.

What is at issue here, then, is not whether we should recognise that people have collective interests, nor whether individual interests should count for more or less than collective interests, nor even whether groups or only individuals can hold rights. It is rather whether we should attribute moral standing to individuals only or whether we can and should ascribe moral standing to groups *qua* groups. If we decide upon the latter, morally, we shall conceive a group as a single integral entity whose moral claims are in no way reducible to the claims of its individual members even though, sociologically, we may agree that the group is constituted only by its members. If the group has rights and if rights are grounded in interests, its rights will be grounded in its interests *qua* group entity ('group-individual') rather than in the several, if identical, interests of its individual members.

What practical difference does it make where we locate moral standing? One answer is that it determines to whom we should listen and to whom we should respond. Imagine that we confront a community which allegedly possesses a common culture but in which people are divided over what that culture requires and perhaps over whether their lives should continue to be governed by that culture. If we give moral standing to individuals, we shall be obliged to listen to all individuals and to take account of all their interests in reaching a decision about how we should respond to the community. That does not mean that, in any clash of wishes between individuals and majorities, we must prioritise individuals over majorities. Nor, as I have already explained, does it mean that we can ignore interests that people share jointly with others or give people's shared interests less significance than their individual interests. What it does mean is that all individuals must count: in reaching our decision, we cannot simply ignore certain individuals as if they were morally of no consequence.

If, on the other hand, we treat the community as a group that has moral standing *qua* group, our approach will be quite different. We shall try to discover the true and single cultural interest of the group *qua* group or, perhaps more likely, to discover whose voice we should treat as the authentic or authoritative voice of the group. Once we have discovered that voice, other voices that express dissenting views will be of no account: if the relevant moral standing lies with the group *qua* group and with no one else, it is only to the single authoritative voice of the group that we should respond.

There are other ways in which these different locations of moral standing make a difference. For example, if we accord standing to groups, the identification of bodies of people as 'groups' for these purposes becomes critically important. Everything will depend upon where the boundaries of groups are drawn and upon whether we regard sets of people, who display a degree of difference, as groups in their own right or as mere sections of larger groups. We are familiar enough with these issues as they bear upon nationhood and rights of national self-determination. Exactly the same issues will arise if we approach cultural diversity as a matter of group moral standing. If, on the other hand, we ascribe moral standing only to individuals, group identifications will not have that sort of primary moral significance. Morally, each individual will count and count equally however we segment humanity.

I shall not pursue the significance of ascribing moral standing to individuals or to groups any further here.[11] I hope I have said enough to establish that where we locate moral standing makes a difference. The point I want to press is that whether we should ascribe standing to individuals or to groups is something that *we* have to decide in approaching cultural diversity. Cultures and their diversity cannot make that decision for us. Recall that, although we may speak of 'being fair to cultures', that is an abbreviated expression. Our real concern is to be fair to people who bear cultures. Thus the critical matter is how we identify people as parties to the diversity with which we are trying to deal. If there is division within a population about how people's lives are to be lived, *we* have to decide which 'units' have standing—individuals or groups? if groups, which groups?—before we can begin responding to them impartially. It is tempting to suppose that, for any particular case, we can allow that issue to be settled by the relevant culture, but we cannot, partly because, in these circumstances, there is likely to be dissensus over what that culture requires, but also because cultures enter the equation only once we have decided *who* has a claim upon us. We might also suppose that, because cultures are group phenomena, evolved by groups and borne by groups, the relevant moral units must be groups. That too is not so. The sociological proposition that cultures are group phenomena is entirely consistent with the moral proposition that cultures matter, ultimately, for what they contribute to the lives of individual persons.

Once again, then, we see that impartiality is not enough. We can be impartial only once we have decided amongst whom we should be impartial. Those who resolve that issue in favour of individuals are often suspected of favouring an individualist mode of life. [12] But the question of who has moral standing is quite separate from the issue of what is the best form of life, either for human beings in general or for a culturally mediated group. Indeed, affirming that individuals are the ultimate units of moral standing is wholly consistent with going on to affirm that the good of individuals is most fully realised in a non-individualist form of life.

SHOULD WE BE IMPARTIAL?

Even when we have settled these issues, other questions will arise about how we might best realise cultural impartiality. In particular, we may confront situations in which the option of allowing each group to live according to its own culture, or of compromising satisfactorily between the claims of different cultures, is not available. For example, if we allow each cultural group to be governed by its own marital conventions and if there is intermarriage between cultural groups, we shall have to decide which set of conventions is to govern intercultural marriages. Even here a degree of compromise may be possible but, insofar as it is not, we shall have to plump for one or other set of conventions, and the only element of impartiality in our decision may be the procedure by which we reach it. However, questions of how we should realise impartiality and of how far we can hope to realise it should not be confused with the question of whether being impartial among cultures is the right or the best thing to be. There are a number of grounds upon which we might reject or qualify the claims of cultural impartiality.

The first of these, which I have already mentioned, challenges the culturalist's conception of the world. Culturalists often congratulate themselves for accepting people on their own terms, but that is what they often fail to do. If people hold religious or scientific beliefs or beliefs about the right or the best way to live, they may very well reject a redescription of those beliefs as cultural constructs. Theorists, like Richard Rorty, use 'culture' as a fundamental category in characterising people's ultimate conceptions or 'final vocabularies', but that category itself belongs to a final and contestable vocabulary (Rorty 1989). [13] Thus we may reject the injunction to be impartial among cultures simply because we reject the conception of the world that that injunction asks us to accept.

A second possible and related reservation concerns the scope we are willing to give impartiality. The approach I have set out implies a comprehensively impartial response to cultural diversity. That approach itself will place some limits on what people may do in the name of their cultures simply because it requires each cultural entity to respect the domain of every other cultural entity. It is on that matter that different views of the relevant 'unit of standing' are likely to be especially significant. But the limits delivered by impartiality itself may not satisfy us: we may find some cultural practices intrinsically intolerable. If we do, and if we insist that these wrongful or harmful practices be stopped, we can do that only by leaving impartiality behind or, at least, impartiality of the sort I have described. We shall be appealing to a notion of wrong or harm that stands independently of any claim of, or for, a culture. That may not lead us wholly to reject impartiality. We may appeal to what we understand to be non-cultural standards of acceptable conduct in setting limits to tolerable practices but allow that, within those limits, impartiality is the right policy. Even so, setting the limits themselves will typically involve taking a stand that departs from cultural impartiality.

Third, we may reject impartiality among cultures because we do not accept that impartiality of the sort I have described is fair. For example, we might think that, within a particular society, the 'host' culture should enjoy a special status and that those who belong to the host community could justifiably complain if their culture were treated on terms equal with migrant cultures. Or we might think that those who belong to an indigenous minority have cultural claims that should count for more than those of migrant minorities (cf. Kymlicka 1995: 10–33, 61–69, 95–101).

Fourth, we may reject both impartiality and fairness as the relevant or overriding considerations. Within a particular society, we may think that social cohesion and commonality of purpose should have greater weight than the claims of diversity and insist that, if those goals require that one culture be patronised and another discouraged, that unequal treatment is entirely justified. (Against this, however, it is often argued that respecting and accommodating differences will serve social unity better than seeking to suppress or eradicate them.)[14]

Fifth, we may reject impartiality not in principle but for pragmatic reasons. Where, for example, a society is peopled by very many groups with different first languages, we may dismiss the proposal that we should secure linguistic equality for all of those groups throughout the public domain simply because implementing that proposal would be unduly costly and would generate unacceptable levels of inconvenience.

I merely note these as possible reasons why we might reject or qualify a commitment to impartiality amongst cultures. What I have argued does not pretend to dispose of these counter-claims. I have argued only that an impartial approach to cultural diversity is available to us, and I have indicated the sort of reasoning that generates a *prima facie* case for that approach. But that leaves the argument between the claims of impartiality and the counter-claims I list here still to be conducted. I myself have no ambition to construct an all-things-considered case for unqualified cultural impartiality.

DEMOCRACY, DIALOGUE, AND DELIBERATION

In spite of the several reasons we might have for rejecting impartiality as a wrong or an undesirable approach to cultural diversity, it is still more common to find that approach dismissed as impossible rather than improper. Some of those who doubt the possibility of an impartial approach have proposed a different tack. Their proposal is that we should deal with cultural diversity through democracy, dialogue and deliberation among all who exhibit that diversity (Young 1990: 116–21, 183–91; Gutman 1993; Williams 1994, 1995; cf. Bellamy 1992: 252–61).[15] I want to conclude by considering whether these mechanisms can enable us to achieve fair arrangements amongst cultural groups while dispensing with impartiality.

A number of thoughts seem to drive this alternative proposal. One, obviously, is scepticism about the possibility of an impartial solution and the accessibility of an external perspective. Even if an external perspective is, in principle, accessible, it may be one that we cannot reasonably expect people to adopt. Perhaps, therefore, we should provide for cultural diversity through a process that allows people to confront one another in their full particularity and to sort out ways of dealing with their differences from their several cultural perspectives.

Second, a sense is abroad that there is something impositional about the impartial approach. It is 'juridical' rather than 'political': rather than allowing the basic structure of a multicultural society or a multicultural world to be settled through a political process, it seeks to reason its way to that structure independently of any political process and makes room for a political process only within the limits set by that structure. By contrast, a 'political' approach would allow all the affected parties to engage discursively with one another and to work out arrangements for themselves. Nothing would be imposed externally; people would determine the character of their own arrangements.

Third, we have seen that the idea of impartiality leaves a number of issues still to be settled, such as what sort of equality should obtain amongst cultures and to whom we should accord standing in dealing with cultural diversity. Democracy and deliberation may seem to offer ways of resolving those issues.

There are, then, a number of things that may be claimed for a democratic process in this context: that it is capable of delivering just results without requiring people to adopt an impartial perspective and to think beyond their cultural particularities; that it enables people to evolve their own just arrangements and avoids the prior imposition of any conception of justice; and that it can supply, comprehensively and specifically, a fair arrangement for a culturally diverse population. Notice that the claim here is not merely that a democratic process is guaranteed to provide *an* outcome; rather it is that it can provide a *just* outcome. How then might democracy have a special role in respect of justice?

It might help if we begin by forestalling confusion between justice and legitimacy. We may hold that no arrangement, including a just arrangement, can *legitimately* govern a society without its first being adopted democratically by that society. But that claim allows that the justice or injustice of an arrangement is identifiable separately from its receipt of democratic endorsement. The members of a demos may know that only their decision will be the legitimate decision, but that does not help them to know what their decision ought to be. So political theorists (and others) can properly argue about which arrangement is the fair arrangement and therefore the one that a demos *ought* to adopt. The claims of democratic legitimacy do not pre-empt the sorts of issue I have set out in this article.

How might we conceive democracy so that it relates more essentially to justice? There are two ways in which democratic processes may be wedded to just outcomes.

The first corresponds to what Rawls calls pure procedural justice (1971: 86–87). In this form, the claim is that we should deem the outcome of a democratic process 'just' merely in virtue of its being the outcome of a process that is itself just. Democracy is an intrinsically just procedure, and the justice of its outcomes resides only in their being the outcomes of that just procedure. Consider the case of a lottery. We can identify the rightful winner of a lottery only by actually conducting the lottery, for the rightfulness of the winner's victory resides only in its being the outcome of a lottery that has been fairly conducted. There is simply no way in which we can identify the just outcome independently and in advance of actually conducting the lottery. Analogously, the claim for democracy here is that we cannot identify an outcome as just independently of the democratic process because the justice of the outcome resides only in its being the outcome of that process. This claim, then, really does make democracy essential for a fair outcome and makes nonsensical any counter-claim that we might figure out the right answer independently of democracy.

Should we be content to deal with cultural diversity through the democratic version of pure procedural justice? Even if we should, we cannot leave everything to that procedure. Pure procedural justice yields outcomes that are just only insofar as the procedure is itself just; the justice of the outcome is wholly and non-contingently dependent upon the justice of the procedure. We must therefore bring some idea of justice to the construction of that procedure. For example, we cannot use the procedure to settle the issue of standing that I raised earlier because the procedure presupposes that that issue has already been settled so that we know who is to have a voice and a vote.

Nor can we use the procedure to determine what are just decision rules since the procedure requires that those decision rules are already in place. Thus we have to look outside the procedure for the source of its own claim to be just.

In addition, we have to consider whether we can really be content to leave everything to pure procedural justice. Fair procedures sometimes yield results that we recognise as palpably unfair. For example, *ceteris paribus*, one person, one vote along with majority decision making constitutes a fair decision procedure but, notoriously, one that can yield substantively unfair results, especially in the context of heterogeneous publics. If we have to rely only upon a procedure, how might we ensure that it will not yield those unfair results? Only, it would seem, by subjecting it to tight constraints that pre-empt unfair outcomes. But those constraints will have to be guided by a prior conception of which outcomes are fair and which unfair.

Notice too that, if the only justice available to us is pure procedural justice, those engaged in the procedure cannot be guided by a conception of what is just. If the just is just only because it emanates from a process, it cannot guide what goes on in that process. Thus, our faith that a democratic procedure will yield a just outcome could not be grounded in a belief that the participants will be guided by a correct conception of what is just. We might think of the participants as motivated only by their own cultural claims yet suppose that the democratic machinery will process those claims into a just outcome. But, once again, the justice of the outcome will depend upon the just design of the machinery. Justice will not be a mere artefact of process.

A variant upon the idea of pure procedural justice is the view that just rules are those upon which a population agrees and that they are just simply because they are agreed. Agreement is constitutive of justice. A democratic political process, conceived as a forum *for* securing agreement, then becomes essential for justice (Williams 1994). We may protest that this view confuses two separate things: the justice of what people might agree to is independent of whether they agree to it. But suppose that we give agreement an essential role. Unless we are willing to accept that agreement under *any* circumstances is a sufficient condition for justice, we need an idea of justice independent of agreement to determine what are just background conditions for agreement. If a minority strikes a deal with a majority, but from an unjustly disadvantaged position, we have no reason to accept that the deal itself is just.

The other way in which democracy may be linked to justice corresponds to Rawls's idea of perfect or imperfect procedural justice (1971: 85–86). Here the link between justice and an associated procedure is contingent rather than essential. The justice of the just outcome resides in its intrinsic quality rather than in its being merely the outcome of a process that we identify as just *qua* process. Procedures are to be accounted perfectly or imperfectly just in relation to their propensity to yield outcomes that we are able to identify as just independently of those procedures. Thus, for example, we know that the just outcome of a criminal trial is the conviction of the guilty and the acquittal of the innocent. We assess the justice of a judicial procedure in terms of its propensity to produce that outcome; but, because it seems impossible to construct a judicial procedure that is certain to get it right every time, even a good judicial process will be an instance of 'imperfect' rather than 'perfect' procedural justice. If we claim that democracy is procedurally just in this way, we must begin by identifying what are just decisions and then go on to claim that democracy has a propensity to arrive at those just decisions. Presumably our claim will be that democracy has not merely some propensity but a unique propensity to yield just outcomes. Even so, as with judicial processes, that claim will be more plausible if it claims 'imperfect' rather than 'perfect' procedural justice for democracy.

Now this way of forging the link between justice and democracy may seem to frustrate any claim that democracy must play a defining role in relation to justice. If we claim that democracy instantiates imperfect procedural justice, we must be able to identify what is just independently and in advance of democracy; only then can we know that democracy functions as an effective instrument for securing just results. But that inference may be too quick. In the case of criminal trials, we know in general terms that justice demands that the guilty be convicted and the innocent acquitted; but, if we take any particular trial, we may have no way of assessing guilt or innocence independently of the judicial process itself. Analogously, we may structure a democratic process in a way that seems likely to secure what, in general terms, we conceive as just outcomes but, when it comes to any specific case, there may be something special about democracy that enables it, uniquely, to disclose what the just response is.

What might that 'something special' be? In the context of cultural diversity, a much favoured answer is that each cultural group has a unique understanding of its own culture (cf. Tully 1995; Williams 1994: 53–58; 1995: 78–81; Young 1990: 156–91). A fully just arrangement will be one that is sensitive to the different characters and needs of different cultures; such an arrangement is achievable only if all of the various cultural groupings for which it provides are able to contribute directly to its creation. Anyone who tries to short-circuit that participatory process by prescribing for cultural diversity from the standpoint of an impartial observer will fail in his endeavour; he will be insufficiently informed about the cultures of others to provide for them completely and fairly.

The best authorities on what a particular culture requires are, indeed, likely to be those whose culture it is. But all they will provide is fuller information about the parties amongst whom we are to be fair. We are still left with the question of what constitutes a fair arrangement among those parties. It is hard to see how those who make up a heterogeneous demos can begin to answer that question without themselves striving to adopt an external perspective from which they can, conscientiously and impartially, assess the claims of all the parties. After all, on this understanding of procedural justice, a just arrangement will emerge from a democratic process only if those who make up the demos do their best to discern what is just and allow that judgement to determine their vote. If they are motivated by something other than justice, such as maximising the return for their own group, we have no reason for supposing that their collective decision will have anything to do with justice. Thus, a democratic process, conceived as an instance of imperfect procedural justice, does not provide an alternative to an impartialist approach since that approach must figure in the reckonings of a demos if there is to be any chance that its collective decision will be just.[16]

We might be more optimistic about what a deliberative process can achieve. We might expect that, through deliberation, people will not merely provide for their differences; they will actually resolve some of those differences so that their diversity will diminish (Gutman 1993: 188–206). But, if we insist on seeing diversity as cultural, there are two reasons why that expectation seems misplaced. First, if cultural differences run as deep as culturalism would have us believe, people may have little common ground from which they can seek, deliberatively, to dissolve their differences. Secondly, if the deliberators conceive their differences as merely cultural, it is unclear why they should come to regard some of those differences as wrong or misplaced and so give them up. If it is set in the context of a diversity that we conceive as 'cultural', deliberation makes more sense as a process through which people provide for their differences rather than seeking to remove them. But providing for their differences justly will take them back to the issues and the perspective I have described, so that we may doubt that deliberation offers a strategy for dealing with cultural diversity that can dispense with impartiality.

My purpose in making these remarks about democracy, dialogue and deliberation is not to deny that these may play an important role in securing fully just arrangements for a culturally diverse population. Rather it is to deny that we can turn to these processes as alternatives to the impartial approach and as alternatives that enable us to avoid, or easily to resolve, the issues associated with impartiality. If we are willing to lower our sights and aim only for a *modus vivendi*, we can dispense with impartiality and accept whatever a political process throws up.[17] But, if we are aiming for an outcome that we have reason to regard as just, mere process is not enough. Some idea of justice must be added to the process, both to ensure that the process is justly structured and to guide what goes on in the process.

CONCLUSION

Cultural diversity, if we take it seriously, calls for a distributive response. The most obvious moral quality we look for in a distributive response is justice or fairness. I have argued that, if we are to respond to cultural diversity justly or fairly, we must deal with it impartially. We may be prepared to lower our aspirations and go for a settlement—any settlement—amongst diverse cultural groups that looks like it works. But if we want a settlement that everyone has reason to regard as fair, we cannot dispense with impartiality. In particular, the belief that we can circumvent impartiality by securing justice through political processes is misplaced.

I do not deny that we shall confront problems and uncertainties in working out precisely what an impartial approach to cultural diversity requires, but no morally defensible approach to cultural diversity is likely to be free of difficulty. Indicating difficulties that an approach has to overcome is not the same as demonstrating that it is simply unavailable as an approach. There are reasons why we might reject impartiality as the wrong approach or why we might qualify our acceptance of impartiality. But we shall have occasion to reject or qualify a policy of impartiality only if it is a possible policy. We are most likely to reject that policy because we believe that something more than merely 'cultural' diversity is at stake. I have indicated that what should be most controversial is not whether we should adopt an impartial approach to cultural diversity but whether we should accept the description of a diversity as merely 'cultural'. But, if we are happy to conceive a diversity as cultural, we should be more rather than less happy to accept that fairness and impartiality are the right values to bring to that diversity.

I have also indicated that impartiality can take different forms so that impartiality presents us with questions to which it does not itself provide the answer. Once again, however, that is not a reason for rejecting an impartial approach to cultural diversity. Rather it might lead those who ostensibly reject impartiality to consider whether they really mean to reject impartiality or whether they mean only to reject inappropriate or inadequate forms of impartiality.

NOTES

1. For a variety of doubts about the culturalist's paradigm, expressed in the context of political theory, see Rorty 1994: 152–66, Tully 1995: 9–14, Waldron 1992: 751–93, Walker 1995: 101–27.

2. For an adept and sophisticated statement of the collective good argument, see Parekh 1994: 203–4, 207–14. See also Ten 1993: 5–16, and Rockefeller 1994: 87–98.

3. In this chapter I make no distinction between impartiality and neutrality, although usage of these terms can be significantly different. See Montefiore 1975: especially 3–30, 199–245.

4. In addition, we can recognise that we should try to deal impartially with cultural diversity without going on to make the absurd claim that people should live their lives in ways that

are somehow culturally impartial. Cf. Barry's distinction between first-order and second-order impartiality (Barry 1995: 11–12, 191ff).

5. I assume, in this instance, that people are committed to their beliefs only as true beliefs. There can, of course, be special circumstances in which someone's interests are served by their continuing to hold false beliefs. Discovering the truth might, for example, cause them undue anxiety or destroy their commitment to a project which, had they persevered with it, would have benefited themselves and others.

6. Kymlicka's approach to cultural plurality does not qualify as fully 'impartial' on my usage of that term here. His characterisation of cultures as primary goods suggests an approach which aims to secure the good of cultural membership equally for all, irrespective of the content of any particular culture. But his more specific characterisation of cultures as 'contexts of choice' implies a more discriminating approach: a culture that affords its members significant choice should rate more highly than one that provides little or no choice. That implies, *ceteris paribus*, that we should set about reforming cultures in the direction of greater choice. Kymlicka could still claim that his approach was *de facto* neutral between cultures if he were willing to maintain both that people's cultures are essential backdrops to choice (however large or small the choice they provide) and that changing or replacing a group's culture is not feasible (because, in practice, attempts to replace or to engineer significant change in a culture will result in its former bearers becoming 'decultured' rather than in their acquiring a new and more choice-rich culture). But, while Kymlicka is sensitive to the psychological and sociological damage that rapid cultural change can cause and also cautious about the justifiability of external intervention, he does not rule out the possibility or desirability of 'liberalising' cultures. See Kymlicka 1989: 162–81; 1992: 142–45; 1995: 80–95, 104–6, 152–72. For critical discussions of the way in which Kymlicka values cultures, see Chaplin 1993; Kukathas 1992a: 118–24, 1992b; Lenihan 1991; Nickel 1994; Tomasi: 1995).

7. For a more developed statement of the distinction between negative and positive neutrality, see Jones 1989.

8. For 'positive' approaches to cultural diversity similar in spirit and character to Kymlicka's, see Rickard 1994 and Margalit and Halbertal 1994. Margalit and Halbertal suggest that granting special rights to cultural minorities requires the state to abandon its neutrality with respect to cultural groups, but that suggestion is misplaced even for the measures they themselves propose since those measures are designed not to 'favour' minorities but only to adjust for inequalities in the circumstances of minorities and majorities.

9. Taylor also offers a Burkean justification for this presumption: 'It is reasonable to suppose that cultures that have provided the horizon of meaning for large numbers of human beings, of diverse characters and temperaments, over a long period of time . . . are almost certain to have something that deserves our admiration and respect' (1994: 72).

10. I say only 'in the first instance' because moral standing clearly leaves much else to be settled, as illustrated by the disagreement between Kymlicka and Kukathas, both of whom hold that, ultimately, only individuals have moral standing.

11. I examine this issue more fully in Jones 1999.

12. See, for example, Thomas Nagel's much-quoted comment on Rawls's original position: that it 'seems to presuppose not just a neutral theory of the good, but a liberal, individualistic conception according to which the best that can be wished for someone is the unimpeded pursuit of his own path' (Nagel 1975: 10). That criticism confuses a commitment to individuals as the parties amongst whom we should be just with a preference for an individualist form of life. Incidentally, while the political liberalism that Rawls 'works up' for societies with liberal democratic political cultures ascribes ultimate moral standing to individuals only, his theory of justice for international society ascribes an irreducible moral standing to groups in the form of 'peoples'. See Rawls 1993a: 41–82, and Jones 1996: 183–204.

13. Rorty would doubtless concede the point.

14. See, for example, Kymlicka 1995: 173–92; Parekh 1990; and Tully 1995: 196–98.

15. In fairness to these authors, I should point out that their commitment to political processes is sometimes hedged with qualification. Gutman, in particular, while giving a central role to deliberation, gives several reasons why we cannot rely upon democratic processes ('political relativism') for a just response to multiculturalism (1993: 178–82).

16. Cf. Williams's argument that a 'spirit of impartiality' is 'essential to have among citizens who participate in a public discourse about justice' (1995: 85).

17. For an argument that a *modus vivendi* is not a second-best but the best there can be, see Gray 1995: 120–84.

REFERENCES

Barry, Brian. 1995. *Justice as Impartiality*. Oxford: Clarendon Press.

Bellamy, Richard. 1992. *Liberalism and Modern Society*. Cambridge: Polity Press.

Chaplin, Jonathan. 1993. 'How Much Cultural and Religious Pluralism Can Liberalism Tolerate?' In *Liberalism, Multiculturalism and Toleration*, ed. John Horton, 32–49. London: Macmillan.

Gray, John. 1993. 'The Politics of Cultural Diversity'. In his *Post-Liberalism*, 253–71. London: Routledge.

Gray, John. 1995. *Enlightenment's Wake*. London: Routledge.

Gutman, Amy. 1993. 'The Challenge of Multiculturalism in Political Ethics'. *Philosophy and Public Affairs* 22: 188–206.

Honneth, Axel. 1995. *The Struggle for Recognition*. Cambridge: Polity Press.

Jones, Peter. 1989. 'The Ideal of the Neutral State'. In *Liberal Neutrality*, ed. Robert E. Goodin and Andrew Reeve, 9–38. London: Routledge.

Jones, Peter. 1996. 'International Human Rights: Philosophical or Political?' In *National Rights, International Obligations*, ed. Simon Caney, David George and Peter Jones, 183–204. Boulder, CO: Westview.

Jones, Peter. 1999. 'Group Rights and Group Oppression'. *Journal of Political Philosophy* 7: 353–77.

Kukathas, Chandran. 1992a. 'Are There Any Cultural Rights?' *Political Theory* 20: 105–39.

Kukathas, Chandran. 1992b. 'Cultural Rights Again: A Rejoinder to Kymlicka'. *Political Theory* 20: 674–80.

Kukathas, Chandran. 1993. 'The Idea of a Multicultural Society'. In *Multicultural Citizens: The Philosophy and Politics of Identity*, ed. Chandran Kukathas, 17–30. St Leonard's: Centre for Independent Studies.

Kymlicka, Will. 1989. *Liberalism, Community and Culture*. Oxford: Clarendon Press.

Kymlicka, Will. 1992. 'The Rights of Minority Cultures: Reply to Kukathas'. *Political Theory* 20: 140–46.

Kymlicka, Will. 1995. *Multicultural Citizenship*. Oxford: Clarendon Press.

Lenihan, Don. 1991. 'Liberalism and the Problem of Cultural Membership: A Critical Study of Kymlicka'. *Canadian Journal of Law and Jurisprudence* 4: 401–19.

Margalit, Avishai, and Moshe Halbertal. 1994. 'Liberalism and the Right to Culture'. *Social Research* 61: 491–510.

Montefiore, Alan (ed.). 1975. *Neutrality and Impartiality*. Cambridge: Cambridge University Press.

Nagel, Thomas. 1975. 'Rawls on Justice'. In *Reading Rawls*, ed. Norman Daniels. Oxford: Basil Blackwell.

Nickel, James W. 1994. 'The Value of Cultural Belonging: Expanding Kymlicka's Theory'. *Dialogue* 33: 635–42.

Parekh, Bhikhu. 1990. 'Britain and the Social Logic of Pluralism'. In *Britain: A Plural Society*, ed. Bhikhu Parekh, 58–76. London: Commission for Racial Equality.

Parekh, Bhikhu. 1994. 'Cultural Diversity and Liberal Democracy'. In *Defining and Measuring Democracy*, ed. David Beetham, 203–14. London: Sage.

Rawls, John. 1971. *A Theory of Justice*. Oxford: Oxford University Press.

Rawls, John. 1993a. 'The Law of Peoples'. In *On Human Rights: The Oxford Amnesty Lectures 1993*, ed. Stephen Shute and Susan Hurley, 41–82. New York: Basic Books.

Rawls, John. 1993b. *Political Liberalism*. New York: Columbia University Press.

Raz, Joseph. 1986. *The Morality of Freedom*. Oxford: Clarendon Press.

Rickard, Maurice. 1994. 'Liberalism, Multiculturalism, and Minority Protection'. *Social Theory and Practice* 20: 143–70.

Rockefeller, Steven C. 1994. 'Comment'. In *Multiculturalism: Examining the Politics of Recognition*, ed. Amy Gutman, 87–98. Princeton, NJ: Princeton University Press.

Rorty, Amelie Oksenberg. 1994. 'The Hidden Politics of Cultural Identification'. *Political Theory* 22: 152–66.

Rorty, Richard. 1989. *Contingency, Irony, and Solidarity*. Cambridge: Cambridge University Press.

Scanlon, T. M. 1982. 'Contractualism and Utilitarianism'. In *Utilitarianism and Beyond*, ed. Amartya Sen and Bernard Williams, 103–28. Cambridge: Cambridge University Press.

Taylor, Charles. 1994. 'The Politics of Recognition'. In *Multiculturalism: Examining the Politics of Recognition*, ed. Amy Gutman, 25–73. Princeton, NJ: Princeton University Press.

Ten, C. L. 1993. 'Multiculturalism and the Value of Diversity'. In *Multicultural Citizens: The Philosophy and Politics of Identity*, ed. Chadran Kukathas, 5–16. St Leonard's: Centre for Independent Studies.

Tomasi, John. 1995. 'Kymlicka, Liberalism, and Respect for Cultural Minorities'. *Ethics* 105: 580–603.

Tully, James. 1995. *Strange Multiplicity: Constitutionalism in an Age of Diversity*. Cambridge: Cambridge University Press.

Waldron, Jeremy. 1992. 'Minority Cultures and the Cosmopolitan Alternative'. *University of Michigan Journal of Law Reform* 25: 751–93.

Walker, Brian. 1995. 'John Rawls, Mikhail Bakhtin, and the Praxis of Toleration'. *Political Theory* 23: 101–27.

Williams, Melissa, 1994. 'Group Inequality and the Public Culture of Justice'. In *Group Rights*, ed. Judith Baker, 34–65. Toronto: University of Toronto Press.

Williams, Melissa. 1995. 'Justice toward Groups: Political not Juridical'. *Political Theory* 23: 67–91.

Young, Iris Marion. 1990. *Justice and the Politics of Difference*. Princeton, NJ: Princeton University Press.

Chapter Two

Human Rights and Diverse Cultures

Continuity or Discontinuity?

The doctrine of human rights is, for the most part, a universalist doctrine.[1] It ascribes rights to all humanity. Yet it has to assert its universal rights in a world characterised by diversity—a world in which people live in different circumstances, bear different cultures, and pursue different forms of life. At best that diversity can seem inconvenient for, and at worst fatal to, the universality claimed for human rights.

In fact, a very large portion of human diversity is quite unproblematic for a theory of human rights. Human individuals exhibit different physical and personal characteristics, but that sort of diversity does not prevent our identifying all of those human beings as human and insisting that all are entitled to the same minimum of concern and respect merely as human beings. In addition, human beings exhibit differences as members of different societies and cultures but, again, much of that diversity need not trouble the human rights theorist. Differences in diet, dress, leisure pursuit, literature, musical form, and the like do not prevent our claiming that the human beings that exhibit those differences possess rights as human beings. On the contrary, the rights commonly claimed for human beings would include rights to express and to pursue those differences. The supposition that a uniform set of rights must presuppose, or must make for, a uniform mode of life is quite mistaken.

So it is not human diversity in general that is troublesome for a theory of human rights. The troubles are caused by a particular type of diversity: diversity of belief and value. We live in a world in which people subscribe to different religious faiths and to different sects within each faith. We also find human beings embedded in cultures which differ in their understandings of the world and in what they prescribe for human life. But differences of belief and value do not stem only from differences in religion and culture. Even those who are supposed to belong to the same culture, or who subscribe to the same religious faith or to no religious faith, can disagree radically about how we should conduct our lives both individually and in relation to one another. Theorists of human rights have, then, to assert their universal values in a world in which values are subject to widespread disagreement.

How should the fact of diversity of belief and value affect our thinking about human rights? One reply might be, not at all. If we have good grounds for ascribing certain rights to human beings indifferently, there is no reason why we should forfeit or modify our commitment to those rights merely because others do not share it. Slavery, for example, is an institution that many in the past have endorsed and that some people still find acceptable; but the mere fact that others take no exception to slavery is no reason why we should forsake or compromise our belief that slavery is wrong. Catholics do not give up on Catholicism just because not everyone is a Catholic; Muslims do not forsake Islam merely because not everyone shares their faith. Why should human rights theorists be any different?

Moreover, the doctrine of human rights is meant to be a fighting doctrine. Its purpose is not to leave the world as we find it but to transform it into a better, more just world. A doctrine of human rights should challenge other ways of thinking; it should confront and seek to displace cultures and ideologies that fail to recognise human rights. We might conclude therefore that, while diversity of belief and value may prove troublesome when we try to implement a theory of human rights, it is utterly without consequence for the theory itself. It need make absolutely no difference to the foundation or form or content of a theory of human rights.

A second possible response is of a directly opposite kind. It holds that, rather than making no difference, the fact of diversity makes all the difference to a putative theory of human rights.[2] For many people, diversity of belief and value provides reason for rejecting any morality that aspires to universality, particularly a morality as ambitiously universal as the doctrine of human rights. Why should we give any more credence to the idea of human rights than to the many other moral notions presented to us by humanity? Why, if the case for human rights is as clear as its proponents would have us believe, has so much of humanity for so much of the time not recognised that case?

Even if it does not lead us to reject the doctrine of human rights out of hand, the fact of diversity may persuade us that it is an unduly arrogant and insensitive doctrine. Those who believe in human rights may have some justification for thinking as they do, but so too do the many adherents of the many other doctrines to be found across the globe. Yet human rights theorists typically claim a privileged status for their position. They are not content to place their theory alongside others and leave it to compete for our allegiance on equal terms with other theories. They insist that human rights must have an overriding status and that the prescriptions of other moralities should be ruled permissible insofar as they conform with, and impermissible insofar as they conflict with, the claims of human rights. Not only do they claim a unique status for their doctrine, but human rights theorists also insist that the institutions of the international community should be mobilised to spread and impose their doctrine across the world.

Yet, in spite of human rights theorists' confidence in their own beliefs, there is often a suspicion that their doctrine is really just one doctrine amongst many with no real claim to specialness. Indeed, the suspicion is often more specific: that the theory of human rights is a doctrine specific to the West during the modern era. It pretends to be a doctrine unique in status and universal in reach but, in reality, it is no more than a local prejudice. Hence the familiar charge of cultural imperialism. The theory of human rights pretends to speak for all, but it is really no more than a doctrine of some, and a doctrine that is all the more insidious for the way in which it licenses its own imposition upon the whole of humanity.

ACCOMMODATING DISAGREEMENT

Are these two diametrically opposed ways of reading the juxtaposition of human rights and human diversity the only ones available to us? Can a theory of human rights recognise and accommodate the fact of human diversity yet retain substance and credibility as a theory of human rights? Before trying to answer that question, we need to address another: should a theory of human rights respond to the fact of human diversity? Clearly, there would be no point in developing a theory designed to accommodate diverse beliefs and values if that accommodation were something we should not attempt. So why should a theory of human rights take account of people's diverse beliefs and values rather than simply dismiss these as so many manifestations of error?

Perhaps the most obvious answer is of a pragmatic kind. A theory of human rights is a practical theory; it is a theory about what people should be able to do and what they should not have to suffer. If we are seriously committed to that theory, we shall want it to be practically effective in securing recognition and respect for the rights it identifies as human rights. Indeed, given that the rights at stake are human rights, we shall want it to be practically effective across the entire globe. But, if we have these practical ambitions for our theory, we must take full account of the world we intend it to shape. If that world is one in which people are strongly committed to a variety of beliefs, we must strive to make our theory as compatible as possible with those beliefs. If we do not, people will simply not take up the theory of human rights and, however laudable it may be as a theory, it will remain only a theory.

This reasoning may seem altogether too calculating and worldly to accompany a high-minded commitment to human rights, but there is much to be said for dirtying our hands and achieving something rather than keeping them clean and achieving nothing. But does this pragmatic approach really make room for human diversity within the theory of human rights? It implies that we should operate with two versions of human rights theory: (i) an ideal version that would incorporate the human rights that people really ought to enjoy and that they would indeed enjoy under ideal circumstances and (ii) a modified version of that ideal calculated to win maximum allegiance in the real world. We would begin with our ideal—complete, undefiled and uncompromised—and then trim and temper it until we were left with a modified rump of claims calculated to appeal to as many people as possible. If that is our approach, diversity will certainly have an impact upon what we claim as human rights, but its effect will be external rather than internal to the theory of human rights. Rather than providing a feature of human existence that properly shapes the rights we have, diversity will figure only as an external impediment to the full realisation of human rights and one to which we should make concessions only because we must if we are to make progress in realising human rights. Every such concession will be made grudgingly and only if, on balance, it serves the cause of human rights.

How, then, might diversity figure in a more principled way in our thinking about human rights? How might it find its way into the theory so that it becomes part of the theory rather than just a constraint upon its realisation? The answer is that, instead of regarding diversity of belief and value as a misfortune that obstructs humanity's full enjoyment of its rights, we might regard it as a normal part of the human condition. We might think of it as a natural and unexceptional feature of humanity rather than as an aberration that we should regret. Given the multitude of traditions that people inherit and their own capacity for reflection, it should not be surprising that human beings see the world in different ways and commit themselves to different forms of life. Sometimes that diversity is said to be unique to the modern era, though in truth there never has been an era during which mankind possessed uniform beliefs and values. Anyway, whatever might be true of the past, what matters is that diversity of belief and value is a feature of humanity now and for the foreseeable future, and it is for now and the foreseeable future that we have to provide. Diversity is for us an essential feature of the human condition and a feature, therefore, that a theory of human rights should not ignore.

REASONABLE DISAGREEMENT

Philosophers sometimes describe acceptable diversity as 'reasonable disagreement'.[3] Is that a description we should accept? That is a complex question and I can comment on it here only briefly. It depends, of course, upon what we mean by 'reasonable' and upon the feature of disagreement that we describe as reasonable. If by 'reasonable disagreement' we mean only disagreement for which there is some reason or perhaps good reason—disagreement that is not merely gratuitous—the description seems acceptable enough.

Sometimes the adjective 'reasonable' is linked to 'reason' rather than merely to 'a reason'. Thus Larmore characterises reasonableness as "thinking and conversing in good faith and applying, as best one can, the general capacities of reason that belong to every domain of inquiry" (1996: 122). Similarly, Rawls describes a plurality of reasonable doctrines as "the natural outcome of the activities of human reason under enduring free institutions" (1993a: xxiv, also xvi, 3–4, 36–37, 129, 135, 144). However, if we use 'reason' to give meaning to 'reasonable', we must give it a very generous sense if it is to yield an appropriately inclusive conception of the reasonable. If, for example, we take 'reason' to exclude revelation, we shall exclude every kind of religious belief for which revealed knowledge is crucial; yet any endeavour seriously to address human diversity cannot begin by excluding from its purview most of the world's major religions.[4]

If we describe a diversity of belief as reasonable, must that mean that it is made up of beliefs all of which are individually reasonable? Should we understand reasonable disagreement as disagreement arising from conflicting doctrines each of which is independently reasonable as a doctrine? That interpretation of reasonable disagreement will be problematic if we want the parties to the disagreement to accept its reasonableness. One difficulty will be that, in a context of diversity, people will be likely to have different ideas about what constitutes reasonableness, so that the reasonableness of a doctrine will be itself a matter for disagreement. A related difficulty is that it has to be possible for the parties to the disagreement to recognise its reasonableness without jeopardising their own beliefs. There may well be a close limit upon the doctrines that they can recognise as reasonable consistently with the doctrine that they themselves hold. If I am a Christian, can I find the tenets of Hinduism reasonable? If I am an atheist, can I endorse the reasonableness of the claims of Islam? The only way out of these difficulties would seem to be to adopt a notion of the reasonableness of doctrines that is extremely weak but, if it is extremely weak, it is not clear what purpose it will serve.

We can understand the notion of reasonable disagreement differently by shifting the focus from doctrines to persons, so that a disagreement will be reasonable in virtue of its being a disagreement amongst reasonable persons. What constitutes reasonableness in persons? We might answer that question in a way that deprives the shift from doctrines to persons of a point. If we identify reasonable persons as persons who hold reasonable doctrines, we shall be no further forward. We can, however, give the reasonableness of persons primacy and insist that we should have regard for people's doctrines because they are doctrines held by reasonable persons rather than because their doctrines have merit that we can identify independently of their holders. This understanding has the advantage of placing rather greater distance between people and the doctrines of others. That is, I can recognise my disagreement with you as a disagreement with a reasonable person without having to take the further step of endorsing the reasonableness of your particular view. I can therefore avoid the problem of having to endorse as reasonable a view directly contrary to my own.

Moreover, this way of interpreting reasonable disagreement seems much truer to what persuades us (if we are persuaded) to describe the world in this way. It is possible to imagine someone, in complete ignorance of the doctrines that people actually hold, assessing one doctrine after another and finding it to be reasonable or unreasonable. But it would be most surprising if the results of that assessment tallied with the doctrines that actually attract significant support in the world and to which we feel obliged to accord recognition. The reality is surely that we are impressed by the range of doctrines that people actually hold and by the fact that the people who hold them are 'reasonable' in the minimal sense of being sane, sensible and not unduly ignorant. In particular, it is difficult to know how we could identify all of the world's major religions as objects of reasonable disagreement except by reference to the people who subscribe to them. Of course, having noticed the existence of this disagreement, we might search for an explanation in the nature and limits of 'reason'. Rawls's 'burdens of judgement' offer one such explanation (1993a: 54–58). But our recognition of disagreement as reasonable still seems one that we arrive at a posteriori rather than a priori. That is, what persuades us to describe as reasonable the large range of very different doctrines that we find in the world is the reasonableness of the people who hold them. It would be disingenuous to pretend that we account those doctrines reasonable because they have passed a test of 'reason' that we have devised independently and in ignorance of the doctrines that people actually hold.

The practical import of accepting that a plurality of beliefs is a normal or reasonable feature of the human condition is that that plurality becomes something that a theory of human rights cannot ignore. Any conception of human rights that overlooks that plurality and supposes that it is something of which humanity either will or should shortly divest itself will be untenable. So both the foundation and the content of a theory of human rights has to be of a kind that makes sense against a background of diversity. But we can ask for more than that; we can also require that it should provide for that diversity. That is, rather than being merely compatible with diversity, we can expect a theory of human rights to tell us something about how we should relate to one another as people with diverse beliefs and values.

PROVIDING FOR DIVERSITY

If we want a theory of human rights that accommodates and provides for diversity of belief and value, we have to confront two types of question:

1. How can there be such a theory? The theory of human rights has its own morality and content. How can it accommodate other beliefs and values and still survive as a theory in its own right? How can it provide for diversity without either suffering emasculation or becoming embroiled in the very diversity for which it aims to provide?
2. If we can devise a theory that reconciles human rights with human diversity, how far should we go? How and where should we set the limits of accommodation so that the theory remains a critical theory?

In dealing with these questions I want to distinguish between two strategies we might adopt in trying to reconcile human rights with human diversity: the continuous and the discontinuous.[5] A continuous strategy would try to establish a continuity between the theory of human rights and the various doctrines to which people are committed. If it is successful, people will be able to recognise that human beings have rights, and to find reason for that recognition, from within their own systems of belief. In that way, the theory of human rights will be 'continuous' with each of the different doctrines that make up the diversity for which it provides. A discontinuous strategy, by contrast, sets out to establish a radical break between the theory of human rights and people's various doctrinal commitments. It deals with diversity by grounding the theory of human rights separately from, and independently of, the different doctrines that make up that diversity. The point of establishing that discontinuity is not to set up a rivalry between the theory of human rights and people's other commitments but, on the contrary, to enable people to subscribe simultaneously to both.

THE CONTINUOUS STRATEGY AND
OVERLAPPING CONSENSUS

If people hold different and conflicting beliefs, how can there be a continuous strategy? How can people acknowledge a common theory of human rights if they each approach that theory from different and conflicting positions? If a continuous strategy is to be feasible, it needs to discover what

Rawls calls an 'overlapping consensus' (1993a: 133–72). Different and conflicting doctrines exhibit an overlapping consensus when, despite their different and conflicting contents, there are points at which they agree. An overlapping consensus describes the domain within which doctrines register identical claims even though outside that domain they continue to register different and conflicting claims. If we apply that idea to the issue of human rights and human diversity, it suggests that our search for a way of reconciling the two should be a search for an overlapping consensus. We might take all of mankind's different cultures, religious faiths, ideologies, and other systems of belief and try to find within them a common core of value. If we succeed, we can use that common core to provide the substance of a theory of human rights. We shall then have a theory that avoids conflict with all of the many other doctrines that people hold. Indeed, we shall have a theory that does more than merely avoid conflict; it will enjoy the positive endorsement of all the various doctrines that contribute to the overlapping consensus.

A number of theorists have been attracted by the prospect of founding a theory of human rights upon a global moral consensus. Alan Milne (1986) and Alison Dundes Renteln (1990) are notable examples.[6] The consensual approach is also sometimes implicit in attempts to ground the idea of human rights in a variety of doctrinal positions. Thus we are presented with the Christian theory of human rights, the Muslim theory of human rights, the Buddhist theory of human rights, the Confucian theory of human rights, the rationalist theory of human rights, and so on. Each of these theories might, of course, turn out to invest human rights with a radically different content, but more commonly they are presented by their proponents in a 'me too' spirit; that is, they are designed to show that these doctrines share a common commitment to human rights.

Despite the obvious attractions of the consensual approach, there are a number of reasons why it is less than satisfactory. I shall document these only briefly.

First, and perhaps most obviously, it is doubtful whether there is any value that has been common to every culture and system of belief to which humanity has subscribed at one time or another and in one place or another. Even if we could find values that have been endorsed by everyone everywhere, these are likely to be so meagre, so denuded of content, that they will provide a set of human rights that is hardly worth having. The lowest common denominator is likely to be very low indeed. Cultures and doctrines that ascribe a fundamentally unequal status to different categories of human being are particularly difficult for the consensual approach.

Secondly, the consensual approach implies a conception of values as modules that are slotted into, and that can be removed without loss from, any system of belief, so that a value remains the same value in whatever system of belief it resides. That ignores the way in which values are not isolatable units but intersections in a nexus of moral relations. For example, it matters not just that a moral system recognises something as 'good' but also how it ranks that good in relation to other goods, how it factors that good into people's responsibilities to one another, how it holds that people have, or can come to have, claims to that good, and so on. These considerations are of the first importance if we are trying to uncover values that we can identify as rights.

Thirdly, the consensual strategy threatens to make a theory of human rights superfluous. Why, if its content has to be limited to values already endorsed by all other theories, do we need a theory of human rights? What will it provide that we do not already have? What do we gain if we merely redescribe a pre-existing moral consensus in the language of human rights?

Fourthly, what would justify that redescription? A theory of human rights is a particular type of theory: a theory that ascribes certain rights to human individuals in virtue of their humanity. The mere fact that a number of moral theories overlap is no warrant for identifying the domain within which they overlap as the domain of human rights, particularly since some or all of those theories may not themselves identify the values within that domain as human rights. It requires more than an overlapping consensus to generate something that we can describe, with justification, as a theory of human rights.

Fifthly, it is not clear what, morally, commends the consensual approach. Certainly our aim is to find a way of thinking about human rights that takes account of the fact of human diversity. But should our thinking about human rights be subordinated so completely to the demands of other doctrines and ideologies? Should we allow any and every doctrine to exercise a veto over the content of human rights? If our concerns are merely pragmatic, it is easy to see the attractions of the consensual approach. But if we want a theory of human rights that has both moral justification and moral purpose, can it defer so comprehensively to every other moral view that people hold or might hold?

Finally, and most importantly for the argument I want to develop, the consensual strategy does not so much address diversity as avoid it. We want a theory of rights appropriate to human beings who hold different and con-flicting beliefs. Even if the search for an overlapping consensus yields a result, all it will pick out is a portion of value upon which people already agree. There is no reason why we should suppose that that portion of value will be of any help to us when we try to figure out how we should relate to one another as persons with different beliefs and cultures. Suppose, for ex-ample, that we discover, amongst all the systems of value that we scrutinise, agreement that, as far as possible, our basic biological needs should be met and that we should neither inflict upon others, nor ourselves have to endure, unnecessary physical pain. That discovery will be of little help when we try to work out how we should organise a world in which people have different and conflicting beliefs about how they all should live. The search for an overlapping consensus is merely the search for an element of uniformity amongst diverse systems of belief. It is a search for something other than diversity rather than a search for a way of dealing with diversity.

THE DISCONTINUOUS STRATEGY

An attempt to reconcile human rights and human diversity by way of a continuous strategy seems, then, unlikely to succeed. How would a discontinuous strategy approach that task?

We are supposing that diversity of belief and value is a normal part of the human condition or at least a normal part of the human world in which we live and for which we have to provide. Given that state of affairs, we can look to a theory of human rights to provide for that diversity rather than simply add to it. That is, we might conceive the theory of human rights as having a different purpose from the various other doctrines we find in the world. People will continue to disagree about the ends to which we should commit our lives; about whether there is a God and, if so, what He requires of us; about whether, if there is no God, there are still standards by which we should live and, if so, what those standards are and upon what they are grounded; and so on. The task of a theory of human rights is not to add yet another voice to that cacophony of disagreement. Its task is to provide for a world in which there is that disagreement. But it is to provide for that world not by itself entering the lists of doctrinal controversy and attempting to declare which doctrine is true and which false. That is not its business. Instead, it should be concerned with how people ought to relate to one another as people with different beliefs. So its proper concern is with people who hold doctrines rather than with the doctrines that they hold.

We might therefore assign a theory of human rights a role quite different from that of other doctrines. We might model its different role by allowing for different 'levels' of concern and by presenting the theory of human rights as a theory whose concerns lie at a different level from those of other doctrines. If we think of doctrines in general, and the disagreements to which they give rise, as constituting a first level of concern, we can think of a theory of human rights (of the sort we are now considering) as functioning at a second level. A theory of human rights neither addresses the issues nor participates in the debates that occur at the first level. It does not set out to compete with other doctrines in that way. Rather, accepting the fact of first-level disagreement, it tells us how individuals should relate to one another as individuals who are caught up in first-level disagreement. In that sense its concerns lie at a second level. That is also the way in which a theory of human rights can be 'discontinuous' with other doctrines. It places itself outside and above the arena of doctrinal disagreement and seeks only to regulate people's relations with one another given that they have to live in that arena of disagreement.

Of course, if a theory of human rights is to be genuinely discontinuous with the disagreement it seeks to regulate, it must be independent of the doctrines that contribute to that disagreement. It must be what Rawls calls a 'freestanding' theory (1993a: 12–13). If it does not have that freestanding character, it will simply be dragged into first-level disagreement, and the parties to that disagreement will have no reason to regard it as an independent theory that stands outside and above their doctrinal disputes and to which they must subordinate the demands of their doctrines. So, for example, in a society populated by Christians, Muslims and Hindus, it will not do to proffer a specifically Christian or Muslim or Hindu theory of human rights, since any such theory would be party to the doctrinal disputes that divide the society. If a theory of human rights is to regulate in a second-level way the lives of people in a multi-faith society, it must be independent of the different faiths present in that society.

The theory of human rights seems well-equipped to perform that task since it is pre-eminently a theory about the status of human persons. Equal rights presuppose equal standing so that a theory that ascribes the same fundamental rights to human persons must be one that ascribes equal moral standing to persons. What people have a right to is what they are owed, so a theory of human rights is a theory of what people are owed merely in virtue of being human. Set in the context of a world in which people have different and conflicting beliefs about how they should live, it most readily issues in the prescription that each person should be free to live according to his or her beliefs. If we allowed one person to impose his beliefs upon others, we should be either according greater standing to the person who imposes than to the persons who are imposed upon, or not taking seriously the idea of reasonable disagreement. Of course, each person's freedom will be constrained by every other person's freedom so that people's freedom to live according to their beliefs will not be unlimited. But the limits that people come up against will be limits imposed by their equal status as persons and not limits grounded in an evaluation of the different merits of their different doctrines.

None of this is intended to imply that the theory of human rights must be or can be entirely free of controversy. On the contrary, I shall indicate in a moment the sorts of controversy to which it will remain subject. But the fact that the theory is primarily a theory about the status of personhood does mean that it is well-suited to playing a second-level role in a context of disagreement. It enables us to set out the rights that people should enjoy in a context of diversity independently of the doctrines that make up that diversity.

It is that separation of people from doctrines that leads discontinuity theorists to claim 'neutrality' or 'impartiality' for the way in which they provide for doctrinal diversity. Claims to impartiality or neutrality have proved peculiarly provocative, often because those who respond adversely to them ignore (sometimes, it seems, wilfully) the limited character of the neutrality or impartiality that is the subject of those claims. The theory of human rights that I am setting out here is neutral with respect to different doctrines only in that it does not aspire to evaluate them but simply to provide for their holders on some ground other than the alleged merits or demerits of their doctrines. In other words, its neutrality resides only in its discontinuity. It does not claim to be neutral with respect to every normative issue—how could any prescriptive theory be comprehensively neutral? Nor, as I shall indicate in due course, is there only one way of dealing with diversity that can claim to do so impartially (see also Chapter 1). Nor, again, need a discontinuous conception of human rights be neutral in its consequences for different doctrines. Suppose one doctrine requires its adherents to impose itself upon non-believers, while another requires its adherents to abstain from any such behaviour. Under the sort of human rights arrangement we are contemplating, the first doctrine will find itself frustrated in a way that the second will not. But that will not show that the theory has betrayed its second-level nature and adopted a first-level view of the relative merits of the two doctrines. Its different impact upon the two doctrines is a merely incidental consequence of its being impartial amongst the people who hold them.

The nature of this role explains why a theory of human rights must enjoy a special status relative to other doctrines. It should have priority over other doctrines in that it should set the terms upon which people are able to act on their beliefs. What justifies its priority is not a claim to epistemological superiority; it does not claim to be 'truer' or 'better' than other doctrines and rightfully to take precedence over them for that reason. It is simply that it functions at a different level from them. It aims to regulate relations between people who hold doctrines, and it could not perform that role if it were subordinated to, or placed in competition with, the doctrines that they hold. So the special status that we should claim for a theory of human rights stems neither from arrogant presumption nor from insensitivity to other beliefs; it derives simply from the regulative (second-level) nature of the theory.

If we adhere to a particular system of belief but are also to embrace this theory of human rights, we shall have to look upon the world from two different vantage points. As adherents of a particular system of belief, we shall see the world as it appears from within our particular system of belief. But, as adherents of a second-level conception of human rights, we must also view the world from a vantage point external to our particular system of belief. That is, we must see the world as populated by people with different and conflicting systems of belief of which our own is merely one. We must appreciate that other people have reasons for believing what they do, just as we have reasons for believing what we do, and that others' beliefs matter to them as ours do to us. We are then in a position to appreciate that the world should be one in which we are each able to live according to our own beliefs, even though we continue to hold that our own beliefs are correct and that others' contrary beliefs are mistaken. Adopting a perspective external to our particular system of belief does not require us to shelve that system of belief. It does not require that we substitute a belief in human rights for whatever other beliefs we might hold. Clearly, if it did, it would defeat the whole point of having a second-level theory of human rights. It requires only that we hold our beliefs with an appropriate awareness that others are committed to their beliefs as we are to our own. We must therefore see the world from both perspectives rather than from only one.

For some people, the world may appear pretty much the same from both perspectives. In other words, the injunctions of their particular system of belief may be the same as, or at least not in conflict with, the demands of human rights. In the society for which Rawls provides in his *Political Liberalism* (1993a), he anticipates that the different comprehensive doctrines held by its members will come to overlap in supporting the political conception of justice that he develops for that society. Thus the conception of justice that he develops in the first instance as a discontinuous and freestanding view is one that he hopes will come to be endorsed by his citizens' different comprehensive doctrines. If his hope is realised, his citizens will experience a continuity of commitment from their different comprehensive doctrines to their shared conception of justice. Analogously, we may hope that people's different and conflicting doctrines will converge in supporting a second-level theory of human rights. But that is not a hope upon which we should rely. There need be no overlapping consensus amongst different and competing doctrines and, even if there is, it need not coincide with a theory of human rights. As I have previously argued, a theory of human rights should not presuppose nor should it depend upon the existence of an overlapping consensus amongst different systems of belief. Indeed, a second-level theory of human rights will be needed all the more, and will be all the more significant in implication, in the absence of an overlapping consensus.[7]

SECOND-LEVEL ISSUES

If a theory of human rights can claim to regulate, rather than to compete or conflict with, first-level doctrines, it is a different matter when it comes up against other second-level theories. Since these compete for the same moral space as the theory of human rights, that theory cannot respond to them in the same detached way that it deals with first-level disputes amongst doctrines.

From the perspective of a human rights theory, issues that arise at the second level divide into two sorts: (i) issues that are 'external' to the theory in that they arise from challenges presented by alternatives to the human rights approach, and (ii) issues that are 'internal' in that they arise within the theory of human rights itself. I look at each in turn.

External Issues

A theory of human rights is not the only sort of second-level position from which we might seek to deal with diversity of belief and value. We might follow the lead of Thomas Hobbes and turn to a collective decision procedure for a second-level solution. That is, rather than construct an order in which we give equal freedom to each individual to live according to his own beliefs, we might subject everyone's beliefs to the decision of a common authority—which could be an authority of any kind, including the most direct of democracies—and require everyone to conform with whatever that authority decrees. There are very many reasons why we should hesitate to do things in that way, but this sort of Hobbesian solution qualifies as a discontinuous strategy provided that it is grounded (as it was for Hobbes) upon something other than a claim that the belief or the value selected by the sovereign authority must be the true belief or the correct value.

Alternatively, a second-level theory might spurn a collective solution and retain the sort of distributive approach we find in a theory of human rights but dissent from another of its features. It might, for example, accord a fundamentally unequal status to different categories of human being. Since my concern in this chapter is to investigate how a theory of human rights might take account of diversity, rather than to justify the very idea of human rights, I shall not stop to defend it against these alternatives. My main concern here is simply to concede that the conception of human rights I have set out in this chapter is not the only kind of split-level approach there can be and that a theory of human rights has to compete with, rather than stand aloof from, other forms of that approach. However, I do want to comment upon one way in which the human rights approach is frequently challenged since it is of particular relevance to the issues raised by diversity of belief and value.

Human rights thinking is often said to be individualistic. That observation is correct insofar as the unit of moral standing in a theory of human rights must be the individual person. But that is the only way in which it need be individualistic. The idea of human rights is not wedded to a belief that a good life must be individualistic in form. On the contrary, the attribution of equal moral standing to individual persons is entirely consistent with a conception of the best life as non-individualistic. The theory of human rights does, of course, place limits upon what may be done to create or preserve a collective form of life; individuals may not be coerced into becoming or remaining members of a community or an association. That, in turn, may be said to make collective forms of life more difficult to sustain than individualist forms. But, if a theory of human rights has that effect (and it is not clear that it must), that will be a consequence of the moral standing it accords to each individual and not of its being committed to the superiority of a particular form of life. Identifying a form of life as good and setting the terms upon which that life may be pursued are two separate exercises.

Even if we accept that, however, we may still feel that the theory of human rights is unduly limiting if the only rights it can recognise are rights that might be held by individual persons. Some of the goods that play a significant role in people's lives are collective in nature, and it seems implausible to suppose that individuals might have rights, *qua* individuals, to those collective goods.[8] If there are rights to collective goods, it would seem that those must be group rights, and it is a common criticism of theories of human rights that they do not, and cannot, recognise groups as possessors of rights.

In the present context, that criticism arises most frequently where a system of belief forms part of a culture. Cultures are necessarily collective in nature; they constitute shared systems of belief and shared forms of life. A belief might be unique to an individual or it might be held by an individual quite independently of the fact that the same belief is held by other people; but that could not be true if the belief formed part of a culture. A culture is necessarily a group phenomenon. Thus, if a culture is important to the well-being of those whose culture it is, it will be a good that is collective to the cultural group; and, if that culture is to be an object of rights, it would seem that those must be rights held by the group *qua* group rather than by its members severally. Consequently, if part of the diversity for which we attempt to provide through a split-level approach is cultural diversity, we may seem stymied if we have to regard individual human beings rather than groups as the bearers of rights.

Can a theory of human rights overcome this apparent difficulty? Can it find a place for group rights? The answer depends upon what we understand a group right to be. We may interpret group rights either as 'corporate' rights or as 'collective' rights. I use these as terms of art to which I attach my own meanings. If we understand a group right as a corporate right, we shall understand it as a right held by a group that has independent moral standing as a group. We shall accord the group an identity and a status that, morally, does not reduce to the several identities and statuses of its individual members. The group will enjoy the same sort of independent and irreducible standing as a right-holding person. If, for example, that is how we understand a cultural group's right of self-determination, we shall ascribe standing to the cultural group *qua* group, and we shall conceive its rights as rights held and wielded by the group as a corporate entity, rather than simply as rights held in some way by the individuals who make up the group at any particular moment. Understood according to this corporate model, group rights will fall outside the compass of human rights since they will be rights borne by corporate entities rather than by human persons, and they will be grounded in whatever gives those corporate entities their moral standing rather than merely in the claims of humanity or personhood.

If, however, we conceive a group right as a collective right, we shall conceive it quite differently. A group right assumes a collective form if we conceive it as a right held jointly by the individuals who make up the group. For example, I, as a single individual, may have a claim to a particular collective good, but that claim, taken on its own, may be insufficient to give me a right to the good. The same may be true of the claim, taken singly, of each other individual who has a stake in the collective good. If, however, we take all of these individuals and treat their several claims as a joint claim, that may well make the case for their having a joint or 'collective' right to the good. A collective right is properly described as a group right since it is a right that the members of the group hold as a group and that none of them holds as an independent individual. But, in contrast to the corporate conception, the collective conception does not require that we ascribe moral standing to the group independently of its members. On the contrary, the moral standing required for the group's right is provided by the standing of its several members rather than by the group as an independent moral entity.[9]

Consider again the specific case of cultural rights. Suppose we have a body of people who form a cultural minority and who, for all the usual reasons, have an interest in the continuance of their culture, but who find their culture in danger of being overwhelmed by that of the majority society. The interest of any single member of the minority in the maintenance of his culture is unlikely to be adequate to justify imposing duties upon the majority society to institute measures to protect and sustain the culture of the minority. But the joint interest of all the individuals who make up the cultural minority in the maintenance of their culture may well suffice, in which case the members of the cultural minority will possess a right jointly that none of them possesses individually. So, in that way, we can ascribe a right to a group of individuals as a group even though we invest the group with no moral standing that is not reducible to the independent moral standing of its individual members. That alone is not enough to show that these collective cultural rights are human rights, since there are additional tests that they have to pass if they are to be human rights. But since collective rights, unlike corporate rights, need appeal only to the moral standing of individual persons, they constitute group rights of a sort that a theory of human rights might accommodate.[10]

If the split-level approach that I am proposing throws up questions about the relevant unit of standing to which it does not itself provide the answers, might that indicate that I have the content of the two levels precisely the wrong way round? Rather than dealing with cultural diversity by way of units of standing, perhaps we should arbitrate amongst different possible units of standing by way of cultures. It will then be cultures that perform a second-level role in relation to competing views about the relevant unit of standing. Each culture will determine for its own population what the unit of standing is to be—individuals or groups and, if groups, which groups.

There are two reasons why this inversion of the content that I have given the split-level approach cannot be satisfactory. One is practical. Disagreements arise within cultures as well as between them and, when we are faced with that sort of dissensus, the issue of standing is thrown back at us: *we* have to decide whose voice is to count and to whose voice we should listen. The other is more theoretical. Can we give moral ultimacy to a culture, as though a culture were itself something possessed of moral standing? Giving ultimate moral standing to a culture, as opposed its bearers, would be rather like giving moral standing to a language or a painting or a musical composition. We may value these things, but we do not normally do so by ascribing them an independent moral standing analogous to the standing we ascribe to human persons or human groups. If cultures matter morally, it is because they matter to and for people and, if that is so, the issue of how people are to count morally must precede rather than follow our encounter with cultures.

Internal Issues

We cannot, then, treat disputes over whether human beings have rights as first-level disputes for which a theory of human rights can perform the role of second-level arbiter. Those disputes belong to the second level, and a theory of human rights is necessarily a party to them. Rather than refereeing a contest in which it takes no part, it must be itself a participant in the contest. That does not mean, of course, that we cannot continue to insist that the human rights approach is the right one. But in insisting upon that approach, we shall be rejecting, rather than regulating, theories that challenge the fundamentals of human rights. [11]

It is not only theories that challenge human rights that raise second-level issues. Those issues may arise even if we limit ourselves to the idea of human rights, since that idea and its implications are open to different interpretations. For example, I have suggested that, faced with first-level differences in belief, a theory of human rights should extend equal freedom to people to live according to their beliefs. However, that proposal may leave room for different possibilities in how precisely we define each person's domain of equal freedom. Many of those who found themselves on different sides in the Rushdie Affair were not in dispute over whether people should enjoy freedom of belief; they disagreed only over the proper make-up of each person's domain of freedom.

Similarly, disputes over who is to count as 'human' for purposes of human rights is a question that belongs to the second level. Imagine there are four adult individuals, A, B, C and D, who disagree over whether D is a person and therefore over whether D has the rights that normally accompany personhood. A and B think D is not a person; C and D himself think D is a person. D might, for example, be black; A and B might be white racists; and C might be white but not a racist. It is fairly obvious that this is not the sort of dispute that we can deal with satisfactorily by turning to a second-level theory of human rights. We proposed dealing with doctrinal disputes about how we should live by retreating from doctrines to persons and by assigning each person a right to live according to his own beliefs. But we cannot similarly deal with a dispute about personhood by retreating to an idea of personhood because that is what is in dispute. If we tried to make that move, how would we decide whether D should or should not figure at the higher level without simultaneously entering into the lower-level dispute about D's personhood? And how could we arrive at any higher-level conclusion that made sense? If we concluded that each person should be free to live according to his own conception of who was a person, A and B might be adjudged free to enslave D since they believe D to be a non-person, while C and D would be free to resist D's enslavement since they believe D to be a person.

All of that is plain enough. In the past, questions of who should count as a person have been real issues; nowadays we rightly give short shrift to suggestions that we might limit the range of 'personhood' or 'humanity' on grounds of race or class or caste. But some variations on this issue are less straightforward. Consider the case of abortion. We might suppose that abortion is a classic example of an issue that we should deal with at arm's length. People differ radically in their views on abortion, so perhaps a theory of human rights should declare itself neither for nor against abortion but, instead, should stand aloof from the issue and prescribe only that each person should be free to act according to his or her beliefs on abortion. That is certainly what many people, including many politicians, think is the right arrangement given the unresolvable nature of disagreements about abortion in our world.

We might, however, conceive abortion as an issue within the idea of human rights rather than one that is settled by that idea. Should a foetus count as a human being for right-holding purposes?[12] If we believe it should, we shall include it in the community of moral beings and exclude it from the class of beings that we may dispose of at will. If, on the other hand, we give the foetus no moral status, we shall be happy to ascribe people the right to practise abortion as they themselves judge fit.[13] In other words, if we locate the issue of abortion within the theory of human rights, it will be a second-level issue and, if we permit people to engage in abortion, we shall be taking a stand, rather than no stand, on that second-level issue.

That is not to say that something like a split-level approach to the issue of abortion is not possible. If we are prepared, at the second level, to treat articulate participants in the dispute about abortion as the only claimants that count, we can respond to that dispute by allowing those articulate participants to engage in abortion, or not, according to their different convictions. But in adopting that strategy, we shall have already decided that it is acceptable that the fate of a foetus should depend upon the different beliefs of different people and that the foetus itself has no moral status that vetoes its disposal by those people. In other words, we shall have already taken sides on an issue that is fundamental to disputes about abortion.[14] We could respond to disagreements about infanticide in a directly parallel fashion: rather than confronting that issue head-on, we might give parents the freedom to dispose or not to dispose of their infant children as their own beliefs dictate. Why do we not do that? Because, in the case of infanticide, almost everyone accepts that infants have independent moral standing and that, consequently, it is entirely unacceptable that their lives should be placed at the mercy of their parents' beliefs.

Thus, the two-level approach to human rights that I have been defending does not provide for cases in which the dispute is about who should count as a human being with rights. Indeed, we might extend that limitation beyond the domain of human rights. Proponents of animal rights might similarly insist that animals should not be placed at the mercy of human beliefs and wishes and, consequently, that a society that allows people to choose between eating or not eating, using or not using, animals cannot claim to remain neutral on the issue of animal rights. My point in making these remarks is not to argue either against abortion or for animal rights; it is simply to acknowledge the limits of a two-level approach. That approach provides for differences of belief amongst the members of the moral community about how they should conduct their lives; it does not provide for disputes about who should count as a member of the moral community. Whatever the merits of the two-level approach as a way of dealing with disagreement, it should not allow us to take for granted that only the articulate have rights.

CONCLUSION

The understanding of human rights that I have presented in this chapter does not, then, provide an easy solution to every sort of disagreement. It places human rights outside and above some disputes, and it enables human rights to respond to those disputes impartially. But it does not extricate human rights from every form of controversy. That need not occasion disappointment. If we could have a moral theory that retreated from, rather than faced up to, fundamental issues concerning the moral status of human beings, would we want it?

In spite of its limits, the two-level approach does, I believe, offer a way of dealing with diversity that has very considerable range. Indeed, if we think a theory of human rights should take seriously and should accommodate the diversity of belief and culture in our world, rather than respond to these as if they were of no consequence, it is difficult to see how it might do that without pursuing a discontinuous strategy.

I do not claim that my account provides comprehensively for human rights. I have considered only how our thinking on human rights might approach the subject of diversity of belief and value. In other areas, human rights will need other arguments. As I have argued elsewhere (Jones, 1994: 117–19), the search for a single grand theory of human rights may be misplaced; different rights may be sustained by different reasons.

NOTES

This chapter was written during my tenure of a Nuffield Foundation Social Science Research Fellowship; I am grateful to the foundation for its support. Earlier versions of the chapter were presented to a conference, 'Human Rights: Sacred or Secular?', held in 1998 at the Milltown Institute of Theology and Philosophy, Dublin, and to a human rights seminar at the University of Essex, as well as to the Newcastle Colloquium on Global Norms and Diverse Cultures. I received much helpful comment from participants in those events.

1. For justification of the qualification 'for the most part', see Chapter 3.

2. For sceptical views of human rights that relate in various ways to diversity of belief and value, see Brown (1997), MacIntyre (1985: 66–71), Nelson (1990), and Pollis and Schwab (1979). For an equally sceptical view that, nevertheless, holds on to the idea of human rights, see Rorty (1993).

3. See Rawls (1993a, especially Lecture II), Larmore (1987: ch. 3, and 1996: ch. 7), and Barry (1995: ch. 7). Although my general approach in this chapter is heavily indebted to the work of John Rawls, the account of human rights that I develop here is fundamentally different from his. For Rawls's account, see Rawls (1993b, 1999). For a critical examination of Rawls's attempt to provide for human rights by way of his political conception of international justice, see Jones (1996).

4. In fact, neither Rawls nor Larmore excludes religious faith from reasonable belief.

5. I borrow these terms from Ronald Dworkin (1990: 16–22).

6. Renteln proposes an anthropological approach that would search empirically for a minimum moral consensus. Milne's approach is more philosophical. He sets out a minimum morality that, he argues, is necessary for social life as such and is therefore to be found amongst all cultures and civilisations. However, he does not rely solely upon that common morality for his account of human rights since he is able to make the transition from that morality to universal human rights only by invoking Kant's humanity principle ('Treat humanity, whether in your own person or in that of another, always as an end withal and never merely as a means'). Although I use Rawls's term 'overlapping consensus' to describe the domain of pre-existing cultural agreement contemplated by Renteln and Milne, Rawls himself uses the notion of overlapping consensus to describe a rather different possibility; see *infra*, note 7.

7. Abdullahi A. An-Na'im (1990a, 1992) argues that a cross-cultural consensus on human rights is not something that we can expect simply to discover but something that we should work to construct. Significantly, Rawls himself does not suppose that an overlapping consensus

is something that lies dormant in a variety of comprehensive doctrines just waiting to be discovered. Rather his hope is that his political conception of justice will provide a focus around which an overlapping consensus can form. That is why his political conception of justice needs, at least in the first instance, its own independent foundation. (Rawls cites An-Na'im's work (1990b), reinterpreting Islam in a form that is consistent with constitutional democracy, as a 'perfect example' of overlapping consensus (Rawls 1997: 782–83).) Analogously, the conception of human rights I am proposing here is not something we should expect to find ready-made within all or most systems of belief, even though we might hope that people will find a way of making their systems of belief "congruent with, or supportive of, or else not in conflict with" (Rawls 1993a: 140) that conception.

8. In fact, there are collective goods that might plausibly be the objects of individual rights; see Réaume (1988).

9. I model what I say here on the conception of collective rights proposed by Joseph Raz (1986: 207–8). The claim about the moral standing required for a collective right is my own, but it is also implicit in Raz's account.

10. I examine more fully the significance of the difference between these two conceptions of group rights in Jones (1999a, 1999b).

11. To avoid undue complication, I have developed my argument as if doctrines or theories had either first-level or second-level concerns. In reality, a major system of belief—such as, for example, a religion—may address both. In that case, a second-level theory of human rights may stand in a regulative non-rival relation to the first-level components of a system of belief but in a competitive non-regulative relation to its second-level components (although, of course, it is quite possible that the second-level aspects of a system of belief may complement, rather than conflict with, human rights thinking).

12. I have previously spoken of human 'persons' and, of course, a foetus does not possess the qualities normally associated with personhood. However, I assume that we can intelligibly ascribe rights to human beings that are not persons, even though there are some human rights that we can intelligibly ascribe only to persons (e.g. rights to freedom of belief and to political participation).

13. The debate about abortion is, of course, much more complex than this, but that does not, I think, affect the general point I am making here about the limits of a two-level approach.

14. Cf. Michael Sandel's use of the cases of abortion and slavery in his critique of 'minimalist liberalism' (1996: 19–24).

REFERENCES

An-Na'im, A. A. 1990a. 'Problems of Universal Cultural Legitimacy for Human Rights'. In *Human Rights in Africa: Cross-Cultural Perspectives*, ed. A. A. An-Na'im and F. M. Deng, 331–67. Washington, DC: Brookings Institution.

An-Na'im, A. A. 1990b. *Toward an Islamic Reformation: Civil Liberties, Human Rights, and International Law*. Syracuse: Syracuse University Press.

An-Na'im, A. A. 1992. 'Toward a Cross-Cultural Approach to Defining International Standards of Human Rights'. In *Human Rights in Cross-Cultural Perspectives*, ed. A. A. An-Na'im, 19–43. Philadelphia: University of Pennsylvania Press.

Barry, B. 1995. *Justice as Impartiality*. Oxford: Clarendon Press.

Brown, C. 1997. 'Universal Human Rights: A Critique'. *International Journal of Human Rights* 1: 41–65.

Dworkin, R. 1990. 'Foundations of Liberal Equality'. In *The Tanner Lectures on Human Values, XI, 1990*, ed. G. B. Peterson, 1–119. Salt Lake City: University of Utah Press.

Jones, P. 1994. *Rights*. Basingstoke: Macmillan.

Jones, P. 1996. 'International Human Rights: Philosophical or Political?' In *National Rights, International Obligations*, ed. S. Caney, D. George, and P. Jones. Boulder, CO: Westview, 183–204.

Jones, P. 1999a. 'Human Rights, Group Rights and Peoples' Rights'. *Human Rights Quarterly* 21: 80–107.

Jones, P. 1999b. 'Group Rights and Group Oppression'. *Journal of Political Philosophy* 7: 353–77.

Larmore, C. 1987. *Patterns of Moral Complexity*. Cambridge: Cambridge University Press.

Larmore, C. 1996. *The Morals of Modernity*. Cambridge: Cambridge University Press.

MacIntyre, A., 1985. *After Virtue*, 2nd edition. London: Duckworth.

Milne, A. J. M. 1986. *Human Rights and Human Diversity*. Basingstoke: Macmillan.

Nelson, J. O. 1990. 'Against Human Rights'. *Philosophy* 65: 341–48.

Pollis, A., and P. Schwab. 1979. 'Human Rights: A Western Construct with Limited Applicability'. In *Human Rights: Cultural and Ideological Perspectives*, ed. A. Pollis and P. Schwab, 1–18. New York: Praeger.

Rawls, J. 1993a. *Political Liberalism*. New York: Columbia University Press.

Rawls, J. 1993b. 'The Law of Peoples'. In *On Human Rights: The Oxford Amnesty Lectures 1993*, ed. S. Shute and S. Hurley, 41–82. New York: Basic Books.

Rawls, J. 1997. 'The Idea of Public Reason Revisited'. *University of Chicago Law Review* 64: 765–807.

Rawls, J. 1999. *The Law of Peoples*. Cambridge, MA: Harvard University Press.

Raz, J. 1986. *The Morality of Freedom*. Oxford: Clarendon Press.

Réaume, D. G. 1988. 'Individuals, Groups, and Rights to Public Goods'. *University of Toronto Law Journal* 38: 1–27.

Renteln, A. D. 1990. *International Human Rights: Universalism versus Relativism*. Newbury Park, CA: Sage.

Rorty, R. 1993. 'Human Rights, Rationality, and Sentimentality'. In *On Human Rights: The Oxford Amnesty Lectures 1993*, ed. S. Shute and S. Hurley, 111–34. New York: Basic Books.

Sandel, M. 1996. *Democracy's Discontent: America in Search of a Public Philosophy*. Cambridge, MA: Belknap.

Chapter Three

Collective and Group-Specific: Can the Rights of Ethno-Cultural Minorities Be Human Rights?

The human rights tradition has viewed the idea of minority rights with ambivalence. On the one hand, the tradition has been protective of minorities simply by virtue of according them the same fundamental rights as majorities. If human rights are universal, minority individuals necessarily have those rights on the same terms as everyone else. Moreover, the protection afforded by universal rights is often of greater significance for minorities simply because, as minorities, they are more vulnerable than majorities to mistreatment or to less than equal treatment.

On the other hand, the kinds of claim associated with minority rights, especially the rights of ethno-cultural minorities, have not always sat comfortably within the human rights tradition. One reason is that minority claims are sometimes collective in nature. Culture, language, nationality, religious affiliation, and the like are collective phenomena, and the rights minorities seek in relation to them often make sense only as collective rights—as rights possessed by the minority as a group rather than by its members severally. Those rights are at odds with the tradition that conceives human rights as rights possessed only by human individuals. While some have dissented from that tradition, the idea that human rights can be held by groups has generally been resisted, either because it has been deemed incoherent or because it has been thought to endanger individual human rights.

Minority rights have also proved difficult for human rights thinking insofar as they are rights that are in some way special to minorities. That specialness is at odds with the belief that human rights are necessarily universal. Consider language rights. If human rights are universal rights, majorities and minorities can have human rights in respect of their language only insofar as they are precisely the same rights. If there is good reason why the language rights of majorities and minorities, or of different minorities, should differ, those different rights cannot be human rights. That simple all-or-nothing dichotomy, forced on us by the demands of universality, seems too stark. There is often good reason why language rights should differ. For example, the cost and inconvenience a society would incur if it were to make a minority's language an official public language on terms precisely equal with the majority language could be prohibitive, especially if the society contained more than one linguistic minority. On the other hand, it might be equally inappropriate that a minority should possess no rights in respect of its language beyond those possessed indiscriminately by all, including a single individual who was the only individual in the society to speak his or her language. If human rights are always and only universal rights, those sorts of consideration would seem to be, of necessity, excluded from the purview of human rights thinking.

In this chapter, I shall challenge the orthodoxies that human rights must be individually held and universally held. I shall argue that human rights can remain authentically 'human' and yet be collective in form and 'group-specific', that is, different for different groups. Human rights thinking need not therefore be embarrassed by the rights of ethno-cultural minorities.

Making an argument of that sort has been complicated by the emergence in recent years of different conceptions of what we should understand a human right to be. The traditional moral conception of human rights takes seriously the 'human' in 'human right', so that a human right is a right we hold in virtue of being human. People may have rights as citizens and other rights as members of non-state associations, but they possess some rights just as human beings. Those are human rights. That has been the dominant conception amongst those who have conceived human rights as moral rights, at least in the first instance, including those who have undertaken philosophical analyses of human rights. I shall follow Pablo Gilabert in describing that traditional conception as 'humanist'.[1] Some contemporary philosophers who keep faith with it are James Griffin,[2] John Tasioulas,[3] and Carl Wellman.[4]

Human rights thinking has always been highly political in inspiration. It has been strongly motivated by what follows politically if people possess human rights; but for humanists those political implications are just that, 'implications'. They are not part of the very idea of human rights. In that respect, the humanist conception contrasts with the 'political' conception espoused by John Rawls,[5] Charles Beitz,[6] and Joseph Raz.[7] On their view, we should understand what a human right is with reference to the meaning the term has, and the role human rights perform, in contemporary political practice. A human right is a right that is legitimately of concern to the international political community and a right whose violation may justify (albeit defeasibly) some form of international intervention—military, economic or diplomatic. Exponents of the political conception differ in their accounts of quite how human rights figure in international political practice, but they agree in conceiving them in terms of their international political role rather than with reference to a supposed link to our humanity.

'Political' theorists do not deny that determining which rights should fall into the category of human rights is properly a matter for moral argument. What makes their view 'political' is their conception of what it is that we justify when we justify a human right. Their thinking can be distinguished from a third school of thought whose conception of human rights I shall describe simply as 'legal'. Legal human rights have existed ever since they were incorporated in international law many decades ago, and the legal conception is not distinguished by mere recognition of that fact. Rather, it is distinguished by the sharp separation it makes between moral human rights and legal human rights. Moral thinking on human rights has often assumed that legal human rights are, or should be, merely moral human rights translated into international law. Allen Buchanan describes that as the 'mirroring' view.[8] He believes it to be profoundly mistaken, since all sorts of consideration other than moral human rights actually feed into, and rightly feed into, the make-up of legal human rights. Moreover, many legal human rights have no moral equivalents. While he does not reject the very idea of moral human rights or deny that moral human rights can sometimes be relevant to the justification of legal human rights, he believes it quite wrong to suppose that a system of international human rights law either can be or should be merely the legal instantiation of a philosophical theory of moral human rights.[9] Patrick Macklem separates legal human rights from moral thinking even more radically.[10] He conceives both the substance of and the case for legal human rights as entirely internal to international law. Legal human rights are rights through which international law has sought to correct pathologies of its own making. In investing sovereign power in states, international law has distributed political power in a way that makes possible seriously adverse consequences; human rights law is the device international law has used to curb the power that it has itself conferred upon states.

In considering whether rights that are collective to and specific to ethnocultural minorities can also be human rights, I shall take seriously the 'human' in human rights. I shall assume, along with the humanist conception, that human rights are rights people hold in virtue of being human. If we do not make that assumption, the issue of whether human rights can be collective or group-specific can easily become a non-issue. If legal human rights are whatever international law declares them to be and if international law declares collective rights or group-specific rights to be human rights, that declaration settles the matter. Similarly, on the political conception, if collective rights or group-specific rights figure amongst the rights that are of legiti-

mate international concern and whose violation can justify international political action, that suffices to make them human rights. So the question of
whether there can be collective human rights or group-specific human rights
remains a significant question only if the 'human' in human rights continues
to have something like its traditional meaning.

In following the humanist tradition in that respect, I do not mean wholly
to reject the claims of either the political or the legal theorists. The political
theorists are right to challenge the assumption that we can leap straight from
human rights traditionally understood to rights that are serious candidates for
international political action. If we take a hard-headed look at the political
structures and the political realities of our world and give due weight to the
limits, costs and dangers of international action, there may well be moral
rights that people possess as human beings which are insufficiently important
to warrant international political action. Not all of the humanist's human
rights need therefore rank as the political theorist's 'international human
rights'. Similarly, the legal theorists make a convincing case against supposing that legal human rights can be, or should be, merely legalised moral
human rights, which take no account of the consequences of making rights
part of international law or of the larger purposes of an international legal
human rights system. There is also no reason to jettison legal positivism's
insistence on separating what law is from what it ought to be, just because the
subject of law happens to be human rights.

On the other hand, the political and legal conceptions can take forms that
render the 'human' in human rights of little or no consequence. If human
rights are no more than rights that the international political community
recognises as sovereignty limiting, why should we persist in describing them
as 'human' rights? We might ask the same of legal conceptions if the 'human' in human rights law turns out to be no more than a conventional but
misleading tag. We have reason to pause before tossing aside the very idea of
human rights along with humanist thinking in general.

In making my arguments, I shall mix modes. I shall use a conception of
human rights largely associated with humanist thinking, but I shall make
extensive use of UN and regional human rights declarations and conventions;
I shall draw, in other words, on soft and hard forms of international human
rights law. I do so partly because examples and instances that are already
recognised formally as human rights are likely to carry greater weight than
rights of my own devising. I also have an eye to extending the relevance of
my arguments beyond humanist approaches to human rights. However, I do
not aim to give a comprehensive account of the human rights currently ascribed to ethno-cultural minorities. I mean only to point out instances in
which those rights are already collective or group-specific in nature, or cases
in which rights could be collective or group-specific consistently with their
remaining human rights.

The term 'ethno-cultural minority' sometimes includes, and sometimes excludes, indigenous peoples. I shall include indigenous peoples in the groups I consider but, since they are now treated as a separate category for human rights purposes, I shall consider them alongside, but separately from, other sorts of ethno-cultural group.

COLLECTIVE HUMAN RIGHTS

Indigenous Peoples and Collective Rights

The human rights instrument that attributes rights to groups most expressly and most abundantly is the United Nations Declaration on the Rights of Indigenous Peoples (UNDRIP), 2007. Here are some examples:

> Article 4
> Indigenous peoples, in exercising their right to self-determination, have the right to autonomy or self-government in matters relating to their internal and local affairs.

> Article 5
> Indigenous peoples have the right to maintain and strengthen their distinct political, legal, economic, social and cultural institutions, while retaining their right to participate fully, if they so choose, in the political, economic, social and cultural life of the State.

> Article 10
> Indigenous peoples shall not be forcibly removed from their lands and territories.

These rights are self-evidently group rights. They ascribe rights to indigenous people as peoples rather than to indigenous people as discrete individuals. Of the thirty-seven articles of UNDRIP that expressly declare rights, twenty-six declare group rights in the form of rights ascribed to indigenous peoples. Of the remaining eleven, nine articles ascribe rights to both indigenous peoples and indigenous individuals. Two ascribe rights to indigenous individuals only.

There may be reason to doubt whether the group rights that UNDRIP ascribes to indigenous peoples should really be understood as human rights. The Declaration's preamble includes the following clause:

> *Recognizing and reaffirming* that indigenous individuals are entitled without discrimination to all human rights recognized in international law, and that indigenous peoples possess collective rights which are indispensable for their existence, well-being and integral development as peoples

That clause may suggest that, while the individual rights of indigenous people are human rights, the collective rights of indigenous peoples belong to a separate category of peoples' rights. Yet the first article of UNDRIP contradicts that interpretation.

> Article 1
> Indigenous peoples have the right to the full enjoyment, *as a collective or as individuals*, of all human rights and fundamental freedoms as recognized in the Charter of the United Nations, the Universal Declaration of Human Rights and international human rights law. (My emphasis)

That article indicates that UNDRIP intends its collective rights to be human rights, so that the rights it ascribes to indigenous people as peoples are also rights that those peoples hold as human beings.[11] Why should there be any objection to that? Why should not indigenous people hold human rights both as individuals and as groups?

Both Human and Collective

For some objectors the answer lies in the very idea of group rights, particularly the idea of group moral rights. Groups, as distinct from their members taken severally, are not, they would protest, the types of entity that are capable of bearing moral rights.[12] Other objectors are willing to accept that groups can hold rights; they deny only that group rights can be human rights. The most common objection to ascribing human rights to groups is succinctly stated by Jack Donnelly.

> If human rights are the rights that one has simply as a human being, then only human beings have human rights. Because only individual persons are human beings, it would seem that only individuals can have human rights. Collectivities of all sorts have many and varied rights, but these are not human rights. (Donnelly 2013: 30)[13]

Before we can assess Donnelly's claim, we need to look more closely at what a group right is. A group right is generally understood as a right that a group holds as a group and only as a group. It is not a right that each of the group's members holds individually, such as the right of a university student to use the university's library or the right of an adult citizen to vote in her country's elections. A right is a group right only if it is possessed by the group as a group rather than by its members taken severally.

When we move beyond that basic idea, we encounter widespread disagreement on how we should conceive a group right. We can, however, distinguish two fundamentally different conceptions, which I shall describe as 'corporate' and 'collective'.

The corporate conception of group rights might also be described as the traditional conception in that it is the way in which group rights have been most commonly understood until recently. On this conception, we should conceive a right-holding group on analogy with a right-holding individual person. A person holds his rights as a single integral entity and so too must a group (which is why I describe this conception as 'corporate'). We might think of the right-holding group as a group-individual or a group-person. In law this can be achieved by the ascription of legal personality to a group; having recognised the group as a legal person, law can then assign that artificial person legal rights and legal responsibilities. The attribution of the properties of a natural person to a group is more problematic, but proponents of the corporate conception need attribute to a group only those natural properties that they reckon are essential for right-holding.[14] For the groups it conceives as moral right-holders, the most fundamental distinguishing feature of the corporate conception is its ascription of moral standing to the group as a group. Moral standing is a precondition of moral right-holding, just as legal standing is a precondition of legal right-holding, and that leads easily to the thought that, if groups can possess moral rights, they must possess moral standing as groups—a standing that is separate from, and independent of, the moral standing of the individuals who make up the group's members.

It is this conception of group rights that most frequently attracts scepticism. The sceptics are unwilling to accept that we should conceive groups as person-like entities or as possessing moral standing in their own right. I shall pass over those issues. Here the relevant question is whether group rights corporately conceived might be human rights. The answer is fairly obviously 'no'. On the corporate conception, the entity that holds a group right is quite different from a natural human being so that, if we take seriously the 'human' in human right, group rights corporately conceived cannot be human rights.

We can, however, conceive group rights in a quite different fashion. We can conceive them as rights that the members of a group hold collectively rather than separately, jointly rather than severally. I describe this conception of a group right as 'collective'. I do so because something that is held 'collectively' is, by implication, something that has more than one holder and, as I use the term, a collective right does indeed have a plurality of holders. By contrast, a group right corporately conceived has a single holder, the group conceived as a unitary entity.[15]

On the collective conception, there is no right-holding group that has a being and moral standing separate from the people who make it up. The right-holding group is simply the set of individuals who constitute the group, and the moral standing that underwrites their collective right is that of the several individuals who make up the group. But the collective right they hold is an authentic group right since it is a right that they hold only together and not separately. The conception here is not therefore one in which individuals hold rights as separate individuals and in which they, or we, somehow aggregate their individual rights into a collective right. On the contrary, a collective right is a right that the group's members hold jointly and *only* jointly. If, for example, we conceive the right of a people to collective self-determination as a collective right, it will be a right possessed by the flesh-and-blood individuals who make up the relevant people and who hold their right only collectively. If a linguistic minority which is concentrated in a particular region of a society has a collective right that public signage in that region should be in the minority's language as well as in the society's official public language, that right will be a right that the individual members of the minority hold jointly but not separately. In both cases, the group's members will hold a right together that none of them holds individually.

Provided a group right takes that form, there is no obvious barrier to its being a human right. Donnelly's objection to the possibility of collective human rights is that, since human rights are held by human beings and since human beings are individual persons, only individual persons can hold human rights. But collective rights *are* held by individual persons; they are distinguished only by being rights that individual persons hold collectively rather than separately.

Of course, whether we should deem a particular collective right a human right will need to be argued. Not all collective rights will be human rights, just as not all individual rights are human rights. But the mere fact that a right is a collective right should not, of itself, stand in the way of its being a human right. We might argue over whether all or any of the collective rights in UNDRIP should figure in a human rights declaration, but that argument should not be foreclosed merely because many of those rights are collective rights.

Ethno-Cultural Minorities and Collective Rights

If we turn from UNDRIP to human rights instruments that are intended to provide for the ethno-cultural groups usually described as 'minorities', we have to search much harder for any hint of group rights. That is because the drafters of those instruments made studied efforts to avoid ascribing rights to groups, perhaps in the belief that, if the rights were to remain human rights, they could not be held by groups. [16]

That is true of the Declaration on the Rights of Persons Belonging to National or Ethnic, Religious, and Linguistic Minorities, 1992 (hereinafter the 'Declaration on Minorities'), and the European Framework Convention for the Protection of National Minorities, 1995 (hereinafter the 'European Framework Convention'). Both ascribe rights not to minorities as groups but to 'persons belonging to minorities'.

In fact that form of words lends itself easily to collective right-holding. 'Persons belonging to minorities' might hold rights collectively just as they might hold rights individually. However, neither the Declaration on Minorities nor the European Framework Convention means to concede that possibility. Both impose upon states obligations that are directed at the collective interests of minorities and, had those interests been made the objects of rights, those would have been rights that minorities possessed collectively. Thus, the first article of the Declaration on Minorities reads,

> States shall protect the existence and the national or ethnic, cultural, religious and linguistic identity of minorities within their respective territories and shall encourage conditions for the promotion of that identity.

The Declaration's fourth article requires states to take several measures that will establish background conditions favourable to the maintenance and promotion of minority identities. The European Framework Convention imposes on parties to the Convention an even wider range of obligations in respect of minorities and, if those obligations were tied to rights, many of those rights would be collective rights. But neither the Declaration nor the Convention takes that extra step.[17]

Even so, neither document wholly ignores the collective character of much that matters to ethno-cultural minorities. Both allow that, while the rights they recognise are always and only rights possessed by persons individually, those persons may nevertheless join with others in exercising their individual rights; so, while the *possession* of rights may be individual, their *exercise* can be collective. Article 3.1 of the Declaration on Minorities provides,

> Persons belonging to minorities may *exercise* their rights, including those set forth in the present Declaration, *individually as well as in community with other members of their group*, without any discrimination. (My emphases)

Similarly, Article 3.2 of the European Framework Convention provides,

> Persons belonging to national minorities may *exercise* the rights and enjoy the freedoms flowing from the principles enshrined in the present framework Convention *individually as well as in community with others*. (My emphases)[18]

If members of minorities have the option of exercising their individual rights in community with others, do they need collective rights? Can they, through collectively exercising their individual rights, be entitled to all to which they would be entitled were they to possess collective rights?

That is a possibility that must tempt those who want human rights to provide for the needs, vulnerabilities and identities of ethno-cultural minorities but who shun the idea of collective human rights. The proposition we need to examine then is that, through exercising their individual rights together, individuals can gain access to the collective goods that are possible objects of collective rights. To test that proposition, consider rights to the two goods that I previously instanced: a linguistic minority's right to public signage in its own language and the right of a people, including an indigenous people, to collective self-determination. Could a group of individuals secure a right to those goods through the simultaneous exercise of their individually held rights?

Individuals can exercise only rights they possess. Might an individual member of a linguistic minority possess, as an individual, a right that the public signage in his region should be in his language? That is highly improbable. The right we are considering is a claim-right and therefore a right that would impose a duty on the rest of the society to provide public signage in the individual's language. Given the cost of making that provision, it is most unlikely that a single person's interest in having public signage in his language would suffice to justify that duty and, if it does not suffice, the individual will possess no corresponding claim-right. If individuals, *qua* individuals, start out with no right to public signage in their language, it is hard to see how they could arrive at a shared right to that signage merely by exercising their individual rights. If, on the other hand, we consider the interest of the entire linguistic minority in having public signage in their language, their combined interest may well suffice to justify the duty. [19] In that case, they will possess a right to public signage collectively that none of them possesses individually.

The case of public signage is an example of a good that is only contingently collective. [20] Having public signage in one's language is a good (let's suppose), but its goodness is not dependent on its being shared with others. Even if a person were the only person in a society to speak his language, he could still have an interest in there being public signage in his language. Some goods are, however, necessarily collective. They can be the goods they are only if they are shared with others. An example is the good for a society of being collectively self-determining. Could a single individual have a right to that good? Logically, that is possible. I could be the only individual in my society who is entitled to its being collectively self-determining, perhaps because my interest in its being self-determining is the only interest that counts; my fellow citizens may possess interests identical with my own but, for some reason, their interests do not count. [21] While that is a logical possibility, it is not a moral possibility that need detain us, since we are operating on human rights assumptions. If I were to have an individual right that my society should be collectively self-determining, I would have a right not only over the organisation of my own life but also over the organisation of the lives of all of my fellow citizens, and that right would be inconsistent with each of my fellow citizens' having a status equal to my own—an equality that is fundamental to human rights thinking. Unsurprisingly therefore, no individual can possess, *qua* individual, a human right to a society's collective self-determination. [22]

Suppose we attribute to each individual a right to that individual's self-determination. Could individuals then exercise their individual rights of self-determination to achieve the collective self-determination of themselves as a group? There is no immediate route from one right to the other. An act of collective self-determination is not the same as a multitude of simultaneous acts of individual self-determination, and individuals cannot, merely through exercising rights over their own lives, turn those rights into collective rights over the lives of one another.

If, however, individual rights of self-determination are alienable, individuals might trade in their rights, partially if not wholly, in order to form themselves into an association. They might, that is, follow the path of John Locke's social contractors and agree to become members of a common association and to subordinate themselves to the authority of that association. They might also each agree that their association should be collectively self-determining. In that case, they will have exercised their individual rights to create a self-determining association which, as an association, can have collective rights to goods that are collective to the association.

The context in which that move from the individual to the collective is most plausible is religious practice. Article 18 of the UDHR gives people the freedom to manifest their religion 'either alone or in community with others', as do the International Covenant on Civil and Political Rights (ICCPR) (Art. 18) and the European Convention on Human Rights (ECHR) (Art. 9). [23] Much of religious practice takes a collective form. People practise their religion through becoming members of religious organisations, such as churches and mosques. They also engage in collective religious practices, such as a *nagar kirtan* (a public religious procession) staged by a Sikh community, or an integrated act of Christian worship in which the participants assume different roles and play different parts. If there is a right to stage a *nagar kirtan*, or a right to a collective act of worship as a collective act, it must be a collective right. Individual participants may have individual rights to participate in the collective act, but those individual rights should not be confused with a right to the collective act as a collective act. That collective right will be held collectively by the participants in the act. Similarly, if we think of the rights of a religious organisation as rights possessed by the organisation's members, those will be rights held collectively by the members. But we can then ask how there came to be those collective rights. If membership of a religious organisation is voluntary and if participation in a collective religious act is also voluntary, the answer will be through individuals' exercising their individual rights of religious freedom. It is through their exercise of those rights that they have become members of religious organisations or participants in collective religious acts.[24] In that way, collective religious rights can be grounded in the exercise of individual religious rights, and the violation of a collective religious right can be, at a deeper level, the violation of several individuals' individual religious rights.

We can, then, tell something like the social contract story to explain how people can, by exercising their individual rights together, gain access to collective religious goods which, if they are objects of rights, will be objects of collective rights. That story depends crucially on people's religious membership and participation being matters of choice, which is not always the sociological reality, especially when religion forms part of an ethno-cultural identity; but, according to the human rights canon, it ought to be the reality. To what extent can we apply that model more generally to the collective aspects of the lives of ethno-cultural minorities? It certainly applies to some. Members of minorities might, for example, exercise their individual rights of freedom of association to establish or join associations devoted to their shared culture, language or history. But it does not apply to all. Consider the two examples I gave previously. People do not join their native language group; they simply find themselves to be members of it. Similarly, they cannot join an indigenous people; they just are, or are not, members of that people. If they are members of an indigenous people, they might opt to abandon that people, either territorially or culturally, just as individuals might choose to give up their native tongue for another language. But they cannot wilfully become members of an indigenous people or wilfully turn a non-native language into their native language. Nor can they wilfully adopt a nationality that is not already their nationality (in the sense of 'nationality' relevant here) or lay claim to a culture of the kind we associate with ethnicity if it is not already their culture. Hence, the contractual route from individual rights to collective goods and collective rights will be more often than not unavailable. We cannot plausibly use the idea of social contract to ground the collective right to self-determination of indigenous peoples in the joint exercise of their members' individual rights. Nor can we use that idea to explain how it is that a linguistic minority might have a right to public signage in its own language.

In large measure, therefore, people will not be able to secure rights to the collective goods associated with their ethno-cultural identities merely by exercising human rights that they possess as discrete individuals. In general, if there are, or ought to be, human rights to those collective goods, they must be collective human rights and, what is more, rights that are fundamentally collective rather than collective rights brought into existence by the exercise of individual rights.

Collective Human Rights: A Threat to Individual Human Rights?

Even if the notion of collective human rights is both coherent and plausible in the form I have proposed, that notion is likely to attract another sort of doubt. People often shun group rights because they fear those rights will be used to the detriment of individuals, particularly the individuals who constitute the group's members. That fear is likely to be exacerbated if we assert group rights in the context of human rights and if the right-holding groups have, like ethno-cultural minorities, involuntary memberships. Should that fear make us reluctant to concede that groups might hold human rights?

The principal source of that fear is the possibility that a group may wield its rights over its own members and do so in a way that significantly impairs their freedom or harms them in some other way. If we accord human rights to groups, we may simultaneously imperil the human rights of those who fall under the authority of those groups. Group human rights may therefore exist to the detriment of individual human rights.

In considering that possibility, the distinction between the corporate and collective conceptions of group rights is once again crucial. A group right corporately conceived creates the possibility that a group will hold rights against its own members. It does so because, on the corporate conception, a right-holding group is an entity that is distinct from its members and that possesses moral standing independently of that of its members. If we separate the group from its members in that fashion, we make it possible for the group as one party to hold rights against its individual members as other parties. On the collective conception, however, there is no group that exists independently of its members; the group is simply the individual members who jointly hold the right. It makes no more sense to hold that the rights jointly held by those individuals might be rights that they hold against themselves than it does to hold that a right held by a single individual might be a right he holds against himself. So, if we operate with the collective conception, a collective right can be directed only outwardly as a claim upon parties external to the right-holding group. It cannot be directed inwardly towards the collectivity's own members.

If that simple logic is less than fully reassuring, the obvious course is to provide that collective human rights must always be consistent with individual human rights. The individuals who hold human rights collectively will be the same individuals who hold human rights individually, so that collective and individual human rights must together form a coherent set. Safeguards for individual human rights of the relevant sort are already written into UNDRIP (Arts 1, 46), the Declaration on Minorities (Arts 3.2, 8.2), and the European Framework Convention (Arts 3.1, 22).[25]

GROUP-SPECIFIC HUMAN RIGHTS

By a group-specific right, I mean a right that is specific to a particular group rather than universal to mankind. Group-specific rights can also be group rights, but they do not have to be. I borrow the term 'group-specific' from Will Kymlicka.[26] Most of the group-specific rights that Kymlicka identified and defended in his *Liberalism, Community and Culture* were also collective rights[27] but, as he has been subsequently at pains to point out, the group-specific nature of those rights was logically independent of their being collective rights, and the issue of whether those rights were rightfully group-specific was quite separate from controversy over whether they could or should be collective rights.[28] A right specific to an ethno-cultural group can be a right held by the group's members severally rather than collectively. For example, Sikhs in Britain have legal rights specific to themselves to ride a motorcycle, or to work on a construction site, without wearing a safety helmet, provided they wear a turban. They also have the right to carry a knife (the *kirpan*) in public, while most other British citizens do not. Those rights are entirely intelligible as rights possessed and exercised by individual Sikhs.[29]

The general run of rights, other than human rights, are group-specific; e.g. rights that people possess as citizens of particular countries or rights they have as members of particular associations. Rights may also be specific to different categories of individual; e.g. rights specific to children or the elderly, such as rights to special care and protection. Thus, the 'group' in 'group-specific' can signify a group that takes the form of a community or an association, but it does not have to. A right can also be group-specific in being specific merely to individuals of a particular type.

The challenge facing the idea of group-specific human rights is readily evident. I have defined group-specific rights in opposition to rights that are universal to human beings, yet human rights are commonly thought to be universal rights. That universality is generally reckoned a defining feature of human rights.[30] How then can a right be both group-specific and human? Before turning to that question, I want to comment briefly on how far the rights currently ascribed to indigenous peoples and ethno-cultural minorities are group-specific.

Indigenous Peoples and Group-Specific Rights

Some of the rights found in UNDRIP are rights ascribed to indigenous peoples or indigenous individuals in common with other peoples or other individuals. Article 3, for example, ascribes to indigenous peoples the same right of self-determination as the first articles of the International Covenant on Economic, Social and Cultural Rights (ICESCR) and the ICCPR ascribe to all peoples.[31] Other articles ascribe rights to indigenous individuals that the UDHR and the international covenants ascribe to everyone. Article 7.1, for instance, states that indigenous individuals 'have the rights to life, physical and mental integrity, liberty and security of person'.[32] Article 2 ascribes to both indigenous peoples and indigenous individuals 'the right to be free from any kind of discrimination, in the exercise of their rights'.[33]

For the most part, however, the rights that appear in UNDRIP are clearly tailored to indigenous peoples—to their specific character, circumstances and historical treatment. Here are three examples:

Article 25
Indigenous peoples have the right to maintain and strengthen their distinctive spiritual relationship with their traditionally owned or otherwise occupied and used lands, territories, waters and coastal seas and other resources and to uphold their responsibilities to future generations in this regard.

Article 28.1
Indigenous peoples have the right to redress, by means that can include restitution or, when this is not possible, just, fair and equitable compensation, for the lands, territories and resources which they have traditionally owned or otherwise occupied or used, and which have been confiscated, taken, occupied, used or damaged without their free, prior and informed consent.

Article 31
Indigenous peoples have the right to maintain, control, protect and develop their cultural heritage, traditional knowledge and traditional cultural expressions, as well as the manifestations of their sciences, technologies and cultures, including human and genetic resources, seeds, medicines, knowledge of the properties of fauna and flora, oral traditions, literatures, designs, sports and traditional games and visual and performing arts. They also have the right to maintain, control, protect and develop their intellectual property over such cultural heritage, traditional knowledge, and traditional cultural expressions.

It is hardly surprising that a declaration devoted to the rights of indigenous peoples should address the specific character, circumstances and experience of indigenous peoples. But, insofar as those rights are specific to indigenous peoples, they confront us with the question of how they can also be human rights.

Earlier I raised and dismissed the suggestion that the collective rights that UNDRIP ascribes to indigenous peoples could belong to a special class of peoples' rights that is separate from human rights. But suppose that suggestion were correct. The issue of universality would still arise. If the rights of peoples are supposed to be universal to all peoples, just as human rights are commonly supposed to be universal to all human beings, how can rights be both rights of peoples and rights specific to indigenous peoples?

Ethno-Cultural Minorities and Group-Specific Rights

If we turn to UN and regional instruments designed to provide for ethno-cultural minorities, we find a mixed picture. We can take as our starting point rights that minorities possess along with everyone else. Some of the rights ascribed to minorities in the Declaration on Minorities and the European Framework Convention are not group-specific at all. Both the Declaration on Minorities (Art. 4.1) and the European Framework Convention (Art. 4.1), for example, assert the right of persons belonging to minorities to equality before the law, a right already ascribed to all in the UDHR (Art. 7) and the ICCPR (Art. 14). The European Framework Convention (Art. 7) replicates the UDHR (Arts 18–20) and the ECHR (Arts 9–11) in asserting the rights of minority individuals to freedom of peaceful assembly, association and expression and to freedom of thought, conscience and religion. Emphasising that minorities possess those rights equally with everyone else is not without practical point since, *ceteris paribus*, minorities are more vulnerable to their denial or infringement, but reasserting those rights does no more than confirm their universality.

The term 'minority rights' is normally reserved for rights that are specific to minorities—rights that are 'special rights recognised to the exclusive benefit of minority groups.'[34] An example is article 27 of the ICCPR.

> In those States in which ethnic, religious or linguistic minorities exist, persons belonging to such minorities shall not be denied the right, in community with the other members of their group, to enjoy their own culture, to profess and practise their own religion, or to use their own language.[35]

No similar article caters for majorities. The Declaration on Minorities and the European Framework Convention similarly ascribe a number of rights specifically to minorities. The Declaration (Art. 2.3) attributes to persons belonging to minorities the right to participate in national and, where appropriate, regional decision-making. The Convention, while allowing policies of integration, requires its parties to refrain from policies or practices aimed at assimilation (Art. 5.2), and it attributes to persons belonging to minorities rights to use their language in private and public (Art. 10.1), to be addressed in a language they understand should they be accused or arrested (Art. 10.3), to use their name and have it recognised in their own language (Art. 11.1), to display signs in their language (Art. 11.2), to manage and maintain their own private educational and training establishments (Art. 13), and so on.

Both documents also oblige states to take measures designed to protect the rights and identities of minorities. The Declaration on Minorities requires states to create favourable conditions enabling persons belonging to minorities to 'express their characteristics and to develop their culture, language, religion, traditions and customs' (Art. 4.2); to secure adequate opportunities for minority persons 'to learn their mother tongue or to have instruction in their mother tongue' (Art. 4.3); and 'to encourage knowledge of the history, traditions, language and culture of minorities existing within their territory' (Art. 4.4). The European Framework Convention includes similar provisions (Arts 5.1, 6.1, 12, 14).

These rights, and the state obligations with which they are associated, are clearly group-specific, but they do not privilege minorities. Rather, they address and aim to provide for the disadvantaged position in which ethnocultural minorities are liable to find themselves relative to majorities. There is no article providing for majorities equivalent to Article 27 of the ICCPR, not because majorities matter less than minorities but because the working assumption is that majorities, since they are majorities, will experience no obstacle to enjoying their culture, professing and practising their religion, or using their language. If that assumption proved misplaced because a minority dominated a society and used its dominance to prevent the majority from enjoying its culture, professing and practising its religion, or using its language, persons belonging to that majority would suffer a violation of their rights (morally if not legally) no less than had they been a minority. Similarly, the special rights and measures set out in the Declaration on Minorities and the European Framework Convention are not replicated for majorities simply because, it is assumed, majorities have no need of them. Thus, while the rights and measures instanced above are clearly group-specific, they aim only to narrow the gap between minorities and majorities by securing states of affairs for minorities that majorities can take for granted. That is why they do not privilege minorities even though they are special to minorities. We might describe them as group-specific devices that are ultimately universal in aspiration.

That description would, however, be less than accurate since there are differences in the end states that current provision for minorities aims to achieve. According to Article 4.2 of the European Framework Convention,

> The Parties undertake to adopt, where necessary, adequate measures in order to promote, in all areas of economic, social, political and cultural life, *full and effective equality* between persons belonging to a national minority and those belonging to the majority. (My emphasis)

On inspection, however, the rights the Convention assigns to minorities fall short of the 'full and effective equality' it ostensibly requires. The Convention does not require, for example, that a minority's language must be an official language of its society.[36] Nor does it require that a minority's culture must figure equally with the majority's in the society's public culture, or that its religion must figure equally with all other religions in the society's public ceremonies, or that a society should not have an officially established religion. There is nothing necessarily untoward in those states of affairs, but they do indicate significant ways in which the rights of ethno-cultural majorities and minorities can be group-differentiated and so group-specific.

Still more striking is the way in which rights of different minorities can differ. The European Framework Convention provides differently for differently situated minorities. It requires parties to the Convention to endeavour, as far as possible, that 'in areas inhabited by persons belonging to national minorities traditionally or in substantial numbers', those persons should be able to use their language in their relations with the administrative authorities (Art. 10.2).[37] In the case of such minorities, the parties should also endeavour to ensure that persons belonging to those minorities 'have adequate opportunities for being taught the minority language or for receiving instruction in this language' (Art. 14.2). It also requires parties to endeavour 'in areas traditionally inhabited by substantial numbers of persons belonging to a national minority' that 'traditional local names, street names and other topographical indications intended for the public' shall be displayed in the minority's language as well as the majority's (Art. 11.3). None of these articles is formulated in the language of rights, but the implication of each is that minorities that meet the qualifying conditions (those that have been 'traditionally' present in an area and/or that exist 'in substantial numbers') have claims that minorities who fail to meet them do not.

The European Framework Convention is more explicit than the Declaration on Minorities on the different provision that should be made for differently situated minorities, but the Working Group on Minorities of the Sub-Commission on the Promotion and Protection of Human Rights, in commenting on the Declaration, is still more forthright.[38] It expressly recognises 'factors that can be relevant in distinguishing between the rights that can be demanded by different minorities'.

> Those who live compactly together in a part of the State territory may be entitled to rights regarding the use of language, and street and place names which are different from those who are dispersed, and may in some circumstances be entitled to some kind of autonomy. Those who have been established for a long time on the territory may have stronger rights than those who have recently arrived.[39]

Again, there is nothing necessarily untoward in these differences in minorities' rights, and I do not cite them in a spirit of criticism. They have eminently reasonable justifications.[40] I cite them only to highlight how the rights that figure in human rights instruments can differ between different minorities as well as between majority and minority. The overall picture is one of rights that differ between groups according to relevant differences in their circumstances.

Making Sense of Group-Specific Human Rights

How then can rights be both human and group-specific? The apparent conflict between these two adjectives arises from the widely shared assumption that human rights must be universal rights. Must they?

The Primacy of Human Status

Take the phrase commonly affirmed by adherents of the humanist conception of human rights: a human right is a right we possess 'in virtue of being human'. What does that phrase mean? It does not present us with a mere biological description; more importantly, it affirms a status, either moral or legal. A human right is a right that we hold in virtue of possessing the status of being human. It is a right that we hold because we are human. In like fashion, a right we hold in virtue of being citizens is a right we hold because we are citizens, and a right we hold in virtue of being a member of an association, such as a natural history society, or a member of an institution, such as a legislature, is a right we hold as a member. That is what a right's being a citizen's right or a member's right connotes. In like manner, a 'human right' connotes a right we possess as human beings.

In the first instance, therefore, the 'human' in 'human right' signals the status in virtue of which the bearer holds the right, rather than the scope of those who hold the right. It will, in the second instance, imply a description of scope if we can infer, as people commonly do, that a right that someone holds in virtue of his or her human status must be a right that every other human person holds, too—if, that is, we can infer universality of right from universality of status. Before proposing that we should not draw that inference, I say a little more about the primacy of human status in the idea of human rights.

The words most commonly used in UN documentation to refer to the moral status that people possess as human beings are 'dignity' and 'worth'. The opening lines of the UN Charter affirm the UN's 'faith in the fundamental human rights' and 'in the dignity and worth of the human person'. That faith is restated in the preamble to the UDHR, which also recognizes 'the inherent dignity' and 'the equal and inalienable rights of all members of the human family'. According to the preambles to the ICESCR and ICCPR, 'the equal and inalienable rights of all members of the human family' are rights that 'derive from the inherent dignity of the human person'. Similarly the preamble to the Vienna Declaration and Programme of Action, 1993, recognizes and affirms 'that all human rights derive from the dignity and worth inherent in the human person, and that the human person is the central subject of human rights and fundamental freedoms'. The word 'derive', rather than indicating only a status that undergirds human rights, may imply that the entire catalogue of human rights can be inferred from human dignity and human worth. That is hard to find plausible, and it is perhaps idle to look for analytic precision in these preambles. Certainly, the term 'dignity' occurs in them with more than one meaning.[41] Nevertheless, amongst those various usages, 'dignity', along with 'worth', is used to indicate that people possess moral status as human beings and that, as bearers of that status, they bear human rights.

Something else affirmed in human rights declarations and conventions, not only in their preambles but also in the rights and standards they set out, is the equal status that people possess as human beings and as the bearers of human rights.[42] We therefore have a double-barrelled claim: human beings have both *status* and *equal* status; they *matter* and they matter *equally*. Thus, whatever rights people hold in virtue of possessing human status must be rights that are consistent with their equal status. If human rights can differ for different people, as I shall suggest, those differences must be compatible with the equal status of their holders. They must be 'horizontal' rather than 'vertical' differences of right; they cannot imply that some matter more than others and are, for that reason, entitled to more and better than others.

The status in virtue of which we hold human rights is also crucial to the political role we look to those rights to perform. In the humanist conception, unlike the political, that role does not figure in the very idea of human rights; rather, it is an implication that follows from the possession of human rights. The status in virtue of which we hold those rights is critical to that implication. If we conceive a right as a right we hold as human beings, we do not conceive it as a gift of the state. It is not granted by the state, nor is the state at liberty to remove it. Even if a human right imposes positive rather than merely negative obligations on the state, it is still not a right we possess by the grace of the state. Thus, if we look to human rights to play their familiar role of limiting the sovereignty of states—limiting what states may do but also what they may not do—the status in virtue of which we hold human rights is crucial to their performing that role.

Both Group-Specific and Human

Why do commentators so frequently suppose that human rights must be universal? The answer may be simply that they treat universality as an axiomatic feature of human rights: human rights, they may suppose, simply *are* rights possessed by all humans. But, amongst humanist theorists, there may be another answer: rights that we possess in virtue of being human must be rights that derive from, and only from, our common human nature, and rights so derived will be rights common to all human beings. However, if human rights are to reach beyond the natural rights of the seventeenth century and to bear any resemblance to the rights incorporated in the UDHR, that view is unsustainable. Certainly human rights need to take account of our nature as human beings, but they must also take account of the conditions and circumstances in which we live. The extent to which the rights in the UDHR are geared to particular socio-political conditions is frequently noticed. Rights relating to judicial processes and to legal punishment, to personal security, to nationality and asylum, to education and to other welfare goods and services provide examples.

The account of human rights given by James Griffin comes close to a 'human nature only' account. For Griffin, the foundation of human rights lies in the human capacity for normative agency; human rights properly conceived are rights that protect the development and exercise of that agency. The most basic of those rights are rights to autonomy, liberty and minimum material provision. But even Griffin accepts that, in order to give determinate shape to those very general rights, we must take account of 'practicalities', including the nature of human societies. [43]

Of course, once we have taken account of those practicalities, the rights that emerge may still be universal rights. Griffin ensures that outcome by allowing practicalities to figure in his argument only insofar as they are practicalities common to the human condition across time as well as space. Why impose such an extraordinarily exacting constraint? The answer seems to lie in Griffin's determination to ensure that human rights will remain universal across both time and space. Others, such as John Tasioulas, suggest that we should impose a time constraint upon the universality of human rights so that we can claim human rights in the contemporary world without their having to make sense for people living in the mediaeval era or the Stone Age. [44] But, if temporal differences can compromise the universality of human rights, why should not other sorts of difference?

In fact, amongst the rights already recognised as human rights by the UN, some do. Consider the rights of children recognised in the Convention on the Rights of the Child, 1989, and its two Optional Protocols. [45] Some of those are also held by adults; e.g. the right to life (Art. 6) and the right not to be tortured (Art. 37). Some are formulated in the same language as the rights of adults but, assuming the Convention does not mean to challenge traditional parental authority (cf. Art. 5), cannot be precisely the same rights; e.g. rights to freedom of association and religion (Arts 14, 15). Still others are rights special to children; e.g. rights to care and protection (Arts 3, 20), the right not to be separated from their parents (Art. 9), rights relating to their development (Art. 27), the right to be protected from any form of exploitation (Arts 32–36), and special rights relating to armed conflict (Art. 38 and Optional Protocol I). All adults will have had a childhood, and most children will go on to have an adulthood so that, in the course of a normal human life, a person will have held rights both as a child and as an adult. But that does not remove the puzzle of how human rights can be universal and yet different for children and adults. However, there is no puzzle if what makes them human rights is the common status in virtue of which the rights are held. Human rights so understood can be rights that provide differently for the conditions of childhood and adulthood, and it would be decidedly odd if they did not.

For the most part, the human rights of women and men are the same, even though women are often more vulnerable than men to violations of some of those rights. But some rights differ because women, unlike men, are capable of pregnancy and child-bearing. Two striking examples are the rights of women not to be subjected to forced pregnancy and to forced abortion.[46] Here too it would be perverse to insist that rights providing against such grotesque wrongs cannot be human rights simply because they are possessed only by women. Their being less than universal is no bar to their being human rights if what makes them 'human' is the status in virtue of which they are held.

Human rights theorists sometimes wring their hands over the case of people who are comatose or who have lost command of their faculties through illnesses such as dementia. Clearly, these conditions will affect the rights of those who suffer them. We do people no favours if we continue to ascribe them freedoms that presuppose a self-direction of which they are no longer capable. But we also have reason to ascribe them rights to special care and protection that non-sufferers do not possess. The non-universality of these rights is entirely consistent with their being human rights—rights that people hold in virtue of their equal status as human beings.

Consider now differences that we might describe as differences of circumstance rather than condition. One such is the different circumstances in which human beings have lived in different centuries. Those differences are inescapably relevant to the content of some rights, such as welfare rights, which in turn creates difficulty for those, like Griffin and Wellman, who insist that human rights must be universal through time as well as space.[47] That difficulty disappears if rights are 'human' in virtue of the status of the holder rather than the universality of the right. The rights that people can possess in virtue of their human status will vary, intelligibly and reasonably, according to the different historical circumstances in which they live.

Now let's return to the human rights of ethno-cultural minorities and consider those that depart from universal rights in the most radical way: the different language rights of differently situated linguistic minorities. We have seen how the language rights of a society's majority may differ from those of its minorities and how the rights of its different minorities may differ according to circumstances, such as their relative size and geographical con-centration. Those differences in right can be entirely consistent with the equal human status of all whose rights are at stake. They hold different rights neither because they are differently valued as persons nor because their lan-guages are differently valued, but because they are differently circumstanced in relation to the make-up of the society to which they belong. The differences in right are neutral with respect to both the identity of particular persons and the identity of their language in that *any* person speaking *any* language in the same circumstances would possess the same rights. Different language speakers can therefore possess different rights in respect of the public use of their language, even though the rights at stake are rights they possess as human beings and are therefore human rights.

The case of linguistic minorities is noteworthy because the language rights of different minorities can differ in extent. In that respect, their rights can be correctly described as unequal but, so long as that inequality is justified, they are unequal in a way that is consistent with the equal human status of those who make up the relevant minorities. The more common case will be rights that differ according to the different conditions and circumstances of groups, but which we have no reason to describe as unequal. The human rights of indigenous peoples exemplify that more common case. In many respects those rights are more complex than the rights of linguistic minorities, since they range over multiple aspects of people's lives and have to provide for people whose specific circumstances and ways of life differ and whose members may adhere in different degrees to the ways of life traditionally associated with their group. Here I shall not enter into any of those complexities. I draw attention only to the way in which rights that indigenous people hold in virtue of their human status can still be rights that are sensitive to their special features and circumstances as indigenous people. Just as Kymlicka has argued that rights can be justifiably group-differentiated even though they are rights that people hold as citizens of the same society,[48] so rights can be justifiably group-differentiated even though they are rights that people hold in virtue of their common status as human beings.[49]

Group-Specific Human Rights: Apparent Rather than Real?

Those who cling to the belief that human rights must be universal can deal in one of three ways with the rights I have suggested are both human and group-specific. They might accept that the rights are indeed human rights but deny that they are (fundamentally) group-specific; or they might accept that the rights are group-specific but deny that they are human rights; or they might deny that they are rights of any kind.[50] How might the first sort of denial be made? How might apparently group-specific rights be reconfigured as universal rights? Two sorts of strategy are available: we might show that an apparently group-specific right is either (a) merely a variant of a universal right or that it is (b) a universal but conditional right—a right that is possessed universally but that applies conditionally. My principal objection to both strategies is that they are wrongly motivated; they are driven by the mistaken belief that rights have to be universal to be human. That said, I comment briefly on each.

Proponents of the first strategy usually characterise a non-universal human right as a right that 'derives' from a higher-level universal right. The derived right is then accounted a human right because of its derivation. Wellman, for example, accepts that both children and pregnant women possess human rights to special care which other people do not.[51] What makes those non-universal rights human rights is their deriving from a basal human right that *is* universal: the right to be rescued from potential harm.[52]

If a human right must be universal, it is unclear how a non-universal right can satisfy that criterion merely by being linked to a right that is universal. That objection might be met by reconceptualising what a derived right is. Rather than being separate from the right from which it derives, as a child is separate from its parent, it may be no more than an aspect or application of a universal right. That is implicit in Griffin's notion that all other human rights cascade from the three basic human rights to autonomy, liberty and minimum provision.[53] But we then need to be convinced that all non-universal rights can be accounted for fully as mere realisations of abstract higher-level rights. The rights in UNDRIP do not lend themselves easily to that task, nor do language rights. James Nickel suggests that the right of minority individuals to use their native language can be derived from the universal right to freedom of expression or communication.[54] That proposal is unconvincing on three counts: the considerations that motivate language rights are quite different from those that motivate the right to free expression; free expression provides no rationale for prioritising native language use over other language use; and it does not explain how different linguistic groups can legitimately have different language rights.

The other possible strategy—the 'conditional' strategy—works by characterising an apparently non-universal right as a right which is held universally but applies only in specific conditions. Wellman presents the right to social security as a right of that sort.[55] The right itself is possessed irrespective of time and place, but its 'application' depends on conditions that make its realisation possible. Thus, while people in the ancient world possessed the same right to social security as people living now, the right did not 'apply' in the ancient world because the circumstances necessary for its enjoyment were absent. That seems little more than a makeshift designed to maintain an appearance of universality. While human status is universal across time, the rights which that status grounds are not. If people in the ancient world were living now, they would have the same right to social security as we have now, and, if we had been living in the ancient world, our right to social security would have amounted only to what was possible then. It is not merely the application of the right that is conditional but the content of the right itself.

Even rights that are more straightforwardly conditional, such as rights to assistance if we are disabled or involuntarily unemployed, are arguably non-universal. If these are human rights, all human beings will be eligible for them, but only those who meet the qualifying condition will actually have the right to assistance. Here again, it is the status that is universal and the eligibility that follows from it, rather than the right. That may seem unnecessarily precise given that unemployment and disability are misfortunes that may befall any of us. But it would not be overly precise if we were to use Wellman's conditional strategy to transform all group-specific into universal rights—if, for example, we were to say that all human beings possess rights relating to pregnancy conditional on their being women, or that all possess the rights in UNDRIP conditional on their being indigenous, or that all possess certain sorts of language right conditional on their belonging to a linguistic minority of a particular type.

CONCLUSION

My main purpose has been to argue that there is scope for the rights of indigenous peoples and those of ethno-cultural minorities to be both collective and group-specific and still be human rights. That argument does not require us either to abandon or to trivialise the 'human' in human rights. On the contrary, we can conceive human rights as rights that we possess in virtue of being human whilst allowing that some of those rights can be collective or group-specific or both. Collective human rights are rights that are held jointly by individuals in virtue of their status as human beings. Typically, they will be rights to collective goods, such as collective self-determination. Group-specific human rights are rights that are specific to a group rather than rights held by all, but are still rights which the group's members hold, either individually or collectively, in virtue of their status as human beings. The universality of the status upon which human rights are founded, and in virtue of which they are 'human', does not entail that rights themselves can be human rights only if they are universal across space or time or both.

In making that argument, I have drawn on UNDRIP and declarations and conventions relating to the rights of ethno-cultural minorities. In doing so, I have not attempted to argue that the rights announced in those documents can be claimed, with full justification, as human rights. My claim has been more limited; I have argued only that their authenticity as human rights need not be in doubt merely because they are either collectively held or less than universal in scope.

In a similar fashion, my conception of what makes a right a 'human right' has been modest and minimal: it is a right that people possess in virtue of their human status. My argument is not therefore tied to any particular justificatory theory of human rights or to any substantive account of the content of human rights. It is a conceptual rather than a normative argument. It therefore stands free of any particular normative theory of human rights, although it may be more congenial to some normative theories than to others.

The idea that rights are 'human' in virtue of the status in which they are held is one that is most associated with the traditional moral thinking about human rights that I have described as 'humanist'. Little distinguishes my argument in this chapter as 'humanist' beyond my use of the idea that human rights are rights we hold in virtue of our human status. Is it the case, even so, that my argument remains trapped within the confines of humanism and has no significance beyond humanist thinking about human rights?

While proponents of the political conception continue to use the language of human rights, their understanding of what a human right is renders the adjective 'human' of little or no significance, although that is more clearly true of Beitz's and Raz's versions of the political conception than of Rawls's. Political theorists are therefore likely to remain unmoved by an argument that rights grounded in human status can be collectively held or group-specific, even though the individualism and universalism commonly associated with the idea of rights held 'in virtue of being human' contribute to Beitz's and Raz's reasons for dismissing that idea.[56]

My argument is more significant for legal conceptions of human rights. Here, of course, the status relevant to the bearing of human rights will be legal rather than moral, even though, if we sought a moral justification for that legal status, we might find it, with Allen Buchanan, in an equivalent moral status.[57] If we conceive legal human rights as rights that are so-called because their legally recognised bearers are human beings, legal human rights can still take the form of collective rights or group-specific rights. The legal ascription of human rights to indigenous peoples and ethno-cultural minorities in those forms need not betoken either adhockery or incoherence at the heart of human rights law. Rather, those rights can be part of a logically coherent scheme of legal human rights.

NOTES

Earlier drafts of this chapter benefited from discussions at the Symposium on Ethno-Cultural Diversity and Human Rights held at the School of Law and Social Justice, University of Liverpool; the inaugural meeting of the Globalising Minority Rights Project held at the Department of Philosophy, University of Tromsø; and a meeting of the Durham and Newcastle Political Theory Group. Special thanks to Gaetano Pentassuglia, Kaspar Lippert-Rasmussen and Annamari Vitikainen.

    1. Pablo Gilabert, 'Humanist and Political Perspectives on Human Rights', *Political Theory* 39 (2011): 439–67.

    2. James Griffin, *On Human Rights* (Oxford: Oxford University Press, 2008).

    3. John Tasioulas, 'The Moral Reality of Human Rights', in *Freedom from Poverty as a Human Right*, ed. T. Pogge (Oxford: Oxford University Press, 2007), 75–102.

4. Carl Wellman, *The Moral Dimensions of Human Rights* (Oxford: Oxford University Press, 2011).

5. John Rawls, *The Law of Peoples* (Cambridge, MA: Harvard University Press, 1999).

6. Charles R. Beitz, *The Idea of Human Rights* (Oxford: Oxford University Press, 2009).

7. Joseph Raz, 'Human Rights without Foundations', in *The Philosophy of International Law*, ed. S. Besson and J. Tasioulas (Oxford: Oxford University Press, 2010), 321–38.

8. Allen Buchanan, *The Heart of Human Rights* (Oxford: Oxford University Press, 2013).

9. Although Carl Wellman, *Moral Dimensions of Human Rights*, aligns himself with the humanist conception of moral human rights, he, like Buchanan, argues that other sorts of consideration bear on the appropriate content of legal human rights.

10. Patrick Macklem, *The Sovereignty of Human Rights* (Oxford: Oxford University Press, 2015).

11. On this issue, see S. J. Anaya, 'The Right of Indigenous Peoples to Self-Determination in the Post-Declaration Era', in *Making the Declaration Work: The United Nations Declaration on the Rights of Indigenous Peoples*, ed. C. Charters and R. Stavenhagen, (Copenhagen: International Work Group for Indigenous Affairs, 2009), 184–98.

12. E.g., Michael Hartney, 'Some Confusions Concerning Collective Rights', *Canadian Journal of Law and Jurisprudence* 4 (1991), 292–314; Jan Narveson, 'Collective Rights?', *Canadian Journal of Law and Jurisprudence* 4 (1991), 329–45.

13. Jack Donnelly, *Universal Human Rights in Theory and Practice*, third edition (Ithaca: Cornell University Press, 2013), 30. See also, James A. Graff, 'Human Rights, Peoples, and the Right to Self-Determination', in Judith Baker (ed.), *Group Rights* (Toronto: Toronto University Press, 1994), 186–214; Griffin, *On Human Rights*, 256–76; Miodrag A. Jovanović, *Collective Rights* (Cambridge: Cambridge University Press, 2012), 166–95; James W. Nickel, *Making Sense of Human Rights*, second edition (Oxford: Blackwell, 2007), 163–66; Jeremy Waldron, *Liberal Rights* (Cambridge: Cambridge University Press, 1993), 339–69; Wellman, *Moral Dimensions of Human Rights*, 66–69.

14. E.g., Peter A. French, *Collective and Corporate Responsibility* (New York: Columbia University Press, 1984).

15. Even so, proponents of the corporate conception most commonly use the adjective 'collective' to describe group rights; e.g. French, *Collective and Corporate Responsibility*; Jovanović, *Collective Rights*; Dwight Newman, *Community and Collective Rights: A Theoretical Framework for Rights held by Groups* (Oxford: Hart, 2011). There is no commonly accepted vocabulary that marks the distinction I make between the two conceptions. I use the terms 'corporate' and 'collective' only because each seems aptly to describe its conception of a right-holding group.

16. The Human Rights Committee, in adjudicating cases relating to Article 27 and other articles of the ICCPR that bear on the rights of ethno-cultural minorities, has been willing to take account of the collective dimensions of minority claims. See Macklem, *Sovereignty of Human Rights*, 112–14, and Yvonne M. Donders, *Towards a Right to Cultural Identity?* (Antwerp: Intersentia, 2002), 176–91. For a comprehensive analysis of judicial discourse on international law relating to minority rights, see Gaetano Pentassuglia, *Minority Groups and Judicial Discourse in International Law: A Comparative Perspective* (Leiden: Martinus Nijhoff, 2009).

17. I do not mean to suggest that either document refrains from recognising a greater range of rights only because those would have been collective rights. The primary purpose of a convention is to set out the obligations of those who are party to it, and it makes sense therefore that its articles should give primacy to those obligations. In addition, both the Declaration and the Convention sometimes require states to take measures of a very general background nature and recognise that the appropriate measures can vary legitimately according to local circumstances; that too may have encouraged sparing use of the language of rights.

18. Article 27 of the ICCPR implies that individuals will exercise the rights it recognises only along with others: 'In those States in which ethnic, religious or linguistic minorities exist, persons belonging to such minorities shall not be denied the right, *in community with the other members of their group*, to enjoy their own culture, to profess and practise their own religion, or to use their own language' (my emphasis).

19. I follow here the reasoning of Joseph Raz, *The Morality of Freedom* (Oxford: Oxford University Press, 1986), 207–9.

20. On the relationship between collective rights and collective goods, see further Peter Jones, 'Collective Rights, Public Goods, and Participatory Goods', in *How Groups Matter*, ed. G. Calder, M. Bessone and F. Zuolo, (London: Routledge, 2014), 52–72.

21. Note that the individual right here is not a right that only the individual right-holder shall determine the course of the society's life since that would not be a right to collective self-determination. Rather the right-holder possesses a right that the society shall be determined by himself along with his fellow citizens. The right-holder might declare to his fellow citizens, 'I have the right that we shall be self-determining'.

22. See further, Peter Jones, 'Human Rights and Collective Self-Determination', in *Human Rights: Moral or Political?*, ed. A. Etinson (Oxford: Oxford University Press, 2017), 441–59.

23. The ECHR uses the same words. The ICCPR's phrasing is, 'either individually or in community with others'.

24. Cf. the European Framework Convention, Art. 8: 'The Parties undertake to recognize that every person belonging to a national minority has the right to manifest his or her religion or belief and to establish religious institutions, organisations and associations'.

25. I consider the issues raised in this section more fully in Peter Jones, 'Cultures, Group Rights, and Group-Differentiated Rights', in *Multiculturalism and Moral Conflict*, ed. M. Dimova-Cookson and P. M. R. Stirk (London: Routledge, 2010), 38–57, at 46–53; and 'Groups and Human Rights', in *Human Rights: The Hard Questions*, ed. C. Holder and D. Reidy (Cambridge: Cambridge University Press, 2013), 100–14, at 109–12.

26. Will Kymlicka, *Multicultural Citizenship* (Oxford: Clarendon Press, 1995).

27. Will Kymlicka, *Liberalism, Community and Culture* (Oxford: Clarendon Press, 1989). E.g. the rights of aboriginal groups to self-government, their rights over their territories, and their right to restrict the mobility, property and voting rights of non-aboriginal people with respect to aboriginal communities and their lands.

28. Kymlicka, *Multicultural Citizenship*, 45–47.

29. For a different view, see Jovanović, *Collective Rights*, 123.

30. 'Generally' here includes my former self; for example, Peter Jones, *Rights* (Basingstoke: Macmillan, 1994), 81–82.

31. 'All peoples have the right of self-determination. By virtue of that right they freely determine their political status and freely pursue their economic, social and cultural development.'

32. Cf. UDHR Art. 3; ICCPR Arts 6.1, 7, 9.1.

33. Cf. UDHR Art. 2; ICESCR Art. 2.2; ICCPR Art. 2.1.

34. Gaetano Pentassuglia, *Minorities in International Law* (Strasbourg: Council of Europe, 2002), 48.

35. The text of the article reappears in modified form in Article 2.1 of the Declaration on Minorities. The Declaration substitutes 'have the right' for 'shall not be denied the right'.

36. 'The Parties' obligations regarding the use of minority languages do not in any way affect the status of the official language or languages of the country concerned.' Council of Europe, *Explanatory Report on the European Framework Convention for the Protection of National Minorities* (Strasbourg, 1995), para. 66.

37. 'This provision does not cover all relations between individuals belonging to national minorities and public authorities. It only extends to administrative authorities.' Ibid., para. 64.

38. *Commentary of the Working Group on Minorities to the United Nations Declaration on the Rights of Persons Belonging to National or Ethnic, Religious and Linguistic Minorities*, E/CN.4/Sub.2/AC.5/2005/2.

39. Ibid., para. 10; see also paras 60–64.

40. The most contentious form of differentiation is the privileging of 'old' over 'new' (i.e. migrant) minorities. For a recent examination of that issue and a qualified defence of the old/new distinction, see Alan Patten, *Equal Recognition: The Moral Foundations of Minority Rights* (Princeton, NJ: Princeton University Press, 2014), 269–97. The European Charter for Regional or Minority Languages, 1992, Art. 1(a), excludes altogether the languages of migrants from its remit; however, the Charter is less concerned to provide for the rights of language-

speakers than to preserve, protect and promote European regional and minority languages as goods in their own right.

41. Charles Beitz, 'Human Dignity in the Theory of Human Rights: Nothing But a Phrase?', *Philosophy and Public Affairs* 41 (2013): 259–90; Jürgen Habermas, 'The Concept of Human Dignity and the Realistic Utopia of Human Rights', *Metaphilosophy* 41 (2010): 464–80. On the idea of dignity more generally, see George Kateb, *Human Dignity* (Cambridge, MA: Harvard University Press, 2012); Michael Rosen, *Dignity: Its History and Meaning* (Cambridge, MA: Harvard University Press, 2012); Jeremy Waldron, *Dignity, Rank, and Rights* (Oxford: Oxford University Press, 2012).

42. On which, see Buchanan, *Heart of Human Rights*, 28–31, 68–72, 88–92, 134–45.

43. Griffin, *On Human Rights*, 37–39.

44. John Tasioulas, 'Taking Rights Out of Human Rights', *Ethics* 120 (2010): 647–78, at 666–72.

45. The UDHR (Art. 25.2), the ICESCR (Art. 10), and the ICCPR (Art. 24) also include children within their purview.

46. Beijing Declaration and Platform for Action, Fourth World Conference on Women: Action for Equality, Development and Peace (1995), Annex II, para. 11.

47. Griffin, *On Human Rights*, 48–51; Wellman, *Moral Dimensions of Human Rights*, 27–28.

48. Kymlicka, *Multicultural Citizenship*. See also Will Kymlicka and Wayne Norman, 'Citizenship in Diverse Societies: Issues, Contexts, Concepts', in *Citizenship in Diverse Societies*, ed. W. Kymlicka and W. Norman (Oxford: Oxford University Press, 2000).

49. For another argument that arrives at the conclusion that human rights need not be universal, though in a different way and in a more radical form, see Rowan Cruft, 'Human Rights, Individualism and Cultural Diversity', *Critical Review of International Social and Political Philosophy* 8 (2005): 265–87.

50. Griffin and Wellman, whose thinking on this issue I consider *infra*, deny that some of the rights I have identified as group-specific human rights are moral human rights or moral rights of any kind. Both deny that young children and severely mentally incapacitated adults possess moral human rights, while allowing that they can be the objects of moral duties. For Griffin, the foundation of all human rights lies in the capacity for normative agency so that those who lack that capacity have no human rights. For Wellman, the capacity for moral agency is a precondition for holding moral rights, so that those who lack that capacity cannot bear moral rights of any sort. (Both allow that children can bear moral human rights once they have acquired a capacity for agency.) Both also deny that groups can bear moral human rights and are sceptical about moral group rights more generally. Griffin, *On Human Rights*, 83–95, 256–76; Wellman, *Moral Dimensions of Human Rights*, 21–22, 27–28, 66–69; Carl Wellman, *Real Rights* (Oxford: Oxford University Press, 1995), 113–32, 157–77.

51. His words echo those of the UDHR Art. 25.2.

52. Wellman, *Moral Dimensions of Human Rights*, 29.

53. Griffin, *On Human Rights*.

54. Nickel, *Making Sense of Human Rights*, 161.

55. Wellman, *Moral Dimensions of Human Rights*, 28–29.

56. Rawls, by contrast, shows no inclination to deviate from a conception of human rights as rights held by human beings individually and universally. For critical discussions of the political conception, see Gilabert, 'Humanist and Political Perspectives on Human Rights'; S. Matthew Liao and Adam Etinson, 'Political and Naturalistic Conceptions of Human Rights: A False Polemic?', *Journal of Moral Philosophy* 9 (2012): 327–52; David Miller, 'Joseph Raz on Human Rights: A Critical Appraisal', in *Philosophical Foundations of Human Rights*, ed. R. Cruft, S. M. Liao and M. Renzo (Oxford: Oxford University Press, 2015), 232–43; John Tasioulas, 'Are Human Rights Essentially Triggers for Intervention?', *Philosophy Compass* 4 (2009): 938–50.

57. Buchanan, *Heart of Human Rights*, 89.

Chapter Four

Equality, Recognition and Difference

In recent years much argument about equality has been argument about which equalities matter. One debate that has contributed to that argument has focused on the relationship between redistribution and recognition. That debate has raised many issues, including whether recognition has displaced or should displace redistribution as the central concern of contemporary politics; whether issues of recognition are separable from those of redistribution and, if they are, whether the demands of recognition pull in the same or in different directions from those of redistribution; and whether the idea of recognition can be broadened to encompass all struggles for equality, including struggles for economic equality.[1] In this chapter I do not want to enter that debate, but I do want to examine the idea of equal recognition that it has brought to the fore.

The idea of equality may seem to apply less readily to issues of recognition than to those of redistribution. Recognition is less easily quantified than income and wealth and is less amenable to precise interpersonal comparisons. But the so-called 'politics of recognition' is clearly a politics that pursues an ideal of equality, and those who have struggled for recognition during recent decades have conceived themselves as struggling for equality.

One way in which equality has become tied into thinking about recognition is through the idea of *mutual* or *reciprocal* recognition. Strictly, recognition might be mutual without being equal: you may recognise me as your inferior and I may recognise you as my superior. We then have recognition that is symmetrical and mutual yet unequal. But that is not how 'mutual recognition' is usually understood. Ordinarily, it is taken to imply an equivalence in the value of the recognition that is exchanged between the recognising parties. Moreover, it is sometimes suggested that I can be satisfied only when I am recognised by someone whom I myself recognise as my equal (cf.

Hegel 1977: 111–19). Whatever the truth of that claim, there is a strong sense abroad that recognition ought to be mutual. James Tully, for example, asserts that 'legitimate recognition is always mutual' (2000: 474).

Recognition can be extended equally to people by recognising them under general descriptions that afford them equal standing. So we might recognise individuals as persons or as citizens or as human beings with rights or simply as 'equals', or we might recognise groups as 'peoples' in the formal sense of that term. Recognising people under those descriptions is a way of placing them on an equal footing, and those who have struggled for recognition have frequently struggled for inclusion in those forms of recognition. In recent years, however, the idea of recognition has been taken up and deployed in a rather different way. The emphasis has been not upon general or 'universal' forms of recognition but upon more particular forms of recognition: recognition that recognises people's differences and, more especially, their different identities. In this article, I examine what sort of recognition that can be, particularly if we aim to secure equal recognition. But, before I do so, I outline the thinking of three prominent authors who have argued the case for recognising difference and whose claims I shall contest.

THE DEMAND FOR RECOGNITION OF DIFFERENCE

Charles Taylor

Much contemporary discussion of recognition has its origins in the work of Charles Taylor, especially his essay on multiculturalism entitled 'The Politics of Recognition' (1994).

Taylor traces the origins of the contemporary concern with identity and recognition to two historical developments: the collapse of social hierarchies and the development of the ideal of authenticity, the ideal of being true to oneself (1994: 26–37). He notices, however, that those developments have given rise to the politics of recognition in two antithetical forms (37–44). Initially they gave rise to the politics of universalism or the politics of equal dignity: to the idea that, contrary to the social hierarchies of the past, all human beings share something in common and, in virtue of their common humanity, are entitled to equal respect and a common set of rights. Like almost everyone else, Taylor links this politics of universalism to Kant and his conception of human beings as rational agents. However, the politics of universalism then gave way, under the influence of the ideal of authenticity, to its opposite: the politics of difference. That politics calls upon us to recognise not people's sameness but their uniqueness; 'what we are asked to recognise is the unique identity of this individual or group, their distinctness from everyone else' (38). It regards the uniformity of recognition associated with universalism as, in reality, an attempt to impose the dominant identity of some upon others who do not share it, and therefore as oppressive and unjust.

What does the recognition of difference demand? It requires, says Taylor, that we recognise 'the equal value of different ways of being. It is this acknowledgement of equal value that a politics of identity-recognition requires' (1992: 51). Thus, if we apply that demand to differences in cultural identity, it requires that we acknowledge the equal value of each culture, 'that we all *recognize* the equal value of different cultures; that we not only let them survive, but acknowledge their *worth*' (1994: 64, emphases in the original).

However, for Taylor, that demands too much—not because cultures are actually of unequal value but because we do not know whether they are of equal value. We lack the judgemental equipment necessary to make that sort of comparative evaluation. Clearly, it will not do to privilege one culture and use its standards to evaluate all others. We need authentically intercultural criteria, but that requires a fusion of the different horizons of different cultures and that we do not have. Without it, he observes, a blunt assertion of the equal value of cultures can be no more than a sham, a patronising pretence (1992: 52; 1994: 70–71).

Taylor does not, though, give up the possibility of according equal recognition to cultures. Rather he argues that we have reason to presume that each culture harbours something of value and, more daringly, that each culture is of equal value. That is only a presumption, a plausible starting hypothesis, which will be vindicated only if and when we have secured the fusion of horizons that enables us to judge its truth (1994: 66–67, 72–73). But Taylor argues for its reasonableness as a presumption and supposes, it seems, that that presumption can provide a basis for satisfying, in some measure, the demand that we accord equal recognition to different cultural identities.[2]

For my purposes, the features of Taylor's argument that I wish to emphasise are his juxtaposition of the politics of universalism to the politics of difference and his insistence that the politics of recognition requires that we accord direct and positive value to each particular identity that we recognise. For Taylor the politics of recognition is very much the politics of *equal* recognition, but what does he suppose that recognising equally must involve? The answer seems to be finding equal value in the identities that we recognise and, in the particular case of cultural identities, finding, or presuming, that the cultures at issue are of equal value.

Anna Elisabetta Galeotti

In a more recent study, Anna Elisabetta Galeotti (2002), has re-presented the case for tolerating minority groups as a case for according them recognition. She accepts that many traditional issues of toleration are now moribund in that they have ceased to be genuinely controversial in liberal democratic societies. But there are other issues, she insists, that are both issues of toleration and very much alive. The two examples to which she gives most attention are issues surrounding Muslims in Western societies, especially the celebrated headscarves issue in France, and issues relating to homosexuality, especially same-sex marriage and the barriers to joining the military that, until recently, gays faced in the United States and many European countries. Whereas traditional issues of toleration concerned the beliefs and values adopted by individuals, these new issues, she argues, concern the ascriptive identities of groups. They also require toleration in a new form. 'Old' toleration followed a privatising strategy in which freedom was extended to individuals in the form of liberal rights that called for no more than non-interference. By contrast, contemporary societies should extend toleration to marginalised and stigmatised minorities by positively and publicly recognising their identities.

In one respect, the recognition that Galeotti seeks for these minorities is general rather than particular in nature. She seeks their full recognition as citizens. That means not merely that they must possess the same formal rights as other citizens, but also that they should cease to be marginalised and humiliated by the majority and suffer damaging slights to their self-respect and self-esteem, so that they are able to participate fully in the life of their society. However, if we are to achieve that goal, it is not enough, she argues, that groups like Muslims and gays should be recognised in ways that remain blind to their particular identities. Rather, societies must extend recognition to Muslims as Muslims and to gays as gays. Therein, she argues, lies the real case for removing the prohibition that prevents French Muslim girls from wearing headscarves while attending state schools, and for instituting provision for same-sex marriage. Measures such as those would (like traditional toleration) extend the freedom of Muslims and gays but that, for Galeotti, would not be their real significance. Their real significance would consist in the recognition that they would accord to Muslim and gay identities. Recognition, she argues, is something that a society can give only symbolically. Measures whose immediate purpose may seem narrow and minor can assume major significance when they constitute gestures of recognition. Liberal democratic societies now need to move beyond their traditional concern with freedom and rights and should seek to secure positive recognition, albeit symbolically, for the minority identities present in their populations.

Axel Honneth

Axel Honneth (1995a, 1995b) has developed a theory of recognition that is far more wide-ranging than those of either Taylor or Galeotti. Indeed, his theory manifests his belief that social struggles in all of their forms can be understood as struggles for recognition.[3] Honneth identifies three forms of recognition that he believes to be essential to an individual's developing a positive and undistorted relation-to-self: love, rights and esteem.

'Love' encompasses emotional relationships between adults, including friendship, but Honneth believes the recognition involved in the early mother-child relationship to be especially significant. The recognition individuals secure through emotional attachments is, he believes, essential to their gaining basic self-confidence. Adult human beings also need to be recognised as morally responsible persons and to be accorded the respect that goes with personhood. Modern systems of law deliver that recognition to citizens by according them equal rights and, nowadays, to all human beings by according them human rights. The social respect that people receive through this form of recognition is essential for the development of their self-respect. However, this universal form of recognition is 'too narrow to include all the aspects that constitute the goal of undistorted and unrestricted recognition' (1995a: 171). People also need to be recognised for the particular people they are. They need social respect, but they also need social esteem, and 'social esteem can only apply to those traits and abilities with regard to which members of society differ from one another. Persons can feel themselves to be 'valuable' only when they know themselves to be recognized for accomplishments that they precisely do not share in an undifferentiated manner with others' (125). Just as social respect is a precondition for self-respect, so social esteem is essential for the development of self-esteem. The condition that a society achieves when its members are able to esteem one another and themselves in this particularised way Honneth describes as 'solidarity' (129).

People, then, can be and need to be and should be recognised in these three different ways. They can also experience disrespect or misrecognition in different ways: through physical abuse, the denial of rights and the denigration of their ways of life. It is their negative experience of these forms of disrespect or misrecognition that motivates people to engage in struggles for recognition.

Thus, unlike many who champion the recognition of people in their difference and particularity, Honneth does not deprecate as misplaced or oppressive general forms of recognition that call upon identities such as personhood. On the contrary, he regards both universal and particular forms of recognition as answering to fundamental human needs. However, while Honneth sees no competition or conflict between recognition of the universal and of the particular, he also conceives these as independent forms of recognition. Recognition of people in their particularity neither derives from nor depends upon their recognition under more general or universal descriptions. Rather, social esteem requires an act of recognition that is separate from, and that needs to be added to, social respect.

THE MEANING OF RECOGNITION

'Recognition' is a word with several meanings, and in discussions of identity and difference it is used in more than one sense.

First, that which perhaps comes most readily to mind in ordinary usage is to 're-cognise': to notice something with which we are already familiar. In this sense, I might recognise an old acquaintance across a crowded room, or my father in a photograph, or someone's handwriting, or the bicycle that was stolen from me a month ago.

A second well-established use is closer to my concerns in this chapter. In this sense to recognise means to be aware of, to appreciate, to accept. Thus I might say that I recognise that I will become a successful athlete only if I train very hard, or that I have behaved badly, or that I have been lucky, or that Bach is a better composer than Haydn.

That sense begins to approach a third for which 'acknowledgement' is often given as the closest synonym. Recognition in this sense goes beyond mere awareness or acceptance and involves a public, expressive element. In this sense, a university might recognise someone's intellectual achievement by awarding him an honorary degree, or an army might recognise a soldier's courage by awarding her a medal. In this same sense, a society might recognise a group by acknowledging and providing for its distinct identity in its law or public arrangements. Things as well as people can be the object of this sort of recognition: a particular drug may be the 'recognised' treatment for an ailment, and a particular language may be the 'recognised' language of a society for public purposes.

The recognition with which theorists of identity are concerned is frequently represented as acknowledgement. But the idea of acknowledgement alone is not quite enough. Acknowledgement can be benign as when we recognise someone's talents or goodness or success. But it can also be neutral or negative. We can recognise someone's talents but also their limitations; we can recognise success but also failure; I may be recognised as a good guy or as a bad guy. A society may recognise a particular identity group, in the sense of officially marking it out and acknowledging its presence, only so that it can persecute and demean it.

Thus we need a fourth sense in which recognition includes positive affirmation as well as acknowledgement. This is the sense intended in the phrase 'the struggle for recognition': people struggle only for something that they wish to have. It is also in this sense that we speak of people deserving or being worthy of or being entitled to recognition. When we 'accord recognition to', we recognise in this sense.

When someone receives this sort of positive recognition, it may be for qualities or achievements that the recognisers regard as admirable. But the positive element in recognition need not be of that sort. Often to be recognised is to be attributed with status or standing. So, when a society accords recognition to a group, it need not applaud the qualities or identity of the group; it may acknowledge only that the group matters, that it should count, that its voice should be heard and its interests given due consideration.

WHY SHOULD WE RECOGNISE IDENTITIES?

The question I want to begin with is why we ought to recognise particular identities. Suppose I am the recogniser and you are the recognised. Why should I recognise your identity? Is it because that identity matters to me or because it matters to you? The obvious answer is because it matters to you.

Let us take Galeotti's example of a Muslim minority in a Western society and the demand that the Islamic identity of that minority should be recognised by the majority population. Given that the majority do not subscribe to Islam, it is difficult to see why they should endorse an Islamic identity merely as such. As non-Muslims, they may take a wholly negative view of Islam. They may regard it as a false system of belief; indeed, since they are not themselves adherents of Islam, they presumably *do* regard it as a false system of belief. Beyond doubting its truth, they may take a negative view of the impact that Islam has upon the lives of those who embrace it. Alternatively, while the majority may be aware of the presence of Muslims in their world, they may be largely ignorant of Islam and view it with indifference. But, even if the majority's view of Islam is more agnostic than negative, it does not provide them with a basis for according recognition to a Muslim identity as such.

Now let us suppose that the majority population takes a more positive view of Islam. While they are not Muslims themselves, they find things to commend in Islam and in Islamic ways of life and so look upon the Muslim identity (or Muslim identities) with a degree of favour. Now they are in a position to accord recognition to a Muslim identity as such. Yet that still seems beside the point. When one section of a society is called upon to recognise another, some people are called upon to recognise other people. The recognition that is demanded is recognition directed at a group of people rather than at a system of belief. If recognition is demanded for the religious identity of that group, that will be because it is the religious identity of those who constitute the group and not because it is a religious identity that has a claim to our recognition independently of its being anyone's identity. In other words, what the majority is called upon to recognise is not Islam but Muslims—not a religious faith but those who subscribe to it. And the imperative for that recognition is grounded not in the value that that identity has for those who do not share it, but in the value it has for those whose identity it is.

Nothing turns here on the particular example I have used. Suppose we reverse roles so that it is Muslims who are called upon to do the recognising and their recognition is demanded for people distinguished by other faiths or by secular forms of life. Again, the obvious ground for that recognition is not the value attributed to those other faiths or to secular forms of life by the Muslim recognisers, but the value that those faiths and forms of life have for the recognised. Not only does that seem the right reason for recognition in this sort of case; it is also the only sort of recognition that we can reasonably demand. If we are content that Muslims should remain Muslims, we cannot ask them directly to endorse atheism or faiths that are in conflict with their own.

If we turn to identities that are cast in terms of 'culture' rather than religion, the same reasoning applies. Why should I accord recognition to your cultural identity? The obvious answer is because it is *your* cultural identity: it should matter to me because, and insofar as, it matters to you. Different cultures need not be conceived as conflicting cultures in the way different religions present conflicting claims to truth. Different cultures can be seen as presenting conflicting sets of beliefs and values, and differences of religious faith may be important to differences amongst cultures. But we might also see different cultures as merely different, as presenting us merely with a range of humanly evolved forms of life and ways of seeing the world. Yet, even if we take a more relaxed view of cultural diversity in which we have no reason to take exception to cultures that differ from our own, the most obvious reason for according recognition to another's culture is the value that culture has for its bearers. I recognise your culture because your culture matters to you, and what matters to you should matter to me because it matters to you.

MEDIATED AND UNMEDIATED RECOGNITION

I have laboured this simple point because its implications fly in the face of so much that is written about recognition, identity and difference. If I should recognise your identity because that identity matters to you, I must accord recognition to you independently of your identity. It is only because you have moral significance for me that your identity should have moral significance to me. So I must first accord recognition to you under some description other than your particular identity if I am to have reason to go on to accord recognition to your particular identity. In other words, the implication of what I have argued about the relevant reason for recognition is that recognition of someone's specific identity must be mediated by their recognition under a more general form of identity.

If, for example, we recognise people as persons, we shall be obliged to treat them as persons. Part of what is involved in respecting people as persons is taking due account of what matters to them, of recognising and responding appropriately to what has significance for them. Thus recognising someone as a person can be a reason for going on to accord them recognition under some more specific description, such as Muslim or Christian or Quebecois or Inuit. It is only by travelling through a general mediating identity, such as 'person', that my recognition of your particular identity can be a recognition I accord you *because* that particular identity matters to *you*.

The general identity 'person' is an obvious one to which we might turn in this context, but it is also one that may encounter resistance because of its Kantian associations. However, we can divest 'person' of its specifically Kantian associations and still be left with a moral category that will do the job. All we need is recognition of people under a description that provides us with reason to take seriously what matters to them, including their specific identities. The identity 'human being' can perform that role, provided we understand that as an identity freighted with moral implication rather than as a merely biological description. Or we might prefer a more extended description such as 'a being of equal moral standing' or 'a being worthy of respect'. Or we might work with a less general identity such as 'citizen'. Or, rather than being an individual identity, the mediating identity might be a group identity such as 'a people'.[4]

This mediated route to the recognition of specific identities is obviously inescapable if we are going to demand that people accord recognition to identities to which they have reason to take exception. How else can a Muslim accord recognition to a Hindu as a Hindu? How else can an atheist or a Christian accord recognition to a Muslim as a Muslim? But I have also argued that, even when we regard a specific identity favourably, our recognition of that identity must take a mediated form, *if* it is to be grounded not in our own favourable estimate of the identity but in the identity's significance for those whose identity it is.

This mediated conception of recognition is at odds with much that is written on recognition and identity simply because recognition of difference or particularity is so commonly juxtaposed to universal forms of recognition. Amongst those who argue for the recognition of difference, 'universal' forms of recognition are frequently rejected as unduly abstract or distorting or oppressive, and the recognition they demand for particular identities is unmediated recognition. But I have shown that, if we take account of the most compelling reason for according recognition to specific identities, forms of recognition that would typically be characterised as 'universal' are indispensable prerequisites for more particular forms of recognition. It is not merely that there are reasons why we should recognise people under both universal and particular descriptions, as if this were a matter of combining together two separate forms of recognition (as Honneth and perhaps Taylor suggest). Rather, it is that the recognition of particularities presupposes and depends upon more general forms of recognition.

One relevant consideration here is that identities are often presented as 'universal' or 'particular' in a misleadingly absolute fashion, as if various forms of identity or category can be assigned straightforwardly to one or the other description. In fact, universality and particularity are always relative to a field of description, and an identity that is universal with respect to one field can be particular with respect to another. Thus, while 'person' is more universal than 'Christian', it is less so than 'sentient being'; and, while 'Christian' is more particular than 'person', it is also less so than 'Roman Catholic' or 'Protestant', both of which are, in turn, less particular than 'Benedictine' or 'Baptist'. An identity, such as 'Muslim' may figure as 'particular' in the context of Western societies but is 'universal' in relation to the Islamic world where, for example, there is an issue of which of several would-be Islamic identities should be recognised as members of the Islamic Ummah. So the tendency of writers on this subject to present themselves as champions of the universal or of the particular is misleadingly simple. An identity is only ever relatively universal (or general) or relatively particular (or specific). My argument uses a relative distinction between the general and the specific, not an absolute distinction between the universal and the particular.

STATUS RECOGNITION AND MERIT RECOGNITION

Before considering the conditions under which recognition is not merely possible but might be accorded equally, I want to introduce another distinction between forms of recognition: merit recognition and status recognition.

One context in which we readily speak of recognition is in relation to achievement or talent or exceptional ability. So we might recognise someone as a highly talented artist or a great composer or a poet gifted with extraordinary insight, or we might recognise someone's athletic prowess or their unusual selflessness in working for the good of others. All of those are examples of merit recognition.

We do not expect merit recognition to be accorded equally simply because we do not expect people to be equally meritorious. Not everyone can be a distinguished poet or a great artist or a fine composer, and not everyone can be a potential Olympic medal winner. We may believe that everyone is equally capable of moral virtue, but we do not expect people actually to be equally virtuous. So we expect merit recognition to be *unequal* recognition; that is part of its point. Merit recognition can, of course, be accorded more or less fairly. It is common to hear the complaint that someone has received less recognition—or, indeed, more recognition—than he or she deserves; but even when merit recognition is apportioned fairly, we do not expect it to be apportioned equally.

Status recognition is a different matter. Of course, status can also be apportioned unequally and has been for most of human history. Hegel notwithstanding, lords have been content to be recognised as lords by their servants, and servants have often been resigned to their recognition as servants by their lords. But status recognition is also open to being accorded equally in a way that merit recognition is not. So, for example, in a democratic age, we suppose that the members of a society should enjoy an equal status as citizens. Or, in more cosmopolitan terms, we think that all human beings should be accorded an equal status as human beings, particularly in relation to those basic rights that we call human rights. That sort of equal status recognition is fundamental to modern moral and legal thinking.

The different ways in which merit and status relate to equality is linked to a difference in the form that the recognising process might take. Sometimes recognising seems to be simply a matter of noticing and acknowledging value, so that the act of recognition in no way contributes to the value that it recognises. The value of what is recognised owes nothing to its being recognised. In other cases, however, recognition has a more constitutive role. Rather than merely noticing and acknowledging value, it confers something of value; it creates rather than discovers value.[5] The distinction between merit and status recognition seems to map onto this difference in the form that the recognising process may take.

For example, when we recognise the achievements of an author, by awarding him or her a literary prize, the value of what we recognise is independent of our recognition. The author has written a great work, and we simply discover and acknowledge its greatness; its greatness is neither created nor contributed to by our recognition. Of course, our recognition does affect the extent to which an author is *conceived* as great; that is what recognition is about. But, when we engage in merit recognition, we conceive the merit that we recognise as a quality that someone or something possesses independently of our recognition. We give the meritorious our recognition, not their merit.[6]

In the case of status, recognition performs a more constitutive role. Status is something that we can bestow through recognition: it is a quality that recognition confers rather than merely notices. In contrast with merit recognition, status recognition creates what it recognises. Consider, for example, a modern institutional status hierarchy such as a judiciary or an army. If someone has the status of a judge or a general, that is a status they have been given; it is not a quality they possess whether or not it is recognised by anyone else. Thus we can make someone a judge or a general, whereas we cannot, in the same sense, 'make' someone a great author or a great athlete.

Recognition of someone as a person or a citizen or as a human being with rights or as an equal is essentially a form of status recognition. So too is recognition of a group as a nation or 'people' as that term is used in international law. These are statuses that we confer through recognition; however, the implication of that point might easily be misunderstood. To say that status recognition, unlike merit recognition, confers what it recognises, rather than simply acknowledges what is already there, is not to say that status recognition manifests an arbitrary act of will. On the contrary, we can have a reason or reasons for according status in the way that we do. Thus status can be accorded in ways that are right and withheld in ways that are wrong. The 'struggle for recognition' has frequently been a struggle for status recognition, and that is a struggle that we can quite properly characterise in terms of justice.

MEDIATED STATUS RECOGNITION, UNMEDIATED MERIT RECOGNITION

I now want to apply this distinction between status and merit recognition to the issue of how we should recognise specific identities. I previously argued that the most compelling reason why we should recognise a specific identity, such as a religious or cultural identity, is because that identity matters to the recognised rather than to the recogniser. That constitutes a reason for recognition provided we suppose that what matters to the recognised should matter to the recogniser because it matters to the recognised. I also argued that recognising for that reason implies a mediated form of recognition in which recognising people under some mediating general identity provides us with reason for taking seriously their particular identity.

The point I now want to add is that that mediating identity is most intelligibly understood as one of status rather than merit. When we recognise people as persons or as citizens or as human beings with rights, we accord them status. Similarly, recognising a group as a nation or a people entails according it status. Certain things follow from that attribution of status, one of which is that we should give due weight to the particular identities embraced by those whom we recognise as persons or citizens or peoples.

If we accord recognition in that way, the recognition that we accord to particular identities is status recognition. It does not involve an evaluation of the merits of the particular identity that we recognise. Thus we can accord recognition to a Muslim identity or Christian identity or Quebecois identity or Inuit identity without having to make any kind of approving judgement of the particular identities that we recognise and without having to compare the relative merits of different identities.

Moreover, it is only if we recognise in this way that we can reasonably expect to secure *equal* recognition. If we recognise people under a description, such as person or citizen, that gives them equal status, we then have reason to give equal status to the particular identities that they embrace. That does not mean that we judge every identity to be of equal value; it means only that we recognise each identity as the identity of someone or some group that enjoys an equal status with others and which we should therefore recognise as the identity of an equal.

Suppose that we do not take this mediated route to recognition. Suppose that we are required—as many people seem to require us—to accord unmediated recognition to particular identities. It is hard to see how that recognition could be any other than merit recognition. If I am required to accord recognition to a Muslim identity, directly and specifically, as a Muslim identity, what can my recognition be about other than the merit (or value or worthiness) of that particular identity? And if that is what recognition entails, how can we possibly suppose that I shall or should find this and other religious identities to be all of equal value or, indeed, of any value? The reply might come back that what I am required to recognise is neither that Islam is meritorious nor that it is of equal value with other religions, but that it is a religion and an identity to which I should give a status that is equal to others. But why should I attribute it with equal status? The obvious answer is the one I have already given: because it is a religion subscribed to by persons of equal status and to which we should give whatever recognition follows from that fact. But that takes us back to mediated recognition. The only other possible answer would seem to be that we should give it equal status because it is of equal merit with other religions or with other identities. That simply makes a claim of equal status dependent upon a claim of equal merit and reintroduces all of the problems associated with engaging in merit recognition in this context.[7]

Taylor and Merit Recognition of Cultures

It is on this issue that, I suggest, Charles Taylor takes a wrong turn in relating the politics of recognition to cultural identities. Taylor supposes that according recognition to a group distinguished by its cultural identity requires recognising its culture, which in turn requires finding value in its culture. Thus, whatever recognition we give a cultural group will be geared to our evaluation of its culture, and we shall be able to accord equal recognition to cultural groups only if we can hold—or, in Taylor's case, presume—that their cultures are of equal value.[8] But, on my understanding of recognition, that gets things the wrong way round. We should begin not with cultures and their relative merits but with people and what matters to them. Our recognition of their cultural identities should be grounded in the recognition that we owe them as people not in the value that we find in their cultures.

That is the only plausible way in which we can accord *equal* recognition to cultural identities. If we recognise people as equals, that is, as beings of equal status, we should give equal status to their cultural identities. Our recognition acknowledges not the value that we ourselves find in the cultures of others but the value that those cultures have for those whose cultures they are. Only if we approach cultural difference in that way can we plausibly insist that different cultural identities should receive equal recognition.

Taylor quite rightly observes that, currently, we have neither the comprehensive knowledge and understanding of different cultures necessary to evaluate their relative merits nor the intercultural criteria needed for their evaluation. It seems unlikely that anyone could ever master the information needed to make an Olympian assessment of humanity's manifold cultures, and the fusion of cultural horizons that Taylor contemplates may also turn out to be an impossible project. But let's suppose that somehow we have gained the comprehensive understanding and generated the standards that we need to assess the relative value of cultures. Is it plausible to presume that, when we apply those standards across all cultures, all will prove to be of equal value? Contrary to Taylor's view, that presumption seems highly implausible. Whatever criteria we apply to the assessment of cultures, it seems virtually certain that some will score better than others.[9] Thus, if we gear our recognition of cultural identities to the value of the cultures from which they derive, we are most unlikely to discover a case for equal recognition.

There are two other ways in which we might relate the value of cultures to equality, but neither is well-placed to deliver recognition. We might hold that different cultures are simply incommensurable in value but, although incommensurability is sometimes elided with rough equality, it really means that the cultures at stake are incomparable rather than equal in value. Alternatively, we might hold that different cultures are in principle commensurable but that, as Taylor observes, we currently lack the evaluative equipment necessary to do the job. But, again, that alone is not enough to justify a presumption of equal value. It is reason only for agnosticism: cultures may be closely equal in value or they may be radically unequal; we simply do not know. Both incommensurability and agnosticism provide reason not to discriminate amongst cultures on the ground that some are better than others, but, without an additional assertion of the positive value of cultures, either in themselves or for their bearers, each is too indeterminate to deliver a case for recognition.

An associated troubling feature of Taylor's approach to recognising cultural identities is exposed by the question, valuable to whom? Let's suppose that 'we' are the potential recognisers and 'they' are the potentially recognised. Because Taylor holds that our recognising their cultural identity entails our finding value in, or presuming the value of, their culture, the value upon which our recognition turns is the value that *we* recognise. Taylor is, of course, fully alive to the difficulties of understanding and judging another's culture, and that is why he is so critical of easy and premature assertions of the value of another's culture. Even so, if and when we actually achieve a fusion of horizons, the value that we can expect to uncover in different cultures will be, it seems, a value that is valuable for everyone; we can expect each culture 'to have something important to say to all human beings' (1994: 66). I do not want to challenge that claim, but I do want to question whether it is right to make it critical to recognition. For Taylor it seems to be critical because he supposes that recognising someone's cultural identity entails recognising the merit of their culture, and that requires that the merit be accessible to, and be recognisable as meritorious by, the recogniser. But that puts the emphasis in the wrong place. Surely cultures are important primarily for the value they have for those whose cultures they are and not for the value they hold for 'outsiders'. Making 'our' recognition of 'their' identity depend upon what 'we', rather than 'they', find valuable seems peculiarly inapt when the identity at issue is a cultural identity.

Galeotti on Toleration as Recognition

Galeotti distances herself from the strong form of recognition that Taylor associates with the politics of difference (2002: 103). She believes that her conception of toleration as recognition requires a revision in liberal thinking and especially an abandonment of 'difference-blind' liberalism. But she shuns liberal perfectionism and believes her revised form of liberalism can satisfy the canons of liberal neutrality. She must therefore have misgivings about what I have characterised as 'merit' recognition, at least insofar as recognition is something accorded by or through the public institutions of a society to different sections of its population. Yet the recognition that she calls for often looks like merit recognition. If we call, as she seems to, for the unmediated recognition of identities, and if we simultaneously spurn the more general 'difference-blind' forms of recognition with which liberalism has been traditionally associated, it is hard to see how our call cannot be for something tantamount to merit recognition. What else can we be demanding if we demand recognition for Muslims *as* Muslims and for gays *as* gays? Galeotti, as I have indicated, wants to avoid the state's giving or withholding its approval to different identities. But she does characterise recognising an identity as accepting and including it in 'the range of the legitimate, viable, "normal" options and alternatives of an open society' (2002: 15). That acceptance and inclusion must involve an appraisal of the identities at issue and must therefore involve 'merit' recognition (in the broad sense in which I have used that term), albeit merit recognition of a modest and limited sort.

The distinction between status and merit recognition is especially relevant for Galeotti's attempt to recast toleration as a form of recognition. In ordinary usage, we 'tolerate' only that which we dislike or of which we disapprove; we have no occasion to 'tolerate' that to which we have no objection. That is an element of the traditional meaning of 'toleration' that Galeotti retains. But if disapproval or dislike remains an essential feature of toleration, it is difficult to see how the recognition in 'toleration as recognition' can be merit recognition. If, on the other hand, the recognition at stake is status recognition, there need be no such difficulty. If I accord you status independently of your identity and, for that reason, accord status to your identity, that gives me reason (at least *prima facie*) to respect your identity and to tolerate your identity if it should be an identity that I view negatively.[10]

Honneth on Social Esteem and Merit Recognition

The context in which Honneth sets the need for recognition of particularity is rather different from the circumstances of cultural diversity considered by Taylor and Galeotti. Although recognition in the form of social esteem is, for Honneth, directed at 'the particular qualities that characterize people in their personal difference' (1995a: 122), that form of recognition is no less needed in culturally homogeneous societies than in those that are culturally diverse. He is also more inclined to regard the 'traits and abilities' of individuals as the targets of this recognition rather than group characteristics of the sort that generally preoccupy identity theorists. Even so, for Honneth as for Taylor, the sort of recognition involved in the attribution of social esteem would seem to be merit recognition.[11] He is clear that, when we recognise individuals as persons possessed of rights, we engage in a form of status recognition. But, when we move from social respect to social esteem, that is not, for Honneth, a form of recognition that is consequent upon, and grounded in, our recognition of individuals as persons. Rather, it is an entirely separate act of recognition that endorses the value of people's particularities.[12] In my terms, it is a form of merit recognition and one that presents Honneth with difficulties similar to those encountered by Taylor.

What sort of particularity should we recognise? There is a measure of ambivalence in Honneth's answer in *The Struggle for Recognition* (1995a). Sometimes he seems drawn to G. H. Mead's idea of functional recognition—that we should recognise each individual's different but valuable contribution, principally through a cooperative division of labour, to their society's collective good. Certainly, his frequent reference to individuals' traits and abilities and to their contribution to 'the realization of societal goals' (122) suggests that sort of functional recognition. At other times, however, he refers more expansively to 'forms of personal self-realization' (125–27, 173), to 'ways of life' and 'forms of life' (127, 134, 172, 175) and, just occasionally, to identities (131, 162).

On what must our recognition of particularity be founded? For Honneth, as for Taylor, the answer is an 'intersubjectively shared value-horizon' (121). That value-horizon can be different for different societies but, within any particular society, it must be shared if the society is to have an 'overarching system of esteem' (126). Honneth presents a strongly communitarian understanding of this shared value-horizon. For any particular society, it will be embedded in that society's cultural self-understanding, and the worth of the individual members of the society will be measured by the degree to which they contribute to the realization of the society's goals (122). Honneth therefore conceives a society as a 'community of value' (122), whose members esteem one another for their different contributions to their 'collectively shared goals' (178). That approach to recognising people in their difference is, again, most obviously suited to recognising them for their different functional contributions to their society. It is not obviously appropriate for according positive recognition to different 'ways of life' or to 'self-chosen life goals' (174). For one thing, different ways of life are much less likely to be united by a shared value-horizon than different functional roles. For another, different ways of life do not obviously promote a goal common to the society in which they are lived and, even if they do, we do not generally suppose that their value resides only or primarily in their contributing to some shared social purpose.[13]

Honneth does make some provision for diversity of value. He speaks of the 'pluralization of the socially defined value-horizon' under modern circumstances (122). By that, he appears to mean not that modern societies are characterised by different and conflicting values, but only that their value-horizons accord value to many different social contributions and ways of life. Can value pluralism solve the problem of particularised recognition for Honneth?

If by a 'pluralized value-horizon' he means no more than one that recognises that people can contribute to the good of a society in different ways, that is not 'value pluralism' as it is usually understood, since the value of these different contributions resides in their serving a common social good. Genuine value pluralism holds out the prospect of our being able to recognise the value of many different forms of life, but Honneth wants recognition for the particular lives that people actually live. So value pluralism will do the trick only if we can anticipate a neat fit between whatever version of that doctrine we embrace and the ways of life actually present in our society. 'We' here refers to the members of a society at large, so a further assumption must be that 'we' can reach consensus on a particular form of value pluralism, even though there is no obvious reason why any version of value pluralism should attract consensus more readily than any other ethical position.

Moreover, if our goal is to secure equal recognition, we must suppose that the version of value pluralism that we settle on will find not only value but also *equal* value in the forms of life it confronts. All of these suppositions are too extravagant to be credible. And, of course, the more generous we make our value pluralism in an effort to maximise the different forms of life it encompasses, the more we shall dilute the recognition it delivers. The more indiscriminate merit recognition becomes, the less esteem it bestows.

In the end Honneth suggests that a 'formal conception of ethical life' might provide a way out of these difficulties (171–79). He sees this formal ethical position as lodged midway between Kantian moral theory and communitarian ethics (172–73). It embraces the Kantian idea of the moral autonomy of human beings, but it goes beyond that in aiming to secure the conditions for self-realization. However, it would stop short of 'the expression of substantive values that constitute the *ethos* of a concrete tradition-based community' (172). Rather it would be concerned with 'the structural elements of ethical life, which . . . can be normatively extracted from the plurality of all forms of life' (172).[14]

What Honneth seems to be aiming for is an approach that will enable a society to endorse the goodness of every way of life pursued by its members and so to accord recognition to each, but one that does not cross over into a substantive conception of the good. A substantive conception would presumably cause problems because it would very likely be controversial and so not be embraced by all, and also because it would almost certainly imply that some forms of life were more worthy of recognition than others and perhaps that some deserved no recognition at all. Yet it is hard to believe that a ghostly 'formal' conception of ethical life would deliver recognition that would do anything for anyone's esteem.[15]

In a reconsideration of these issues, Honneth gives a rather different and more sure-footed account of the sorts of difference or particularity a society should recognise (Fraser and Honneth 2003: 110–97, 237–67). He also confronts issues raised by 'identity politics' more directly than before (160–70). He unequivocally limits his third form of recognition, in which a society accords esteem to its members severally, to the (primarily work-based) contributions individuals make to their society's collective good.[16] The value upon which this recognition is based he describes as the 'achievement principle' (140–60). So where should we locate, and how should we respond to, demands for the recognition of ethnic, cultural, sexual, gender and other sorts of identity whose focus is on something other than social contribution and individual achievement? Honneth suggests that, insofar as these demands stem from complaints about the disadvantage and discrimination suffered by certain identity groups, they really fall within, and can be met by, 'the normative framework staked out by the equality principle of legal recognition' (164; also 163–66, 169). But how should we regard demands for recognition that go beyond that principle? How should we respond to a group's demands that we should esteem, rather than merely respect, its identity, values and goals? Honneth observes that those demands are not catered for by any of the three forms of recognition he identifies and would require a new fourth principle of recognition (161, 169). However, because of the nature of the normative demand it would make, he does not concede the case for that additional form of recognition. Recognition of a culture as intrinsically good or valuable is not something that can be publicly required; it can arise only 'spontaneously or voluntarily' depending upon the standards that people bring to their evaluation of the culture (168).[17]

Thus Honneth arrives at a position not so very different from that for which I argue in this chapter. Demands for recognition of identities are most satisfactorily grounded in the equal status of those whose identities they are, and complaints of the inadequate recognition of differences are most persuasively presented as complaints that genuine equality of status has not been secured. Demands that we recognise the intrinsic merit and the equal merit of different identities may very well be demands that ask for more than we can give.

SOME ISSUES

Essentialism

One of the great bogeys of those who write on identity and difference is essentialism. Essentialism is a sin that everyone deplores but to which no one pleads guilty. I shall not depart from that pattern. Essentialism is the tendency to ascribe identities to individuals or groups in ways that imply that those identities are fixed rather than shifting and givens over which their bearers have no control. Normatively, essentialism can lead on to the view that each person has an authentic and objectively discernible identity; that is the identity to which they should remain true, and it is that identity that should determine how they are treated by others. To have one's identity recognised in that essentialist fashion can clearly be tyrannous and suffocatingly restrictive.

The approach to recognising identities for which I have argued in this chapter is well-placed to avoid essentialism. That is because the mediated status approach to identity is one in which we should recognise and give significance to an identity because and insofar as it is an identity that matters to the person who bears it. Thus, it is the recognised rather than the recogniser that determines what we recognise. Unmediated merit recognition is perhaps more susceptible to essentialism because it must find value in an identity independently of its being an identity that someone embraces.

Seeking Merit Recognition

While I have pointed out the difficulties involved in a group's demanding merit recognition rather than status recognition for its identity, nothing I have said is meant to suggest that a group should not seek merit recognition. In cases in which a group conceives its identity as having value beyond the value it has as its identity, it is perhaps natural that it should want others to recognise that value. So, for example, a group distinguished by its culture may embrace its culture not merely because that culture defines who its members are but because it believes its culture harbours much of intrinsic value that can and should be recognised by others. However, merit recognition is more safely pursued *in addition to*, rather than instead of, status recognition. In part that is because, as I have tried to show for the sorts of case at issue here, status recognition has a more secure rationale than merit recognition. Indeed, in some circumstances, merit recognition will be impossible because it demands what the values of the putative recognisers cannot concede. It is hard to see how, in a context of conflicting values, mutual recognition can get beyond status recognition. I have also shown that, if our goal is equal recognition, that equality is secured much more readily and dependably through status than through merit recognition.

But there is a further point. If we rely on merit recognition alone, the claims of the group seeking recognition will depend entirely on the approval of those from whom it seeks recognition. That is an unduly hazardous and other-dependent basis on which to ground the fate of a group. If, on the other hand, a group seeks merit recognition in addition to status recognition, it can fall back upon its status, and the rights it has because of its status, if its quest for merit recognition is unsuccessful. So, for example, the case for same-sex marriage can be grounded on the equal status of gays as persons who, as persons, are entitled to enjoy the same legally recognised relationships as heterosexuals. It is entirely intelligible that gays should, in addition, want the non-gay population to recognise the value of same-sex relationships. But, if that merit recognition is not forthcoming, that will not jeopardise the case for same-sex marriage based upon the mediated status of the gay population.[18] Indeed, people sometimes spurn merit recognition just because seeking it can seem to imply that the way they are entitled to live should depend upon the approval of others. It is resentment at that implication that often lies behind people's protests that they do not care what others think of them (even though they usually do).

The Point of Recognition

It might be alleged that I have missed the point of recognition. That point, for many theorists of recognition, is the meeting of a psychological need. According people status and respecting what matters in their lives has significant implications for the legal, political and social arrangements under which they should live. It also has implications for how we should interact with one another in less formal settings. Even so, status recognition might be thought inadequate to give people the direct reassurance and the particularised endorsement that they need; perhaps that psychological need can be met only by merit recognition. The psychological dimension of recognition is clearly important for Taylor, who emphasizes the psychological harm that can result from misrecognition or non-recognition (1994: 25–26), and for Honneth, who conceives the goal of recognition as promoting a positive and undistorted 'practical relation-to-self', which incorporates self-confidence, self-respect and self-esteem (1995a: 129). For Galeotti too the case for recognition turns very much on the need to enhance the self-respect and self-esteem of marginalised minorities.

Perhaps I should say again that I do not intend to argue either that people should not seek merit recognition or that others should be predisposed to withhold it. Nor should we be dissuaded from re-examining our beliefs about who or what is meritorious. But we can genuinely recognise as meritorious only what we genuinely reckon to be meritorious. Even if people do have a deep need for their way of life (or some other aspect of their identity) to be recognised as good, that fact is not evidence that their way of life is indeed good, nor therefore a reason why others should conceive it as good. We can guarantee, or accept an obligation, to meet this alleged psychological need in every possible case in which it may arise only if we are willing to engage in the sort of hollow pretence of recognition against which Taylor so rightly protests.[19]

Recognising Difference

Much of what is described as 'recognition of difference' is not 'recognition' in the sense in which I have used that term predominantly throughout this chapter. It is concerned neither with the attribution of status nor with the acknowledgement of merit. Rather it describes recognising in the sense of noticing and taking due account of differences because they are relevant or significant. When people counterpose the recognition of difference to difference-blindness, that is often all that they mean. They mean to protest that differences are being ignored that should be taken into account if a society's arrangements are to treat people in a genuinely fair and equal fashion.

Suppose, for example, that we provide for Muslim women to wear headscarves and for Sikh men to wear turbans in circumstances in which these depart from normally prescribed dress codes, and we then describe ourselves as 'recognising difference'. What does that mean? It does not mean that we applaud the wearing of headscarves and turbans by the people concerned.

Nor need it mean that we attribute status to Muslim and Sikh identities *qua* identities. It means only that we recognise the significance that headscarves have for Muslim women and that turbans have for Sikh men and that we take due account of that significance. The recognition involved here is closest in sense to the second meaning of the term that I identified earlier, in which 'to recognise' means to be aware of, to appreciate, or to accept, and then to act consistently with that recognition. It is better thought of as 'recognising that' rather than as 'according recognition to'.

These two sorts of recognition may often be closely related, as they are in the examples I have just given. But recognition of difference need not always be consequent upon, or tied to, according recognition to an identity. For example, it is generally accepted that, when we allocate according to need, we must recognise the different quantities and qualities of people's needs and modulate our allocation accordingly. When we do that, we recognise difference, but the differences we recognise need not be differences associated with particular identities.

Equally, the demands of groups distinguished by their identities are often demands not that their difference be recognised so that they will be treated differently but, on the contrary, demands that they should not be treated differently because of their difference. As Iris Young observes,

> the public political claims of such groups . . . rarely consist simply in the assertion of one identity as against others, or a simple claim that a group be recognized in its distinctiveness. Instead, claims for recognition usually function as part of or means to claims against discrimination, unequal opportunity, political marginalization, or unfair burdens. (2000: 104)

Moreover, the equal recognition that identity groups demand does not have to be in every case recognition for their specific identities; it may be a demand for recognition, or for more complete recognition, of more general sorts such as recognition as persons or as citizens or as human beings possessed of rights. These more general forms of recognition have value in their own right and not only as conduits for more particular forms of recognition.

General Principles and Particular Cases

My concern in this chapter has been to examine the form that identity recognition must take if it is motivated by the significance an identity has for those who bear it and if different identities are to be objects of equal recognition. I do not pretend that the analysis I have offered will enable us to 'read off' a right answer each time we confront any of the myriad of particular cases in which questions of recognition arise. Issues concerning how much can be demanded in the name of status recognition and the practices and institutional forms through which it should receive expression have still to be settled.[20]

So too have issues concerning limits to the identities, or to the details of identity, to which we should accord recognition. Some of those limits may be set by the demands of equal status recognition itself, but others will be set by judgements, which will often be 'merit' judgements, concerning the limits of what we find tolerable in the beliefs, values and practices of others. We may not be able to settle everything by reference to status. Considerations of practicability must also figure in our calculations. For example, language is often an important feature of cultural identity but, if extending equal recognition to different linguistic groups means giving their languages an equal place in the public life of a society, that sort of recognition is simply not practicable in the circumstances of most modern multicultural societies. Thus, with recognition, as with many other issues that political philosophy addresses, general principles may not be able to take us all the way in settling particular cases. Nevertheless, the differences between mediated and unmediated recognition and between status and merit recognition remain of fundamental significance for the recognition that we might reasonably demand for ourselves and that others might reasonably demand from us.

NOTES

Earlier versions of this chapter were presented to the Conference of the Association for Legal and Social Philosophy 2004, the Newcastle Applied Philosophy Group (APIS), the Department of Politics of the University of Durham, and the Political Theory Group of the University of York. I am grateful to the participants in those occasions for making me clarify and rethink several aspects of my argument, and to the Leverhulme Trust for enabling me to conduct research for this article. Thanks too to David Middleton, Ian O'Flynn, Jonathan Seglow and Steven Smith for their detailed comments.

1. The distinction between issues of redistribution and recognition has been most associated with Nancy Fraser (1997b, 1997c). She argues that, while practically the two sorts of issue are entwined, they can be distinguished analytically and that remedies for injustices of distribution can, in some measure, pull in different directions from those for injustices of recognition. For debate on the relationship between issues of redistribution and recognition, see also Fraser 1997d, 1998, 2000, 2001; Fraser and Honneth 2003; Young 1990, 1997; Butler 1998; Phillips 1999; Yar 2001; Benhabib 2002: 68–81; Armstrong 2003; Parekh 2004.

2. Taylor phrases this presumption in more or less modest terms. Sometimes he claims only that we can presume that all cultures have *something* of value to offer all mankind. 'As a presumption, the claim is that all human cultures that have animated whole societies over some considerable stretch of time have *something* important to say to all human beings' (1994: 66, my emphasis; see also 72–73). Clearly the presumption that each culture contains *something* of value is much less daring than the presumption that each culture is of *equal* value, but Taylor seems willing to defend both (68–69, 72–73).

3. Honneth subsequently reasserted the comprehensive reach of struggles for recognition: 'resistance to an established social order is always driven by the moral experience of in some respect not receiving what is taken to be justified recognition' (Fraser and Honneth 2003: 160, see also 125–37, 150–60).

4. Because the identities at issue here are typically group identities, demands for recognition are commonly demands made by or on behalf of groups. However, that leaves open the question of whether the moral standing that underwrites claims of recognition should be con-

ceived as a standing possessed by the group as a single integral entity or by its members severally. On that issue, see Jones 1999.

5. This difference in the form that the recognising process might take has been previously noticed by Patchen Markell (2000: 496) and Arto Laitinen (2002: 473–75).

6. I do not mean to deny that what we consider meritorious is socially constructed or that people may seek merit recognition by attempting to redefine what is meritorious. My point is rather that, once we have fixed upon a conception of merit, that conception will dictate who we can and cannot recognise (without pretence) as meritorious.

7. Nancy Fraser has also argued, though in a rather different way, that we should model equal social and political recognition on status recognition. See especially Fraser 2001 and Fraser and Honneth 2003: 26–48. Although Iris Young makes limited use of the term 'recognition' in her *Justice and the Politics of Difference*, issues of recognition figure prominently in her concerns in that book. Some of what she argues for seems to push in the direction of merit recognition; e.g. her emphasis on the 'positivity' of group difference (1990: 166f). On the other hand, many of her concerns are really with status and with the policies required to make equal status a social reality; she indicates, on several occasions, that her argument is underwritten by the universalist principle that all persons are of equal moral worth (1990: 37, 105, 158, 169).

8. Taylor occasionally uses the word 'status' (1994: 39, 69) to describe what is at stake in the recognition of difference and more frequently connects that recognition with 'respect' (e.g. 42, 64, 66, 70). But he seems to suppose that, when we recognise difference, our attribution of status and respect must depend upon our positive appraisal of the merit of the difference that we recognise. So, for Taylor, recognising a cultural identity remains primarily (in my terms) an instance of merit recognition and only secondarily and dependently an instance of status recognition.

9. Since the horizons to be fused are those of the different cultures at issue, the claim might be that their fusion will necessarily yield a conception of those cultures as equally valuable. But Taylor's hesitancy indicates that that is not his view. See also Taylor 1995.

10. I examine Galeotti's attempt to recast toleration as recognition at greater length in Jones 2006, where I also question the appropriateness of applying the idea of toleration to identities as opposed to beliefs, values and practices.

11. Honneth himself has described the principle at work in social esteem as 'the merit principle' (Fraser and Honneth 2003: 170).

12. Honneth examines at length the historical 'uncoupling of legal recognition from the forms of social regard in which subjects are recognized according to the socially defined worth of their concrete characteristics' (1995a: 121; see also 121–26).

13. Honneth often suggests otherwise. E.g. 'within value-systems (which have emerged via conflict) the social standing of subjects is indeed measured in terms of what they can accomplish for society within the context of their particular forms of self-realization' (1995a: 127). 'Since individuals must know that they are recognized for their particular abilities and traits in order to be capable of self-realization, they need a form of social esteem that they can only acquire on the basis of collectively shared goals' (1995a: 177–78, see also 89–90, 111–12, 126). What is odd about this view is not the claim that a society can esteem only forms of life that score positively when judged by the values that make up the society's 'cultural horizon' (134). Rather it is the claim that a society can or will or should esteem a form of life only insofar as it promotes goals that are collective goals of the entire society. Why should we recognise value in forms of life only insofar as they promote goals that are common to all of us? That implies a curiously restricted and self-referential conception of value. It also begins to suggest an oppressively collectivist restraint upon recognition.

14. The suggestion that we derive our value-horizon from ethical features common to all forms of life present in a society may seem to render the whole recognising process fraudulent, for we are then allowing forms of life to dictate to us the standards by which we judge them. However, that need not be an objection if all that we are concerned to secure is mutual recognition amongst the members of a particular society. If we can find ethical features common to all forms of life, that discovery will enable everyone to recognise something of value in everyone else's form of life. But we might still suspect that these common ethical features, if they can be found, will be too thin to have much recognition value.

15. For further discussion of the problem of value in Honneth's theory, see Kauppinen 2002 and Honneth 2002.

16. Although recognising the value of people's contribution to their society does not encounter some of the problems created by the demand that we recognise the value of different cultures or ways of life, it clearly presents problems for the idea of *equal* recognition. In fact, Honneth suggests that the mutual esteem amongst the members of a society that constitutes 'solidarity' can mean only a general symmetry of esteem rather than a precise equality of esteem.

> The fact that 'symmetrical' cannot mean here that we esteem each other to the same degree is already clear from the essential openness to interpretation of every societal value-horizon. It is simply impossible to imagine a set of collective goals that could be fixed quantitatively in such a way that it would allow for an exact comparison of the value of individual contributions; 'symmetrical' must mean instead that every subject is free from being collectively denigrated, so that one is given the chance to experience oneself to be recognized, in the light of one's own accomplishments and abilities, as valuable for society'. (1995a: 129–30)

Honneth also observes that, while we can say that subjects 'equally deserve recognition' of all three types, we can expect that to be equal recognition only in the case of legal recognition (Fraser and Honneth 2003: 182, 187–88).

17. Honneth goes on to suggest that it may make sense to speak of 'an indirect, secondary claim to well-meaning attention and consideration [of a minority's culture] by the majority, so that the process of intercultural communication can get started' (Fraser and Honneth 2003: 168).

18. For a robust defence of this point using the example of homosexuality, see Barry 2001: 274–79.

19. On this issue, see also the comments of Nancy Fraser who argues that we should conceive the point of recognition not as engineering psychological change but as securing 'parity of participation' in social life (Fraser 2001; Fraser and Honneth 2003: 26–48).

20. For an identification and discussion of these issues that is generally favourable to the claims of recognition, see Seglow 2003. For an assessment that concedes much less to the claims of recognition, see Barry 2001.

REFERENCES

Armstrong, Chris. 2003. 'Equality, Recognition and the Distributive Paradigm'. *Critical Review of International, Social and Political Philosophy* 6(3): 154–64.

Barry, Brian. 2001. *Culture and Equality*. Cambridge: Polity.

Benhabib, Seyla. 2002. *The Claims of Culture*. Princeton, NJ: Princeton University Press.

Butler, Judith. 1998. 'Merely Cultural'. *New Left Review* 227: 33–44.

Fraser, Nancy. 1997a. *Justice Interruptus: Critical Reflections on the 'Postsocialist' Condition.* London: Routledge.

Fraser, Nancy. 1997b. 'From Distribution to Recognition? Dilemmas of Justice in a Post-Socialist Era'. In Fraser 1997a: 11–39.

Fraser, Nancy. 1997c. 'Culture, Political Economy and Difference: On Iris Young's *Justice and the Politics of Difference*'. In Fraser 1997a: 189–205.

Fraser, Nancy. 1997d. 'A Rejoinder to Iris Young'. *New Left Review* 223: 126–29.

Fraser, Nancy. 1998. 'Heterosexism, Misrecognition and Capitalism: A Response to Judith Butler'. *New Left Review* 228: 140–49.

Fraser, Nancy. 2000. 'Rethinking Recognition'. *New Left Review* 3: 107–20.

Fraser, Nancy. 2001. 'Recognition without Ethics?' *Theory, Culture and Society* 18(2–3): 21–42.

Fraser, Nancy, and Axel Honneth. 2003. *Redistribution or Recognition? A Political-Philosophical Exchange*. London: Verso.

Galeotti, Anna Elisabetta. 2002. *Toleration as Recognition*. Cambridge: Cambridge University Press.

Hegel, G. W. F. 1977. *Phenomenology of Spirit*, trans. A. V. Miller. Oxford: Oxford University Press.

Honneth, Axel. 1995a. *The Struggle for Recognition: The Moral Grammar of Social Conflicts*. Cambridge: Polity Press.

Honneth, Axel. 1995b. *The Fragmented World of the Social: Essays in Social and Political Philosophy*. Albany: State University of New York Press.

Honneth, Axel. 2002. 'Grounding Recognition: A Rejoinder to Critical Questions'. *Inquiry* 45: 499–520.

Jones, Peter. 1999. 'Group Rights and Group Oppression'. *Journal of Political Philosophy* 7(4): 353–77.

Jones, Peter. 2006. 'Toleration, Recognition and Identity'. *Journal of Political Philosophy* 14(2): 123–43.

Kauppinen, Antti. 2002. 'Reason, Recognition, and Internal Critique'. *Inquiry* 45: 479–98.

Laitinen, Arto. 2002. 'Interpersonal Recognition: A Response to Value or a Precondition of Personhood?' *Inquiry* 45: 463–78.

Markell, Patchen. 2000. 'The Recognition of Politics: A Comment on Emcke and Tully'. *Constellations* 7: 496–506.

Parekh, Bhikhu. 2004. 'Redistribution or Recognition? A Misguided Debate'. In *Ethnicity, Nationalism and Minority Rights*, ed. Stephen May, Tariq Modood and Judith Squires, 199–213. Cambridge: Cambridge University Press.

Phillips, Anne. 1999. *Which Equalities Matter?* Cambridge: Polity.

Seglow, Jonathan. 2003. 'Theorizing Recognition'. In *Multiculturalism, Identity and Rights*, ed. Bruce Haddock and Peter Sutch, 78–93. London: Routledge.

Taylor, Charles. 1992. *The Ethics of Authenticity*. Cambridge, MA: Harvard University Press.

Taylor, Charles. 1994. 'The Politics of Recognition'. In *Multiculturalism: Examining the Politics of Recognition*, ed. Amy Gutmann, 25–73. Princeton, NJ: Princeton University Press.

Taylor, Charles. 1995. 'Comparison, History, Truth'. In his *Philosophical Arguments*, 146–64. Cambridge: Cambridge University Press.

Tully, James. 2000. 'Struggles over Recognition and Distribution'. *Constellations* 7(4): 469–82.

Yar, Majid. 2001. 'Beyond Nancy Fraser's "Perspectival Dualism'." *Economy and Society* 30(3): 288–303.

Young, Iris Marion. 1990. *Justice and the Politics of Difference*. Princeton, NJ: Princeton University Press.

Young, Iris Marion. 1997. 'Unruly Categories: A Critique of Nancy Fraser's Dual Systems Theory'. *New Left Review* 222: 147–60.

Young, Iris Marion. 2000. *Inclusion and Democracy*. Oxford: Oxford University Press.

Chapter Five

Bearing the Consequences of Belief

THE ISSUE

Should people suffer social disadvantage because of their beliefs? There is a strong element in the liberal tradition which holds that they should not. According to that tradition, people should be free to adopt and to live in accordance with whatever beliefs they find persuasive. People can be considered 'free' to adopt and to live in accordance with a set of beliefs only if they are not subject to persecution and harassment for holding those beliefs. If there are any 'settled convictions' of liberalism, this commitment to freedom of belief is surely one of them. One offshoot of that conviction is an antipathy to discrimination against people on grounds of religious faith in matters such as employment and education. In some societies discrimination against people on grounds of religious faith is legally prohibited along with discrimination on other grounds such as race and sex. In other societies, religious discrimination remains legally unproscribed but is still frowned upon in their official and unofficial cultures. Yet just what ought to count as 'discrimination' in relation to religious belief and just what 'toleration' requires of us are often far from clear. Consider the following celebrated case. [1]

Mr Ahmad, a devout Muslim, was employed as a full-time schoolteacher by the Inner London Education Authority (ILEA). His faith required that, if possible, he should attend a mosque for prayers on Friday afternoons. At first Mr Ahmad taught in a district too far from a mosque to enable him to fulfil this injunction. But when he was transferred by ILEA to a district within reasonable distance of a mosque, he insisted that, thenceforth, he should attend the mosque each Friday afternoon. His doing so meant that he was absent for the first three-quarters of an hour of teaching time on Friday afternoons and his absence had to be covered by other teachers. ILEA advised the head-teachers of the schools at which Mr Ahmad taught that he should not be given permission to absent himself in this way. However, Mr Ahmad continued to attend the mosque.[2] Eventually ILEA informed Mr Ahmad that, if he insisted on absenting himself on Friday afternoons, he would have to relinquish his appointment as a full-time teacher. The Authority offered to re-employ him as a part-time teacher for four and a half days a week, though of course that would have meant a commensurate reduction in his salary. Mr Ahmad found the offer of part-time employment unacceptable and resigned from his full-time post.

Mr Ahmad contended that his treatment by ILEA amounted to unfair dismissal and appealed to an industrial tribunal. The tribunal dismissed his appeal, a decision that was subsequently upheld by the Employment Appeal Tribunal. Mr Ahmad then took his case to the Court of Appeal where, by a majority decision, his appeal was again rejected, the dissenting judgement in his favour coming from Scarman L.J. Finally Mr Ahmad petitioned the European Court of Human Rights but still without success; his application was found by the European Commission to be manifestly ill-founded and declared inadmissible.[3]

Was Mr Ahmad treated fairly? My concern here is not with the legal niceties of his case which turned, in large part, upon the precise interpretation that should be placed upon section 30 of the British 1944 Education Act and section 9 of ILEA's staff code, both of which made provision for the religious convictions of teachers. Rather I want to focus on the general point of principle underlying the case. In part, this was a question of what constituted equitable treatment of different faiths. This was a worry expressed by Scarman L.J. in the Court of Appeal who pointed out that the established five-day working week created no problem for Jewish teachers in relation to Saturdays or for Christian teachers in relation to Sundays. But a rigid adherence to the five-day working week would mean that a devout Muslim, who took seriously his duty to attend Friday prayers, could never become a full-time teacher.[4]

However, beneath this question of equity lay a more fundamental issue. On whom should the 'costs' of belief fall? Who should bear the consequences of belief? Should the inconvenience and the loss of working time involved in a teacher's attending an act of worship during the working day be borne by the education authority? Or should the costs consequent upon belief fall upon the believer himself? In the Court of Appeal, Lord Denning M.R. and Scarman L.J. differed not only in their interpretation of the legal details that bore upon the case but also in their general approach to this question. Lord Denning, while 'upholding religious freedom to the full', clearly regarded the demands of Mr Ahmad's beliefs as a burden that Mr Ahmad should bear and construed his claim that he should be able to attend the mosque, on full pay, as a demand that the Muslim community be given 'preferential treatment over the great majority of the people'.[5] By contrast, Scarman L.J. argued that the educational system should be sufficiently flexible to accommodate the beliefs and observances of all religions and held that, if it did not accommodate a demand like Mr Ahmad's, Muslims could properly complain of 'discrimination'.[6]

In Mr Ahmad's case, then, it is not enough to be told that we should not engage in religious discrimination for, in a case like his, it is not clear what should count as 'discrimination'. Nor is anything settled by insisting that all religious beliefs should be 'tolerated', for the issue here is not so much whether or why we should tolerate Mr Ahmad's beliefs, but rather of 'how' his beliefs should be tolerated, of what toleration itself requires. Is it enough that we simply leave Mr Ahmad to pursue his faith and to bear whatever burdens that brings his way? Or should a society arrange things so that believers are spared the incidental but adverse effects that might otherwise be consequent upon their beliefs?

The general issue underlying Mr Ahmad's case arises in many other forms in the contemporary world. For example, is it acceptable that Orthodox Jews should find their employment opportunities curtailed because they refuse to work on Saturdays? Should Christian Sabbatarian traders have to suffer commercial disadvantage, relative to their non-Sabbatarian competitors, because they refuse to trade on Sundays, or should law prohibit all commercial activity on Sundays so that Sabbatarians and non-Sabbatarians enjoy 'equal terms of trade'?[7] Should churches be taxed like other organisations or should they receive tax concessions so that their members do not incur financial burdens because they possess religious beliefs? Should people be safeguarded from conduct which they find offensive because of their religious beliefs, or should their offended condition be regarded as a consequence of their beliefs which they should therefore have to endure? Should religious groups who want their children to be separately educated be required to meet the additional expense that that involves, or should their separate education be financed entirely from the public purse?

In contemporary Western societies these issues are likely to arise most frequently in relation to minorities, several of whom will be ethnic as well as religious minorities. It is worth noting therefore that the question of beliefs and their consequences is not inherently one about the status of minorities. In principle, it could be a majority that is required to suffer disadvantages consequent upon its beliefs. For example, in a society in which the majority were Sabbatarians and in which people were required to bear the consequences of their beliefs, it would be the majority that would find itself commercially disadvantaged relative to the minority.

Nor is this issue limited to religious belief. In this chapter, I shall confine myself to the case of religious belief since the issue of consequences arises particularly obviously and acutely in relation to that form of belief. But the question of who should bear the consequences can arise in relation to any sort of belief that is treated as a matter of private conviction. 'Private' here obviously does not mean 'behind closed doors'; people can and do make public expressions of the beliefs with which I am concerned. Nor does 'private' necessarily mean 'individual'. We might treat groups rather than individuals as the bearers of beliefs; that would make no material difference to the issue of consequences. Rather, these beliefs are appropriately described as 'private' only because and insofar as a society treats them as outside the proper realm of public decision-making.

A society cannot remove all matters of belief from the public domain. Some matters have to be the subject of public decision, and the outcomes of those decisions must be regarded as matters of public responsibility. Suppose, for example, that the majority of a society believes that, for reasons of social justice, taxation should be increased while the minority strongly opposes any such increase. If taxation were then increased, it would hardly do for the minority to argue that, since the increase in taxation is a consequence of the beliefs of the majority, only the majority should have to pay that increase. That would not do because taxation is properly a matter of public decision, and public decisions properly apply to all members of the public. Henceforth, when I use the term 'belief' I shall use it to refer only to those beliefs that a society treats as matters of private conviction. I shall pass over the question of why we should not treat all matters of belief as properly the subjects of public decision.

Generally the liberal tradition has held, or perhaps taken for granted, that people should bear the consequences of their beliefs. John Rawls will serve as an example.[8] Indeed, Rawls is a particularly apt example since he is willing to go a considerable way in requiring the members of a society to take responsibility for one another's well-being. He regards the distribution of natural abilities amongst people as morally arbitrary; no one has a claim to a better lot in life merely because he or she has been favoured by nature. Thus, a just society would distribute its resources so that those of its members who had been least favoured by nature were not materially disadvantaged because of that fact about themselves. In particular, Rawls's difference principle allows inequality in the distribution of income and wealth only insofar as that inequality works to the advantage of the least well-off group in society. So Rawls does not allow that individuals should have simply to endure whatever consequences happen to follow upon their possessing or not possessing natural abilities.

However, he handles people's beliefs quite differently from their natural abilities. He places individuals' beliefs, including their religious beliefs, within what he calls their 'conceptions of the good'. In Rawls's scheme of things, the basic rules of a society are set without reference to the different content of people's conceptions of the good. Subject to the difference principle, liberties and resources are apportioned to people equally. People are then at liberty, within the structure established by that just distribution, to pursue whatever conception of the good they choose. That may mean, of course, that some conceptions of the good—those demanding more resources or more than one's allotted portion of liberty—are more difficult to fulfil than others. But individuals must take responsibility for their conceptions of the good, and there can be no complaint of 'injustice' merely because a more demanding conception is harder to realise than a less demanding conception.[9] Thus, if some beliefs turn out to be more demanding than others, and therefore less easy to fulfil, that is an outcome that the believers have to endure. By the same token, individuals have to look to themselves and to other like-minded individuals to cope with the consequences of their beliefs. They cannot, in fairness, impose those consequences upon others.

Why should that be? Why should people bear the consequences of their beliefs? Why does justice not require us to even out those consequences so that no body of believers is more or less well-placed than any other?

FOUNDATIONS

Belief and Choice

One consideration which may be invoked to justify our making people bear the consequences of their beliefs is choice. People do not choose their race or their sex, and it is unfair that their opportunities in life should be prejudiced by these unchosen features of themselves. Similarly people do not choose their abilities and talents—insofar as those abilities and talents are determined by each individual's genetic endowment rather than by the subsequent development of that endowment. We might argue therefore, like Rawls, that a society should try to arrange things so that those who have not been favoured in the genetic lottery do not suffer economic and social disadvantage as a consequence of their having been disadvantaged by nature. By contrast, people's beliefs are not a given part of themselves like their race or sex or genetic make-up. People choose what they believe, and they can therefore be held responsible for what they believe and, by extension, for the consequences of what they believe. The consequences of people's beliefs are the consequences of their choices; they must therefore shoulder the burden of those consequences themselves rather than expect that burden to be shouldered by others.[10]

In some ways the language of choice goes quite naturally with that of belief. For example, we might casually remark to someone, 'If that is what you choose to believe, that is up to you'. But there is also reason to question whether people can really be said to 'choose' what they believe.

First, people are greatly influenced in what they believe by the social context in which they develop. In reality, it might be said, people do not adopt beliefs via a process of autonomous, critical reflection. They simply imbibe beliefs from the social and cultural context in which they find themselves. Thus, although people do not come into the world already possessed of beliefs, the process of socialisation ensures that their beliefs are just as 'unchosen' as their race or their sex.[11]

This is a large and complicated matter. Insofar as the link between socialisation and belief is an empirical matter, different things are likely to be true of different circumstances and different individuals and, perhaps also, different beliefs. There is reason to resist the claim that, in Richard Rorty's phrase, socialisation 'goes all the way down' for everyone, everywhere.[12] Clearly many people can and do shed beliefs which were part of their upbringing, and they can and do adopt beliefs that were not a part of their upbringing. This fluidity is more likely to characterise the sort of society with which we are concerned here: a plural society which, just because it is plural, causes its members to be aware of beliefs other than those which form their immediate context. However I can do little to settle this issue here, and I do not wish to deny the tremendous importance of socialisation in the formation of beliefs. I suggest only that there is reason to hesitate before accepting that people are the entirely helpless victims of inherited systems of belief.

How we regard this issue is likely to be biased by how we conceptualise it. I have characterised it in terms of beliefs, but nowadays it is also likely to be characterised by reference to 'cultures'. It is part of the idea of a 'culture' that it is something which envelops those who belong to it. Individuals do not make their own cultures, nor do they choose a culture. Their culture is something that they find themselves within, and the culture to which they belong constitutes part of their given identity. The idea of 'choosing' a culture has the same absurdity about it as the idea of deciding to start a tradition. Cultures and traditions do not work like that. Thus, insofar as we treat people's beliefs as ingredients of their culture, we will be predisposed to treat those beliefs as part of their given identity rather than features of their lives over which they have control.

However, we should not allow our thought to be tyrannised by concepts like 'culture'. That term takes in a large array of very different aspects of people's lives—their language, diet, manners, mores, dress, and so on. Some of these, such as language and dress, would not normally be objects of critical reflection. But beliefs have epistemic content. They make claims about the way the world is and about how we should behave in it. They can be assessed as true or false, more or less supported by evidence, more or less plausible, and so on. Beliefs are therefore open to critical appraisal in a way that is quite irrelevant to many of the other ingredients of culture. Anyone who takes his beliefs seriously must be concerned about the truth or merit of their content. He cannot regard his own beliefs as a mere quirk of culture. A person's culture may be invoked in a *causal* explanation of his beliefs, but it cannot be offered by the believer himself as a *reason* for his believing what he does. In addition, the notion, which has been voiced in some quarters recently, that it is somehow disloyal and traitorous to do other than accept the truth or the rightness of the beliefs that form a part of one's inherited culture is both silly and sinister.[13]

Once again, I do not mean to be dismissive of the significance of culture. I mean only to question whether societies and cultures imprison their members in systems of belief from which there is no escape. At the very least, the appeals to socialisation and culture would seem insufficiently conclusive to remove all reason for holding people responsible for their beliefs.

However, there is a second and less contingent way in which the idea of 'choosing beliefs' may be questioned. Do I 'choose' what to believe? Do I not simply believe? I do not choose to believe Pythagoras's theorem; I simply believe it. I do not choose to believe that New York is in the United States; I just believe that that is where it is. The use of 'choice' in conjunction with 'belief' implies an act of choosing which is separate from that of believing: we choose what to believe and then we believe it. But that is not how belief works. I can choose to go to France for a holiday, and that act of choosing can be distinguished from my subsequently going to France. I can decide to buy a car, and that act of deciding can be distinguished from my actually buying the car. But there is not a similar act of choosing or deciding to believe which is distinguishable from a subsequent and separate act of believing. There is just believing. I may, of course, gradually come to believe something, and my beliefs may be the outcome of a long process of deliberation. But 'coming to believe' is not the same as choosing to believe something and then going on to believe it.

In addition, 'choosing to believe' implies an optionality of a sort that is not normally a part of the believing process. I choose to go to France for a holiday when I might have chosen to go to Spain or Italy. Similarly I choose to buy a car when I might have chosen to buy a yacht or to have spent my money on something else. But it is not similarly open to me to choose to believe that the square on the hypotenuse is not equal to the sum of the squares of the two other sides of a right-angled triangle. Nor can I simply opt to believe that New York is in Canada or Mexico rather than in the USA. Thus, when people are told that their beliefs are the offspring of their choices, they may reasonably object that, on the contrary, they have no choice about what they believe. They cannot but believe what seems to them to be the case. Their beliefs are no more at their disposal than their physical make-up.

At this point, it may be that we should begin to distinguish between different sorts of belief. What is morally right or what is religiously true are not, it might be said, matters on which people find themselves confronted with indisputable states of affairs which they cannot but recognise. Thus, in these areas, there remains a significant element of choice. Even if there is no scope for people to choose what to believe about Pythagoras's theorem or about the location of New York, there is scope for them to choose which God or gods to believe in. However, even that is disputable. Some believers would protest that their religious beliefs are so manifestly true to themselves, even if not to others, that they have no choice but to believe. Those who accept that there is scope for different people to arrive intelligibly at different beliefs in religious matters might still object that the language of choice misdescribes the process by which particular individuals come to hold particular beliefs.[14] Since the role of choice, or of processes akin to choice, in believing is likely to remain controversial, let me add one further comment on the alleged centrality of choice to the issue of consequences.

Even if some feature of a person is a product of that person's choice, it does not follow that others are justified in treating that person any old how in respect of that choice. Suppose we accept that I have the right to adopt any religion that I 'choose'; it does not follow that others are free to persecute me for my religious beliefs just because those beliefs are 'chosen'. On the contrary, it is implicit in my having a *right* to adopt the religion I choose that others are duty-bound not to persecute me in that way. If we move from outright persecution to discrimination, we may still say that my having chosen a particular religion does not justify others' discriminating against me in matters such as employment and education. If I have the right to adopt whatever religion I choose, my choice ought to be respected, and others ought not to deprive me of opportunities because they dislike the particular choice I have made.

Of course, much depends on how we define the right at issue here. Assuming that the right to adopt and to pursue a religion is, in jurisprudential terminology, a claim as well as a liberty, the scope of that claim can be drawn more or less generously. Libertarians, for example, would normally accept that the right to religious liberty constitutes a claim upon others to refrain from religious persecution, but not a claim which properly limits the freedom of employers to hire and fire whomsoever they choose, for whatever reason they choose. We should note, however, that the libertarian's objection centres on the right of private employers to determine the make-up of their own workforce. It is not therefore special to laws prohibiting religious discrimination and counts equally against the legal prohibition of racial and sexual discrimination.[15] But, if we do not share this general aversion to anti-discrimination measures, it does not seem extravagant to hold that, if the freedom to adopt and to pursue a religion has the status of a fundamental right, people should not have to suffer unfavourable treatment because of the use they make of that fundamental right. But that, in turn, simply takes us back to the question of what is to count as 'suffering unfavourable treatment'. If people have a right to hold the beliefs they do—whether or not those beliefs are 'chosen'—does requiring them to bear the consequences of their beliefs amount to a violation of that right? We may find a clearer answer to that question if we shift our focus from the idea of choice to that of freedom of belief.

Freedom of Belief

I shall simply take for granted that people should be accorded freedom of belief and leave unstated the many cogent arguments that may be urged in favour of that freedom. That people should possess freedom of belief is not an extravagant assumption in this context for, in the absence of that freedom, the issue of who should bear the diverse consequences of diverse beliefs could hardly arise. By 'freedom of belief' I understand not only the liberty to believe but also the liberty to act upon one's beliefs. Limits may have to be imposed upon that freedom and, in a plural society, just where those limits should fall, and why, are likely to be controversial matters. Again, I shall not pursue those matters here. Rather, I want to suggest that, if we accord people freedom of belief, it is reasonable to require them to bear the consequences of what they believe.

Freedom of belief, I have said, includes not just the freedom to believe but also the freedom to shape one's life in accordance with one's belief. Indeed, it is the latter freedom that has been the more significant in that it has been the more vulnerable. It is, of course, possible to control what people believe—sadly more so nowadays than in previous ages. But, for the most part, what goes on in the recesses of people's minds has been of less concern to others and less vulnerable to interference and suppression than the external manifestations of belief. In particular, given that our concern is with the consequences of belief, it is not merely believing but 'practising' one's belief that is more pertinent.

Now, as long as my beliefs shape only my life, I can reasonably keep others at bay. My beliefs, I can protest, are properly no one's concern but my own. In particular, as long as I bear the consequences of my belief, I can maintain that my beliefs remain purely my affair. However, if I expect others to bear those consequences, that ceases to be true. What I believe then affects lives other than my own. The more burdensome the consequences of my beliefs, the more those beliefs will burden the lives of others. That provides reason for others having some control over what I believe. Of course, they may be unable to alter what I believe, and it may be highly undesirable that they should if they could. But they are capable of controlling how far I *act* on my beliefs and, if they are going to have to meet the costs of my actions, why should they not spare themselves that expense by preventing my acting in costly ways? In other words, why should they not be entitled to limit my freedom rather than bear its consequences? If my acting on my beliefs significantly affects the lives of others, it becomes implausible for me to claim an inviolable and exclusive right to determine how I should behave in matters of religious faith. The force of this line of argument is all the greater for its arising in a context of conflicting beliefs. It is bad enough that others should have to bear the costs of my freely chosen actions. How much worse that they should have to bear the consequences of my beliefs, which beliefs they may reckon (perhaps with good reason) to be false, wrong or evil. How much stronger the case for protecting people from becoming the unwilling 'victims' of another's freedom.

It will not do to reply that any such pre-emptive strategy should be vetoed in the name of 'freedom', for it is not just my freedom that is at stake. If others have to bear the consequences of my beliefs, my use of my freedom can unilaterally diminish the freedom of others. We should be concerned not only with freedom but also with its equitable distribution, and it is difficult to see how an arrangement which places the freedom of some at the mercy of the freedom of others can be consistent with any standard of equitable distribution.

Thus, I suggest, the reason why people should bear the consequences of their beliefs is that that is a natural concomitant of their enjoying freedom of belief. Those who claim that freedom must accept responsibility for the use they make of it. We could, of course, turn this around and argue that people have to bear the consequence of one another's beliefs and that freedom of belief should be curtailed accordingly. But that, I suspect, is an option which will appeal to no one.[16]

Promoting Diversity

The argument I have developed here may be regarded as altogether too negative in spirit. Is not the diversity of a plural society something that we should cherish and celebrate rather than merely tolerate? Is it enough merely to refrain from persecuting or impeding ways of life other than our own? Should we not take positive steps to see that all ways of life flourish? This more positive, promotive approach to diversity might be used to argue that the consequences of belief should be treated as a burden to be borne by society as a whole. By taking collective responsibility for those consequences, we will ensure that no system of belief labours under any special disadvantage and that a hundred flowers can bloom.

There are many forms of human diversity, and many of those forms are quite intelligibly cherished and fostered. A society may be said to be richer for having a diversity of forms of literature, music, food, and so on. It may therefore be in the interests of all of us that we should ensure that that diversity should continue and develop; if that requires a sharing of costs, so be it. But what are we to say of a diversity of beliefs about the true, the right and the good? Can we similarly celebrate the propagation and proliferation of beliefs which we ourselves believe to be erroneous, evil and wrong? It is one thing to refrain from preventing people holding and acting upon beliefs which we ourselves believe to be false. It is quite another positively to contribute towards the maintenance and promotion of those erroneous beliefs. It borders on absurdity to suppose that a group of people with a system of belief about the true and the right should welcome and feel duty-bound to support a rival system of belief which they hold to be false and wrong.

This objection is likely to be felt particularly keenly by those who possess a religious faith. Atheists, of course, can regard religious beliefs as pernicious as well as false. But the non-believer might also take a more relaxed and benign view of religion. He might regard it as a relatively harmless delusion which adds to the range of human experience and which has some fortunate social and cultural side-effects. He might therefore be relatively undisturbed by having to play some small part in its continuance. But it is hard to see how the religious adherent could be similarly relaxed about his having to sustain a rival system of belief—unless he subscribes to the rather odd belief that all religions, without distinction, are equally valid and valuable paths to God (or the gods?). Imagine how Muslims and Hindus in contemporary India would respond to the suggestion that they should help to maintain and promote one another's beliefs. At a minimum they would be likely to react with indignation and incredulity and I, for my part, could not fault those reactions.

However, there is another sort of argument that might be used to justify our adopting a more positive attitude and assisting with the consequences of others' beliefs. Instead of appealing to an alleged collective interest that we all have in the maintenance of a diversity of beliefs, we might focus upon each person's 'good' and how that good is related to that person's beliefs. People, it might be argued, should be able to flourish in whatever lives they lead, and a society ought to ensure that all of its members have genuinely equal opportunities to lead equally fulfilled lives. What constitutes 'flourishing' and 'fulfilment' for individuals or groups must be tied to their fundamental beliefs. That is, they can flourish and find fulfilment only in forms of life to which they themselves are committed. We have to accept that people believe what they believe and work from there. Thus a society ought to do its utmost to assist its members to maintain and promote their beliefs, not because that society has a collective interest in the continuance of all of those beliefs, but because its members ought to flourish equally in whatever lives they themselves believe to be right.[17]

This argument raises large and fundamental issues about the character of a just society, and here I can do no more than point to various reasons for rejecting it. Notice that it is an argument which demands far more than that we should cancel out whatever material inequalities happen to be consequent upon differences in belief. It shifts the focus of justice from the distribution of resources to the relative levels of individuals' fulfilment. A just society ceases to be one which distributes resources fairly amongst people and then leaves them to use those resources in the pursuit of whatever goals they think good, right or desirable. Instead it becomes one in which a society is made responsible for ensuring that people attain equal levels of fulfilment in whatever forms of life they commit themselves to.

There would clearly be massive practical problems in implementing this principle of equal fulfilment. Large philosophical doubts must also hang over the intelligibility of 'equal fulfilment' in the context of radically different forms of life. The most obvious candidate for reducing different forms of life to commensurability would be some form of utilitarianism, but a utilitarian measure would be both inappropriate and improper in the context of forms of life which were non-utilitarian in character.[18] Even if equal fulfilment were feasible, we might still question whether it would be just. If people are left free to pursue any form of life, should some have to suffer because of the extravagant, eccentric or ill-judged use that others make of that freedom? As I argued earlier, if some have to pay the price for the use that others make of their freedom, including their freedom of belief, the legitimacy of that freedom is very much in doubt. In addition, the view that people's 'good' consists in fulfilment in *whatever* form of life they pursue is obviously a highly contestable form of perfectionism and is a conception of the good which is most unlikely to be shared by the members of a religiously plural society.[19]

There is much more to be said on the ideal of equal fulfilment, but I hope that these brief remarks are sufficient to intimate why a society should not assume collective responsibility for securing equal levels of 'belief fulfilment' for each of its members.

IDENTIFYING CONSEQUENCES

Even if we accept that, in principle, people should bear the consequences of their beliefs, we are not yet out of the woods. We have still to establish what *are*, or what are to *count as*, the consequences of belief. That is far from straightforward.

Consider Mr Ahmad's position. His predicament arose not merely from his duty (as he understood it) to attend a mosque on Friday afternoons. It arose because Friday afternoon forms part of the normal working week in Britain. If the working week had run from Sundays to Thursdays, with Fridays and Saturdays counting as the 'week-end', Mr Ahmad's beliefs would not have had problematic consequences. It would then have been Christian

Sabbatarians who would have been in trouble. So was Mr Ahmad's inability to perform his teaching duties to the full a consequence of his beliefs? Might he not claim that it was rather a consequence of the particular set of days that children were required to attend school in Britain?

In some cases we may be able to say that an outcome is a 'natural' consequence of a belief such that no one but the believer can be held responsible for that outcome. For example, if a Jehovah's Witness contracts an illness which can be cured only by a blood transfusion and if he refuses to receive a transfusion, his death can be characterised as a natural consequence of his belief.[20] But most controversial cases will not be like that. They will result not from a conjunction of beliefs and 'nature' but from a confluence of beliefs and humanly established circumstances.

Here it may help to distinguish between two different ways in which systems of belief can make demands upon their adherents. Demands which are intrinsic to a system of belief I shall call *burdens* of belief. Those which are extrinsic to the system of belief I shall call *consequences* of belief. The 'burden' of a belief is intrinsic to the belief in that it is imposed by the belief itself. Thus it is part of the burden of Islamic belief that one must pray five times a day. It is part of the burden of Catholic belief that one should attend Mass on Sundays. It is part of the burden of Orthodox Judaism that one should not work between nightfall on Friday and nightfall on Saturday. (What I describe as a 'burden' of belief may, of course, be experienced as joyous rather than onerous by the believer.) By contrast what I label the 'consequences' of belief are distinct from the belief itself in that they are not essential requirements of the belief even though that belief is essential to their occurrence. If, for the sake of argument, we accept Mr Ahmad's own interpretation of the demands of his faith, it is part of the 'burden' of his belief that he should attend a mosque on Friday afternoons, but it is not a part of that burden that he should refrain from performing the duties of a full-time teacher. That is simply a 'consequence' of his belief which arises in the context of the British educational system. Similarly, refraining from working on the Lord's Day is part of the 'burden' of Sabbatarian belief, but suffering commercial disadvantage is not; that may be a 'consequence' of Sabbatarian belief, but 'suffering commercial disadvantage' is not something enjoined by Sabbatarianism itself.

Given all that I have argued up to now and, in particular, assuming that we reject the equal fulfilment principle, we should require people to bear the 'burdens' of their beliefs, for those burdens are imposed only by their beliefs. But assigning responsibility for what I have distinguished as the 'consequences' of belief is altogether more complicated since those consequences are not uniquely determined by belief. Let me identify two fundamentally different approaches to this issue.

The first possibility is that we establish a set of social arrangements independently of people's religious beliefs. Those arrangements would be set according to certain standards of fairness or rightfulness and would constitute a 'fixed background'. People would then be free to live according to their beliefs within the constraints set by that background. Whatever consequences, advantageous or disadvantageous, arose from the conjunction of a particular set of beliefs with those background arrangements would have to be borne by believers themselves. This approach is implicit in the work of liberal theorists such as Rawls and Ackerman.[21]

The second possibility is more even-handed in character. If an outcome is the result of two (or more) factors, it would hold both (or all) factors responsible for the outcome and proceed accordingly. Believers should be held jointly rather than solely responsible for the consequences which emanate from the conjunction of their beliefs and social circumstances. That points to a policy of compromise, mutual accommodation or cost sharing or, where no such middle way is possible, a decision which is reached only after due weight has been given to all of the interests involved, including those of religious believers.

For the sake of clarity it might help to mention a third approach which would be the obverse of the first: beliefs should be treated as fixed features of the social landscape, and believers should bear no responsibility at all for consequences which emanate from the interaction of those beliefs with social circumstances. The purpose of the second part of this chapter was to rule out this third approach. But how should we decide between the first and second?

That question is not easy to answer within the limits of this chapter, or indeed outside of them, since it turns not on the status to be given to beliefs and to the demands of belief, but on the status to be given to the circumstances and arrangements which combine with beliefs to yield consequences. Thus, where one stands on this issue will depend upon where one stands on some of the most fundamental questions of political philosophy. People of significantly different political persuasions will give significantly different answers not because they give different values to belief and to the demands of belief, but because of their different evaluations of the social and political contexts in which beliefs are held and acted upon. It is not therefore easy to make progress in this area. Here I shall confine myself to pointing out that the two approaches I have described need not be thought of as mutually exclusive and that some mix of the two has considerable appeal.

Suppose a religion requires that a temple be constructed for the glory and worship of God. According to the distinction I made a moment ago, it will be part of the 'burden' of belief of that religion that a temple should be constructed. Constructing the temple will take time, effort and money. But the expenditure of that time, effort and money is not itself part of the 'burden' of belief. It is a 'consequence' of the belief. The belief requires only that there be a temple; it does not prescribe that its adherents, and its adherents alone, must sacrifice specific amounts of time, effort and money to construct the temple. Those costs arise for the believers only because non-believers will not share in financing the temple and/or because, and to the extent that, people charge for the expenditure of labour and for materials in the society concerned. Now we have shown that believers should not be entirely absolved of responsibility for the consequences of their beliefs. The temple should not, therefore, be financed wholly out of general taxation. But might we argue that, since the costs of constructing the temple arise only in part because the faithful believe it ought to be constructed, and since they arise also because people are unwilling to provide labour and materials at less than the going rates, those costs are jointly brought about by believers and non-believers and therefore should be met jointly by the two groups? The temple might then be financed partly from the private funds of believers and partly from general taxation.

That proposal would not, I suspect, win much approval—from either believers or non-believers. The reason is not that current rates for labour and materials (whether fixed by the market or by the state) contribute nothing causally to the costs incurred in building the temple. Clearly they do. Rather it is because material and labour costs set a 'background' against which people are to make decisions about their lives and against which, in the ordinary course of things, they are required to take responsibility for the costs of their own projects. Of course, what that 'background' should be is open to disputes of a familiar sort—a range of possibilities is on offer from the libertarian to the liberal socialist. But, given that those background arrangements are 'just', believers should have to bear the financial consequences of having to construct temples, to go on pilgrimages, to stage festivals, and the like. For moral and political purposes, those consequences are to be deemed exclusively consequences of belief.

I myself would respond to Sabbatarianism in this way. Other things being equal,[22] people should be free to enter into whatever voluntary arrangements they choose, with whom they choose, and when they choose. If some people possess beliefs according to which it is wrong to trade or work on Saturdays or Sundays, they should be free to abstain from trading and working on those days. But any commercial disadvantage they suffer as a consequence should be regarded as a consequence of their beliefs and not as a consequence of others not sharing those beliefs. That disadvantage should not therefore rank as a reason for removing or limiting the freedom of non-Sabbatarians to trade and work as they see fit, and it would be quite wrong to deal with this issue in a utilitarian, or quasi-utilitarian, fashion by simply weighing up the competing interests involved.

But, however one sets those background constraints, there may also be cases which arise *within* them, cases in which private or public projects are at odds with, or in competition with, the demands of religious belief and which are properly dealt with by weighing and, if possible, accommodating the competing interests involved. Consider the once contentious issue of Sikhs and motorcycle crash helmets. In 1972 the British Parliament passed a law empowering the Minister of Transport to require all motorcyclists to wear crash helmets, which he duly did. That caused problems for biking Sikhs who would not remove their turbans. In 1976 the law was amended to exempt Sikhs from this requirement. Should Sikhs have been accommodated in that way?

In a case that went to trial before the law was amended, a Sikh claimed that his religious beliefs provided adequate excuse for his not wearing a crash helmet. In response a judge presiding at the trial commented that no one was bound to ride a motorcycle, and the law prescribed simply that, if you rode a motorcycle, you had to wear a crash helmet; members of the Sikh community might find themselves unable to ride motorcycles, but they were prevented 'not because of the English law but by the requirements of their religion'.[23] In other words, a Sikh's inability to ride a motorcycle was to be deemed a consequence not of the law but of his beliefs. But that construction seems much less plausible in this case. Why? In part, no doubt, the answer is that compelling people to wear crash helmets is a largely paternalistic measure, and Sikhs have a reason, special to themselves, for taking a different view of what is for their good. However, that is not the only consideration. Other-regarding interests are also at stake in this issue, but those interests do not seem sufficiently special to trump all competing considerations.[24] Consequently, in this sort of case, it seems appropriate that interests should be weighed and the law adjusted accordingly.

One further comment on this alternative. An argument commonly used in relation to religiously plural societies is that their constitutions and policies should not be grounded upon religious principles. The justification usually given is that public rules and public policies should be based upon reasons of a kind that are accessible to, and that can be acknowledged by, all members of the public; in a religiously diverse society, religious doctrine cannot provide that shared form of reason.[25] But that argument does not require that public decisions should ignore the interests that people have as holders of religious beliefs, nor does it require that any non-religious concern should routinely trump any interest that has its foundation in a religious belief. It does not therefore require us to adopt the 'background' approach to the complete exclusion of the approach that I have just described.

However, as I have already indicated, I cannot settle the question of how beliefs should rank alongside other factors which contribute to consequences. All I have sought to establish is that a society does not have a *general* duty to relieve people of the consequences of their beliefs. If, in a particular instance, there is a case for relief, that case must be grounded not in any such general duty but in a claim that, morally as well as empirically, the relevant consequence is not to be considered a consequence of belief alone.

Since I began with the case of Mr Ahmad, perhaps I should conclude with it. Applied to that case, the thrust of my argument is that Mr Ahmad had no general claim, *qua* believer, that others should bear the consequences of his not being available for teaching on Friday afternoons. However, there is obviously more to be said. Mr Ahmad's beliefs caused difficulty only in the context of the working week in Britain. The pattern of that week cannot pretend to be a fact of nature, nor can the use of Sunday as a day of rest pretend to be religiously neutral, either in effect or, more importantly, in intention. For those who take the view that Britain and other Western societies are, or ought to be, 'Christian societies', there is nothing untoward in that; those societies' arrangements are rightly Christian in character, and other religions have to take their chances against that background. Insofar as Saturdays are also non-working days for many people in Christian societies, that is simply fortunate for members of the Jewish faith; insofar as Fridays are working days for almost everyone in Christian societies, that is simply unfortunate for members of the Islamic faith. (*Mutatis mutandis*, the same might be said of Islamic or Jewish societies.) But for those who hold that, in its laws and its public policy, a society should aspire to be neutral between religions, the 'inequitable' character of the British week must be a source of concern. It would of course be possible to make the non-working day neutral between religions by shifting it to, say, Tuesday or Wednesday, or by altering its frequency, so that it would be equally inconvenient for all religions. But to invert the Pareto principle in that way ('make some people worse off while making no one better off') would seem entirely without merit. As long as Sundays retain their traditional status in societies like Britain, Mr Ahmad and Muslims like him have some claim to be accommodated.[26] Whether, all things considered, they should be accommodated must depend upon the feasibility and the costs of that accommodation.

NOTES

An earlier version of this article was given to a seminar on 'Political Theory and Toleration' organised by Sally Jenkinson and Preston King for the annual conference of the Political Studies Association of the United Kingdom, 1991. I am grateful to both of them and to the other participants in the seminar, particularly Mark Goldie, John Horton and Deborah Fitzmaurice, for their comments on the chapter. I am also grateful for their helpful advice to Kay Black, Robert Goodin, Tim Gray and Albert Weale.

1. *Ahmad v. Inner London Education Authority.* Employment Appeal Tribunal: [1976] I.C.R. 461. Court of Appeal: [1978] 1 Q.B. 36; [1977] 3 W.L.R. 396. The case is described in detail in Sebastian Poulter, *English Law and Ethnic Minority Customs* (London: Butterworths, 1986), 247–52. See also St John A. Robilliard, *Religion and the Law* (Manchester: Manchester University Press, 1984).

2. Whether the demands of employment provide sufficient reason for not attending Friday prayers seems to be disputed within the Muslim community. ILEA pointed out that it employed hundreds of Muslim teachers, none of whom had made the same request as Mr Ahmad; [1978] 1 Q.B. 39, 40–41, 43–44.

3. *Ahmad v. UK* (1981) 4 EHRR 126.

4. *Ahmad v. ILEA* [1978] Q.B. 47, 50.

5. Ibid., 41.

6. Ibid., 48, 50. See also Lord Scarman, 'Toleration and the Law', in *On Toleration*, ed. Susan Mendus and David Edwards (Oxford: Clarendon Press, 1987), 49–62.

Mr Ahmad's case is not unique in English law. For another case arising from a conflict between patterns of work and Muslim religious obligations, see *Hussain v. London Country Bus Services Ltd*, Incomes Data Services (IDS) Brief 283 (Aug 1984), 5. For similar cases, concerning other faiths, see *London Borough of Tower Hamlets v. Rabin*, IDS Brief 406 (Oct 1989), 12, and *Fluss v. Grant Thornton Chartered Accountants*, IDS Brief 360 (1987), 6 (both concerning Jews); *Esson v. London Transport Executive*, [1975] I.R.L.R. 48 (concerning a Seventh-Day Adventist); and *Post Office v. Mayers*, IDS Brief 397 (May 1989), 4 (concerning a member of the World Wide Church of God). There have also been a number of notable cases concerning specific religious festivals; see *Ostreicher v. Secretary of State for the Environment*, [1978] 1 All ER 591, [1978] 3 All ER 82 (C.A.); *Prais v. EC Council*, [1977] ICR 284; and *Naiz v. Ryman Ltd*, IDS Brief 376 (July 1988), 6.

This chapter was originally published in 1994 and, at that time, law in the United Kingdom prohibited direct and indirect discrimination on grounds of race and sex but, with the exception of Northern Ireland, not on grounds of religious faith. However, in the case of groups such as Jews and Sikhs, a high degree of coincidence between ethnic identity and religious belief meant that, under the 1976 Race Relations Act, those groups received a measure of legal protection against adverse treatment related to their religious beliefs. The House of Lords ruled that Sikhs were a racial group (by reference to their 'ethnic origins') within the meaning of the Race Relations Act 1976, in *Mandla v. Dowell Lee*; [1983] 2 A.C. 548. Lord Fraser gave 'a common religion' as one of several characteristics that might contribute to the identification of a community as an 'ethnic group' (562). In the same case, the Court of Appeal had previously ruled that Sikhs were a religious rather than a racial group who therefore, *qua* Sikhs, fell outside the protection afforded by the Race Relations Act; [1982] W.L.R. 932. In an unreported case, *Dawkins v. The Crown Suppliers* (*P.S.A.*), a tribunal decided that Rastafarians were an ethnic group, rather than merely a religious group, and therefore came within the provisions of the Act; see Dave Marrington, 'Legal Decisions', *New Community* 16 (1990): 296–98. However, that decision was subsequently overturned; [1991] I.R.L.R. 327; [1993] I.R.L.R. 284.

If British law had provided against religious discrimination on the model of laws which then prohibited racial and sexual discrimination, Mr Ahmad could not have complained of direct discrimination since he did not lose his full-time post because he was a Muslim. Rather he lost his post because he failed to comply fully with ILEA's requirement to teach on Friday afternoons. But he might well have complained of indirect discrimination in respect of that requirement since he, and Muslims like him, were prevented by their religious beliefs from complying fully with that requirement and suffered disadvantage as a consequence. It would then have fallen to ILEA to show that that requirement was 'justifiable' in spite of its disadvantageous effect for devout Muslims.

For two significant American cases, raising issues similar in character to the case of Mr Ahmad, see *T.W.A. v. Hardison*, 432 U.S. 63 (1977), and *Ansonia Board of Education v. Philbrook*, 55 USLW 4019 (1986). For investigations of these issues in the context of American law, see David E. Retter, 'The Rise and Fall of Title VII's Requirement of Reasonable Accommodation for Religious Employees', *Columbia Human Rights Law Review* 11 (1979): 63–86; Michael W. McConnell, 'Accommodation of Religion', in *The Supreme Court Review*, ed. P. Kurland, G. Casper, D. J. Hutchinson (Chicago: University of Chicago Press, 1986), 1–59; William L. Kandel, 'Current Developments in EEO: Religious Accommodation after *Philbrook*', *Employee Relations Law Journal* 12 (1987): 690–97; and Gloria T. Beckley and Paul Burstein, 'Religious Pluralism, Equal Opportunity, and the State', *Western Political Quarterly* 44 (1991): 185–208.

7. Cf. Albert Weale, 'Toleration, Individual Differences and Respect for Persons', in *Aspects of Toleration*, ed. John Horton and Susan Mendus (London: Methuen, 1985), 16–35, at 27; Susan Mendus, *Toleration and the Limits of Liberalism* (Basingstoke: Macmillan, 1989), 84. There are, of course, many arguments for and against keeping Sundays 'special' which do not turn on the issue that I am concerned with here.

8. John Rawls, *A Theory of Justice* (Oxford: Oxford University Press, 1971).

9. Rawls underlined this feature of his theory in articles he wrote after the publication of *A Theory of Justice*. See especially, 'Fairness to Goodness', *Philosophical Review* 84 (1975): 536–54; 'Justice as Fairness: Political not Metaphysical', *Philosophy and Public Affairs* 14 (1985): 223–51; 'The Priority of Right and Ideas of the Good', *Philosophy and Public Affairs* 17 (1988): 251–76.

10. That religious faith, unlike race, is a 'chosen' rather than an 'unalterable' feature of people was a consideration that weighed with the English Court of Appeal in reaching its decision, in *Mandla v. Dowell Lee*, that Sikhs did not constitute an 'ethnic group'. In particular, Oliver L.J. thought the expression 'ethnic group' was 'entirely inappropriate to describe a group into and out of which anyone may travel as a matter of free choice; and freedom of choice—to join, to remain or to leave—is inherent in the whole philosophy of Sikhism'; [1982] W.L.R. 932 at 941–42; see also the similar views of Kerr L.J. at 945–49. The House of Lords recognised that people may convert into and out of Sikhism but held that that did not preclude Sikhs being an ethnic group; [1983] 2 A.C. 548 at 562–63, 569.

11. Cf. Susan Mendus, 'The Tigers of Wrath and the Horses of Instruction', in *Free Speech*, ed. Bhikhu Parekh (London: Commission for Racial Equality, 1990), 3–17.

12. Richard Rorty, *Contingency, Irony and Solidarity* (Cambridge: Cambridge University Press, 1989), xiii.

13. Cf. Ali A. Mazrui, 'The Satanic Verses or a Satanic Novel? Moral Dilemmas of the Rushdie Affair', in *Free Speech*, ed. Bhikhu Parekh (London: Commission for Racial Equality, 1990), 79–103, at 80–81, 101.

14. Cf. Mendus, *Toleration and the Limits of Liberalism*, 32–35.

15. Even the libertarian need not be wholly indifferent to discrimination. First, to say that employers have an unlimited right to decide whom they employ is not to say that they cannot be criticised for the use they make of that right. Secondly, even in the minimal state there will be a public sector, and the libertarian's claim that anti-discrimination measures violate the rights of private employers has no obvious equivalent in that sector.

16. For a British case which comes close to this alternative, see *Singh v. British Rail Engineering Ltd*, [1986] I.C.R. 22. Singh was not allowed to continue with his job because he refused to remove his turban so that he could wear a hard hat. Part of the justification offered by the employer was that, if Singh continued with the job wearing only his turban and then incurred injury, the fact that the injury was a consequence of Singh's beliefs would not absolve the employer of legal liability for that injury. In other words, that the employer would have to bear the financial consequences of Singh's acting on his beliefs—that is, the costs that would be consequent upon Singh's sustaining injury through wearing a turban rather than a hard hat— became a reason for depriving Singh of the freedom to continue with his job while wearing a turban.

17. Cf. Charles Taylor, 'Atomism', in his *Philosophy and the Human Sciences*, vol. 2 (Cambridge: Cambridge University Press, 1985), 187–210.

18. For a close examination of the idea of equal fulfilment, see Ronald Dworkin, 'What Is Equality? Part I: Equality of Welfare', *Philosophy and Public Affairs* 10 (1981): 185–246. See also my 'The Ideal of the Neutral State', in *Liberal Neutrality*, ed. Robert E. Goodin and Andrew Reeve, 9–38, at 14–17. For a defence of a utilitarian form of 'equal fulfilment', but one cast only in terms of 'preferences', see Richard J. Arneson, 'Liberalism, Distributive Subjectivism, and Equal Opportunity for Welfare', *Philosophy and Public Affairs* 19 (1990): 158–94; see also his 'Neutrality and Utility', *Canadian Journal of Philosophy* 20 (1990): 215–40.

19. See further my 'Liberalism, Belief and Doubt', *Liberalism and Recent Social and Political Philosophy*, ed. R. Bellamy, ARSP, Beiheft 36 (Stuttgart: Steiner, 1989), 51–69, at 63–68 (republished in my *Essays on Toleration* [London: ECPR Press/Rowman & Littlefield, 2018],

153–76, at 167–72). I use the term 'perfectionism' in the special sense given to it by Rawls, *Theory of Justice*, 25, 325–32.

20. One could resist that only by claiming that others were duty-bound to override the Jehovah's Witness's freedom of belief and to force a blood transfusion upon him; his death could then be characterised as a consequence of their failure to perform that duty.

21. Bruce A. Ackerman, *Social Justice in the Liberal State* (New Haven, CT: Yale University Press, 1980).

22. I include this phrase only to provide for restrictions upon freedom of contract other than those at issue here.

23. *R v. Aylesbury Crown Court ex parte Chahal*, [1976] R.T.R. 489, at 492.

24. I have in mind here the distress caused to those involved in accidents causing serious injury to others. Hospital treatment and other supportive public expenditure following injury are also at issue, although those are not always straightforwardly unpaternalistic in character; see my 'Toleration, Harm, and Moral Effect', in *Aspects of Toleration*, ed. John Horton and Susan Mendus, 136–57.

25. The exclusion of religious reasons from public policy is implicit in the approaches of Rawls and Ackerman. See also Jeremy Waldron, 'Theoretical Foundations of Liberalism', *Philosophical Quarterly* 37 (1987): 127–50, and Thomas Nagel, 'Moral Conflict and Political Legitimacy', *Philosophy and Public Affairs* 16 (1987): 215–40. For critical examinations of this approach, see Kent Greenawalt, *Religious Convictions and Political Choice* (New York: Oxford University Press, 1988), and Joseph Raz, 'Facing Diversity: The Case of Epistemic Abstinence', *Philosophy and Public Affairs* 19 (1990): 3–46.

26. The number of those within a religious group making demands like Mr Ahmad's has implications which point in opposite directions. The smaller the number, the more easily they can be accommodated. But, the smaller the number, the greater must also be doubts about whether they *rightly* make that demand. Suppose Mr Ahmad were *mistaken* in believing that, within Islam, the exigencies of employment did not provide adequate reason for not attending a mosque (on which see note 2 above). Should that make a difference? In principle, surely it should, since Mr Ahmad's claims about what his own religion required of him would be false. In practice, public bodies would probably be reluctant to become embroiled in questions of correct doctrine. This is one respect in which a 'group' approach might yield a different answer from an 'individual' approach, i.e. an approach which identifies beliefs and the demands of belief by reference to groups rather than individuals. This issue arose in Britain in *Saggers v. British Railways Board*, a case concerning exemption from a trade union closed shop on grounds of religious belief; [1977] I.R.L.R. 266. Saggers, a Jehovah's Witness, believed that his religion was incompatible with his membership in a trade union even though membership in trade unions was not proscribed by the doctrine of Jehovah's Witnesses. The Employment Appeal Tribunal ruled that (as far as the law relevant to that case was concerned) 'belief' referred to the belief of the relevant individual and not to the established creed or dogma of the religious body of which that individual was a member.

Chapter Six

Belief, Autonomy and Responsibility

The Case of Indirect Religious Discrimination

How much should the adherents of a religious faith be able to demand of others? In liberal societies and in many non-liberal societies, there is broad consensus that religious adherents should be able to make negative demands of others: they should not be persecuted, nor should they be prevented from pursuing their faith or be made to comply with a different faith. Adhering to a religious faith cannot of course license just anything, particularly not practices that inflict harm or violate the rights of others, and how precisely we should circumscribe religious freedom has been, and remains, a rich source of controversy. But, in general, freedom of religion as a liberty that imposes obligations is widely accepted. Indeed, we need not think of it as specifically religious liberty; we can conceive it as merely one aspect of the general freedom people should enjoy to live their lives as they see fit.

The demands that religious believers can reasonably make of others become more controversial when we move beyond those basic negative obligations. A much-discussed case is the clash that can arise between a law that is genuinely non-religious in purpose but that cuts across the demands of a religious faith such that its effect, though not its intention, is to impose a special burden on the faith's adherents. A society has then to decide whether it should leave the faithful to bear their legally imposed burden or remove it by granting them an exemption from the law. Here I give practical import to my discussion by focusing on a related but different sort of case: law governing indirect religious discrimination. I focus on the British version of that law, which requires employers and providers of goods and services to modify their rules and arrangements to accommodate the demands of people's religious beliefs, though British discrimination law on religion and belief shares much in common with the law of many other European countries.[1] I use that law as a vehicle for examining the larger question with which I began: how much should the bearers of a religious faith be able to demand of others? Answering that question requires investigation of some broader and deeper issues, including the ways in which autonomy and authenticity relate to religious belief and how they bear on the demands that religious believers can reasonably make of others.

INDIRECT RELIGIOUS DISCRIMINATION

In Britain, the Equality Act 2010 designates 'religion or belief' a 'protected characteristic'.[2] The Act protects people in respect of all such characteristics from both direct and indirect discrimination in employment and in the provision of goods and services. A discriminates against B *directly* 'if, because of a protected characteristic, A treats B less favourably than A treats or would treat others' (Pt 2, Ch. 2, s. 13). An employer is, for example, guilty of direct religious discrimination if she refuses to employ or promote someone because he is a Muslim or because he is not a Muslim. A discriminates against B *indirectly* if A applies to B 'a provision, criterion or practice' (PCP) that, relative to others, disadvantages people who share B's characteristic, even though the disadvantage is an incidental and unintended consequence of the PCP.[3] If, for example, an employer has a dress code for her employees and if it is more difficult for Muslims than for others to comply with that dress code, she is guilty, *prima facie*, of indirect religious discrimination. She can, however, escape the charge of indirect religious discrimination if she can show that her PCP is 'a proportionate means of achieving a legitimate aim' (Pt 2, Ch. 2, s. 19).

The claim that direct discrimination, including direct religious discrimination, is unfair is unlikely to be challenged. The claim that indirect discrimination, particularly indirect religious discrimination, is unfair is altogether more controversial. Consider the following case.

Sarah Desrosiers owned and ran a small hairdressing salon in North London named Wedge. She advertised for an assistant stylist, and Bushra Noah applied for the position. Noah was a Muslim who wore a headscarf that covered her hair entirely. In itself that was not an obstacle to Desrosiers's employing Noah. However, in the course of an interview, Desrosiers discovered that Noah would refuse to remove her headscarf while she was working in the salon. That was a problem for Desrosiers, since she required the hairstyles of her hairdressers to be visible to the salon's customers. Her salon offered an 'alternative' form of hairdressing, which she described as 'ultramodern' and 'urban, edgy and funky'. She wanted her hairdressers to use their own hair to model the salon's style, a practice that is common in British hairdressing salons. As Noah was unwilling to comply with that practice, Desrosiers told Noah that she could not offer her the position. Noah responded by registering claims of direct and indirect discrimination against Desrosiers.

An Employment Tribunal (ET) heard the case during spring 2008.[4] It dismissed Noah's claim of direct discrimination: Desrosiers had refrained from appointing Noah not because she was a Muslim but because she would not show her hair while working in the salon and Desrosiers would not have appointed any applicant who, for whatever reason, religious or non-religious, refused to reveal her hair to the salon's customers.

The ET did, however, find Noah's claim of indirect discrimination well-founded. Desrosiers's practice of requiring her employees to show their hair placed female Muslims, who, like Noah, wore a headscarf for religious reasons, at a disadvantage compared with the adherents of other faiths or none. That itself was not conclusive, since Desrosiers would have escaped the charge of indirect discrimination had she persuaded the Tribunal that her PCP constituted a 'proportionate means of achieving a legitimate aim'. The ET accepted that Desrosiers's practice was a legitimate aim for her business; many salons required their hairdressers to reflect the salon's image, and that practice was especially relevant for Desrosiers's business, given her promotion of a particular brand image and her use of that image in her strategy for attracting and retaining clientele. However, the fact that Desrosiers could not provide concrete evidence that discontinuing the practice or exempting Noah from it would have had, or would have risked having, a significantly adverse impact on her business, led the ET to conclude that her PCP was not a proportionate means for achieving her legitimate aim. (The fact that circumstances at the salon developed so that Desrosiers did not ultimately appoint anyone as an assistant stylist and, for that reason, would not have appointed Noah even if her hair covering had not been an issue, was deemed irrelevant.)[5]

Noah claimed compensation of £34,000. The Tribunal awarded her £4000 in respect of 'injury to feelings'. Of greater moment for Desrosiers was the estimated £40,000 she had to sacrifice in preparing for the trial and the prospect of bankruptcy.[6]

How should we view the outcome of this case? Was it a triumph for fairness, since it upheld Noah's right not to be deprived of an employment opportunity on account of her religious faith? Or was it an injustice, since it deprived Desrosiers of the right to run her business according to her own preferred (and not unreasonable) practice, because that practice did not suit a religious believer whose beliefs Desrosiers did not share?

In some ways the issues raised by law governing indirect religious discrimination (hereinafter IRD) are akin to those raised by statutory exemptions granted to the religious. Both measures are designed to accommodate the diverse religious beliefs present in a population, and the law on IRD itself requires a form of exemption: it does not require an employer or provider to abandon a PCP that a court would deem to be not 'a proportionate means of achieving a legitimate aim'; rather, it requires that she should not apply the PCP to a person whom it disadvantages for reasons of religion or belief. On the other hand, in its basic provisions, IRD legislation takes the form of a general rule rather than an exception to a general rule, and it provides a form of religious accommodation that is more general in scope and systematic in content than the handful of assorted laws that provide for religiously based exemptions. It also differs from legal exemption in that its locus is civil society rather than the state. In the case of statutory exemptions, such as those in Britain relating to ritual slaughter or to the carrying of knives in public by Sikhs, it is the state that does the accommodating. In the case of IRD, it is members of civil society—employers and providers of goods and services (including government departments and agencies in those roles)—that are required to accommodate. Those members of civil society can be large impersonal organisations, such as business corporations and local authorities, but they may also be individuals, like Sarah Desrosiers. I have cited the case of *Noah v. Desrosiers* partly because the issue is thrown into particularly sharp relief when it takes a citizen-to-citizen form and one individual has to bear the costs of another individual's belief.

The case of IRD is particularly interesting because it is caught up with the issue of choice. People's religious beliefs, it is often claimed, are unlike their race or gender in being chosen and, because they are chosen, they warrant different treatment from characteristics such as race and gender.

In fact, even if religious beliefs are chosen, it does not follow that discriminating on grounds of religion is acceptable. Direct discrimination, in which people are denied employment or access to goods and services simply because of their religious affiliation, still seems improper and unjust, unless religious affiliation is genuinely relevant to the employment or access. Consider the analogous case of political opinion. (Discrimination on grounds of political opinion has not been expressly prohibited in Britain but has been in Northern Ireland, along with religious discrimination, since 1976.[7]) Political opinions may be more readily characterised as chosen than religious beliefs, yet we would still normally think it improper that someone should be denied a job because of his political opinions, unless, once again, political opinion was genuinely relevant to the job at stake.

In the case of indirect discrimination, however, choice may seem a good deal more relevant. If my religious beliefs are chosen, and if the demands of my religious beliefs clash with an employer's practice, and if the employer is then required to sacrifice her practice to the demands of my religious belief, my choice may seem to be unfairly privileged over the employer's practice. Certainly people should be free to adopt whatever religious beliefs they like, but they cannot expect others to pick up the bill for the choice they make. If I choose a belief, I should bear the consequences of my choice. I cannot reasonably expect to choose a belief, the demands of which make me less eligible for employment, and yet be able to offload the costs of my choice onto an employer.

The issue here is close to the central concern of luck egalitarianism. For luck egalitarians, people's opportunities in life should not be affected by brute luck. It is unjust if features of themselves or their circumstances, for which they cannot be held responsible, affect people's life chances. If, however, people fare better or worse as a consequence of their own choices, that is a different matter. It would be unfair if the consequences of people's choices were equalised such that those who had chosen prudently or cheaply had to contribute towards the higher costs incurred by those who had chosen imprudently or extravagantly. Luck egalitarians differ over exactly where the division between chance and choice should be located, but not over the relevance of that cut for the just distribution of resources.[8] The argument about what luck egalitarianism requires has been conducted mainly with reference to tastes and preferences, but its two leading, and feuding, protagonists have both signalled that the same logic should apply to beliefs of the sort that I am concerned with here (Cohen 1989: 935–39; Dworkin 2000: 285–99).

Luck egalitarianism implies that people have a better claim to export the costs of their religious beliefs if those beliefs are matters of chance rather than choice. More particularly, it implies that the case for prohibiting IRD is more easily made if people's religious beliefs are unchosen. That reverses the normal implications of autonomy. We might suppose that, more commonly, people will do better if their beliefs are conceived as autonomously held. If they have arrived at their beliefs via a route that is consistent with their autonomy, we would seem to have reason to take their beliefs more seriously as *their* beliefs and as their *authentic* beliefs. If, on the other hand, their beliefs have been planted in their heads by circumstance and are held unreflectively, we would seem to have less reason to respect their beliefs. In the present case, however, it appears that believers would do better if their beliefs were not autonomous, since, according to the rules of luck egalitarianism, they would then have a claim upon their society's resources that autonomous believers would not.[9]

CHOOSING TO BELIEVE

Should we then treat people's religious beliefs as chosen? One reason for doubting that we should resides in the nature of belief itself. We cannot simply choose or decide what to believe in the way that we might choose to take a holiday in Spain or decide to pursue a career in law. We can believe only what seems to us to be the case. If I have good reason to believe that Barcelona is in Spain or that a law career is well remunerated, I cannot choose to believe otherwise. Beliefs therefore would seem to be (in a suitable sense) imposed upon us by the world.

That line of reasoning is open to challenge on a number of grounds. First, choice does not have to be arbitrary if it is to be meaningful. Our choices may sometimes be arbitrary acts of will, but more commonly we have reasons for choosing as we do and we do not think that the presence of those reasons eliminates choice. Even when my reasons identify a particular option as inescapably the best option, we would still find nothing untoward in characterising that option as an object of my choice. I may conclude that, all things considered, Spain is my ideal holiday destination and that a career in law is the right career for me, but Spain can still be my chosen holiday destination and law my chosen career. That said, choosing to holiday in Spain or to pursue a career in law is still rather different from 'choosing' to believe that Barcelona is in Spain or that, in general, law careers are well remunerated. So perhaps it is not reasons as such but certain *types* of reason that pre-empt choice.

That makes relevant a second consideration: the non-evidential, or incompletely evidential, basis of religious belief. This is tricky territory. Religious faiths and variants of religious faiths come in different forms, so the nature of what people believe in religiously is highly varied in character. Equally, the reasons that people might have, or that they might advance, for holding a religious belief can be very different. Broad generalisation in this area is therefore hazardous. Nevertheless, religious belief is a matter of faith in a way that believing that Barcelona is in Spain, or that law careers are well remunerated, is not. That is one reason why we speak of religious belief as 'belief', whereas we might say simply that we 'know' that Barcelona is in Spain and that, on average, lawyers are well paid. The non-evidential, or non-fully-evidential, nature of religious belief means that it affords people a domain of epistemic discretion that they do not have in relation to simple factual matters. People can and do have scope to arrive at different religious beliefs and, to that extent, that sort of belief offers a domain of choice.

If that were not so, the idea of 'freedom of religious belief' would make little sense. That freedom might describe only people's freedom to pursue a religious faith, which is consistent with their having no discretion over the particular faith they pursue. But 'freedom of religious belief' is normally understood to include the freedom to adopt, to change and to reject religious beliefs, which would make no sense if religious belief was so given, so pre-emptive of autonomy, that it was a freedom we were incapable of exercising. That is why we do not normally speak in a parallel fashion of freedom of race or freedom of gender.[10]

While this issue is normally debated in the language of choice, that language is not entirely felicitous for what is at stake. If we think of choosing a holiday or choosing a career as a paradigmatic instance of choice, embracing a religious faith will often seem a very different sort of process. For the believer, the experience of believing or coming to believe will often seem unlike choosing, or at least not like making a choice of the sort involved in choosing a holiday or a career.[11] But the relevant consideration for our concerns is whether religious faith constitutes a domain of epistemic discretion that makes autonomous judgement both possible and meaningful and, if it does, whether it is reasonable to hold people agentially responsible for their religious beliefs. My claim is that the character of religious faith does indeed present such a domain of discretion and that we can reasonably ascribe to religious believers agential responsibility for what they believe.

A quite different sort of reason for rejecting any association between religion and choice lies in the facts of sociology. For the majority of the world's believing population, their religious beliefs are a consequence of their socialisation, either by their family or by the larger community or society in which they live. Catholic communities beget Catholics, and Muslim societies beget Muslims. Of course, that generalisation requires considerable qualification. People can and do shed the religious beliefs to which they are heir, and they can and do take up new religious beliefs or spurn religious belief altogether. They probably do so now more than ever before, particularly in the liberal, plural societies in which issues of accommodation are most likely to arise. But, considered in the context of the world's believing population as a whole, religious converts are a tiny minority. The role of family and community in shaping people's religious beliefs is too obvious to need labouring.

The role of social context in shaping people's religious beliefs may induce us to conceive their beliefs as 'givens' which, like their race or gender, are features of themselves over which they have no control. That, in turn, may lead us to doubt that we should hold people responsible for believing what they do or for meeting the demands of their faith. Insofar as their beliefs generate demands, we might conceive those demands as burdens or handicaps with which believers have been saddled by circumstance and for which they can properly look to others for aid or relief.

In response to that sort of determinism and its apparent implications, I want to appeal to an argument made by, amongst others, Brian Barry (1991: 156–58), Thomas Scanlon (1986: 116–17) and Ronald Dworkin (2000: 289–96). It matters less how people have come to have the beliefs they do than how they now hold them. There may be a large element of inheritance in people's beliefs but, if they now embrace and endorse those beliefs (as believers normally do), they can hardly present their beliefs to others as disabilities or handicaps with which they have been encumbered and for which they can seek compensation from others. We can employ the test afforded by Dworkin's imaginary pill (2000: 292). Suppose a pill were available which, if taken, would 'cure' people of their beliefs. If people really disidentified with their beliefs, if they really viewed their beliefs as incubi that burdened their lives, they would be willing to take the pill. If they are not so willing, their unwillingness signals they do not genuinely disidentify with their beliefs and reckon themselves to be handicapped by them. Much more simply, if people disidentify with their beliefs, they can give them up. And, if for some reason they find themselves incapable of doing so unaided, they might, in the absence of Dworkin's pill, be offered therapy. Why palliate when we can cure?

But all of this is plainly fanciful. In reality, when people make claims in respect of their beliefs, they do so not by presenting them as burdens with which they have been saddled by circumstance and which they would rather be without. Quite the contrary, they insist that others must take their beliefs seriously because they themselves take their beliefs seriously. It is because they embrace and endorse their beliefs that they expect others to respect their beliefs. Others may reject the truth of the beliefs at stake, but it is still incumbent upon them to respect those beliefs out of respect for their adherents as believers. So it is the fact that people strongly identify with their beliefs, rather than their claim to disidentify with them, that grounds the demands that believers make in respect of their beliefs. They register their demands not as helpless victims of chance and circumstance but as people whose beliefs are manifestations of their autonomy and who are capable of taking responsibility, and who do take responsibility, for what they believe.

They are wise to do so. If people present themselves as the helpless victims of sociological determinism, they invite us to treat their current beliefs as other than their authentic beliefs and, if we can, to engineer their coming to hold other beliefs that have a better claim to authenticity. In reality, sociological determinism may not make a case against freedom of belief all things considered, since the costs of liberating people from their unwarranted and disabling beliefs may be too great, both for them and for us. But, in principle, the deterministic argument can work as an argument for setting aside freedom of religious belief, both as a liberal and as a non-liberal principle, and no body of believers is likely to wish that for themselves.

FREEDOM OF BELIEF AND ITS IMPLICATIONS

To these arguments I want to add another that is different in kind but similar in thrust. That argument concerns what is implicit in the principle of freedom of religious belief, a principle which I assume all parties to the issue I am examining will endorse. I understand that principle to entitle people to embrace, revise and pursue whatever religious belief they deem fit (subject to the usual qualification that they do not pursue their faith in a way that violates the rights of others).

What would an equitable version of that principle require? It would require that people should bear the consequences of the use they make of that freedom. People cannot reasonably expect to enjoy freedom of belief yet also to be able to export to others the costs of the use they make of it. If they could, one person in embracing a belief could unilaterally burden the lives of others, and that seems plainly inequitable. Thus freedom of belief, properly understood, comes as a package. People should be free to embrace and pursue whatever religious faith they see fit but, when they avail themselves of that freedom, they must bear the consequences of the use they make of it. They cannot, in fairness, impose those consequences upon others. Autonomy and authenticity may remain relevant to our valuing freedom of belief, but the argument here turns not on the phenomenology of belief but on the 'rules of the game'. If the game is played according to the rules of freedom of belief, it is implicit in those rules that people must take responsibility for the consequences of their beliefs.

The principle of freedom of belief involves the notion that your beliefs are 'none of my business'. It does, of course, leave me free to make my own assessment of your beliefs. However, even if I assess your beliefs as bizarre, implausible, heretical, benighted or lacking merit in some other way, the principle debars my impeding or interfering with your freedom to hold and pursue whatever beliefs you possess. But that remains plausible only so long as the pursuit of your beliefs does not burden my life. If your beliefs become a source of positive rather than merely negative claims against me, so that I have, for example, to forfeit resources or to adjust my behaviour out of deference to your belief, then—to that extent—your belief reasonably becomes 'my business'. If your belief is going to burden my life, it is entirely reasonable that I should be able to judge it and, if I find it wanting, dismiss it as a reason for my having any positive obligation in respect of it. I do not mean that, in these circumstances, your freedom of belief should be suspended in every respect but only that there is no clear reason why your embracing a belief that justifies your making a burdensome claim upon me should count for more than my rejection of that belief and its burdensome implications.

We can add to that the more general point that freedom of belief is supposed to work both ways around: it is freedom to embrace and freedom to reject a belief. If X's embracing *p* is reason for Y's incurring positive obligations with respect to X, why should that reason not be cancelled by Y's believing in not-*p*? Why should my belief that Christ was the Son of God count for more than your belief that he was not, and why should your belief that Muhammad was God's Prophet count for more than my belief that he was not? After all, we find it no more acceptable that people should be made to comply with religious beliefs they reject than that they should be prevented from complying with religious beliefs they accept. Indeed, people's religious beliefs can make it wrong for them to assist in the maintenance or promotion of other (conflicting) beliefs.

Since my main point of practical reference in this chapter is discrimination law, I want to pause briefly to consider how the practice of courts in Britain relates to the general argument I am making here. Their practice is to refrain from subjecting religious beliefs to any sort of test of correctness, plausibility or even reasonableness. They do subject beliefs to a limited moral screening: a court will not protect manifestations of belief that are inconsistent with 'basic standards of human dignity and integrity'. In addition, judges have ruled that to be recognised as a 'belief' within the meaning of Article 9 of the European Convention on Human Rights (ECHR), and by implication in other areas of UK law, [12] the belief must satisfy some other criteria. It must relate to 'more than merely trivial' matters, it 'must possess an adequate degree of seriousness and importance' and 'be a belief on a fundamental problem'. It must also be 'coherent in the sense of being intelligible and capable of being understood', but 'too much should not be demanded in this regard'. [13] But, when we turn from form to content, the courts abstain from making any judgement on the reasonableness or plausibility of religious beliefs.

Moreover, it is not the orthodoxies of organised religions that the courts protect in human rights law or discrimination law; it is the belief of the individual claimant, provided a court is satisfied that the claimant sincerely holds the belief he or she professes. Judicially, therefore, a belief's authenticity is a matter of whether it is sincerely held by the claimant rather than whether it conforms to an established body of doctrine. In the celebrated words of Lord Nicholls,

> emphatically, it is not for the court to embark on an inquiry into the asserted belief and judge its 'validity' by some objective standard such as the source material upon which the claimant founds his belief or the orthodox teaching of the religion in question or the extent to which the claimant's belief conforms to or differs from the views of others professing the same religion. Freedom of belief protects the subjective belief of an individual. [14]

It is easy to appreciate why the courts have adopted that position, not only in the UK but also in many other countries, including the United States and Canada. [15] It is not the role of the courts to uphold orthodoxy or to suppress heresy. The law's purpose is to protect believers rather than belief, and civil courts are not equipped to rule on contentious points of theology. But, intelligible and defensible as this judicial state of affairs is, it means that the religious beliefs that enjoy legal protection are virtually bereft of any form of quality control. [16] In the absence of that control, in the absence of any assessment of a religious belief's plausibility and reasonableness, it is hard to accept that one person, merely by embracing a religious belief, should be able to burden the lives of others.

BELIEFS AND BEARING RESPONSIBILITY
FOR CONSEQUENCES

The thrust of my argument so far has been that we should require people to take responsibility for their religious beliefs and for meeting the demands of their beliefs. They cannot reasonably expect others to assist them with, or to compensate them for, meeting the demands of their faith. If, for example, the religious adherent is a Christian who desists from the recreational activities in which others engage on Sundays, or an Orthodox Jew who is similarly abstemious on Saturdays, he should not expect others to make good the opportunity costs he incurs because of his Sabbatarianism. Even without the argument I have made, this would be a difficult area in which to deploy the idea of compensation, since it is not clear that, for the believer, fulfilling the demands of his belief should count as a negative experience. But, even if the believer were to experience the demands of his faith as burdens, they are not burdens that he should expect others to assist him in carrying or for which he should expect compensation.

However, the 'consequences' that attract controversy are not usually of that kind. They are not usually consequences that are entirely internal to— that arise only from—a system of belief. Rather, they arise from the intersection of a set of beliefs and a social arrangement that is external to those beliefs. It is this sort of 'mixed' consequence that is relevant to IRD. Discrimination of that sort arises when a PCP used by an employer or provider clashes with the demands of an adherent's faith. So, for example, the Sabbatarian Christian is unlikely to complain—at least not in a way that registers a demand for remedy—about the injustice of his having to observe the Lord's Day while non-Sabbatarians are adding to their income or enjoying themselves shopping or playing tennis. But he may well complain if he is unable to take a job because his prospective employer has a PCP that requires her employees to work on Sundays. He may also complain if he is an avid football supporter whose favoured football club stages matches on Sundays that he is unable to attend. We might also think that, in these latter cases, he has reason to complain since the relevant 'consequence' is not one for which he alone is responsible. Agentially, the clash would seem to be one for which the believer and the employer or service provider bear joint responsibility.

The issue here bears some resemblance to the issue of expensive preferences as conceived by Jerry Cohen. In his later writings on this issue, Cohen

(1999, 2004) stressed that the bad luck incurred by those who possessed expensive involuntary preferences (preferences that they had not themselves cultivated) lay not so much in having the preferences but in their being expensive to satisfy. As Dworkin (2004: 344) reformulated Cohen's view, those with expensive tastes suffered from bad *price* luck rather than bad *preference* luck. Presenting the issue in that way shifts the emphasis from the make-up of the person who has the preference to the external circumstances he or she confronts. In particular, Cohen pointed out that a preference that might be expensive to satisfy in one set of circumstances might not in another. Thus expensiveness could be a contingent feature of a preference. In a similar fashion, the believer might point out that the obstacles or costs he encounters in a society are not intrinsic to his belief; they are contingent upon the particular arrangements of the society in which he finds himself.

Although there is a degree of similarity between the issues of expensive preferences and costly beliefs, I do not want to conflate the two issues. Beliefs are not the same as preferences and religious beliefs have features special to themselves, so I want to maintain my focus on the specific case of religious belief. The argument I want to resist is that, if the costs the believer incurs are a joint consequence of the demands of his belief and those of an employer's or a provider's PCP, meeting those costs should become the joint responsibility of the two parties or the sole responsibility of the employer or provider. Even if the two parties bear joint causal responsibility for the costs that fall upon the believer, it does not follow that they bear joint moral responsibility for meeting them.

Consider the sorts of economic cost that are routinely associated with religious belief and practice. The adherents of a religious faith usually need buildings—churches, mosques, synagogues, temples—in which they can conduct acts of worship and other ceremonies that are important to their faith. They also require other artefacts for their rites and ceremonies such as special forms of vestment, church organs, prayer mats, cleansing areas, and Torah scrolls. Some faiths require or exhort their adherents to undertake pilgrimages. In providing for the needs of their faith, the faithful incur economic costs. But those costs do not arise from their faith alone. They also arise because those who provide the goods and services they need charge for labour and materials at the going market rate. Thus the economic costs the religious incur in relation to their faith are not consequences of their faith only; they are a combined consequence of their demand for goods and services and the willingness of others to provide them only if they receive a normal economic return.

Are we then to accept that, since believers and suppliers are jointly responsible for there being costs, the two parties should bear joint moral responsibility for meeting them? For example, those whose faith requires them to undertake a pilgrimage might meet half of the travel costs themselves, while leaving the travel company to pick up the bill for the other half or to be reimbursed by a public subsidy. Similarly, the costs arising from the construction and maintenance of places of worship might fall equally on the worshippers and the providers or the taxpayer. No one is likely to endorse such a proposal. The reason is simply that, provided believers have been treated in the same way as others in their society's background allocation of resources, whether that be a market-based or state-based allocation or some mix of the two, it is fair that they, rather than others, should bear the costs of pursuing their beliefs.

I want here to make use of John Rawls's approach to this issue, particularly his idea of a society's 'basic structure'. For Rawls, a society's basic structure describes 'the way in which the main political and social institutions of society fit together into one system of cooperation, and the way they assign basic rights and duties and regulate the division of advantages that arises from social cooperation over time' (2001: 10). His theory of justice aims to provide the principles that should shape a society's basic structure, particularly its distribution of freedoms and resources. The basic structure should be set, Rawls argues, without reference to the different comprehensive doctrines (including religious doctrines) to which the members of a society subscribe or to the conceptions of the good they wish to pursue. Once the basic structure is in place, people are entitled to use their freedoms and resources to pursue whatever ends they have, religious or non-religious.

I shall not invoke the details of Rawls's theory of justice since they are unnecessary for the position I wish to defend here. All I want to borrow from Rawls is the general idea that a fair distribution of freedoms and resources should be determined independently of any particular individual's comprehensive doctrine or conception of the good. The implication of the arguments I made earlier—that individuals should take responsibility for their beliefs and for meeting the demands of their beliefs—is that the basic structure should be set without reference to those beliefs. Some individuals should not be accorded greater freedoms or more resources than others simply because they hold religious beliefs or because their religious beliefs are more costly to pursue than the beliefs of others. Rather, freedoms and resources should be distributed independently of the demands of any particular individual's beliefs; believers should then meet the demands of their faith from their own freedoms and resources rather than help themselves to the freedoms and resources of others.

How does all of this bear on legal provision for IRD? I want to suggest that reference to something like the idea of a basic structure is implicit in British law on indirect discrimination, and rightly so. As previously indicated, that law provides that an employer or provider is not guilty of IRD as a legal offence if she can show that her PCP is 'a proportionate means of achieving a legitimate aim'. Henceforth, I shall describe that provision as the

PMLA test or PMLA threshold. An employer or provider is obliged to accommodate the beliefs of others only insofar as her PCP falls below the threshold set by the PMLA test. Once her PCP reaches that threshold, her obligation to accommodate ceases. The PMLA test therefore sets an order of priority and one that holds even if the PCP serves the employer's or provider's interest less than it disserves the interest of the believer.

The spirit of the PMLA threshold seems to be that normal organisations should be able to pursue their normal aims through appropriate means without being impeded by the religious beliefs of others. Insofar as they can avoid rules and arrangements that incidentally disadvantage people who have religious commitments, and they can do so consistently with pursuing their aims through proportionate means, they should. But, insofar as they cannot, they have no legal obligation to accommodate. The freedom of organisations and individuals to pursue their legitimate aims through proportionate means forms part of the basic structure of society, and it is against that background that religious believers have to take their chances, as do other members of society.

What understanding of proportionality does this interpretation of the PMLA test imply? The proportionality of a means should be judged with reference to the aim at which it is directed, assuming that aim to be legitimate. If it is well-attuned to the aim, it is proportionate and therefore trumps the competing demands of the believer. We can allow that a PCP which fails to be more accommodating than it could be without suffering any loss in its efficacy might properly be deemed 'disproportionate' simply for that reason. But, even if we make that part of the calculation, it is still primarily the efficacy with which a means realises its aim that identifies it as proportionate or not. Understood in this way, the burden to which the PMLA test makes employers and providers liable can be described as 'insignificant'; it is 'insignificant' in that it will not impede their ability to pursue legitimate aims through proportionate means. Were the burden to exceed that limit, we could describe it as 'significant'. Making employers or providers liable only to insignificant burdens does not imply that the benefits experienced by believers as a consequence of that liability will also be insignificant. The burden shifted from the believer (e.g. a barrier to employment) can still be highly significant and far more significant for him than the burden shifted onto the employer (an insignificant exemption from her PCP) is for her.

Everything I have stated here about the PMLA test is consistent with what British legislation on indirect discrimination actually *says* but, for reasons I shall now explain, I have to present it as an understanding of what the law ought to be rather than an account of what the law actually is. Tribunals and courts often incorporate in the PMLA test the nature and degree of a PCP's disadvantageous impact for a religious group. Thus in *Noah*, the ET remarked that the function of the legislation on IRD was 'to outlaw particular means of pursuing what may be found, in principle, to be entirely legitimate aims, *because of their disproportionately discriminatory impact*.[17] If we incorporate the degree of disadvantageous impact in the proportionality test, we could have two PCPs that were equally efficacious in relation to their aims, but one could be judged disproportionate and the other proportionate because one affected a group of believers more disadvantageously than did the other, or because it disadvantaged a larger number of believers.[18] The interpretation of the PMLA test given by the ET in *Noah* is an instance of an approach to proportionality often described as 'balancing'. In the words of another ET, 'a proportionate means is one which is achieved as a result of a balancing exercise between all the interests involved'.[19] Clearly that 'balancing' understanding of the proportionality test is very different from the 'prioritising' interpretation I have offered. According to the argument I have made, the even-handed approach of balancing is objectionable because it allows religious believers to impose the costs of providing for their beliefs upon others in ways and to degrees that, for those others, are 'significant'.

We do well to remember that the law on IRD and the PMLA test apply not just to commercial organisations whether they are large corporations or small businesses like Sarah Desrosiers's. They apply to any organisation that is an employer or a provider of goods or services, including government departments, government agencies, local authorities, hospitals, charities, schools and universities.

Lest my argument should appear hostile to religion, I should point out that its beneficiaries include religious organisations. They too should be able to pursue their legitimate aims through proportionate means without being hobbled by the religious beliefs of others. In general, religious organisations are well served by the Equality Act 2010. Both 'organised religions' (e.g. churches and mosques) and organisations with an 'ethos based on religion' (e.g. religious charities and faith schools) are entitled to discriminate on grounds of religion in employment, provided their religious requirement is a genuine occupational requirement and meets the PMLA test. Given their purpose, it would be absurd if they could not. In addition, organised religions, though not organisations characterised only by an ethos based on religion, may discriminate in employment on grounds of gender, gender reassignment, sexual orientation and marital status, provided that such discrimination is required for compliance with the religion's doctrines or to avoid conflict with the strongly held convictions of a significant number of the religion's followers. In matters other than employment, 'organisations relating to religion or belief' can take account of religion or belief and sexual orientation in imposing restrictions on membership of their organisation; on participation in its activities; on those to whom it provides goods, facilities and services; and on the use and disposal of its premises. Once again, restrictions relating to sexual orientation are permitted only insofar as they are necessary to comply with the organisation's doctrines or to avoid conflict with the strongly held convictions of a significant number of the religion's or belief's followers. Some of these exemptions from the general rules governing direct and indirect discrimination have been matters of controversy. Nevertheless, they embody the same principle that organisations should not be prevented by obligations to accommodate others from pursuing their core aims and activities through proportionate means. [20]

THE CASE FOR PROVIDING AGAINST
INDIRECT RELIGIOUS DISCRIMINATION

Is there, then, any case for seeking to combat IRD at all, even when the burden that falls on an employer or provider is 'insignificant' in the sense I have indicated? There is a marked contrast in the ways discrimination law and human rights law have dealt with IRD. In considering employment cases in relation to Article 9 of the ECHR, which provides for freedom of thought, conscience and religion, courts have generally responded unsympathetically to claims of an indirectly discriminatory kind. Where an employee's religious convictions have clashed with an employer's requirements, they have generally taken the view that the employee's right to manifest his religion has not been interfered with, since the employee chose to accept the employment and retains the option of resigning from it. In relation to the workplace, the judicial view has been that 'the freedom to leave one's job acts as sufficient protection of one's fundamental human rights'. [21] Britain's domestic legislation on IRD has therefore gone a good deal further than European human rights law (as it has generally been interpreted) in safeguarding believers from the possible adverse socio-economic consequences of their beliefs. Given what I have argued in this chapter, is it right to do so?

There are many considerations that bear on the case for IRD legislation other than those that have been my central concern. One is the need to provide against covert direct discrimination. If there were no provision against IRD, employers who wished to discriminate against a particular religious group could avoid doing so openly; they could achieve the same effect by adopting a requirement with which members of the group could not comply. [22] The test of whether a PCP is a proportionate means for achieving a legitimate aim might be interpreted as a test of employers' and providers' good faith.

Secondly, if practices and policies persist that significantly disadvantage some peoples' employment opportunities or their access to goods and services, but there is no good justification for those practices and policies, simple utilitarian reasons argue for their removal. That consideration is especially relevant for many European societies, including Britain, that have been historically largely mono-faith (even if multi-denominational) and have become multi-faith societies only recently. Their public arrangements have often been influenced by the historically dominant faith (e.g. the structure of the working week, the timing of public holidays) and so do not present all faiths with a level playing field. Introducing measures to combat IRD is one way of making people address traditional arrangements and amend them, or provide alternatives, if the status quo reflects a bias that is no longer defensible.

Thirdly, considerations of social policy may argue for measures prohibiting indirect as well as direct discrimination. If some beliefs conflict with basic features of a society, such as its workplace practices, their adherents may find themselves significantly disadvantaged, both socially and economically. That disadvantage is clearly bad for them, but it may also be bad for the society generally insofar as it damages social cohesion and becomes a source of social discontent and unrest. If differences of religious faith track ethnic divisions so that religious disadvantage compounds racial disadvantage, as it now does in many European societies, there will be even greater reason to worry about IRD. This sort of concern has clearly been significant in motivating British public policy on religious diversity.

These considerations argue powerfully in defence of measures proscribing IRD. However, I do not mean to rely upon them only and to discount entirely the consideration that has been my more immediate concern in this chapter: the claims that people have simply as conscientious bearers of religious belief. If we are committed to freedom of belief, it is entirely intelligible that we should regret clashes between the demands of a religious belief and a society's public or private arrangements that result in believers being 'burdened' in ways that other people are not. Such burdens may not remove people's freedom of belief but they are a form of cost or disadvantage, and we may reasonably regret that people's conscientiously held beliefs should be a source of social disadvantage for them. A society committed to freedom of belief can therefore reasonably wish to mitigate the burdens that people incur when their beliefs clash with its public or private arrangements, insofar as that mitigation is fair.[23] But we are then left with the question of what sort or degree of mitigation is fair. The answer I have given in this chapter is: mitigation that does not impose significant costs upon others. Of course, determining how that general principle applies to particular cases will often be far from straightforward, as the case of *Noah v. Desrosiers* illustrates; but, on my reading of that case, Desrosiers was unfortunate to be the loser.

NOTES

I am grateful for discussions of earlier drafts of this chapter to participants in several events: the workshop on 'Autonomy, Authenticity and Belief' organised by Geoffrey Brahm Levey, hosted by the Royal Flemish Academy for Science and the Arts, Brussels, 2010; seminars in politics at the University of Manchester and in philosophy at the University of Hull; the AHRC/ ESRC Religion and Society Conference on 'New Forms of Public Religion', St John's College, Cambridge, 2012; and the workshop on 'Religion and Public Life', Queen's University Belfast, 2014, organised by Matteo Bonotti. Special thanks for their comments to Cécile Laborde and Geoffrey Brahm Levey.

1. See Doe 2011: 64–78. British law on religious discrimination has its origins in the EU: Council Directive 2000/78/EC, 27 November 2000.

2. The other protected characteristics are age, disability, gender reassignment, marriage and civil partnership, pregnancy and maternity, race, sex, and sexual orientation; Equality Act 2010 Pt 2, Ch. 1, s. 4. The Act designates 'religion or belief', rather than only religion, a protected characteristic. It defines 'belief' as 'any religious or philosophical belief' (Pt 2, Ch. 1, s. 10). A belief would appear to be 'philosophical' if it is akin to religious belief. The Employment Equality (Religion or Belief) Regulations 2003 (now superseded by the Equality Act 2010) stated that 'religion or belief' meant 'any religion, religious belief, or *similar* philosophical belief' (regulation 2, my emphasis). Under those Regulations, an ET ruled that 'belief' did not include political beliefs since they were not similar to religious beliefs; *Baggs v. Fudge* ET case number 1400114/2005. A later EAT ruled that a belief in man-made climate change and its resulting moral imperatives was 'philosophical'; *Grainger PLC & Others v. Nicholson* [2009] UKEAT/0219/07/ZT. See further Sandberg 2011: 46–56. To date, legal cases that have arisen under discrimination law on religion or belief have related overwhelmingly to religious belief and practice.

3. The actual wording of this section of the Act (Pt 2, Ch. 2, s. 19) runs as follows:

> a provision, criterion or practice is discriminatory in relation to a relevant protected characteristic of B's if—
>
> 1. A applies, or would apply, it to persons with whom B does not share the characteristic,
> 2. it puts, or would put, persons with whom B shares the characteristic at a particular disadvantage when compared with persons with whom B does not share it,
> 3. it puts, or would put, B at that disadvantage.

4. The case therefore preceded the Equality Act 2010 and was pursued under the Employment Equality (Religion or Belief) Regulations 2003, but, for the most part, the substance of those regulations remained unchanged in the Equality Act 2010.

5. My account of *Noah v. Desrosiers* is based on details given in the unpublished report of the Employment Tribunal, case number 2201867/2007.

6. Report, including an interview with Desrosiers, *Mail Online*, 18 June 2008, http:// www.dailymail.co.uk/femail/article-1027300/How-I-nearly-lost-business-refusing-hire-Muslim-hair-stylist-wouldnt-hair.html (accessed 17 December 2019).

7. Fair Employment (Northern Ireland) Act 1976, and Fair Employment and Treatment (Northern Ireland) Order 1998.

8. In fact, as the debate has progressed, the choice that is central to Dworkin's version of luck egalitarianism has become increasingly complex and less recognisable as 'choice' in any ordinary sense. Right from the start, Cohen's principal criticism of Dworkin has been that Dworkin holds people responsible for features of themselves and their situation that they cannot plausibly be said to have chosen. See Dworkin 2000: 285–99; Cohen 1989; Matravers 2002.

9. In linking luck egalitarianism to this issue, I do not mean to embrace it as a general theory or to imply that it provides the foundation for the arguments that follow. Those arguments stand or fall on their own merits. As a general theory of equality or justice, luck egalitarianism has attracted some trenchant criticism. See, for example, Anderson 1999; Schef-

fler 2003, 2005; Shiffrin 2004. Even so, for the specific knot of issues that are my concern in this chapter, the intuitions driving luck egalitarianism retain considerable force.

10. It is now possible for people to alter some physical features commonly associated with race, such as skin colour, and to change their sex but, Michael Jackson and gender reassignment notwithstanding, these 'options' are still of a very different order from those relating to changes in one's religious beliefs.

11. There are cases in which people's choices in relation to religious faith are not so very different. Some people set off in search of a way of life, rifle amongst those offered by different faiths, and then choose to 'believe in' the faith that they find the most appealing option. Others 'convert' to a different faith simply because they marry a spouse of that faith, either because they wish to harmonise the marriage or because the spouse's new faith requires their conversion if, in the eyes of that faith, the marriage is to be legitimate.

12. Section 3 of the Human Rights Act 1998 requires courts to construe domestic law compatibly with the ECHR.

13. *R (Williamson) v. Secretary of State for Education and Employment* [2005] UKHL 15, para. 23.

14. Ibid., para. 22. On these issues, see Addison 2007: 6–11; Knights 2007: 41–43; and Sandberg 2011: 39–58.

15. The justification for courts' adopting this approach to the authenticity of belief is not, however, wholly straightforward, as I argue in Chapter 9. See also Eisenberg (2015). Note too that UK courts have ruled that Judaism and Sikhism fall under the remit of law prohibiting racial discrimination; *Seide v. Gillette Industries Ltd* [1980] IRLR 427; *Mandla v. Dowell Lee* [1983] AC 548. Legally, race includes 'nationality' and 'ethnic or national origins' as well as 'colour'. If a person's religion is treated as a matter of 'ethnic origin', that would seem necessarily to require an *objective* test of authenticity; viz. is the belief that a person professes, or the practice in which he or she engages, really a part of that person's ethnicity?

16. A court might hear expert evidence on a faith or belief, as it did for example in *R (Ghai) v. Newcastle City Council* [2009] EWHC 978 (Admin)—a case concerning Mr Davender Kumar Ghai's wish, as a Hindu, to be cremated by open pyre; see paras 21–45, 54–60. But that would be to enhance their understanding of the relevant faith or belief, rather than to evaluate it. In his judgement in that case, Mr Justice Cranston noted the uncertainties surrounding the requirements of Hindu cremation, but went on to say, 'Notwithstanding all this, the starting point for me is the claimant's genuine belief, held in good faith, that he must be cremated on an open air pyre and the fact . . . that this is a manifestation of his religious belief' (para. 100). Later in the judgement he added, 'It is beside the point that typically Hindus in this country do not share that belief' (para. 160). *Ghai* was a case pursued under human rights law, and my claim requires some qualification in relation to discrimination law. The Equality Act 2010, Pt 2, Ch. 2, para. 19, includes the following in its definition of indirect discrimination as it applies to a protected characteristic: 'It puts, or would put, *persons with whom B shares the characteristic* at a particular disadvantage when compared with people with whom B does not share it' (my emphasis). It is unclear how demanding this reference to a group is when the protected characteristic is religion or belief, but there have been cases in which it has been significant, notably *Eweida v. British Airways* [2010] Civ 80. For discussions of this issue, see Sandberg 2011: 112–14, and Vickers 2008: 126–31.

17. *Noah v. Desrosiers* [2008] ET case number 2201867/2007, para. 160, my emphasis.

18. For example, in a case concerning a care-worker at a children's home who was a Christian Sabbatarian and who claimed indirect discrimination against her employer because she was required to work on Sundays, the home's PCP requiring Sunday working was said by an Employment Appeal Tribunal to be proportionate in part because it affected adversely only a small number of Christians (those who were strict Sabbatarians) and that it might have been adjudged disproportionate had it adversely affected Christians more generally. *Mba v. The Mayor and Burgesses of the London Borough of Merton* [2012] UKEAT/0332/12/SM, para. 46.

19. Quoted in *Eweida v. British Airways* [2008] UKEAT/0123/08/LA, para. 18. This balancing approach has its origins in judicial interpretations of earlier laws governing indirect discrimination on grounds of sex and race; see Bamforth et al. 2008, pp. 299–304, 321–25.

20. Equality Act 2010, schedule 3, para. 29; schedule 9, paras 2 and 3; schedule 23, para. 2. For the details and qualifications relating to the broad-brush picture I paint in this paragraph, see Sandberg 2011: 117–28.

21. Vickers 2008: 87. See generally, Vickers 2008: 86–94, and Ahdar and Leigh 2005: 165–68. In a recent case, the European Court of Human Rights signalled that it may in future adopt a less parsimonious approach to the right of employees to manifest religious belief in the workplace; *Eweida and Others v. The UK* (2013) 57 EHRR 8, paras 79–84, 89–95. For discussion of that case and its significance, see Leigh and Hambler 2014.

22. Arguably, however, a PCP that was deliberately contrived to be discriminatory would be an exercise in direct rather than indirect discrimination.

23. For a fuller defence of this view, see Chapter 7.

REFERENCES

Addison, Neil. 2007. *Religious Discrimination and Hatred Law.* London: Routledge Cavendish.
Ahdar, Rex, and Ian Leigh. 2005. *Religious Freedom in the Liberal State.* Oxford: Oxford University Press.
Anderson, Elizabeth S. 1999. 'What Is the Point of Equality?' *Ethics* 109: 287–337.
Bamforth, Nicholas, Maleiha Malik and Colm O'Cinneide. 2008. *Discrimination Law: Theory and Context.* London: Sweet and Maxwell.
Barry, Brian. 1991. 'Chance, Choice and Justice'. In his *Liberty and Justice: Essays in Political Theory 2*, 142–58. Oxford: Clarendon Press.
Cohen, G. A. 1989. 'On the Currency of Egalitarian Justice'. *Ethics* 99: 906–44.
Cohen, G. A. 1999. 'Expensive Tastes and Multiculturalism'. In *Multiculturalism, Liberalism and Democracy*, ed. Rajeev Bhargava, Amiya Kumar Bagchi and R. Sudarshan, 80–100. Delhi: Oxford University Press.
Cohen, G. A. 2004. 'Expensive Tastes Ride Again'. In *Dworkin and His Critics*, ed. Justine Burley, 3–29. Oxford: Wiley.
Doe, Norman. 2011. *Law and Religion in Europe: A Comparative Introduction.* Oxford: Oxford University Press.
Dworkin, Ronald. 2000. *Sovereign Virtue.* Cambridge, MA: Harvard University Press.
Dworkin, Ronald. 2004. 'Replies to Critics'. In *Dworkin and His Critics*, ed. Justine Burley, 339–95. Oxford: Wiley.
Eisenberg, Avigail. 2015. 'What Is Wrong with a Liberal Assessment of Religious Authenticity?' In *Authenticity, Autonomy and Multiculturalism*, ed. Geoffrey Brahm Levey, 145–62. London: Routledge.
Knights, Samantha. 2007. *Freedom of Religion, Minorities and the Law.* Oxford: Oxford University Press.
Leigh, I., and A. Hambler. 2014. 'Religious Symbols, Conscience, and the Rights of Others'. *Oxford Journal of Law and Religion* 3: 2–24.
Matravers, Matt. 2002. 'Responsibility, Luck, and the "Equality of What?" Debate'. *Political Studies* 50: 558–72.
Rawls, John. 2001. *Justice as Fairness: A Restatement.* Cambridge, MA: Harvard University Press.
Sandberg, Russell. 2011. *Law and Religion.* Cambridge: Cambridge University Press.
Scanlon, T. M. 1986. 'Equality of Resources and Equality of Welfare: A Forced Marriage?' *Ethics* 97: 111–18.
Scheffler, Samuel. 2003. 'What Is Equality?' *Philosophy and Public Affairs* 31: 5–39.
Scheffler, Samuel. 2005. 'Choice, Circumstance, and the Value of Equality'. *Politics, Philosophy and Economics* 4: 5–28.
Shiffrin, Seana Valentine. 2004. 'Egalitarianism, Choice-Sensitivity, and Accommodation'. In *Reason and Value: Themes from the Moral Philosophy of Joseph Raz*, ed. R. Jay Wallace, Philip Pettit, Samuel Scheffler, and Michael Smith, 270–302. Oxford: Clarendon Press.

Vickers, Lucy. 2008. *Religious Freedom, Religious Discrimination and the Workplace*. Oxford: Hart.

Chapter Seven

Liberty, Equality and Accommodation

Fifty years ago, polyethnic multiculturalism was a minor feature of European societies; today it is a major subject of public policy.[1] Political theorists were initially rather slow to appreciate its significance for them, but for the last two decades multiculturalism has been firmly lodged at the centre of their concerns. No one has done more to forge the connections between the political philosophy and the public policy of multiculturalism than Bhikhu Parekh. As well as bringing the acute analytical skills of a political theorist and the scholarly expertise of an intellectual historian to the study of multiculturalism, he has brought to it a wealth of knowledge of different cultures, some of it from the 'inside', and the experience of a practitioner who has had to grapple with the details and implementation of public policy. His *Rethinking Multiculturalism* is remarkable for its sheer sweep, scholarship, breadth of vision, grasp of detail and intricacy of argument. It has rightly won recognition as one of a small number of seminal texts on the subject.

In this chapter I want to focus on just one aspect of Parekh's wide-ranging thinking on the issues raised by cultural diversity: his thinking on the issue of accommodation. 'Accommodation' is a term that can be used more or less generously. When a society moves from being largely mono-cultural and mono-faith to being significantly multicultural and multi-faith, it has to make a variety of changes in its rules and arrangements to provide for its new circumstances. In Britain there have been a multitude of such changes, including changes in the content and administration of law, greater sensitivity to cultural differences in the delivery of health care, efforts to secure greater representation of ethnic minorities in the police, adjustments to the arrangements for and the content of state-provided school education, and so on. Most of these changes might be described as 'accommodation' insofar as they are designed to 'make room' for people whose ethnicity, culture and religion are relatively new to Britain. Here, however, I shall mean by 'accommodation' something more specific: measures that provide differently for different cultural and religious groups. Accommodation in this narrower sense is commonly associated with exemptions, such as the exemptions enjoyed by turban-wearing Sikhs from the law that requires motorcyclists to wear crash helmets and by Jews and Muslims from the law that requires animals to be stunned before slaughter. Accommodation through differential treatment is most conspicuous when, as in these cases, some groups are allowed to depart from a rule with which others must comply. But accommodation includes more than these piecemeal exemptions. It can also be provided through general rules, such as law on indirect discrimination.

While I want to suggest that accommodation takes in a broader range of measures than is commonly recognised, I do not want to exaggerate its importance for multiculturalism. Multiculturalism as a policy is especially associated with 'difference-sensitivity' rather than 'difference-blindness', and that may lead us to suppose that the issue of whether policy should be multicultural is reducible to the issue of accommodation as I have characterised it. But that would be a mistake. Most measures prompted by sensitivity to cultural difference simply take account of the range of differences present in a society and aspire to provide for them fairly without resorting to arrangements that provide differently for different groups. Certainly, when a society becomes culturally diverse, securing equality amongst its population will require revisions to its arrangements, but those revisions can move it towards greater equality without the use of accommodation in the narrow sense I have identified. Thus, those, like Parekh, who appeal to equality in arguing the case for accommodation should not be understood to argue that, in multicultural circumstances, equality *always* requires accommodation of the specific sort that I focus on in this chapter.

ACCOMMODATION AND OPPORTUNITY

In *Rethinking Multiculturalism*, Parekh examines a catalogue of cases in which the practices of cultural minorities have clashed with existing societal norms and considers whether, in those cases, the minority practices should be accommodated and, if so, on what grounds. He gives particular attention to the ways in which the principles of equal treatment and equal opportunity bear on the case for accommodation. He does not insist that equality is the only value relevant to accommodation or that it should always be the overriding value. Other values, such as social harmony, the value of diversity, and securing and maintaining a common sense of belonging, should also figure in the assessment (2006: 262–63). Nevertheless, the demands of equality remain central to his prescriptions for a multicultural society, and much of his argument on accommodation is devoted to determining what equal treatment requires, and how equality of opportunity should be understood, in circumstances of cultural diversity.

One of his principal claims is that, in a multicultural society, we need to consider how cultural differences affect the opportunities available to people. The ideas of 'opportunity' in general, and of 'equal opportunity' in particular, should not be limited to the brute circumstances that people confront. Our conception of people's opportunities should also take account of the cultural attachments they bring to those circumstances.

> Opportunity is a subject-dependent concept in the sense that a facility, a resource, or a course of action is only a mute and passive possibility and not an opportunity for an individual if she lacks the capacity, the cultural disposition or the necessary cultural knowledge to take advantage of it. (2006: 241)

By way of illustration, he cites a number of different groups whose cultures or religions can become barriers to opportunities that are available to others.

> A Sikh is in principle free to send his son to a school that bans turbans, but for all practical purposes it is closed to him. The same is true when an orthodox Jew is required to give up his yarmulke, or the Muslim woman to wear a skirt, or a vegetarian Hindu to eat beef as a precondition for certain kinds of jobs. (2006: 241)

The constraints he is concerned with here are not constraints that are intrinsic to a culture or religion itself. He is not pointing out, for example, that the Sikh is deprived by his culture of the opportunity not to wear a turban or that the Hindu is deprived by his religion of the opportunity to eat beef. Rather he is indicating the way in which a person's culture or religion might close off opportunities that we might think of as 'external' to the culture or religion. If a school has a uniform policy that is inconsistent with the turban, the opportunity to attend that school will not be available to a Sikh; if a department store requires its female employees to wear a uniform that incorporates a knee-length skirt, the opportunity to work in that store will be removed for a Muslim woman; if a Jew can join the army only if he removes his yarmulke, a military career will not be open to him; and so on.

Parekh's characterisation of opportunity as a 'subject-dependent concept' provoked a characteristically robust response from Brian Barry, who argued that, on the contrary, people's opportunities consist in the choice sets objectively available to them. People may have preferences that lead them not to take up a particular opportunity, but their preference not to exploit an opportunity does not mean that the opportunity is not genuinely available to them. Similarly, people's cultures or religions may impose constraints upon the opportunities that they are willing to take up, but the existence of those subjective constraints is no reason to hold that the forsaken opportunities are not real opportunities. Nor can subjective constraints justify complaints of inequality of opportunity. For Barry, therefore, opportunity is an entirely objective matter, and there is no case, on grounds of equality of opportunity, for permitting departures from general rules in order to accommodate the cultural or faith-based wishes of particular groups. On the contrary, such departures are both unequal and unfair.[2]

In this chapter, I want to consider Parekh's claim that opportunity is a subject-dependent concept. I shall argue that subject-dependent considerations are relevant to a society's response to the way in which people's culture or religion affects their options, but I shall suggest that cultural or religious 'constraints' are different in nature from constraints such as lack of resources or lack of capacity, and that our reasons for taking those constraints seriously should also be different. I also want to consider the relationship between equality and accommodation. It is common ground for Parekh and Barry that the issue of accommodation should turn largely, though not wholly, on the demands of equality. I shall not claim that equality has no relevance for accommodation, but I shall suggest that, in some of its instances, accommodation can find a more compelling justification elsewhere. I shall also suggest that, even when equality is involved, we often need to look to other values to make sense of and to justify accommodation. In making that case, I shall focus on the forms that polyethnic and multi-faith accommodation has taken in Britain, but those forms are not unique to Britain and my argument is intended to apply generally to accommodation in polyethnic and multi-faith societies.[3]

ACCOMMODATION AND EQUALITY

In what form might equality relate to accommodation? In answering that question, I want to make use of the distinction between telic and deontic equality (Parfit 2002). If we are committed to equality as a *telic* ideal, we shall regard equal outcomes as good simply because they are equal and preferable to unequal outcomes. We may seek telic equality as an intrinsic good, that is, as something to be valued for its own sake. Or we may seek it as an instrumental good; we may seek it, for example, because we believe that a more equal society will be more harmonious and more at ease with itself. If we are committed to *deontic* equality, we shall regard equality as right rather than good, and we shall regard it as right, not because we value equal outcomes merely as equal outcomes, but because we value equality for some other moral reason, most commonly because we regard it as a requirement of justice or fairness. When we invoke the ideas of equal respect, equal treatment and equal opportunity—the principles of equality to which Parekh most frequently appeals—we typically do so in a deontic spirit. Certainly, when Parekh mobilises the idea of equality in defence of accommodation, he does so in a way that is implicitly deontic: in a context of cultural difference, accommodation is an instrument of equality, and it matters because a more equal society is a fairer or more just society (2006: 132–33, 211, 240–41). Accordingly, in considering the relationship between equality and accommodation, I shall focus primarily on deontic equality.

Let's begin with three instances of cultural or religious accommodation in Britain that are particularly well known. Turban-wearing Sikhs are exempted from the requirement to wear a crash helmet if they ride a motorcycle[4] and from hard hat rules if they work on a building site.[5] Sikhs who carry the kirpan as their faith requires are exempt from the law that bans the carrying of knives in public.[6] Jews and Muslims are exempt from animal welfare legislation requiring that animals be stunned before slaughter so that they can slaughter animals according to the rites of their religion.[7]

Can we defend these exemptions as instruments of equality? In a simple telic sense, they may seem to make for greater equality. If there were no exemptions, the rules at issue would affect some groups more disadvantageously than others; in precluding that uneven impact, the exemptions remove a potential inequality between the exempted groups and other members of the society. Sikhs become able to ride motorcycles, like others; Jews and Muslims become able to eat meat, like others; and so on. However, the link between exemptions and telic equality is not straightforward. Is subjecting everyone to the same law less consistent with telic equality than subjecting some but not others? The answer depends, of course, on the 'telos' we are seeking to equalise. A defence of exemptions as instruments of telic equality would seem most plausible if we are seeking to equalise people's welfare, but the ideal of equal welfare is notoriously difficult to interpret and operationalize (Dworkin 2000: 11–64). Moreover, if these exemptions are part of a general endeavour to equalise welfare levels amongst a society's members, they form a strangely piecemeal, heterogeneous and limited set.

Are they better conceived as instruments of deontic equality? Do they preclude a potential unfairness? The way that Sikhs, Jews and Muslims would be adversely affected by the relevant laws, in the absence of accommodation, seems more unfortunate than unfair. The laws at issue do not engage in a form of distribution in which Sikhs, Jews and Muslims receive less than others and less than their due. Rather they aim to secure goals whose pursuit has unfortunate side-effects for those communities. The laws at stake are not even particularly 'cultural' in character. Seeking to reduce head injuries, knife crime and animal suffering are goals that virtually all cultural communities in Britain would endorse, including Sikhs, Jews and Muslims. In general purpose, those laws do not run counter to the culture of any significant group; they prove problematic only insofar as their pursuit through particular measures clashes with the particular practices of some communities. It is not easy, then, to represent those clashes as arising from a majority's efforts to impose its culture upon minorities who think differently. Nor is it easy to see a requirement that Sikhs, Jews and Muslims should comply with the relevant laws as instances of unequal treatment.

Rather than seeing the exemptions as vehicles for an equality that is either deontic or telic in inspiration, the accommodations are more plausibly seen as efforts to ameliorate the conflicts between cultures and public policies that arise when a society becomes multicultural and multi-faith. Inevitably there will be clashes and incongruities between the established rules, practices and mores of a society and the cultures of communities who are relatively new to the society. We then have to ask how, all things considered, those clashes and incongruities are best dealt with. Sikhs have reason not to wear crash helmets and hard hats, and reason to carry knives in public, that other members of the population do not. Jews and Muslims have reason not to stun animals before slaughter that other people do not. It is entirely reasonable for a society to notice and to take account of those reasons.

It should also take account of considerations that compete with those reasons, so that what is best done in the particular case will involve an on-balance judgement. So, for example, given the availability of other forms of transport, the loss of the opportunity to ride a motorcycle does not seem a terribly onerous burden to impose on devout Sikhs, particularly by comparison with the very onerous burden they would experience if they were not allowed to carry the kirpan in public.[8] On the other hand, the potential costs of not wearing a crash helmet are largely borne by Sikh bikers themselves, so that, when these and other relevant considerations are weighed against one another, there is a good on-balance case for exempting Sikhs.[9] The loss of the opportunity to eat meat that devout Jews and Muslims would suffer if the ritual slaughter of animals were not allowed would affect their lives far more centrally. Here again, other factors have to be taken into consideration, particularly the additional animal suffering that ritual slaughter entails. Current UK policy would seem to reflect an on-balance judgement that any additional suffering that animals may undergo is insufficiently great to outweigh the case for allowing ritual slaughter. If the evidence were to change and to indicate that the additional suffering was much greater than had been supposed, that might tip the balance of considerations the other way. Cases such as these seem altogether too *sui generis* for the idea of equality to contribute very much to their resolution. To question the argument for accommodations in terms of equality is not to suggest that accommodations are unfair or unequal; it is to suggest only that the considerations that bear upon these instances of accommodation lie elsewhere.

The 'balance of considerations' approach that I am proposing here is, in fact, very much in tune with Parekh's own approach to the satisfactory resolution of the conflicting claims that inevitably arise in a culturally and religiously diverse society. In considering how a society should resolve actual or potential conflicts between minority cultural practices and its 'operative public values', he gives a series of compelling examples of the sort of intercultural dialogue through which majorities and minorities should resolve those conflicts (2006: 264–92). All of those examples exhibit the sort of on-balance reasoning I have been describing. But even when Parekh makes the case of accommodation by mobilising the idea of equality (2006: 239–63), the lion's share of his reasoning consists in identifying and weighing the many different and competing considerations that bear on each particular instance of accommodation.

A more general vehicle for accommodation that is present in most European societies, including Britain, is the European Convention on Human Rights (ECHR), particularly Article 9. That Article gives everyone 'the right to freedom of thought, conscience and religion', including the freedom 'either alone or in community with others and in public or private, to *manifest* his religion or belief, in worship, teaching, practice and observance' (my emphasis). The second clause of the Article, however, subjects the freedom to manifest one's religion or belief 'to such limitations as are prescribed by law and are necessary in a democratic society in the interests of public safety, for the protection of public order, health or morals, or the protection of the rights and freedoms of others'. Cases concerning Article 9 that come before the courts are typically cases in which a person claims that his right to manifest his religion in particular circumstances has been interfered with, while others either resist that claim of interference or argue that it is justified by the limitations listed in the Article's second clause. They raise the question of whether someone has the right to manifest his particular religion in particular circumstances, and, in resolving that question, courts take account of the specific demands of a person's faith as well as of the specific features of the circumstances in which he wishes to manifest his faith. They are typically, that is, cases in which the issue is whether and how far a person's wish to manifest his religion should be accommodated by others.

Thus, in Britain, such cases have concerned the right of a Christian employee to be exempt from his employer's practice of requiring Sunday working;[10] the right of a Muslim teacher to attend Friday prayers, even though his doing so entailed his being absent from school during teaching hours;[11] the right of a Muslim schoolgirl to attend school wearing a jilbab, rather than the *shalwar kameez* provided by the school's uniform;[12] the right of a Christian schoolgirl to wear a 'purity' ring contrary to her school's no jewellery policy;[13] and the right of a Hindu on his death to be cremated by open pyre rather than by the enclosed form of cremation currently provided in Britain.[14] In resolving these sorts of case, courts typically engage in on-balance judgements in which they weigh the claims of the religious against the considerations listed in the second clause of Article 9. Here again, it is not a simple matter of reading off what equality requires but of considering whether someone has the right to manifest a particular aspect of their religious faith in the context of all the relevant circumstances. That is why, in these cases, courts frequently insist that their decisions are 'fact specific', that is, specific to the particular facts relating to the particular case. Certainly, the rights at issue in the ECHR are conceived as rights that people possess equally, but that idea of equality contributes little to determining the kind and degree of accommodation to which someone is entitled in virtue of their right to freedom of thought, conscience and religion.

ACCOMMODATION, EQUALITY, AND DISCRIMINATION

There are, however, other instances of accommodation in which equality is much more to the fore. Arguably, the most significant measure now providing for accommodation in Britain is the 2010 Equality Act. The Act brought together and harmonised the various anti-discrimination measures that had been enacted in Britain over several decades. It provides against both direct and indirect discrimination. Laws providing against direct discrimination, including racial and religious discrimination, are clearly defensible in terms of equality, both deontic and telic. But, equally clearly, prohibiting direct discrimination is not an exercise in accommodation: it does not attend to, and provide differently for, the different demands of different racial or religious groups, even though, *de facto*, the protection it provides is likely to be more significant for some groups than for others.

By contrast, laws on indirect racial and religious discrimination *are* exercises in accommodation. They seek to safeguard people from disadvantages that might arise in relation to employment and the provision of goods and services from *particular* features of their ethnicity or religious faith. For the sake of simplicity, I shall focus here on the case of employment. Stated informally, an employer discriminates indirectly against an actual or potential employee if she applies a provision, criterion or practice (PCP) to the employee that, for racial or religious reasons, disadvantages the employee in comparison with other employees (Equality Act 2010, Pt 2, Ch. 2, para. 19). An employer may apply a PCP with scrupulous equality to all of her actual and potential employees, but if, because of their ethnicity or religious faith, it is more difficult for some employees than for others to comply with the PCP, the employer is guilty, *prima facie*, of indirect discrimination. If, for example, she has a PCP requiring her employees to be clean-shaven, she is guilty, *prima facie*, of indirect discrimination if she applies that PCP to male Sikhs. However, an employer is not guilty of indirect discrimination if applying her PCP is, in spite of its discriminatory effect, a 'proportionate means of achieving a legitimate aim' (ibid.). If, for example, she is able to persuade a court or tribunal that her production process requires strict standards of hygiene that are incompatible with facial hair, the application of her PCP to male Sikhs will not be illegal in spite of its disadvantageous impact upon them. [15]

The law on indirect racial and religious discrimination effectively requires an employer to accommodate the demands of an employee's ethnicity or religion up to the point at which doing so conflicts with her use of proportionate means to pursue her legitimate aim as an employer. Suppose, for example, that she has a PCP specifying the particular weeks of the year during which her employees may take time off for holidays. A particular employee wishes to take his 'holiday time' outside of the specified period so that he can celebrate a religious festival. The employer is then legally obliged to accede to his request unless she could prove to an employment tribunal or a court that yielding to that request was incompatible with her proportionate pursuit of her legitimate aim. The legal wrong of indirect discrimination does not reside in the PCP itself; it consists in applying the PCP to someone who, in respect of a protected characteristic, is disadvantaged by it. Provided she exempts that person, the employer can retain the PCP and she has no obligation to yield to similar requests relating to unprotected characteristics. So, for example, the employer who is legally obliged to allow an employee time off to celebrate a religious festival is not obliged to allow employees time off for other sorts of reason, such as enabling them to attend a party political conference or to go bird-watching during the only two weeks in the year that a rare bird visits Britain's shores.

How does this form of accommodation relate to equality? It may seem that indirect discrimination is another phenomenon that is more unfortunate than unfair. To be disadvantaged as the side-effect of an innocently motivated PCP is rather different from being the victim of a deliberate act of discrimination. Arguably, however, considerations of deontic equality are at stake here. If I am an applicant for a job and my chance of success, relative to those of others, is jeopardised unnecessarily by a PCP, I can reasonably complain that I have been deprived of a fair chance of success even though the PCP was not put in place deliberately to disadvantage people like myself. Success in the competition for a post should depend upon the applicants' competence to perform the tasks it entails; if an applicant's chances are prejudiced by other factors, we can deem that unfair no matter how wilfully or unwilfully irrelevant factors have been allowed to prejudice the appointment process. More generally, deploying a PCP in a way that unnecessarily or unjustifiably limits people's eligibility for employment is inconsistent with the deontic principle of equal opportunity in employment. Of course, how far we can understand measures proscribing indirect discrimination in these terms depends upon how straightforwardly fairness maps onto the law on indirect discrimination. 'Proportionate means of achieving a legitimate aim' is not a precise test, and courts and tribunals have interpreted it less generously in some cases than in others. An employer may have a relevant reason and a good reason for her PCP, yet it may still be adjudged to fall short of the proportionality test. But, if, in a particular case, a PCP's failing that test is tantamount to its being unnecessary or lacking reasonable justification, we can say that measures providing against indirect discrimination protect people from unfairness rather than mere misfortune.

Even in the case of indirect discrimination, however, more than equality is at stake. For one thing, the law providing against indirect discrimination still incorporates a balance of considerations: a balance between the interests of the potential claimant and the interests of the employer or provider of goods and services. Claimants are protected up to the point, but only up to the point, at which the employer's or provider's PCP becomes a proportionate means of achieving a legitimate aim. That limit is likely to leave some claimants less well-placed than others; it is likely to mean, for example, that niqab wearers will have fewer employment opportunities than hijab wearers. We might not think that unfair all things considered, since it would be unfair if people's cultural or religious commitments were allowed to impose costs and disadvantages upon employers or providers without limit. Even so, the presence of that limit indicates that more is at stake than merely ensuring that people's cultural or religious commitments do not result in their having unequal access to employment opportunities and to goods and services.

More fundamentally, provision against indirect discrimination raises the question of why people should be protected in relation to their culturally or religiously based wishes but not in relation to wishes that have other foundations. The law could, but does not, require the accommodation of *any* request that is not inconsistent with an employer's or provider's using proportionate means to pursue a legitimate aim. That would provide comprehensive and apparently even-handed cover against indirect discrimination.[16] So why should people's cultural and religious commitments be 'protected characteristics' (Equality Act 2010, Ch. 2, para. 19) when so many other aspects of their lives are not? Why, in the example that I cited earlier, should the employer have a *prima facie* obligation to accommodate an employee's wish to be away from work at the time of a religious festival but no similar obligation to accommodate another employee's wish to be away at the time of a political rally or a unique bird-watching opportunity, or indeed to deal with a family emergency or to visit a dying relative?

That question returns us to Brian Barry's objection to accommodation: responsibility for coping with the consequences of cultural and religious commitments should lie with those whose commitments they are. Cultural and religious commitments are no different in status from expensive preferences. People who have expensive preferences are liable to find that they suffer lower levels of preference satisfaction than those who have cheaper tastes, but that gives them no claim to additional resources or freedoms that will enable them to achieve satisfaction levels equivalent to those enjoyed by others. And so it should be with cultural and religious commitments. If the bearers of those commitments find them costly, they must bear the costs themselves; they are not entitled to exemptions or other forms of accommodation that relieve them of those costs and shift them elsewhere (Barry 2001: 32–62).

OPPORTUNITY: SUBJECTIVE OR OBJECTIVE?

In considering how we might meet Barry's objection, I want to return to the specific claim made by Parekh to which he took exception. That claim was that opportunity is a 'subject-dependent' concept in that an ostensible opportunity is really no opportunity for someone who 'lacks the capacity, the cultural disposition or the necessary cultural knowledge to take advantage of it' (2006: 241). How are we to understand that claim?

An obvious possibility is as an assertion of cultural determinism. People develop in accordance with, are shaped by, and become the people they are through the culture they inherit. Their outlook on the world and the choices they feel able to make are predetermined by the cultural context in which they have developed. Thus, an option for one person may be no option for another if, for that other, the option has been closed off by the culture that has shaped his very being. People's cultures are as fixed and unalterable features of themselves as their skin colour or gender.

In fact, Parekh rejects cultural determinism of that simple sort. Certainly people find themselves embedded in a culture and none can escape the influence of culture, but that does not mean that they are unable to take a critical view of their culture or to 'rise above its constitutive beliefs and practices and reach out to other cultures' (2006: 157; see also 158, 336, 350). The degree to which people are shaped by their inherited culture will vary with circumstances and will depend particularly on how far their culture is isolated from others (2006: 158). One of the merits Parekh claims for a multicultural society is that it enables its members to appreciate the limits of their own culture and to become aware of alternative ways of seeing and living in the world. 'They are able to see the contingency of their culture and relate to it freely rather than as a fate or a predicament' (2006: 167; see also Parekh 2002: 141–42).

Parekh's argument does not therefore rest upon the claim that people are helpless constructs of their cultures. If it did, it would seem the wrong sort of argument as well as one of questionable truth. It matters less how people have come to hold their beliefs and values than how they now regard them. If they now embrace and endorse those beliefs and values (as they normally do), they can hardly present them as disabilities or handicaps with which they have been saddled by their cultures and for which others must make special allowance. If people really did disidentify with their beliefs and values, if they really viewed them as incubi that burdened their lives, they should be willing to shed them (Dworkin 2000: 289–96). If they find they could not do so unaided, the appropriate solution would lie in therapy rather than indulgence.

The reality of course is that, when people make claims in respect of their beliefs, they do not present them as burdens with which they have been encumbered by culture or circumstance. Quite the contrary, they insist that others must take their beliefs seriously because they take them seriously. It is because they embrace and endorse their beliefs that others must respect their beliefs. Others may not share the beliefs at stake, but it is still incumbent upon them to respect those beliefs out of respect for their holders. So it is the fact that people strongly identify, rather than that they disidentify, with their beliefs that typically grounds the demands that believers make in respect of their beliefs. Rather than suggesting that people are the mental slaves of culture and are incapable of thinking beyond its limits, Parekh observes that giving up a cultural norm or practice is hardest for an individual when it is 'constitutive of the individual's sense of identity and self-respect' and when it 'cannot be overcome without a deep sense of moral loss' (2006: 241). That implies a reason for accommodation very different from mere determinism; it implies a reason that appeals to reasons rather than to causes.

A further possibility is that a person may be deprived of an opportunity by constraints imposed by the cultural community to which he belongs. If he were to fail to conduct himself according to the culture or religion of his community, he would incur the opprobrium of that community and might find himself ostracised from it. This account concedes something to 'subjectivity', since incurring the hostility of one's fellows will constitute a constraint only if it is a penalty that a reasonable person would be unwilling to undergo, but, given what we know about human psychology, this would be a sanction that most people would be reluctant to incur. Nor need we be of a particularly communitarian cast of mind to concede the constraining nature of this pressure. It was, for example, a central concern of J. S. Mill's in *On Liberty* (1974).

David Miller argues that this sort of consideration is relevant to the choice set available to a person. Considering the case of *Mandla v. Dowell Lee*, in which a Sikh boy was barred from attending a school because his turban contravened the school's rules on dress and appearance, he argues that

> if you grow up in a cultural community and identify with it, then violating one
> of the community's norms in a way that will effectively exclude you from

further participation in the life of that community imposes unreasonable costs. (2002: 53)

Jeremy Waldron pleads a similar case on behalf of the person who encounters a conflict between the norms of his religion or culture and those of state law.

> His being pulled in the direction of the cultural or religious practice (contrary to state law) has *social* reality; it is not just a matter of subjective conviction. Because of the positive existence of a scheme of regulation rivalling the state law, the person we are considering is already under a socially-enforced burden, established as part of an actual way of life, a burden grounded in the actually-existing and well-established regulation and coordination of social affairs afforded by a religious or a cultural tradition. (2002: 24)

These arguments stress the pressures placed on the members of a religious or cultural community to conform with its norms, and those pressures need occasion neither protest nor regret; we may view them merely as sociological facts of life and an inevitable part of what being a member of a cultural or religious community entails.

The sociological constraints invoked by Miller and Waldron may well be part of the overall picture,[17] but should we make the case for accommodation depend on them? Once again, this argument seems to put the emphasis in the wrong place: it implies that, but for community pressures to conform, a person would be free to set aside his cultural or religious commitments. Moreover, suppose community pressures were absent or ineffective. Would that make a critical difference to our thinking? Would we then think it right not to concede exemptions or to concede them only to those who were subject or vulnerable to community pressures?

OBLIGATION, OPPORTUNITY, AND FREEDOM

Consider again the examples Parekh gives to illustrate his claim that opportunity is subject-dependent.

> A Sikh is in principle free to send his son to a school that bans turbans, but for all practical purposes it is closed to him. The same is true when an orthodox Jew is required to give up his yarmulke, or the Muslim woman to wear a skirt, or a vegetarian Hindu to eat beef as a precondition for certain kinds of jobs.

These cases share a conspicuous common feature: they are all cases in which the 'subjects' consider themselves under an obligation that makes it wrong for them either to do what their faith forbids or not to do what their faith requires.[18] Being 'under an obligation' of that sort is quite different from being prevented by legal restrictions or lack of resources or lack of mental capacity. It would not be out of the ordinary for the Sikh to protest that he was 'not free' to dispense with his turban or the Jew to give up his yarmulke or the Muslim woman to wear a knee-length skirt or the Hindu to eat beef. But the freedom at issue here is of a quite different order from the freedom that is removed by sanctions or absence of resources or lack of capacity. It is to be morally or religiously unfree, to be morally or religiously not 'at liberty', to do those things that one has an obligation not to do. Writers on freedom have become suspicious of this sort of usage because of the tricks that might be played by moralising the concept of freedom, but in fact it is entirely commonplace. For example, if you were to ask why I am not 'free' to meet you this evening, my answer could very well be that I have already promised, and therefore am under an obligation, to meet someone else; and, if I should protest that I am not 'free' to go on a blind date, my explanation could be simply that I am married.

While I think it quite in order that we should use the language of freedom in this way, it points to a notion of unfreedom quite different from that which is the staple fare of analyses of negative freedom (nor does it have much to do with the idea of positive freedom). One thing that is common to that staple fare is the notion that freedom and unfreedom are interpersonal conditions. I can protest that I am unfree to do x only if I can point to someone who is preventing my doing x either by subjecting me to physical restraint or sanctions of some sort, or by withholding from me the means to do x. But in the case of moral unfreedom, there is no one whom I can hold responsible for my condition. I am simply under an obligation. It would, of course, be possible to tell a psychological story about the origins of my sense of obligation, in which I trace that sense to the influence of my parents or my schooling or my community, and so to represent myself as having been internally shackled by an external influence. But that would be to switch from an idea of moral unfreedom to one of sociological or psychological unfreedom and, as I have already argued, people do not normally conceive their deepest moral commitments in that way.

My guess is that the unwillingness of commentators like Barry to take account of this sort of unfreedom in describing the opportunities available to people stems from the kind of unfreedom it is. It is internal to the subject. It is not an unfreedom that I can hold anyone else responsible for my being under; nor can I look to others to relieve me of that condition in the way that they might alleviate my poverty or enhance my education. It would also be a mistake to deal with this issue by assimilating being under an obligation to being physically restrained or subject to duress. H. L. A. Hart (1961) pointed out long ago that 'having an obligation' is very different from 'being obliged', where 'being obliged' means being coerced or placed under some other form of duress.[19]

Even so, obligations do limit what people are free to do and what they have the opportunity to do. If a society introduces a law requiring all motor-cyclists to wear crash helmets, the turban-wearing Sikh finds himself unfree (in the sense that I have indicated) to ride a motorcycle. By contrast, Barry's biker—for whom nothing compares with the thrill of 'riding a Harley-David-son at full throttle down a deserted freeway' and who protests that 'a bare head is essential to the value of the experience' (2001: 47)—is not rendered unfree to ride a motorcycle by legislation requiring him to wear a crash helmet. His *preference* for not wearing a crash helmet does not preclude his donning a crash helmet and riding a motorcycle, whereas the devout Sikh's *obligation* not to discard his turban would, in the absence of an exemption, preclude his riding a motorcycle. In the same sense, the Jew and the Muslim would not be free to eat meat if ritual slaughter were prohibited; the Muslim woman would not have the option to work as a shop assistant if the shop's uniform required her to expose her legs; and the devout Jew would lose the opportunity to join the military if its uniform required him to discard his yarmulke. That, I suggest, is the truth in Parekh's claim that opportunity is 'subject-dependent'.

Even if we accept that argument, however, we do not have a full case for accommodation. We might accept that Sikhs and others are governed by obligations and that those obligations affect what they are religiously or morally free to do, but still question why that should weigh with others. Why should the religious not bear the consequences of their beliefs, just as others have to bear the consequences of their tastes and preferences? Why should the Sikh's obligation not to discard his turban count for any more than the thrill seeker's desire to ride a motorcycle bare-headed?

The answer lies, I believe, in the special significance that we give to people's conscientious commitments and to their belief that there are certain things that they are morally or religiously required to do or not to do. That respect for people's sincerely held convictions shows through most clearly in cases when we confront, but recoil from, the option of compelling people to act contrary to their convictions, such as making a conscientious objector fight in a war, or an Orthodox Jew testify in court on a Saturday, or a Catholic priest divulge the secrets of the confessional. An example particu-larly pertinent to accommodation is the exemption granted by discrimination law to 'organised religions' allowing them to discriminate in employment, not merely on grounds of religion but also on grounds of gender, sexual orientation, gender reassignment and marital status, provided that such dis-crimination is required for compliance with the religion's doctrines or to avoid conflict with the strongly held convictions of a significant number of the religion's followers (Equality Act 2010, schedule 9, para. 2).[20] Contro-versial as those exemptions have been, without them discrimination law would require some organised religions to defy their own doctrines.

In the forms of accommodation I have focused on in this chapter, the options are not so stark. If the accommodation were withheld, the unaccommodated would face lost opportunities or incur other sorts of cost or disadvantage rather than be obliged to act in ways that, for them, would be morally or religiously wrong. Nevertheless, if we are committed, insofar as possible, to allowing people to live according to their own convictions about how they should live, it is an intelligible extension of that commitment that we should regret clashes between the demands of a religious belief and a society's public or private arrangements that result in believers being 'burdened' in ways that others are not. It is also intelligible that we should wish to mitigate those burdens insofar as we can do so reasonably. The qualification 'reasonably' reintroduces the need to weigh the case for accommodation against other considerations, particularly against the possibility that we might remove costs from the accommodated only to impose them upon others. If accommodation could be bought only at that price, we would have powerful reason to object to it.[21] It is significant, however, that the types of accommodation on which I have focused impose minimal or insignificant costs upon others. The costs of not wearing motorcycling crash helmets or hard hats on construction sites are largely borne by Sikhs themselves, and the costs of allowing Sikhs to carry kirpans are non-existent or minimal;[22] the additional suffering to animals involved in ritual slaughter is assumed by public policy to be too insignificant to warrant prohibition. Courts in interpreting Article 9 of the ECHR have been conspicuously chary of allowing people's religious beliefs to impose costs on others, especially in the area of employment (Vickers 2008: 86–94). The law on indirect discrimination is less parsimonious but still requires accommodation only insofar as it is consistent with an employer's or provider's proportionate pursuit of a legitimate aim.

My thinking here clearly connects with the idea of liberty of conscience, and that may seem too Protestant an idea to be serviceable in multi-faith circumstances. But I intend nothing so specific. It entails no particular theory of morality and certainly none that turns on a theory of conscience narrowly conceived. Rather it draws on the idea, which seems to be widely shared amongst faiths and not only amongst faiths, that people attach a special significance to what they believe to be right such that there is something peculiarly wrong about others not respecting their beliefs and something especially wrong about their being made to betray their beliefs. Certainly people across all major faiths seem to respond with much greater outrage, indignation and anguish when they or their fellows face obstacles to complying with the requirements of their faith than when their other wishes are frustrated or disappointed.

My thinking might also be questioned because of the emphasis it places upon 'obligation'. I have used that term because it readily conveys the notion that people are not at liberty to do this or that. Sometimes, whether a practice is obligatory or discretionary may be relevant to the case for accommodating it.[23] However, I do not mean to make too much of that distinction for two reasons. First, the distinction between the right and the good, or between the wrong and the bad, might not be present in a faith or moral tradition, or it may be present only in a very fuzzy way. Secondly, quite independently of the contingencies of particular faiths, the idea of obligation may set the stakes too high. If, for example, someone wants to live the best possible Christian or Islamic life, should we really discount that commitment because it exceeds the minimum level of conduct their faith requires, supposing that to be a distinction we can make?

FROM RELIGION TO CULTURE

So far I have made my argument primarily with reference to religion, making only occasional references to culture. How does that argument transpose to the idea of a multicultural, rather than a multi-faith, society? The answer is very easily in the case of societies like Britain, where cultural differences are caught up so closely with religious differences, especially where those are differences of faith rather than denomination (or its equivalent). But religion is not the whole of culture, and our conceptions of, and modes of thinking about, religion and culture can be very different.

In sympathy with Parekh's thinking, my argument has been that the 'subjective' constraints that people are under contribute significantly to the case for cultural accommodation. The case provided by those constraints is a *pro tanto* rather than always an all-things-considered case, but reasons have force even if they are not always conclusive reasons. The constraint of which I have made most, in some measure differently from Parekh, is that of being subject to an obligation or to some other form of normative imperative. The logic of my argument applies therefore as much to non-religious as to religious imperatives, including those that would be appropriately described as 'cultural'. In that respect, the argument comports with Article 9 of the ECHR, which protects 'thought' and 'conscience' as well as religion, and with current British discrimination law which applies to 'religion or belief' rather than to religion alone.

If that is so, why does religion figure so much more prominently than non-religious belief in the reality of accommodation? Part of the answer lies in the way in which religion figures so centrally in the cultures of minority communities—communities who are most likely to encounter a clash between their cultures and the norms and practices of the larger society, especially the civil society, in which they reside. But it also lies in the greater propensity of religious than non-religious belief to throw up norms that are likely to clash with the wider society's arrangements, such as norms providing for special forms of dress, diet, religious festivals, holy days, and prayer times.

My argument therefore applies to an aspect of, rather than to the whole of, culture, but that need not be a failing. Given the comprehensive and all-enveloping character of 'culture', at least in idea, and given the impossibility of transposing cultures to a polyethnic society in the complete and uncompromised form in which they existed in their societies of origin, we cannot give equal significance to every element of culture. Moreover, we should remember that a person's 'culture' is all that shapes his or her being and mode of existence, not just the 'exotic' features that relate to a person's ancestry. Hybridity is therefore a feature of virtually everyone's real culture, especially in a multicultural society. In that respect, too, 'culture' comes too close to absorbing everything to provide an undifferentiated claim to accommodation.

However, I must acknowledge two limits to the range of my argument. First, it does not apply—and it does not aspire to apply—to every legitimate instance of accommodation. Secondly, it need not be the only justification for cultural accommodation, nor need it apply to every instance of justified cultural accommodation.

The first of these limitations is almost too obvious to need stating and is clearly illustrated by indirect discrimination law in Britain. That law applies to a wide range of 'protected characteristics': age, disability, gender reassignment, marriage and civil partnership, race, religion or belief, sex, and sexual orientation (Equality Act 2010, Ch. 2, para. 19). If we suppose that the accommodation of each of these characteristics is justified, it is clear that their bearers' beliefs about the obligations and normative imperatives to which they are subject will not provide the relevant justification for accommodating most of them.

The way in which current British law has wrapped up all of the characteristics in a single piece of legislation and protects all of them in largely the same way might suggest that the case for the accommodation of each should be identical. That, however, is difficult to accept. The approach favoured by luck egalitarians might suggest that it is the choice/chance distinction that provides the common thread: people should be accommodated for features of themselves for which they are not responsible, but not for those that are consequences of their choice. But, aside from the complex case of 'religion or belief', several other of these characteristics are not straightforwardly unchosen.[24]

A more prosaic possibility is that the protected characteristics are simply those that happen, as a matter of contingent fact, to be the most common grounds of discrimination. In principle, it is wrong that *any* characteristic of a person that is not genuinely relevant to a particular form of employment or to the receipt of a particular good or service should affect his or her opportunities. In practice, *some* characteristics are more likely than others adversely to affect people's opportunities, and it is those for which the law provides. That argument can be deployed quite persuasively in relation to the characteristics that are currently protected, or not, from direct discrimination. It can be deployed much less plausibly in defence of the current law on indirect discrimination, given the multitudinous ways in which PCPs can adversely affect people's opportunities. If we are to defend the current law on indirect discrimination, we have to explain why some characteristics merit protection from the adverse effects of indirect discrimination while others do not. Given the heterogeneous nature of the current set of protected characteristics, it is unlikely that our explanation can or should be the same in every case.

Turning to the second limitation, it is often the case that more than one reason can be offered in defence of a public policy and does, in fact, motivate the policy. So, for example, concerns for social cohesion might justify attempts to ameliorate the differential impacts of public policies or PCPs. So too might the wish to mitigate the extent to which religious and cultural disadvantage compounds racial inequality. Parekh (2000, 2006) rightly insists on the plurality of considerations that bear on multicultural issues and that should receive their due in intercultural dialogue. Consistently with his view, I do not claim that the argument I have made constitutes the only defence that might be offered for cultural accommodation. However, even if we conceive the normative imperatives to which people are subject as cultural rather than religious, the fact that they are imperatives helps to explain why there is a case for their accommodation. As I have already observed, if we set normativity aside, culture merely as such is too inclusive and indiscriminate a phenomenon to be a plausible candidate for accommodation. The law on racial discrimination (direct and indirect) defines race as including 'colour', 'nationality', and 'ethnic or national origins' (Equality Act 2010, Ch. 1, para. 9). It therefore protects claims of culture insofar as those can be represented as claims of national or ethnic identity. But identity is a complex and controversial phenomenon, as Parekh (2008) has shown in depth and detail, and it is not clear why the aspects of people's cultural identity that are 'racial' as defined by law should matter more than others.[25] Moreover, as multicultural societies become increasingly intercultural and as lived cultures assume eclectic and fused characters, the less people's real cultural identities will be assignable to primordial nationalities or ethnicities that are supposedly theirs.

CONCLUSION

Like Parekh, and unlike Barry, I have argued that the range of opportunities available to people can be, in part, 'subject-dependent'. Parekh traced that subject-dependency to the way in which cultural differences can render people differently able or disposed to take advantage of opportunities objectively open to them. I have suggested that we should find the explanation in the different normative imperatives by which people believe themselves to be governed. Morally we are not free to do what we are obligated not to do, nor are we free not to do what we are obligated to do, even when we cannot hold others responsible for those unfreedoms. The lost opportunities that should be a society's concern are not those debarred by the normative imperatives themselves, but those that disappear as a result of the intersection of the demands of those imperatives with the society's rules and arrangements. The imperatives involved in those unfortunate interactions need not be religious in foundation but, in the multicultural circumstances of a society like Britain, they most frequently will be.

The mere loss of options does not, of itself, make the case for accommodation. That case depends upon our finding reason, at least *prima facie*, why a society should relieve or mitigate the burdens that people incur when their society's arrangements combine with their own imperatives to deprive them of options that remain available to others. Given the difference in the conditions of the burdened and unburdened, we might expect the idea of equality, especially deontic equality, to provide that reason. Equality can indeed contribute something to the case for accommodation, but it cannot resolve the issue alone. We have to find reason why we should give people's conscientious convictions, religious or non-religious, a status different from their preferences, whose satisfaction might be no less frustrated by a society's arrangements. We have to also weigh the case for accommodation against the diverse considerations that argue against it. One of the messages running through Bhikhu Parekh's work on multiculturalism, particularly his *Rethinking Multiculturalism*, is that there is no simple template for the proper organisation of a multicultural society. Much has to depend upon context and circumstance, and upon the particular considerations that relate to each particular case. And so it is with accommodation.

NOTES

1. This chapter was first published in a collection of essays honouring the work of Bhikhu Parekh (Uberoi and Modood 2015).

2. Barry allows that considerations other than equality might bear on the case for accommodation. But he limits those to pragmatic considerations which, for the most part, justify only temporary continuation of an accommodation that is already in place (2001: 48–62).

3. I follow Will Kymlicka (1995) in contrasting 'polyethnic' societies with 'multination' societies. Multination societies include societies such as Canada, Australia and New Zealand that possess settler populations and indigenous peoples, and in those societies the issue of accommodation takes a rather different form.

4. Initially by the Motor Cycle Crash Helmets (Religious Exemptions) Act (1976) and later by the Road Traffic Act (1988), s. 16(2). For further details of the law relating to this exemption, see Poulter 1998: 297–301.

5. Employment Act (1989), s. 11. The legal position was complicated by EU Regulations governing Personal Protective Equipment at Work that came into force in 1992 and that included no exemptions. See Poulter 1998: 313–22, and Singh and Tatla 2006: 134–35, 137.

6. Criminal Justice Act (1988), s. 139. For my doubts about whether we should interpret permission to carry knives for religious reasons as an 'exemption', see note 8 below.

7. Now under schedule 12 of the Welfare of Animals (Slaughter and Killing) Regulations, 1995; but legal exemptions to permit ritual slaughter date back to the nineteenth century. See Poulter 1998: 132.

8. There is reason to question whether the right of Sikhs to carry the kirpan in public constitutes an 'exemption'. The law that excepts Sikhs, and others who have religious reasons for carrying knives, also excepts those for whom knives are an occupational tool or part of their national dress (such as Scotsmen for whom Highland dress includes a dirk inserted into a sock). The law aims to prevent the carrying of knives by people who intend, or who are liable, to use them to harm others; the three excepted categories of people carry knives for innocent reasons and fall outside the law's target group. Thus, the law effectively provides that people should not carry knives in public unless they have good reason for doing so. Read in that way, the law as it relates to Sikhs seems much less like an exemption. In particular, it does not run counter to the purpose of the law in the way that exempting Sikhs from crash helmet and hard hat rules, and Jews and Muslims from animal welfare legislation, clearly does run counter to the purpose of the laws from which they are exempt. For the history of the issue of accommodating the kirpan in Britain and elsewhere, see Singh and Tatla 2006: 135–37.

9. It is possible that a court would reduce the compensation claimable by an injured Sikh motorcyclist to the extent that it deemed his wearing a turban rather than a crash helmet to have contributed to the injury he suffered. See Poulter 1998: 297–301. The law is clearer in the case of construction workers and hard hats. The Employment Act (1989) provides that, if a turban-wearing Sikh incurs injury, loss or damage for which another party is liable, that party is liable 'only to the extent that injury, loss or damage would have been sustained by the Sikh even if he had been wearing a safety helmet' (s. 11[5]).

10. *Copsey v. WWB Devon Clays Ltd*, [2004] UKEAT/0438/03/SM; [2005] EWCA Civ 932.

11. *Ahmad v. Inner London Education Authority*, Employment Appeal Tribunal: [1976] ICR 461; Court of Appeal: [1978] 1 QB 36; [1977] 3 WLR 396. I examine this case in Chapter 5.

12. *R (Begum) v. Denbigh High School*, [2004] EWHC 1389 (Admin); [2005] EWCA Civ 199; [2006] UKHL 15.

13. *R (Playfoot) (A Minor) v. Governing Body of Millais School*, [2007] EWHC 1698 (Admin).

14. *R. (Ghai) v. Newcastle City Council* [2009] EWHC 978 (Admin); [2010] EWCA Civ 59.

15. This example is based on *Panesar v. The Nestle Company Ltd* [1980] IRLR 60 EAT and [1980] IRLR 64 CA.

16. Cf. Barry's argument (2001: 54–62) that, if an employer has good reason for a rule, that rule should remain and the employer should be able to make compliance with it a condition of employment; but, if there is inadequate reason for the rule, the employer should be required to dispense with it altogether, so that all employees, and not only those who are adversely affected by it for religious or cultural reasons, would be freed from its restrictions.

17. Cf. the example of marriage and duress discussed by Parekh 2006: 248.

18. Virtually all the other examples Parekh cites in Chapter 8 of *Rethinking Multiculturalism* are also religious in foundation.

19. Arguably, legal freedom and unfreedom should be understood primarily with reference to obligation. If a law to which I am subject prohibits x, I am unfree to do x in that I am under a legal obligation not to do x, and only secondarily and contingently because I am liable to be punished if I do x. Whether a rule proscribes a freedom is a matter quite separate from whether a punishment is annexed to the rule.

20. In addition, 'organisations relating to religion or belief' are permitted to restrict their memberships and to whom they provide goods and services on grounds of sexual orientation,

provided such restrictions are necessary to comply with the organisation's doctrines or to avoid conflict with the strongly held convictions of a significant number of the religion's or belief's followers (Equality Act 2010, schedule 23, para. 2).

21. For an account of that 'powerful reason', see Chapter 6.

22. See notes 8 and 9 above.

23. It was deemed relevant, for example, in *Eweida v. British Airways* [2010] EWCA Civ 80, though mainly with reference to the question of whether the disadvantage suffered by the claimant was one that would be suffered by 'persons of the same religion or belief' as the claimant.

24. Marital status and gender reassignment are two obvious such cases. The law also makes no distinction between congenital disability and disability resulting from culpable risk-taking. For an extensive list of accommodations relating to chosen or semi-chosen features of people, though one focusing primarily on US cases, see Shiffrin 2004. Two celebrated and opposing exponents of luck egalitarianism are Dworkin (2000) and Cohen (1989, 1999). Shiffrin (2004) and Quong (2006) provide arguments for accommodation that expressly reject luck egalitarianism. For an analysis and discussion of the chance/choice distinction as it relates to the dispute between Parekh and Barry, see Mendus 2002.

25. One well-known instance of the uneven protection afforded to cultural identities by racial discrimination law was the way in which the Race Relations Act (1976) secured protection for the religiously based claims of some groups but not others. Unsurprisingly, in 1980, the courts defined Jews as a racial group within the meaning of the Act so that Judaism gained protection as an ethnic characteristic (*Seide v. Gillette* [1980] IRLR 427). A few years later and more controversially, the House of Lords defined Sikhs as a racial group within the meaning of the Act, thus protecting Sikhs in respect of features of themselves that were clearly religious in nature (*Mandla v. Dowel Lee* [1983] 2 AC 548). Other religious groups, such as Muslims, were and are denied protection under racial discrimination law because their religion is not definitive of a particular ethnic or national identity, even though it is central to the culture of many ethnic and national groups. Those groups gained legal protection from religious discrimination in relation to employment only in 2003 and, in relation to the provision of goods and services, only in 2006. In spite of the introduction of laws prohibiting religious discrimination, Sikhs remain able to pursue discrimination cases on grounds of race rather than religion; see, for example, *R (Watkins-Singh) v. The Governing Body of Aberdare Girls' High School* [2008] EWHC 1865 (Admin).

REFERENCES

Barry, Brian. 2001. *Culture and Equality: An Egalitarian Critique of Multiculturalism*. Cambridge: Polity.

Cohen, G. A. 1989. 'On the Currency of Egalitarian Justice'. *Ethics* 99(4): 906–44.

Cohen, G. A. 1999. 'Expensive Tastes and Multiculturalism'. In *Multiculturalism, Liberalism and Democracy*, ed. Rajeev Bhargava, Amiya Kumar Bagchi and R. Sudarshan, 80–100. Delhi: Oxford University Press.

Dworkin, Ronald. 2000. *Sovereign Virtue*. Cambridge, MA: Harvard University Press.

Hart, H. L. A. 1961. *The Concept of Law*. Oxford: Clarendon Press.

Kymlicka, Will. 1995. *Multicultural Citizenship*. Oxford: Clarendon Press.

Mendus, Susan. 2002. 'Choice, Chance and Multiculturalism'. In *Multiculturalism Reconsidered*, ed. Paul Kelly, 31–44. Cambridge: Polity.

Mill, J. S. 1974. *On Liberty*, ed. Gertrude Himmelfarb. Harmondsworth: Penguin.

Miller, David. 2002. 'Liberalism, Equal Opportunities and Cultural Commitments'. In *Multiculturalism Reconsidered*, ed. Paul Kelly, 45–61. Cambridge: Polity.

Parekh, Bhikhu. 2000. *The Future of Multi-Ethnic Britain: The Parekh Report*. London: Profile Books.

Parekh, Bhikhu. 2002. 'Barry and the Dangers of Liberalism'. In *Multiculturalism Reconsidered*, ed. Paul Kelly, 133–50. Cambridge: Polity.

Parekh, Bhikhu. 2006. *Rethinking Multiculturalism: Cultural Diversity and Political Theory*, 2nd edition. Basingstoke: Palgrave Macmillan.

Parekh, Bhikhu. 2008. *A New Politics of Identity: Political Principles for an Interdependent World*. Basingstoke: Macmillan.

Parfit, Derek. 2002. 'Equality or Priority?' In *The Ideal of Equality*, ed. Matthew Clayton and Andrew Williams, 81–125. Basingstoke: Palgrave Macmillan.

Poulter, Sebastian. 1998. *Ethnicity, Law and Human Rights*. Oxford: Oxford University Press.

Quong, Jonathan. 2006. 'Cultural Exemptions, Expensive Tastes, and Equal Opportunities'. *Journal of Applied Philosophy* 23(1): 53–71.

Shiffrin, Seana Valentine. 2004. 'Egalitarianism, Choice-Sensitivity, and Accommodation'. In *Reason and Value: Themes from the Moral Philosophy of Joseph Raz*, ed. R. Jay Wallace, Philip Pettit, Samuel Scheffler, and Michael Smith, 270–302. Oxford: Clarendon Press.

Singh, Gurharpal, and Darshan Singh Tatla. 2006. *Sikhs in Britain: The Making of a Community*. London: Zed Books.

Uberoi, Varun, and Tariq Modood (eds.). 2015. *Multiculturalism Rethought: Interpretations, Dilemmas and New Directions; Essays in Honour of Bhikhu Parekh*. Edinburgh: Edinburgh University Press.

Vickers, Lucy. 2008. *Religious Freedom, Religious Discrimination and the Workplace*. Oxford: Hart.

Waldron, Jeremy. 2002. 'One Law for All? The Logic of Cultural Accommodation'. *Washington and Lee Law Review* 59(3): 3–34.

Chapter Eight

Religious Exemption and Distributive Justice

Religious exemptions necessarily treat some differently from others. An exemption makes an exception to a law or rule so that, while some are free to depart from the law or rule, others are not. The 'some' are usually a minority and the 'others' a majority, although they do not have to be. Exemptions are therefore open to the charge that they favour those they exempt and do so unjustly. Yet religious exemptions are frequently defended as instruments of justice.[1] So far from privileging the exempted group, they merely correct for the group's disadvantage. The group finds itself adversely affected by a law or rule in ways that others are not, and the exemption, by removing the disadvantage, simply returns the group to a level playing field. Religious exemptions are often recast as 'cultural' exemptions, and that re-characterisation is especially associated with the egalitarian defence. When religious exemptions are defended in this fashion, the justice their defenders invoke is distributive: exemptions are devices that can and should be used to secure a just distribution, or redistribution, of freedoms and opportunities. Even if exemptions fail to achieve unqualified distributive justice, they still make the world less distributively unjust than it would otherwise be.

In this chapter, I want to cast doubt on whether we should look to equality or to any other distributive principle for the primary justification of religious exemptions. I do not dismiss distributive justice as of no relevance to exemptions, and I shall concede that one sort of exemption is rightly conceived as distributive in purpose. But I argue that distributive justice, for other sorts of exemption, is at best a secondary consideration and that the reasoning primarily relevant to whether there should be an exemption has a different focus. In making this argument, I do not mean to imply that exemptions treat people unequally or that they are distributively unjust. My claim is simply that the issue of exemption mostly lies elsewhere.

My argument addresses only religious exemptions. Law in the UK and elsewhere is replete with exemptions, and it seems grossly implausible that all of those many and varied exemptions could be catered for by a single justificatory theory. The existence of so many other sorts of exemption does perhaps give us reason to question just how special we should suppose that religious exemptions are or need to be, but here I do not stray very far from the religious case. I do mean to include religious exemptions that are recast in the literature as cultural exemptions. Like many commentators, I am persuaded that a plausible general case for religious exemption must also be a case for conscientious non-religious exemption, but here I focus mainly on the religious case.

Exemption is closely associated with the idea of accommodation, but exemption is only one form of accommodation. For example, making non-alcoholic drinks and vegetarian food available at a reception to cater for those who are religiously forbidden from drinking alcohol or eating meat is a form of accommodation, but one that makes no use of exemption. My arguments apply to exemptions only and not to all other forms of religious or cultural accommodation.

In the UK, people can gain exemptions through human rights law and through indirect discrimination law, both of which I consider below. However, the model case of exemption is usually one granted, directly and specifically, by law, such as the exemption in Britain enabling Sikhs to carry kirpans or Jews and Muslims to practise ritual slaughter. I describe these as 'statutory exemptions'.

One final point of clarification. For purposes of this chapter, I shall suppose that distributive justice is always comparative; that is, the justice of a distribution will turn on how the holdings of some compare with those of others. That supposition is not wholly accurate. Desert theories, for example, are usually accounted theories of distributive justice, yet they are not comparative in the way I have just described. However, the distributive justice that is invoked in relation to religious or cultural exemptions is almost always comparative; most commonly it is conceived as an equal distribution of some kind, such as equal freedom or equal opportunities. I equate distributive with comparative justice to avoid having constantly to qualify my references to distributive justice, but nothing I argue should be invalidated by exceptions to that equation. I want to retain the term 'distributive justice' since, while the distinction between comparative and non-comparative justice is significant for what I argue, so too is that between a distribution and its distribuend (what the distribution distributes).

DISTRIBUTION AND DISTRIBUENDS

Exemptions that are described as 'religious' can aim to secure for their bene-ficiaries either or both of two sorts of distribuend. One is religious freedom: the freedom to embrace, pursue and live in accordance with a religious faith. The other is the opportunity to enjoy non-religious goods, an opportunity that may be diminished for some because they subscribe to a particular religious faith.

In Britain and many other European countries, this distinction is marked by the distinction between two bodies of law: human rights law and discrimi-nation law. Under the European Convention on Human Rights (ECHR), everyone has the right to 'freedom of thought, conscience and religion'. That right includes the freedom of each, 'either alone or in community with others and in public or private, to *manifest* his religion or belief, in worship, teach-ing, practice and observance' (Article 9, my emphasis). In 2000, the EU issued a directive for the prohibition of direct and indirect discrimination on grounds of religion or belief. In Britain, that directive was translated into law governing religious discrimination in employment in 2003 and in the provi-sion of goods and services in 2006. With minor modifications, the content of those laws was incorporated in the Equality Act 2010, which consolidated and harmonised discrimination law in Britain. [2]

In some measure, these two bodies of law overlap in the conduct they regulate, but they have clearly different aims. Human rights law aims to protect people's freedom of religion or belief. Discrimination law aims to protect people from discrimination in employment and in the provision of goods and services in respect of a number of 'protected characteristics', of which 'religion or belief' is one.

If we turn to statutory exemptions, it is sometimes possible to infer from their content by which distribuend they are driven. For example, the exemp-tion of organised religions (churches, mosques, etc., as opposed to individual believers) from law prohibiting discrimination in employment on grounds of gender, gender reassignment, sexual orientation and marital status clearly aims to preserve the religious freedom of organised religions. [3] Without it, many would find themselves legally obliged to defy their own doctrines. The Abortion Act 1967 (s. 4) exempted doctors and other medical staff who conscientiously object to abortions (for religious or non-religious reasons) from the obligation to participate in their performance, and they are also exempt under the Human Fertilisation and Embryology Act 1990 (s. 38). That exemption most obviously protects freedom of conscience; it aims to avoid legally obliging doctors and nurses to do what they conscientiously believe they should not.

By contrast, the exemption allowing Sikh motorcyclists not to wear safety helmets, [4] provided they wear turbans, is more readily intelligible as an effort to retain for them a non-religious good: the option of riding a motorcycle. Loss of that option cannot easily be represented as a significant impediment to practising the Sikh faith. Similarly, the exemption of turban-wearing Sikhs from the legal obligation to wear a safety helmet if they work on a construction site[5] is more obviously designed to preserve for them the non-religious opportunity to be a construction worker than the religious opportunity to be a Sikh.

Very often, however, it is quite unclear which distribuend an exemption is designed to protect. People's religious freedom is clearly curtailed if a law has the effect of rendering a religious practice impermissible. But it is also commonly thought impaired if a law makes a religious practice more costly. If a government were to impose a special tax upon a religious group merely for being that religious group, we would deem that tax an infringement of the group's religious freedom, even though it did not render impossible the group's practice of its faith. Laws that give rise to the issue of exemption are unlike that case in that they do not normally set out deliberately to disadvantage a religious group. Rather they are religiously neutral in purpose; it just so happens that, in pursuing that purpose, their side-effect is to disadvantage a religious group. A disadvantage is, even so, no less real for being unintended, and we may therefore account it, like the imposition of a special religious tax, an impairment of the group's religious freedom. That sort of impairment is usually described as 'burdening'.

If we follow common practice and conceive burdening as impairing religious freedom, it becomes virtually impossible in many cases to know how we should characterise an exemption's distribuend. How should we describe the disadvantage that Muslims and Orthodox Jews would incur if there were no exemption permitting ritual slaughter? Would the relevant disbenefit be their loss of a non-religious good—the option of eating meat—or would it be the burdening of their religious practice? In Britain, rules governing passport photographs require people to be photographed without a head-covering, unless they wear one for religious or medical reasons. In the medical case, the exemption clearly aims to preserve for its beneficiaries the opportunity to travel internationally. Does the religious exemption have the same aim, or is its aim to avoid burdening the wearer's religious freedom? Even the two Sikh cases cited previously are not without ambiguity: being rendered unfree to ride a motorcycle or to work in the construction industry might be said to burden Sikhs' practice of their faith. And, to reverse another example given above, the principal aim of the exemption of pro-life medical staff from the obligation to participate in abortions could be to remove a potential impediment to their medical careers rather than to spare their consciences.

Of course, it need not be one distribuend or the other. It could be both. In consonance with that possibility, disadvantaging persons because of their religion or belief can fall foul of both human rights law and discrimination law, and the disadvantaged individual can seek remedy under both sorts of law. That does not, however, make the distinction between the two sorts of distribuend inconsequential. If an individual does seek remedy under both bodies of law, a court might reject his complaint with respect to one law but uphold it with respect to the other.

The difference between the two distribuends also matters for the justification of an exemption. In the case of upholding religious freedom, it clearly matters that the freedom is *religious*, and accordingly much argument about religious exemption has focused on the question of what, if anything, is special about religion (e.g. Garvey 1996; Koppelman 2006, 2009; Leiter 2013; McConnell 2000; Nussbaum 2008: 164–74; Trigg 2012). In the case of discrimination, religion *qua* religion does not matter in the same way and may not matter at all. What matters is that religion as a personal characteristic might block an opportunity for its bearer that it ought not to block. It is not the particular nature of the blocking characteristic that matters; it is the mere fact that it may block an opportunity and would do so without justification. To that extent, religious discrimination is no different from discrimination on grounds of race or gender or sexual orientation. It is not quite that simple[6] but, if we take our cue from discrimination law, our starting point will be indifference to religion as a characteristic beyond its potential to give rise to unjustified discrimination.

EXEMPTION AND RELIGIOUS FREEDOM

I begin by supposing that the distribuend motivating an exemption is religious freedom. I also suppose that all adult members of a society are equally entitled to that freedom. In other words, religious freedom is a good that should be distributed equally amongst all citizens. We address the issue of exemption after the main event is over—the 'main event' being the equal distribution amongst citizens of the freedom to embrace, pursue and practice a religious faith.

The issue of exemption arises when we confront occasional and awkward cases in which people's religious practice intersects with a public law or a private rule to their disadvantage. There are two sorts of limiting case that we can set aside. One is that of a law or rule that deliberately disadvantages a religious group, perhaps for religious reasons such as the lawmaker's belief that the group's religion is heretical or blasphemous. Any such law is at odds with the principle of equal religious liberty and can be set aside as unjust. In the other sort of case, a law deliberately curtails a group's religious freedom, but this time with full justification, for example, in order to prevent child sacrifice or less extreme forms of child abuse. Setting the boundaries that delimit these cases is not always straightforward; consider, for example, current controversy over the ritual circumcision of male children (Ahdar and Leigh 2013: 332–37). But, in general idea, the two sorts of case are reasonably clear.

The issue of exemption arises out of neither but, as we have already noticed, out of a law or rule that is religiously neutral in purpose but that affects, incidentally and disadvantageously, the religious practice of a group or an individual. We have then to decide whether the law or rule should prevail over the practice, or whether the group's practice should be exempt from the law or rule, or whether we should settle for a third option—if one is available—that concedes something to both sides. My main claim is that, when we resolve that issue, we are not deciding how we should distribute religious freedom. That has already been decided: we should distribute it equally. Rather, we are determining the proper make-up of the religious freedom to which people are entitled. We are deciding what is the proper content of the distribuend rather than how the distribuend should be distributed.

The question we are resolving concerns the rightful scope of religious freedom in the specific circumstances of the case before us. In the case of Sikhs and kirpans, for example, we have to decide whether people should be free to carry knives in public for reasons of religious faith or whether the danger posed to others by knife carrying rightly pre-empts that freedom. When we decide that issue, we should of course do so impartially; we should treat the religious claims of Sikhs neither better nor worse than those of others, and we should give due weight to all of the other interests at stake. But the question we address remains one of the scope of the religious freedom to which a person (any person) is entitled in the specific circumstances of the case. It is not a question of how religious freedom, suitably circumscribed, is justly distributed.

The religious freedom to which a person (any person) is entitled can itself be a matter of justice. If someone is denied a religious freedom to which they have a right, they are treated unjustly. But the injustice they suffer is non-comparative justice.[7] If a government denies an individual or a group the religious freedom to which they have a right, we do not need to know how it treats others before we can know that it has treated the individual or group unjustly. However, we should not expect too much of the idea of non-comparative justice. When we weigh the claims of religion against claims of other sorts and determine the proper scope of religious freedom, we are determining what is non-comparatively just. The idea of non-comparative justice does not itself contribute to that weighing process.

Non-comparative justice and distributive justice are not, of course, mutually exclusive. A government may simultaneously subject a group to (i) non-comparative injustice in denying them a religious freedom to which they have a right and (ii) distributive injustice in denying them a religious freedom that others enjoy. But that is no reason to conflate the question of (i) what should be the make-up of a good that is to be distributed amongst a population with (ii) how that good should be distributed amongst them.

I want now to reinforce this argument by looking at how the issue of exemption figures in human rights law and in jurisprudence relating to the US Constitution's 'free exercise' clause.

EXEMPTION AND THE HUMAN RIGHT
TO FREEDOM OF RELIGION OR BELIEF

As we have seen, Article 9 of the ECHR provides that the right to freedom of thought, conscience and religion includes everyone's freedom 'to manifest his religion or belief, in worship, teaching, practice and observance'. However, the second clause of the Article subjects that freedom to 'such limitations as are prescribed by law and are necessary in a democratic society in the interests of public safety, for the protection of public order, health or morals, or for the protection of the rights and freedom of others'. When someone alleges a violation of their human right to manifest their religion or belief, a court has to determine two things: (i) whether the complainant's freedom to manifest has indeed been interfered with, and, if it has, (ii) whether that interference is nonetheless justified by the considerations listed in the second clause of Article 9.

In weighing a person's freedom to manifest against the considerations listed in clause 2, a court is, in effect, addressing an issue of accommodation: in what degree are others, such as government departments, employers and service providers, obliged to accommodate a person's wish to manifest his religion or belief? Very often the accommodation someone seeks takes the form of exemption. For example, a Christian girl who wanted to wear a purity ring and a Muslim girl who wanted to wear a jilbab, each claimed that she was entitled by her right to manifest her religion to do so while attending school, even though her school's uniform policy provided otherwise.[8] Employees have similarly claimed the right to display religious symbols while they were at work, contrary to their employer's rules.[9] A local authority registrar, who was an evangelical Christian, claimed the right to be exempt from the obligation to officiate at civil partnership ceremonies; and another evangelical Christian, who worked for the charity Relate, claimed the right not to provide sex therapy for same-sex couples, contrary to Relate's equality policy.[10] A Christian Sabbatarian claimed that Article 9 entitled him to exemption from his employer's requirement that employees work on Sundays, and a Muslim schoolteacher claimed the right to attend his local mosque on Fridays, even though he was then unavailable for teaching for part of Friday afternoons.[11] A Hindu claimed the right on his death to be cremated by open pyre rather than by the enclosed form of cremation provided by his local authority. [12]

In deciding human rights cases, a court is determining the proper scope of a person's (any person's) right to manifest her religion or belief. It is important to notice that, in the weighing process, it is not the human right that vies with the considerations listed in clause 2 of Article 9. Rather the vying is done by the claimant's interest in religious freedom. There is a human right only to so much religious freedom as is justified taking into account all of the considerations that bear upon the particular case. So the precise details of the religious freedom to which a person (any person) has a right are determined by the weighing of considerations that the court undertakes. The human right does not contribute to that weighing process; rather its content, like the content of non-comparative justice, is defined through that process.

That is how human rights law works but, if we think about human rights morally rather than judicially, perhaps we should think about them differently. We may certainly find reason to quibble with the wording of Article 9's second clause, but, even conceived non-legally, the judicial approach to determining the content of a human right is hard to fault. Political theorists often represent a right as vying with competing considerations so that, if the competing considerations prevail, the right is 'overridden'. But, if the competing considerations rightly prevail, they set the moral limit of the right. Beyond that limit, there is no right. [13]

The wording of Article 9 may suggest that the religious interest provided for in its first clause is a fixed quantity, while the interests listed in its second clause are variable in character and so may or may not trump the claims of religion or belief in a particular case. But weighing has to be done on both sides of the calculation. It must matter how greatly a law or rule burdens the practice of a religious faith. For example, a law that rendered Sikhs unable to carry kirpans would burden the practice of their faith far more directly and seriously than one that prevented their riding motorcycles. It might also matter whether the religious practice at issue is obligatory or discretionary within its faith, or whether it is conceived as obligatory or discretionary by the claimant. It may matter too whether a practice is central or peripheral for a faith. [14] Some commentators object to judges prying into religious questions of this sort (Ahdar and Leigh 2013: 166–69, 173–75; Trigg 2012: 116–17), and courts themselves are usually keen to avoid grappling with contentious issues of religious doctrine insofar as they can. But, even if there is prudential justification for keeping judges away from these questions, they remain relevant in principle and, arguably, if individuals or groups seek an exemption, they cannot reasonably demand that a court should treat these questions as off-limits (Greene 2009: 998–1000). [15]

The considerations that can figure in the other side of the calculation are immensely varied, and courts have rightly taken a generous view of the range of considerations that Article 9's second clause admits. What constitutes 'interference' with the manifestation of a religion or belief can also be a contentious matter.[16] Arriving at an overall judgement often requires a court to commensurate incommensurables, but what that judgement determines is the religious liberty to which a person (any person) has a right in the particular circumstances of the case. People are equally entitled to that liberty, but it is the constitution of the liberty rather than the equality of the entitlement that is at issue.

EXEMPTIONS AND 'FREE EXERCISE'

The First Amendment of the US Constitution deprives Congress of the power to prohibit the free exercise of religion. US religious exemptions, whether legislative or judicial in origin, and whether mandatory or permissive in character, are commonly grounded in the Constitution's free exercise clause. The distribuend for which they provide is therefore, at least ostensibly, religious freedom rather than other sorts of good.[17] What sort of reasoning undergirds those exemptions?

The best-known and most thoroughgoing effort to provide an argument for religious freedom that is both egalitarian and consistent with US constitutional jurisprudence has come from Christopher Eisgruber and Lawrence Sager (2007). They set their faces against the tradition that holds that the First Amendment gives a special status to religion. They also reject the 'balancing' approach to religious freedom with which that tradition has been associated (81–87). Instead, they argue, religious freedom should be subsumed within a larger principle of equal liberty, which prescribes fair terms of cooperation for a religiously diverse population (4, 15). According to that principle, no member of a political community 'should be devalued on account of the spiritual foundations of their important commitments and projects' (4, 15, 18, 52, 95). That is no more than a demand that the religious should be treated equally with others; the equal liberty approach provides that 'we have no constitutional reason to treat religion as deserving special benefits or as subject to special disabilities' (6, 52). Rather, the bearers of projects and commitments, religious or non-religious, should be treated with 'equal regard' (13, 75, 89). Why then does religion receive special attention in the First Amendment? It receives 'special constitutional solicitude', Eisgruber and Sager suggest, only because religious interests are peculiarly vulnerable to hostility and neglect; the Constitution's religious-specific goal is to prevent discrimination against religion (9, 52, 58–59, 62, 69). The principle of equal liberty also includes a more general commitment to constitutional liberties: all persons, religious or non-religious, should enjoy 'rights of free speech, personal autonomy, associative freedom, and private property' (4, 53, 94–95). These liberties allow religious practice to flourish, but they are in no way special to religion. Indeed, religious liberty is conspicuously absent from Eisgruber and Sager's list of constitutional liberties. Its inclusion would contradict their thesis that there is nothing special about religious liberty; it is merely part of a larger freedom to which all are equally entitled.

Eisgruber and Sager's approach is designed to provide comprehensively for the constitutional and legal governance of religion in the US context, and it therefore takes in both non-establishment and free exercise.[18] Here I consider their thesis only as it applies to exemptions. According to that thesis, what justifies an exemption for religious adherents is its securing *equal* liberty for those adherents, be that equality with the adherents of other religions or equality with those pursuing non-religious commitments and projects. 'Equal liberty . . . calls on government to exempt religious observers from burdens that are not shared fairly with others' (87), though it also demands that the religious should bear their fair share of the burdens and limitations that go along with membership of an organised society (87, 241–42, 246).

I want to examine Eisgruber and Sager's approach to exemptions by focusing on two legal cases they use in making their argument. The first of these is the celebrated *Sherbert* case.[19] Adell Sherbert had worked a five-day week at a textile mill in Spartanburg County, South Carolina. In 1959 the mill switched to six-day working and, as a consequence, Sherbert resigned from her position. She was a Seventh-Day Adventist and was obliged by her religion not to work on Saturdays. She could find no other employment in the county's mills that did not require Saturday working and so claimed unemployment compensation benefits. South Carolina's State Commission rejected her claim on the ground that she had wilfully resigned from her former post and so was failing, 'without good cause', to accept suitable work that was available to her. Sherbert went on to claim that the State Commission, in denying her unemployment benefits, abridged her First Amendment right to free exercise. Both the Court of Common Pleas of Spartanburg County and the South Carolina Supreme Court upheld the Commission's decision. The US Supreme Court took a different view. It held that the Commission's rejection of Sherbert's claim infringed her right of free exercise and that no 'compelling state interest' justified that infringement.

Eisgruber and Sager conceive *Sherbert* as a case in which the critical value was equality and which could be readily determined by their equal liberty principle.[20] A South Carolina statute provided that, if in times of national emergency textile plants were authorised by the State Commissioner of Labor to operate on Sundays, 'no employee shall be required to work on Sunday . . . who is conscientiously opposed to Sunday work', and the employee should not 'jeopardize his or her seniority by such refusal or be discriminated against in any other manner'.[21] Thus, mainstream Christians in

South Carolina who refused to work on their day of rest were protected from adverse consequences that they might otherwise incur, whereas Seventh-Day Adventists, like Sherbert, were not. It was that inequality of treatment, Eisgruber and Sager argue, that provides the principal reason why the Supreme Court should have found in Sherbert's favour (14–15, 40–41, 97).

That was not how the Court itself saw the main issue, and they were right not to. For the Court, the two principal issues were (i) whether Sherbert's disqualification for unemployment benefits burdened her free exercise of her religion (the Court judged it did) and (ii) if it did, whether a compelling state interest justified the imposition of that burden (the Court judged it did not). In other words, the Court's primary focus was on whether Sherbert's religious freedom had been infringed and whether the considerations adduced by the state of South Carolina sufficed to justify that infringement. The primary issue was one not of equal treatment but of non-comparative justice.

Justice Brennan did go on to observe, 'The unconstitutionality of the disqualification of the Sabbatarian is . . . *compounded by* the religious discrimination which South Carolina's general statutory scheme necessarily effects'.[22] In other words, to the fundamental wrong that Sherbert had suffered was added the further wrong of being treated unequally with those whose religious day of rest was Sunday.[23] That notion of a double wrong makes perfect sense. Sherbert was the victim of non-comparative injustice in having her right to religious freedom violated and of distributive injustice in being allowed less religious freedom than others. But the demands of non-comparative justice were primary. It would be odd to require that two parties should be treated equally while remaining indifferent to whether the equal treatment they received amounted to either more or less than their due. And if equal treatment had really been the primary concern, South Carolina could have fallen into line by ceasing to exempt Sunday worshippers rather than by exempting Seventh-Day Adventists. That might invite the riposte that, even if the exemption for mainstream Christians were removed, Sunday would remain, in ordinary circumstances, a non-working day in South Carolina so that mainstream Christians would remain better placed than Seventh-Day Adventists. But that difference in circumstance would not conclude the issue since, if mainstream Christians were merely the chance beneficiaries of Sunday's being set aside as a uniform non-working day, their chance benefit would not signal that Seventh-Day Adventists suffered unjust treatment in not enjoying the same benefit when they declined to work on Saturdays.[24]

Eisgruber and Sager are rightly critical of the 'compelling state interest' test that was used by the Court in *Sherbert* (40–48, 82–85), sidelined many years later in *Smith* (the 'peyote case'),[25] and resurrected by the Freedom Restoration Act 1993, which the Supreme Court then ruled unconstitutional as it applied to states and localities, though not to federal law, and which Congress reinstated in part for states and localities in the Religious Land Use and Institutionalized Persons Act 2000. That an interest, if it is to override the claims of free exercise, must be 'compelling' tells us very little. The test also implies a fixed threshold, whereas, given that interferences with free exercise can be more or less serious, the test should be one of proportionality, as Eisgruber and Sager suggest (85). But some such test is indispensable; treating religious claims with 'equal regard' is no substitute for it.

Courts should, of course, treat cases consistently insofar as they are comparable. If a court has settled a basic issue of rightful treatment in case A, it can use its judgement in that case as a benchmark for its decisions in other cases. But when it treats the parties in cases B, C and D in the same way as it treated those in case A, it does not forsake non-comparative justice for distributive justice since the justice of its decisions in cases B, C and D remains parasitic upon the non-comparative justice of its decision in case A. Moreover, it is misleading to say that, in using case A as a benchmark for other cases, it is securing equal treatment for the parties across all of the cases. Rather, it is using its decision in case A to guide its decision on what constitutes non-comparative justice in each of cases B, C and D. The justice (or injustice) of the treatment meted out in each case must be capable of standing on its own two feet, even if decision in one case has been guided by decision in another.

A second case Eisgruber and Sager use is of a rather different kind. It concerned two Muslim police officers, Faruq Abdul-Aziz and Shakoor Mustafa, who grew beards contrary to the rules of the Newark Police Department of which they were members.[26] Their reasons for doing so were religious: they believed that as Muslims they were obliged by commands in the Qu'ran and the Sunnah to grow beards. The Newark Police Department refused to exempt them from its no-beard rule and initiated disciplinary action. Aziz and Mustafa responded by filing a complaint that the Department had violated their right of free exercise. Both the District Court and the Court of Appeals ruled that Newark Police had indeed violated their right of free exercise.

Although Newark Police would not tolerate religiously motivated departures from its no-beard rule, it did allow exemptions on medical grounds. In particular, officers who suffered from the skin condition pseudo folliculitis barbae were allowed to wear beards. The existence of that medical exemption played a prominent role in the case made by Aziz and Mustafa and in the judgement of the Court of Appeals. Following some earlier Supreme Court judgements, the Court held that the department's permitting medical exemptions but disallowing religious exemptions was suggestive of discriminatory intent, and that the department's reasons for treating the two cases differently should therefore be subject to 'heightened scrutiny'. It found that the department's reasons did not survive that scrutiny.

In the Court's view, the police department, in providing for exemption on medical but not religious grounds, had accorded unequal treatment to secular and religious interests. The larger significance of the Court's judgement for Eisgruber and Sager is that it constituted an effort to secure equal liberty between the secular and the religious and indicated a method for determining what that equality required. A case like *Sherbert* lends itself easily to the equal liberty approach since it enables that approach to appeal to equality between religions and equality between directly comparable religious practices—abstaining from work on a religion's day of rest. However, equal liberty requires there to be equality not only between religions but also between religious and secular commitments and projects. How are we to know what that second sort of equality requires? Eisgruber and Sager argue that certain arrangements provide benchmarks by which we can judge whether the religious and the secular are treated equally. One such benchmark is the provision made for medical conditions. If we find, as in the Newark Police case, that people are exempted on medical but not religious grounds, we can conclude that secular and religious interests are not treated with equal regard; the state is then failing 'to show the same concern for the fundamental needs of all its citizens' (89).

It is not easy to know quite how much Eisgruber and Sager, or the Court of Appeals, are claiming for this sort of argument. The claim could be the modest one that, if an organisation allows medical exemptions, we have reason to suspect that it should also allow religious exemptions. Eisgruber and Sager themselves say that 'disparities in treatment between what seem comparable secularly grounded interests and religiously grounded interests . . . *suggest* a failure of equal regard' (2007: 102, my emphasis). But, if the disparity only 'suggests' that failure, the case for a religious exemption will remain to be made.

Eisgruber and Sager seem to contemplate something tighter and more significant than a merely suggestive relationship.[27] Yet there are problems in making the case for religious exemption depend upon the prior existence of a medical or other sort of exemption,[28] or in tying the cases for the two exemptions together, so that we can rest the case for religious exemption on equality. First, in the absence of a medical exemption or a case for one, we would be left with no case for a religious exemption; but that cannot be acceptable, as Eisgruber and Sager recognise (105–6). Secondly, there are well-rehearsed objections to treating health-based claims and religion-based claims as highly similar in character, so that we treat a religious belief as tantamount to a disability (Barry 2001: 36–37; Dworkin 2000: 291–96; White 2012: 111–12). Thirdly, the equality to which Eisgruber and Sager aspire is a pan-societal form of equality that spans a multitude of commitments and projects; it is hard to accept that a particular instance of medical exemption can set or signal, reliably and intelligibly, what that comprehensive standard of equal treatment should be. Fourthly, the equality that is supposed to be of primary concern in equal liberty is equality in people's liberty to pursue 'commitments and projects', religious and non-religious; but medical conditions are neither commitments nor projects.

Eisgruber and Sager's linking medical to religious exemptions also indicates that they mean to argue as much for inequality as for equality. They do not suggest that police officers who wish to wear beards merely for reasons of personal appearance should, like Muslims and folliculitis sufferers, be free to do so. Their theory depends upon the idea that the state 'must not discriminate between religious convictions and *comparably serious* secular convictions; it does not depend on the idea, which is manifestly false, that the religious convictions are comparable to *any* secular conviction or impulse, however frivolous' (101, my emphases). So some wishes are to count differently from others. Their appeal to the special treatment accorded to medical conditions forms part of an argument for the similarly special treatment of religious belief. So what are the commitments and projects that are entitled, and equally entitled, to that special treatment? Sometimes Eisgruber and Sager suggest they are 'deep' commitments (81, 87, 101, 103); sometimes they are described as 'life projects', which include 'philosophic, political, educational, familial, vocational, artistic', as well as religious projects (88, 108). Yet there is little indication that Eisgruber and Sager regard any of the non-religious life projects they list as enjoying the same claim to exemption as the religious.[29]

The one type of commitment which, they indicate, does merit the same consideration as religious commitment, is non-religious conscientious commitment (112–15). Those who have, for example, a sincere non-religious conscientious commitment to pacifism are entitled to the same exemptions as those whose pacifism is religiously grounded. So the liberty to which all are equally entitled begins to look very much like liberty of conscience. There is nothing wrong with that, but, as a foundation for exemption, equal liberty of conscience is very much narrower than equal liberty. Moreover, faced with a specific issue of exemption, knowing merely that liberty of conscience is a liberty to which all are equally entitled will not tell us how a claim of conscience should weigh against the considerations with which it competes. Fundamentally, the issue of exemption in the Newark Police case reduces to the same twofold question as in *Sherbert*: (i) was there an interference with the plaintiff's free exercise? and, (ii) if there was, did the considerations that could be offered in its defence justify the interference?

One other way in which Eisgruber and Sager relate medical conditions and religious belief to equality is by pointing to the impact that both have on their bearer's opportunities: 'If a police department prohibited all officers from wearing beards, the regulation would have much the same impact on folliculitis sufferers and Muslims: neither group could serve in the police force' (104). Indeed they could not, but here the distribuend has changed. It is no longer religious freedom but a non-religious good: the opportunity to serve as a police officer. I consider exemption relating to that sort of good below.

STATUTORY EXEMPTIONS AND RELIGIOUS FREEDOM

If we turn to statutory exemptions—exemptions granted specifically and directly through legislation—the same reasoning applies. If a prospective law will cut across a religious practice in a way that will burden the practice or render it illegal, legislators have to decide whether the law should incorporate an exemption. That, in turn, requires them to weigh the adverse impact of the law upon religious freedom against the 'costs' consequent upon the exemption, especially the degree to which it would frustrate the law's purpose. If the good at stake in the potential exemption is religious freedom rather than a non-religious good, instructing lawmakers to treat the potential exemptees equally with others will be decidedly unhelpful.

Consider religious exemptions from discrimination law, such as that mentioned earlier exempting organised religions from laws forbidding discrimination in employment on grounds of gender, gender reassignment, sexual orientation and marital status. It is difficult to see how an exemption of that sort can be justified on grounds of equality. Indeed, opponents of the exemption commonly object to it precisely because it derogates from equal treatment. The most obvious justification for the exemption is that, without it, (some) organised religious would be legally compelled to defy their own doctrines, which would be a direct and serious violation of their religious freedom. If the exemption is justified all things considered, the reason must be that the religious liberty at stake is sufficiently significant to trump considerations to the contrary. In making that argument, we may call upon the principle of 'equal religious liberty' but, if we do, it will be the 'liberty' rather than the 'equality' in the principle that delivers the case for exemption.

Religious exemption from discrimination law proves difficult for Eisgruber and Sager's equal liberty thesis, since they have difficulty in finding an equivalent non-religious arrangement that can vindicate their claim that exemptions treat religion equally rather than specially. They draw on the constitutional values of privacy and freedom of association in an effort to interpret religious exemption from discrimination law as no more than a token of a more general type (2007: 62–66, 249–52). But the non-religious legal case to which they appeal fails to provide a convincing analogy (Laborde 2014: 20–21), and shifting the ground of exemption from free exercise to privacy and freedom of association is little more than a makeshift designed to keep their equal liberty thesis afloat. If we do not allow ourselves to be distracted by that thesis, exempting religion from the full rigours of discrimination law is an obvious instance of preserving free exercise.

Another type of religious exemption, which is clearly driven by respect for religious liberty, is the exemption from military service and military-related activity of those who believe themselves religiously forbidden from participating in it. Eisgruber and Sager argue (2007: 112–15) that those who possess conscientious but non-religious objections to war and war-related activity should enjoy the same exemption. If we give the claims of the non-religious conscience a status inferior to those of the religious conscience, we violate the principle of equal liberty. That argument is entirely sound, but it does not deal with the primary issue with which pacifist convictions present a society: whether pacifists, religious or non-religious, should be exempt from military and military-related service and, if so, over what range of activities. That is an issue of liberty rather than equality.

As we move away from cases in which no-exemption would result in the loss of religious liberty to those in which no-exemption would 'burden' but not remove it, the identity of the dominant distribuend (religious or non-religious?) becomes less clear. But, insofar as the distribuend remains religious liberty, either wholly or in part, the primary issue for exemption will be what people's religious liberty should entitle them to, rather than how that liberty should be distributed.

RELIGIOUS EXEMPTION AND INDIRECT DISCRIMINATION

I turn now to the other sort of distribuend that might motivate the accommodation of people's religious commitments: the opportunities they possess to access non-religious goods, opportunities which they may find diminished because they possess religious commitments. I previously indicated that this sort of distribuend is catered for by law on discrimination, and I focus on that law in this section for two reasons. First, in the UK and many other countries, that law imposes on employers and providers of goods and services an obligation to accommodate people's religious commitments. Secondly, I consider in the next section whether we might plausibly understand statutory exemptions as having the same rationale as indirect religious discrimination law.

I have argued that, insofar as religious exemption aims to provide for people's freedom to practise their religion, the principal issue is the constitution of that freedom rather than its distribution. That is not true of discrimination law. That law is not concerned to map out a specific set of non-religious opportunities that should be available to all and the absence of which would constitute a non-comparative injustice. The opportunities a society presents for employment and for accessing goods and services is a largely contingent matter. It depends upon the opportunities that public agencies, private firms and a variety of other types of employer and provider opt to make available. Discrimination law aims to ensure that those opportunities, whatever they happen to be, should be fairly available to all and should be unprejudiced by 'protected characteristics' such as religion or belief. There are, of course, occasions on which it is entirely proper that an opportunity should be conditional upon a person's religion or belief; it is quite right, for example, that only Roman Catholics should be eligible for the Roman Catholic priesthood. In what follows, I suppose that the opportunities at issue are not of that kind, so that a person's religion or belief should be deemed an irrelevant consideration.

In what form, then, does discrimination law require the accommodation of religion or belief? The prohibition of *direct* religious discrimination—for example, refusing to employ someone because he is a Muslim, or to promote him because he is not a Muslim—requires nothing that warrants the term 'accommodation'. The prohibition of *indirect* religious discrimination does demand a form of accommodation. In British discrimination law, a person, A, discriminates indirectly against another person, B, 'if A applies to B a provision, criterion or practice [a PCP] which is discriminatory in relation to a relevant protected characteristic of B's'. A PCP is discriminatory if it 'puts, or would put, persons with whom B shares the characteristic at a particular disadvantage when compared with persons with whom B does not share it'. So, for example, if A, an employer, has a PCP requiring her employees to comply with a dress code, and if B, a prospective employee, subscribes to a religion whose demands are incompatible with A's dress code, and if A nevertheless requires B to comply with her dress code, A discriminates indirectly against B. Her dress code places B, and those who share his religious belief, at a disadvantage compared with those who hold other religious beliefs or none. However, A's guilt is only *prima facie* since, if she can show that her PCP (her dress code) is 'a proportionate means of achieving a legitimate aim', she will not be guilty of indirect discrimination as a legal offence.[30] I shall refer to this proportionality defence as the PMLA defence or the PMLA test.

Indirect discrimination law requires a form of exemption. It requires A, in the absence of a successful PMLA defence, to exempt B from her PCP. It does not require her to set aside her PCP altogether; it requires only that she refrain from applying the PCP to B. For example, if, as before, A's PCP were a dress code, A would have to exempt B from it, but she could continue to require her other employees to comply with it (assuming that it did not disadvantage any of them for reasons of religion or belief or in respect of another protected characteristic).

Although non-legal discussions of exemption often overlook indirect discrimination law, one of the most frequently cited instances of exemption in

Britain arose from that law: the case of a Sikh boy who wished to attend a private school with a Christian ethos while wearing a turban, contrary to the school's uniform policy. The House of Lords ruled that the headmaster, in refusing to exempt the boy from the school's uniform rules, was guilty of indirect discrimination.[31] If the case of the two Muslim police officers who fell afoul of Newark Police Department's no-beard rule had arisen in Britain, it would have been a paradigm case for indirect discrimination law. The opportunity to be a police officer was more obviously at stake in that case than the freedom to be a Muslim. The issue in *Sherbert* could also be recast as one of indirect religious discrimination rather than, or as well as, one of free exercise.

Insofar as indirect religious discrimination (IRD) law requires exemptions from the PCPs of employers and providers, its rationale lies most obviously in distributive justice and, more specifically, in the idea of fair equality of opportunity. Let's say for the moment that, if a PCP fails the PMLA test, it is unnecessary. If it is unnecessary, it will limit without good reason the opportunities of those who cannot comply with the PCP and will therefore deprive those people of opportunities unjustly. Unlike direct discrimination, indirect discrimination is not maliciously unjust. Typically it arises as the unintended side-effect of a PCP whose purpose is genuinely non-discriminatory with respect to the characteristic it affects disadvantageously. But an effect can be unjust even though unintended. The injustice consists in a person's being deprived unnecessarily of opportunities that are available to others, whatever the genesis of that state of affairs. Thus, we can say that the rationale for the exemptions required by IRD law is distributive justice and, more particularly, fair equality of opportunity. That conclusion needs, however, to be set in the context of the full order of things secured by IRD law.

First, to describe a PCP that fails the PMLA test as 'unnecessary' is too simple. 'Unnecessary' implies that the PCP is entirely without justification, but a PCP can have a reasonable rationale and still be adjudged less than proportionate in some circumstances. An employer may, for example, have a set period of the year during which her employees may take their annual holiday. The rationale for that PCP may be that she finds it more practicable to have all of her employees on leave at the same time and to cease production during that period rather than try to maintain continuity of production with a depleted workforce. Suppose an employee wishes for a religious reason to take his leave at another time of year; he may wish, for example, to celebrate a religious festival. In that case, a court may decide that he is entitled to take leave outside the employer's specified period. The court's decision need not imply that the employer's PCP is entirely without justification; it need entail only that its justification in the case of the religious employee falls short of the PMLA defence. As I indicate below, different interpretations of that defence trade off the rival interests of employer and employee in different ways.

Secondly, in many instances an employer's or provider's PCP will pass the PMLA test, so that those who are disadvantaged by the PCP for reasons of religion or belief have to remain disadvantaged. IRD law does not therefore aim to eliminate all religiously based disadvantaged. Sabbatarians and those who wear burkas or niqabs, for example, may find they have fewer employment opportunities than others.[32] That may be unfortunate, but it may also be entirely fair and indicates that IRD law is about fair *inequality* of opportunity as well as fair equality of opportunity.

Thirdly, the PMLA defence can itself be interpreted in different ways. It is most obviously intelligible as a simple threshold test. The proportionality of the means (the PCP) should be judged according to the aim at which the means is directed, assuming that aim to be 'legitimate'. Up to the threshold set by proportionality so understood, the employer or provider has a duty to accommodate the believer; beyond that threshold she has none (see further Chapter 6). However, rather than judging the proportionality of a PCP with reference only to the employer's or provider's aim, courts have been inclined also to include in 'proportionality' the degree to which a PCP adversely affects religious believers and the number of believers it adversely affects. Understood in that fashion, the PMLA test ceases to be a simple threshold test and becomes a quasi-utilitarian weighing of all the interests affected. We might push the PMLA test still further towards the believer's interest, as Jonathan Quong (2006) apparently thinks we should. He argues that justice requires that all citizens should be able to combine their conceptions of the good (including religious conceptions) with equal opportunities in employment '*even if doing so is costly, inefficient, or inconvenient for society more generally*' (2006: 66, emphasis in the original). Taken at face value, this implies that employers have an unlimited obligation (perhaps with financial assistance from society at large) to accommodate the demands of people's religious beliefs, no matter how costly or inconvenient that proves.[33]

These issues are too complex to pursue further here. They indicate that it is overly simple to characterise IRD law as an uncomplicated and uncontroversial instrument for promoting equality of opportunity. The exemptions required by IRD law certainly mitigate the extent to which people have to sacrifice opportunities in employment and access to goods and services in order to comply with the demands of their faith. But the limited scope of that mitigation is also a matter of distributive justice. Beyond that limit, wherever it lies, employers and providers can properly complain that they are treated unjustly if they have to incur further costs and endure yet more hobbling of their endeavours in order to accommodate the religious beliefs of others. In other words, in the domain of discrimination law, distributive justice dictates not only the exemptions people should enjoy but also their limited scope.

STATUTORY EXEMPTIONS AND NON-RELIGIOUS GOODS

Let's turn now to statutory exemptions and consider how we should understand their rationale if they aim to secure non-religious goods rather than religious freedom. If we suppose, for example, that turban-wearing Sikhs are exempt from legal obligations to wear safety helmets not in order to preserve their religious freedom but to secure their opportunities to ride motorcycles and to work on construction sites, can we understand the rationale of those exemptions on the model of IRD law?

Prima facie, that may seem plausible. We might say that, without an exemption, safety-helmet legislation would discriminate indirectly against turban-wearing Sikhs since it would affect them disadvantageously relative to those of other faiths or none. But we have to remember that IRD exemptions are subject to the PMLA test. The thought behind that test is that there can be cases in which an employee or client can be exempted from a PCP consistently with the employer's or provider's continuing to use proportionate means to achieve her legitimate aim; in such cases, the employee or client should be accommodated. Can we say that exempting Sikh bikers from a safety-helmet law is consistent with that law's using proportionate means to achieve its legitimate aim? The answer cannot be 'yes' because rather than being consistent with the law's aim—the reduction of head injuries—the exemption runs counter to it. If turbans afforded a degree of protection similar to that provided by helmets, we could hold that requiring biking Sikhs to wear helmets instead of turbans was not a proportionate means for achieving the law's aim. But, since turbans provide much inferior protection, it is hard to see how the exemption could survive the PMLA test. Requiring an exemption on these grounds would be like requiring a manufacturer of widgets to employ someone even though the employee would positively impede the production of widgets.

The same applies to exemption for ritual slaughter. That case is more controversial since there is dispute over whether ritual slaughter causes animals any more suffering than pre-stunned slaughter. If it does not, we could say that prohibiting ritual slaughter was not a proportionate means for achieving the law's aim—minimising the suffering experienced by slaughtered animals. But the more common assumption is that, while there may be uncertainty over quite how much additional suffering ritual slaughter entails, it inflicts *some* additional suffering, in which case allowing ritual slaughter is inconsistent with realising the law's purpose.

It does not follow, however, that there is no case for these exemptions. Exemptions are common in law and cater for cases in which special features provide reason for different treatment. Sikhs have reason peculiar to themselves for wishing not to wear a safety helmet. They understand themselves to be required by their faith to wear a turban and, since they cannot wear both a turban and a safety helmet, they are not at liberty, religiously, to wear a safety helmet. Hence, a law that requires all motorcyclists to wear safety helmets effectively closes off for devout Sikhs the option of riding a motorcycle. The law does not similarly remove the option of motorcycling from those who merely prefer not to wear a safety helmet, or who, like Brian Barry's biker (2001: 47), gain a special thrill from riding a Harley-Davidson, bare-headed, at full throttle down a deserted freeway. I shall not repeat here the defence of exemptions I give in Chapter 7. I mean only to illustrate how an argument can be made for a religious exemption even when the exemption's object is a non-religious good.

Of course, any such case has to compete with considerations that militate against it, particularly the aim of the law from which exemption is sought. The risks of motorcycling without a helmet are no less for Sikhs than for others, and public policy has no reason to give less weight to the health and well-being of Sikhs than to those of others. On the other hand, safety-helmet legislation is largely paternalist in aim, and we should therefore take account of the way in which adherence to their faith makes the all-in interests of Sikhs different from those of others. The legislation is not entirely paternalist, since allowing biking Sikhs not to wear safety helmets can have adverse consequences for others; but these will fall largely on the Sikh community and, insofar as they add to the costs of public health care, those additional costs may be sufficiently modest to be tolerable. My interest here is not in whether, all things considered, the case for the exemption goes through (which I think it does) but in the sort of reasoning that is relevant to assessing whether it does.

Orthodox Jews and some Muslims[34] similarly have reason, which other members of the population do not, for slaughtering animals without first stunning them. If they are legally prevented from acting on that reason, they will be religiously unfree to eat meat. An exemption therefore preserves for Orthodox Jews, and for those Muslims who believe that halal meat requires unstunned slaughter, the option of eating meat. The obvious counter to that case is the suffering ritual slaughter inflicts on animals additional to that inflicted by pre-stunned slaughter. Public policy in many countries, including Britain, Germany and the Netherlands, embodies the judgement that the additional suffering is insufficiently great to override the case for exemption. Public policy in several others, including France, Denmark and Norway, takes the opposite view. Here again my interest is not in whether, all things considered, the exemption is justified but in the kind of reasoning relevant to deciding whether it is.

The legal exemption in Britain that comes closest to meeting conditions analogous to those required by IRD law is the exempting of those who carry knives for religious reasons from law forbidding the carrying of knives in public. The intended beneficiaries of that exemption are, of course, Sikhs who carry kirpans. With no exemption, devout Sikhs would be legally unable to enter public space without violating a requirement of their faith and, since it is virtually impossible for them, or anyone else, to live entirely within a private space, an exemptionless law would effectively compel them to defy their faith. That yields a powerful case for exemption based on religious freedom, but also for one based on the non-religious good of being free to enter and frequent public space. That exemption has still to pass the PMLA test, but in Britain (to my knowledge) there have been no recorded incidents of Sikhs using kirpans to injure others (cf. Singh and Tatla 2006: 135–37), and that record suggests that exempting kirpans is consistent with the law's proportionate pursuit of its legitimate aim. The exemption qualifies as a Pareto improvement: it makes some people better off and no one worse off.

Even this exemption, however, is not entirely straightforward. There has been disquiet in several countries about Sikh boys being free to carry kirpans while attending school. In neither the United States nor the UK are Sikhs incarcerated in prison allowed to carry kirpans and, since 9/11, it has become common for airlines to require Sikhs to surrender their kirpans during flights. In countries other than Britain, there have been instances of Sikhs using kirpans in fights (Hamilton 2005: 114–18) and clearly, if a pattern of violent use began to develop in Britain, the case for exemption would quickly disappear. This is an example of an exemption that is tolerable only so long as it remains consistent with the law's aim.

It would make for a neat symmetry if we could understand all religious exemptions that provided for religious liberty as primarily exercises in non-comparative justice, and all religious exemptions relating to non-religious goods as exercises distributive justice. However, legal exemptions in Britain are altogether too particular, occasional and limited in number for that to be plausible. Rather than constituting parts of some comprehensive egalitarian scheme designed to ensure that legislation never results in a religious group's being disadvantaged relative to others, those exemptions are better conceived as exercises in adhockery. It should be unsurprising that public policy occasionally throws up laws whose demands are out of kilter with a faith's religious practices and that, when it does, there is reason to consider whether a way can be, and should be, found of removing the conflict. We need not suppose that, if there is a case for an exemption, it must be grounded in justice. Nor need we suppose that exemptions, religious or non-religious, should relate only to issues of great moment. It should be enough that an exemption constitutes a 'sensible' or 'reasonable' arrangement in all of the relevant circumstances. The Act which exempts those who carry knives for religious reasons from the ban on public knife carrying also exempts those who carry knives for use at work or as part of a national costume (Criminal Law Act 1988, s. 139). We are unlikely to conceive those other exemptions as part of some grand scheme of distributive justice. The authors of the law have simply recognised that some people are specially circumstanced in relation to the carrying of knives, and have seen fit, all things considered, to make special provision for them.

MAJORITIES AND MINORITIES

Those who understand exemptions as instruments of equality often conceive the inequalities they believe exemptions should remedy as inequalities between majority and minority. The story is one in which societies are dominated by their majority populations and those majorities organise public arrangements to suit themselves.[35] Minorities are merely passive recipients of whatever arrangements majorities put their way and are frequently disadvantaged as a consequence. Exemptions help correct that unequal state of affairs. The condition of the majority sets a benchmark, and exemptions are conceived as mechanisms through which minorities can be moved closer to, and ideally would reach, that benchmark.

Sometimes the dominant majority is conceived as a religious majority, for example, those whom Eisgruber and Sager describe as adherents of a society's 'mainstream religion'. Sometimes it may be non-religious, with the religious of any kind being cast in the role of the minority. And sometimes the majority may shift with the issue, so that it encompasses everyone in the society apart from the religious minority that is disadvantaged on the relevant issue. The recasting of religious exemptions as a cultural issue, in which the culture of a 'host' population is pitted against those of migrant groups, almost inevitably yields a majority/minority story.

There are a number of things to be said in defence of conceiving a majority/minority division as the context for religious exemption. One is that the beneficiaries of exemptions are almost always minorities. Another is that an exemption, in relieving a group of a relative disadvantage, necessarily renders its condition in that respect equal to, or less unequal than, that of the rest of the society. A third is that it is evident that societies do commonly possess arrangements that suit the religious allegiance, or the lack of religious allegiance, of their majority populations. An obvious example is the structure of the working week and the timing of public holidays in societies with a Christian heritage. The PCPs of employers can also be geared to majority norms. The increased incidence of Sunday and 'holiday' working has done something to diminish that difference, and Christians have become increasingly prominent as aggrieved parties in legal actions on human rights and indirect religious discrimination. Moreover, the historical majority whose religious interests have shaped a society's arrangements is often nowadays no longer a majority. But none of those observations invalidates the claim that societies often present religious minorities with rules and arrangements that suit them less well than the rest of the population.

I want, even so, to suggest that locating the case for exemptions in a narrative of majority dominance and minority victimhood is often a mistake. Consider the statutory exemptions on which I focused in the previous section. The laws from which they provide exemptions have a variety of purposes. Safety-helmet legislation aims to reduce the incidence of death and injury from blows to the head. The ban on carrying knives aims to prevent death and injury through the use of knives as weapons. The requirement that animals should be stunned before slaughter aims to minimise the suffering they experience. It would be bizarre to represent those purposes as manifesting the sectional interests or values of a majority. It would be equally bizarre to suggest that Sikhs are indifferent or hostile to efforts to reduce head injuries or knife crime or that Jews and Muslims are indifferent to animal suffering. On the contrary, we can presume that the exempted groups applaud the aims of the laws from which they are exempt. They seek exemption not because they reject the law's aim but only because the specific measure their society uses for its pursuit conflicts with their religious practice.

We can go further. Suppose there were a society in which the majority of the population were Sikh. There would be nothing incoherent or nonsensical in that society's banning the carrying of knives other than kirpans, or in its requiring motorcyclists and construction workers who do not wear turbans to wear safety helmets. Those measures would simply recognise that the balance of reasons applying to the well-being of non-Sikhs differs from that applying to the well-being of Sikhs. Similarly, there would be nothing incoherent or nonsensical in a majority Jewish society's requiring that all slaughter, other than ritual slaughter, should use pre-stunning, or in a majority Muslim society's having a rule, like the UK, that no headgear should be worn for passport photographs except for religious or medical reasons.

As I observed in the previous section, in a religiously diverse society we should not expect there to be a perfect congruence between the society's public policies and all of the norms of all of the religions present amongst its population. Legal exemptions respond to that social fact. They need be conceived neither as symptoms of injustice nor as correctives to majority oppression. Rather they can be part of the normal arrangements of a plural society.

CONCLUSION

I began this chapter by distinguishing two distribuends for which religious exemption might aim to provide: religious liberty and access to non-religious goods. I have argued that, insofar as the distribuend is religious liberty, the primary issue with which exemptions confronts us is the scope of the liberty that people should enjoy rather than the way in which that liberty should be distributed amongst them. That is not to deny, absurdly, that distributive justice has no bearing on religious liberty; that liberty is, of course, one that should be distributed equally. It is to hold only that, when the object of a putative exemption is religious liberty, the issue is what, in the circumstances relevant to the exemption, should be the scope of the religious liberty to which all are equally entitled. There can, of course, be cases like *Sherbert* in which there is strong reason to hold that one religious group has been treated less favourably than another. But, even in that sort of case, correcting the inequality by granting an exemption implies that the exemption is justified in its own right and would stand even in the absence of a comparator group. Determining the rightful scope of religious liberty logically precedes distributing that liberty justly.

Protecting the religious from disadvantage in their access to non-religious goods has a different logic. If we take the exemptions from PCPs that are provided by way of IRD law, the object of those exemptions is to ensure that, up to a point (the point set by consistency with the employer's or provider's using proportionate means to achieve a legitimate aim—the PMLA test), people are not disadvantaged, relative to others, by their religion or belief. Beyond that point, they are disadvantaged but not unjustly. Discrimination law is concerned not with what opportunities there should be but with the just distribution of people's access to whatever opportunities happen to exist.[36]

I have resisted the possibility that we might understand statutory religious exemptions, insofar as they aim to secure non-religious goods, on the model of IRD law. Some religious groups may well be relatively disadvantaged by law in a way that mimics indirect discrimination, but most would have a hard time showing that the law failed the PMLA test so that they were due an exemption. If we take statutory religious exemptions in the UK as our test case, these are most plausibly understood as exercises in adhockery, as are the multiplicity of statutory non-religious exemptions. They do not form parts of a comprehensive scheme of distributive justice, nor need they be instantiations of non-comparative justice which, in turn, does not imply that they are unjust. They are *ad hoc* efforts to deal with special cases in ways that are reasonable, if not necessarily uncontroversial, given all of the circumstances of the case.

NOTES

This chapter is based on a paper I gave to a conference on 'Religion in Liberal Political Philosophy', organised by Cécile Laborde and Aurélia Bardon at University College London in 2015. I am grateful to participants in the conference, and particularly to Cécile Laborde and Aurélia Bardon, for their helpful comments on that paper.

1. See, for example, Eisgruber and Sager 2007; Kymlicka 1995: 108–15; Miller 2002; Nussbaum 2008; Parekh 2006: 239–63; Quong 2006.

2. The distinction I make here is complicated by the fact that people may also suffer discrimination in relation to their religious freedom. Article 14 of the ECHR provides that the rights and freedoms set out in the Convention shall be secured "without discrimination" of various sorts, including discrimination on grounds of sex, race, religion, and national or social origin. To avoid confusion, I use the term 'discrimination law' in this chapter to refer only to law protecting people from discrimination with respect to goods such as employment and the provision of goods and services; i.e. protection from discrimination of the sort provided by the Equality Act 2010.

3. Equality Act 2010, schedule 9, paras 2 and 3.

4. Initially by the Motor Cycle Crash Helmets (Religious Exemptions) Act (1976) and later by the Road Traffic Act (1988), s. 16(2). For further details of the law relating to this exemption, see Poulter 1998: 297–301.

5. Employment Act 1989, s. 11.

6. Arguably, we can and should require people to take responsibility for the religion or belief they hold, whereas we cannot hold them similarly responsible for their race or gender. That, in turn, may be reason for indirect discrimination law to treat claims relating to religion or belief less generously than those relating to race and gender, but UK discrimination legislation recognises no such difference. I consider that issue in Chapter 6.

7. On non-comparative justice, see Feinberg 1974; Hoffman 1993; Montague 1980; and Olsaretti 2004: 33–37.

8. *R (Playfoot) (A Minor) v. Governing Body of Millais School* [2007] EWHC 1698 (Admin); *R (Begum) v. Denbigh High School* [2006] UKHL 15.

9. *Eweida and Others v. The UK* (2013) 57 EHRR 8.

10. Ibid.

11. *Copsey v. WWB Devon Clays Ltd*, [2005] EWCA Civ 932; *Ahmad v. Inner London Education Authority*, [1978] QB 36.

12. *R (Ghai) v. Newcastle City Council* [2009] EWHC 978 (Admin); [2010] EWCA Civ 59.

13. That blunt assertion needs qualification, since there can be cases in which a right is properly said to be 'overridden', even though the overriding might be thought justified all things considered. For example, the right not to be imprisoned without trial may be overridden by the use of internment in time of war, and the right of free speech may be overridden not because the speaker says something he has no right to say but because silencing him is the only way to prevent a riot. The distinguishing feature of such cases is that the right-holder is wronged and might therefore be owed compensation. Such cases are different from the ordinary run of cases in which competing considerations simply and properly define the scope of a right.

14. Two examples of human rights claims that failed, in part, because the practice at issue was deemed insufficiently central to the claimant's religion are *R (Williamson) v. Secretary of State for Education and Employment* [2005] UKHL 15, and *R (Playfoot) (A Minor) v. Governing Body of Millais School* [2007] EWHC 1698 (Admin).

15. For a systematic account of the weighing process I describe in this paragraph, see Laborde 2017: 221–29.

16. As it was, for example, in *Begum* in which judges in the House of Lords reached the same conclusion in different ways, some judging that there had not been interference and others that there had. Those who thought there had been interference all found against Begum for clause 2 reasons. *R (Begum) v. Denbigh High School* [2006] UKHL 15.

17. Whether all exemptions that claim a foundation in the free exercise clause really have the aim of protecting religious freedom rather than their beneficiaries' access to non-religious goods is, as I suggest below, more doubtful.

18. Their thesis has received much critical attention. See, for example, Berg 2007; Greenawalt 2007; Greene 2009; Koppelman 2006; Laborde 2014; Lupu and Tuttle 2007; McConnell 2000; and White 2012.

19. *Sherbert v. Verner*, 374 U.S. 398 (1963).

20. 'In our view, equality was what was really at stake in Adell Sherbert's case, and equality was what lent appeal to the proposition [which Eisgruber and Sager reject] that religion enjoyed some sort of unique presumption of immunity to otherwise applicable regulation' (2007: 15).

21. Quoted in *Sherbert v. Verner*, 406.

22. Ibid., my emphasis.

23. Nussbaum (2008: 137) takes a different view of Brennan's judgement: 'Equality is not advanced as an extra consideration, over and above the idea of substantial burden; it is one constituent of the idea of substantial burden'.

24. Cf. Justice Harlan's comment in his dissenting opinion: 'Plainly, under our decisions in the "Sunday law" cases, [the] appellant can derive no support for her position from the State's general statutory provisions setting aside Sunday as a uniform day of rest'; *Sherbert v. Verner*, 406 note 3.

25. *Employment Division v. Smith*, 494 U.S. 872 (1990).

26. *Fraternal Order of Police Newark Lodge No. 12 v. City of Newark*, 170 F.3d 359 (3rd Cir. 1999).

27. They describe medical needs as 'plainly analogous' to religious needs (91) and the failure of equal regard, if they are treated differently, as 'easy to recognise' (91). Exemptions for those with medical conditions, as in the Newark Police case, provide 'immediate and clear benchmarks for comparison in Equal Liberty cases' (120). If the state is 'appropriately responsive to health concerns . . . the resulting accommodations can easily form the basis of Equal Liberty claims on behalf of religious accommodation' (96–97).

28. While Eisgruber and Sager believe health-exemption analogies 'are an especially fruitful source of comparisons for Equal Liberty's anti-discrimination principle' (97), they believe that other sorts of exemption can also do the job (97–99).

29. Their list includes familial projects but, when Eisgruber and Sager consider similar religious and familial claims (115–17), they conclude that, while the religious claim should be met with an exemption, the familial claim should not. For a more developed critique relating to the issues I raise in this paragraph, see Laborde 2014.

30. Equality Act 2010, Pt 2, Ch. 2, s. 19.

31. *Mandla v. Dowell Lee* [1983] 2 AC 548. That case is famous for the House of Lord's decision that Sikhs constituted a 'racial group', within the meaning of the Race Relations Act 1976. Legally, therefore, Mandla was a victim of indirect racial, rather than religious, discrimination. At the time, there was no law in Britain prohibiting religious discrimination (though there was in Northern Ireland). Had there been such a law, it is hard to believe that the House of Lords would have deemed Sikhs a racial rather than a religious group, but, since *Mandla*, Sikhs have remained a racial as well as religious group for purposes of discrimination law.

32. E.g. *Azmi v. Kirklees Metropolitan Borough Council* [2007] UKEAT 0009 07 3003; *Mba v. The Mayor and Burgesses of the London Borough of Merton* [2012] UKEAT/0332/12/ SM, [2013] EWCA Civ 1562.

33. It is hard to believe that that is what Quong really means, although he does ground his argument on Rawls's lexical ordering of the principles of justice. He rules out exemptions that would be unfair because they afford the exemptee more than his fair share of societal benefits; e.g. an exemption that allowed the exemptee to work for fewer hours than others but for the same salary (2006: 65). But there could be cases in which an exemption, while not advantaging the exemptee relative to others, still significantly impeded pursuit of the employer's aim. Quong (2006: 64–65) gives an example in which Jonah, an Orthodox Jew, wishes to become a police officer but is denied that opportunity because the police force requires all of its officers to be available for weekend working and Jonah is religiously unfree to work on Saturdays. In those circumstances, Jonah's opportunity-set is unequal to the set enjoyed by others, such as Jeff, a liberal Protestant, who has no objection to working on weekends: Jeff can combine his religious practice with service as a police officer while Jonah cannot. Quong argues that the inequality of opportunity should be removed by Jonah's being exempted from Saturday working. (Jonah would still work the same number of hours as other officers and so would not be advantaged relative to them.) But suppose that there were a large number of Jonahs, rather than only one, all wanting to become police officers. Are the police duty-bound to accommodate all of them, irrespective of the problems that would create for policing on Saturdays and of the

impact upon the Jeffs who, as a consequence, found themselves working every Saturday? Compare Quong's imaginary example with the real-life case of *Mba*, cited in the previous note, in which a care-home worker, who was a Christian Sabbatarian, claimed a right to exemption from Sunday working, even though the home with its relatively small staff had to provide around-the-clock care for disabled children seven days a week.

34. The *Results of the 2018 FSA Survey into Slaughter Methods in England and Wales* (published Feb. 2019), p. 10, show that, of animals slaughtered by halal method, only a minority of each species was slaughtered without first being stunned. Available at https://assets.publishing.service.gov.uk/government/uploads/system/uploads/attachment_data/file/778588/slaughter-method-survey-2018.pdf (accessed 19 November 2019).

35. For example, Eisgruber and Sager 2007; Kymlicka 1995: 113–15; Nussbaum 2008.

36. Which is not, of course, to deny that there may be other grounds on which a society should guarantee some specific opportunities for its citizens.

REFERENCES

Ahdar, Rex, and Ian Leigh. 2013. *Religious Freedom in the Liberal State*, second edition. Oxford: Oxford University Press.

Barry, Brian. 2001. *Culture and Equality*. Cambridge: Polity.

Berg, Thomas. 2007. 'Can Religious Liberty Be Protected as Equality?' *Texas Law Review* 85 (5): 1185–215.

Dworkin, Ronald. 2000. *Sovereign Virtue*. Cambridge, MA: Harvard University Press.

Eisgruber, Christopher L., and Lawrence G. Sager. 2007. *Religious Freedom and the Constitution*. Cambridge, MA: Harvard University Press.

Feinberg, Joel. 1974. 'Noncomparative Justice'. *Philosophical Review* 83(3): 297–338.

Garvey, John H. 1996. 'An Anti-Liberal Argument for Religious Freedom'. *Journal of Contemporary Legal Issues* 7: 275–91.

Greenawalt, Kent. 2007. 'How Does "Equal Liberty" Fare in Relation to Other Approaches to the Religion Clauses?' *Texas Law Review* 85(5): 1217–46.

Greene, Abner. 2009. 'Three Theories of Religious Equality . . . and of Exemptions'. *Texas Law Review* 87(5): 963–1007.

Hamilton, Marci A. 2005. *God vs. the Gavel: Religion and the Rule of Law*. Cambridge: Cambridge University Press.

Hoffman, Joshua. 1993. 'A New Theory of Comparative and Noncomparative Justice'. *Philosophical Studies* 70(2): 165–83.

Koppelman, Andrew. 2006. 'Is It Fair to Give Religion Special Treatment?' *University of Illinois Law Review* 3(3): 571–603.

Koppelman, Andrew. 2009. 'Conscience, Volitional Necessity, and Religious Exemptions'. *Legal Theory* 15(3): 215–44.

Kymlicka, Will. 1995. *Multicultural Citizenship: A Liberal Theory of Minority Rights*. Oxford: Clarendon Press.

Laborde, Cécile. 2014. 'Equal Liberty, Non-Establishment and Religious Freedom'. *Legal Theory* 20(1): 52–77.

Laborde, Cécile. 2017. *Liberalism's Religion*. Cambridge, MA: Harvard University Press.

Leiter, Brian. 2013. *Why Tolerate Religion?* Princeton, NJ: Princeton University Press.

Lupu, Ira C., and Robert W. Tuttle. 2007. 'The Limits of Equal Liberty as a Theory of Religious Freedom'. *Texas Law Review* 85(5): 1247–72.

McConnell, Michael W. 2000. 'The Problem of Singling Out Religion'. *DePaul Law Review* 50(1): 1–47.

Miller, David. 2002. 'Liberalism, Equal Opportunities and Cultural Commitments'. In *Multiculturalism Reconsidered*, ed. Paul Kelly, 45–61. Cambridge: Polity.

Montague, Phillip. 1980. 'Comparative and Non-Comparative Justice'. *Philosophical Quarterly* 30(119): 131–40.

Nussbaum, Martha. 2008. *Liberty of Conscience: In Defense of America's Tradition of Religious Liberty*. New York: Basic Books.

Olsaretti, Serena. 2004. *Liberty, Desert and the Market*. Cambridge: Cambridge University Press.

Parekh, Bhikhu. 2006. *Rethinking Multiculturalism: Cultural Diversity and Political Theory*, second edition. Basingstoke: Palgrave Macmillan.

Poulter, Sebastian. 1998. *Ethnicity, Law and Human Rights*. Oxford: Oxford University Press.

Quong, Jonathan. 2006. 'Cultural Exemptions, Expensive Tastes, and Equal Opportunities'. *Journal of Applied Philosophy* 23(1): 53–71.

Singh, Gurharpal, and Darshan Singh Tatla. 2006. *Sikhs in Britain: The Making of a Community*. London: Zed Books.

Trigg, Roger. 2012. *Equality, Freedom and Religion*. Oxford: Oxford University Press.

White, Stuart. 2012. 'Religious Exemptions: An Egalitarian Demand?' *Law and Ethics of Human Rights* 6(1): 97–118.

Chapter Nine

Conscientious Claims, Ill-Founded Belief and Religious Exemption

In the enduring controversy over religious exemptions, one matter seems reasonably settled. That is the matter of how courts should handle the religious beliefs of those who register a claim to exemption. Provided a court is satisfied that a claimant sincerely holds the belief he professes, it should take the belief at face value. In particular, it should not subject the belief to any test of merit, plausibility or reasonableness. That statement is subject to some qualification which I shall acknowledge in due course, but the general position is that a court should not vary the status or weight it gives a belief according to its estimate of the belief's merit or validity. Nor for judicial purposes should an individual's belief be subject to appraisal by a religious authority, including an authority that speaks on behalf of an organised religion of which the individual is a member.

Accordingly, when the question of exemption arises and the claimant's interest is weighed against various other sorts of consideration in deciding whether the claimant should receive an exemption all things considered, the weight the court accords the claimant's interest should not vary according to its estimate of the plausibility or reasonableness of the claimant's belief. As well as being generally accepted judicial practice, that position is pretty much an orthodoxy amongst liberal commentators on religious freedom in general and religious exemption in particular.

In this chapter, I want to question that orthodoxy. Perhaps I should say that I 'interrogate' it since I eventually acknowledge a justification for it. I do not call into question religious liberty in general. Rather, I take for granted that individuals have a right to embrace a religious faith, or none, as they themselves see fit and that others, including judges, are duty-bound to respect their use of that right. I question the immunity of religious belief from official appraisal only in a more limited way. Suppose that B, a religious believer who subscribes to faith X, believes that his faith requires him to do y and to refrain from z. Suppose too that we have reason to doubt the correctness of B's belief; we reckon, with good reason, that he is mistaken in believing that X requires y or forbids z. His belief is 'ill-founded'. Should that affect the weight or the status we give to B's belief?

In some respects, it should not. Courts in applying Article 9 of the European Convention on Human Rights (ECHR) treat the freedom to hold a belief as absolute. If B's belief is ill-founded, that is a reason why he should not hold it, but it does not diminish his right to do so. It also does not affect his right to manifest his belief by doing y or refraining from z. The ill-foundedness of B's belief becomes practically relevant when it impinges on and competes with the (legitimate) interests of others and, more particularly, when B seeks an exemption enabling him to engage in a practice manifesting his belief. B then presents his belief as a reason why he should not be subject to a law or rule with which others have to comply and very often as a reason why others should endure costs and inconvenience so that he can manifest his belief. To the extent that B's exemption would adversely affect the public or private interest of others, his belief ceases to be his business only and becomes the business of others too. That is reflected in the weighing process through which a decision should be made on whether someone should receive an exemption all things considered.

Why should that weighing process not take account of the well- or ill-foundedness of B's belief? If B's belief is ill-founded, he is not justified in holding it and, if he is not justified in holding it, how can his holding it justify his making positive demands upon others? At the very least and *ceteris paribus*, does not an ill-founded belief have a weaker claim to accommodation than a well-founded belief, and might its ill-foundedness jeopardise its claim to accommodation entirely?

These questions, of course, beg many others. One of the more obvious is how we are to determine whether B's belief is indeed well- or ill-founded. Even though we are to judge not the well-foundedness of B's religious faith (X) but only his belief about what his faith requires (y and not-z), that may still be a challenging task. But, *prima facie*, it is surprising that a belief's well- or ill-foundedness should make no difference to its bearer's claim to an exemption.

My examination of the questions raised by the issue of ill-foundedness unfolds as follows. I begin by giving some real-life instances of belief-based practices that exemplify the issue I have described. I then say more to explicate that issue and sketch the current orthodoxy, with reference to Lord Nicholls's well-known remarks, that courts should abstain from subjecting religious beliefs to any sort of evaluation. What might justify that abstinence? Two, rather different, answers are commonly given. One appeals to principled considerations, particularly the moral right to religious liberty, which make it wrong to take account of the well- or ill-foundedness of a belief in considering the believer's claim to an exemption. I find that case not made. The other is more practical in nature: courts lack the knowledge and ability needed to arrive at a reliable assessment of a belief's well-foundedness. While not accepting that that claim is obviously true, I do find reason why judges should wish to avoid 'entanglement' with religious questions. Finally, I consider whether we might circumvent the problem of entanglement by using a group test as a proxy for testing well-foundedness.

EXAMPLES

In December 2013, an employee working on a cash register in the food section of Marks & Spencer refused to serve a customer, albeit politely, because his shopping included alcohol and she declared that, as a Muslim, she was forbidden to handle items containing alcohol. She asked the customer to join the queue for another register. In response to this incident, a boycott was mooted by indignant customers, and the store quickly declared that it would no longer employ staff at its registers if they refused to handle alcohol. The issue had previously arisen in another supermarket chain, Sainsbury's, which had allowed its Muslim staff not to handle alcohol or pork. An objecting Muslim who was working at a cash register was allowed to summon another member of staff to put the offending item through the register in his or her stead. Once their indulgence attracted public comment, Sainsbury's took advice from Muslim authorities on whether Islam did indeed forbid the mere handling of alcohol or pork; having been advised that it did not, the supermarket changed its policy.

This is the sort of case in which we might question whether the objector's belief was soundly based and, if it was not, whether the employers either were, or should have been, duty-bound to accommodate it. As far as I know, a case concerning the handling of alcohol or pork by Muslims has not been tested in law in the UK. If Muslim objections were not accommodated and that, in turn, gave rise to a claim of indirect religious discrimination, I strongly suspect that an employer's requirement that its sales staff should be willing to handle all items sold by a shop would be deemed a 'proportionate means of achieving a legitimate aim' and so not indirectly discriminatory. But in that case the determining factor would be the proportionality test, whereas the issue I am raising concerns the merit of the belief with which that test competes and how its merit (or demerit) should affect the consideration it receives.

More recently, a dispute arose in Birmingham over a four-year-old girl whose parents wished her to wear a hijab while attending a Catholic primary school, contrary to the school's uniform policy.[1] Birmingham City Council's equality chief, Waseem Zaffar, claimed (probably incorrectly) that the school's uniform code banning headwear, including Islamic headscarves, breached the Equality Act 2010. However, the case attracted attention not only as yet another clash between the claims of religion and a school's uniform policy but also because of the parents' zealotry in making a four-year-old girl wear a hijab, a zealotry which was widely deemed misplaced since Islam normally requires girls to cover their heads only when they reach puberty. This too was a case in which the questionable justification of a religious practice might be thought adversely to affect, if not to rule out altogether, its claim to accommodation.

That case, like the case of handling alcohol or pork, was not tested at law. A much older case that was and that provides a clear example of the issue I mean to raise concerned an employee of British Rail (BR) in the days of the closed shop when BR existed as a nationalised industry and required its employees to belong to a trade union.[2] Mr Saggers was a Jehovah's Witness who claimed that his religious beliefs forbade trade union membership. The Industrial Relations Act 1971, under which his case fell, had originally provided that employees could escape the closed shop requirement if they objected to trade union membership on 'conscientious' grounds. In 1974, the Act was amended so that the ground for exemption became 'religious belief' in particular rather than conscientious objection in general. Nothing in the doctrines of the Jehovah's Witness Church proscribed membership in a trade union, as Mr Saggers himself acknowledged. For that reason, the Industrial Tribunal that heard his case decided that he did not qualify for exemption. On appeal, the Employment Appeal Tribunal (EAT) ruled that the Industrial Tribunal had applied the wrong test. Provided the Industrial Tribunal was satisfied that Mr Saggers himself sincerely believed that, for religious reasons, he should not join a trade union, he qualified for exemption. It mattered not that his belief was at odds with the official doctrines of the organised religion to which he subscribed.

The EAT remitted the case for rehearing by the Industrial Tribunal on the factual question of whether Mr Saggers's objection was really grounded in his religious belief. On remission, the Industrial Tribunal accepted the sincerity and genuineness of Mr Saggers's attitude that his objection to joining a trade union was based on his religious belief, but still held that, in fact, his objection was based upon more general grounds of conscience. Mr Saggers again appealed, and the EAT again decided, by a majority, that the Tribunal had erred in law.[3] Provided it was accepted (as it was by the Tribunal) that Mr Saggers was sincere and genuine when he declared, 'I do not think that a Christian can be a trade unionist', that sufficed to establish that his objection was 'due to religious belief'.[4]

Here I do not want to question whether the EAT was right in law. Rather, I want to ask whether it *should* have been right in law. Since Mr Saggers made his claim *as* a Jehovah's Witness and since we can reasonably suppose that his command of the doctrines of his church was inferior to that of the church itself, do we not have reason to doubt the well-foundedness of his belief? And, if we do, should that not make a difference to the legal status of his claim?

A more recent and better-known case, which raised similar questions about the subjective and objective dimensions of the religious belief protected by law, is the Canadian case of *Syndicat Northcrest v. Amselem*.[5] The case concerned the Jewish festival of Succot, during which religiously observant Jews are to 'dwell' in a succah (a small enclosed temporary hut) for the nine days of the festival.[6] A number of practising Orthodox Jews who lived in co-owned luxury buildings in Montreal wanted to erect succot on the balconies of their units, contrary to the by-laws governing the building which prohibited decorations, alterations and constructions on balconies. The case turned partly on how the rights of the claimants to freedom of religion weighed against the rights of other co-owners and the steps taken by Syndicat Northcrest to accommodate the beliefs of the claimants, particularly its offer to provide a communal succah in the garden attached to the buildings. But it also turned on the nature of the religious belief whose freedom was protected by the rights enshrined in the Quebec Charter of Human Rights and Freedoms, and it is upon that aspect of the case that I focus here. The specific point at issue was not whether the claimants were mandated by their faith to observe the festival of Succot; all parties accepted that they were. Rather it was whether their freedom of religion entitled each to construct a private succah on his balcony rather than use the communal succah offered by the Syndicat (an offer approved by the Canadian Jewish Congress) or a succah at some other location.

The original trial judge ruled that, to be protected by the right to freedom of religion under the Quebec Charter, a claimant must prove that the practice at issue was required by the teachings of his or her religion. Sincere belief alone did not suffice.

> Freedom of religion can be relied on only if there is a connection between the right asserted by a person to practise his or her religion in a given way and what is considered mandatory pursuant to the religious teaching upon which the right is based. A sincere belief must be supported by the existence of a religious precept. . . . The rite must have a rational, reasonable and direct connection with the teaching. How a believer performs his or her religious obligations cannot be grounded in a purely subjective personal understanding that bears no relation to the religious teaching as regards both the belief itself and how the belief is to be expressed (the rite).[7]

Having heard evidence that Judaism did not require Jews to erect their own succot and that there was no commandment governing where succot should be erected, the judge concluded that the by-laws governing the Syndicat's building did not prevent Jews from fulfilling their religious obligations and so did not infringe their freedom of religion.[8]

A majority of the Court of Appeal agreed.[9] A majority of the Canadian Supreme Court thought differently. They held that the lower courts' interpretation of freedom of religion was unduly restrictive. Speaking for the majority, Iacobucci J insisted that the freedom of religion protected by both the Quebec and the Canadian charters was essentially 'personal' or 'subjective' and cited several judicial comments and decisions in support of that view.[10]

> In my opinion, these decisions and commentary should not be construed to imply that freedom of religion protects only those aspects of religious belief or conduct that are objectively recognized by religious experts as being obligatory tenets or precepts of a particular religion. Consequently, claimants seeking to invoke freedom of religion should not need to prove the objective validity of their beliefs in that their beliefs are objectively recognized as valid by other members of the same religion, nor is such an inquiry appropriate for courts to make.[11]

While a claimant had to show sincerity of belief, he or she did not need to show that the belief was 'valid'. To be protected by 'freedom of religion', the belief had to have 'a nexus with religion', but that nexus could be entirely subjective.[12] Accordingly the majority found that the Syndicat's rules, in preventing the appellants' constructing succot on their balconies, did interfere with their freedom of religion, and went on to find no justification for that interference.

Three members of the Supreme Court dissented.[13] In a shared judgement, they rejected the majority's understanding of freedom of religion.

> A religion is a system of beliefs and practices based on certain religious precepts. A nexus between personal beliefs and the religion's precepts must therefore be established. . . . Religious precepts constitute a body of objectively identifiable data that permit a distinction to be made between genuine religious beliefs and personal choices or practices that are unrelated to freedom of conscience. Connecting freedom of religion to precepts provides a basis for establishing objectively whether the fundamental right at issue has been violated.[14]

Thus, as well as establishing that the claimant's alleged belief was sincerely held, a court had also to be satisfied that it was genuinely connected to the religion that the claimant shared with others. That connection was subject to an 'objective test', and that was a test that, the dissenting minority concluded, the appellants' claim did not pass.[15]

The disputes evoked by *Amselem* provide a model instance of judges taking different positions on the question of whether claimants should be treated as self-authenticating authorities on the demands of their religion, or whether claims made in the name of a religion should be subject to scrutiny in respect of that religion. While the disputes formally concerned what Canadian law was, they also included judicial comment that clearly took sides on the issue of what the law ought to be.

Frequently, the subjective/objective issue relates not to whether a practice can plausibly claim a foundation in a particular faith but to the status the practice has within that faith. One such issue is what should count as 'manifestation' of a belief for purposes of Article 9 of the ECHR and the protection it affords religion or belief. Strasbourg case law has distinguished an act or practice that 'manifests' a belief from one that is merely 'motivated' or 'influenced' by the belief. In *Arrowsmith*, the case in which the European Commission first made the distinction, the Commission decided that the claimant's activity of distributing leaflets exhorting British soldiers not to serve in Northern Ireland, while it may have been motivated by the claimant's pacifism, was not a manifestation of her pacifism since the leaflets contained no mention of pacifism.[16] It was not therefore protected by Article 9 (1). As that case made clear, the judgement of whether an act manifests, or is merely motivated by, a belief is an objective one. It is a judgement to be made by the court, not one to be outsourced to claimants and their sincere understanding of what their own beliefs demand of them.

Thus, for example, in *Williamson* the court held that use of corporal punishment was a manifestation of the belief of the Christian groups who were the claimants,[17] while in *Playfoot*, it decided that the claimant's act of wearing a 'purity ring' contrary to her school's uniform policy was not a manifestation of her Christian belief on sexual abstinence before marriage, even though it may have been motivated by her belief.[18] Let us return to the case of the Muslim supermarket workers who objected to handling alcohol or pork and suppose that their employer refused to accommodate their objections. The employees might have responded not by appealing to the law on indirect religious discrimination but by claiming that the employment laws which obliged them to comply with their employer's instructions on handling alcohol or pork had interfered with their human rights under Article 9 of the ECHR. In such an event, the judgement of a court might well have been that, while the employee's refusal to handle alcohol and pork was a belief-related preference, it did not manifest the belief that consuming alcohol or pork was *haram*; it was simply a preference motivated or influenced by that belief.[19] Similarly, had *Amselem* arisen as a case in European law, the dispute over the scope of the belief protected by law might have been recast as one concerning the distinction between manifestation and motivation.

Of course, the manifestation/motivation distinction retains a subjective element in that, in Strasbourg case law, it is the demands of the claimant's belief, not the orthodoxies of the religious faith with which he or she identifies, that are subject to assessment. Even so, that assessment involves a court's inquiring into the claimant's belief and reaching a judgement on its demands, a judgement that may well differ from the claimant's own conception of those demands. Use of the manifestation/motivation distinction has been criticised for that reason.[20] Moreover, a religious believer may find it harder to persuade a court that an act or practice manifests a belief if it is not so conceived by a significant number of others who subscribe to the same faith.

Suppose now that it is agreed on all sides that a practice does manifest a religious belief. A decision on an exemption requires that the claim of the believer be weighed against the other considerations with which it competes, such as how significantly the exemption would frustrate the aims of the law or rule from which the believer seeks exemption and how great are the costs and inconvenience the exemption would shift onto others. That weighing process requires us to assign a notional, if inevitably imprecise, weight to the believer's claim, which, in turn, requires attending to two considerations. First, how *severely* does the law or rule impinge upon the believer's faith? For example, other things being equal, a law or rule that frustrates an obligatory practice will be more severe in its effect than one that frustrates a practice that is only discretionary. Secondly, how *directly* does the law or rule frustrate the practice? If, for example, a law or rule effectively prohibits a practice, its adverse effect will be more direct than if it renders performance of the practice only more costly or inconvenient; if it does the latter, the less the cost or the inconvenience, the less direct will be the effect. Thus, the more severe and direct the effect, the weightier will be the believer's claim for an exemption.[21]

My interest here is in the criterion of severity. Some commentators insist that courts should refrain from investigating people's religious beliefs in an effort to assess how severely those beliefs are disadvantaged.[22] However, if there is to be a weighing process, it is hard to see how that can be avoided or why it should be deemed illegitimate. As Abner Green has observed, if people seek an exemption on religious grounds, they cannot reasonably expect to veto any judicial entanglement with their religious beliefs.[23] Two distinctions that commonly arise both in judicial comment and in moral and political thinking on exemption are those between (i) obligatory and discretionary religious practices and between (ii) central or core practices and those that are more peripheral to a faith. Other things being equal, burdening a practice that is obligatory or central to a faith affects it more severely than burdening one that is discretionary or peripheral. Although these distinctions are eminently reasonable, they are not always easily deployed, and they apply to some faiths more readily than to others. I pass over those difficulties. The relevance of the distinctions here is that they provide another occasion for the subjective/objective question: obligatory or discretionary, central or peripheral, according to whom?[24]

ILL-FOUNDEDNESS AND JUDICIAL AGNOSTICISM

The cases cited in the previous section exemplify the sorts of case in which we might think that the well- or ill-foundedness of an individual's belief should affect the weight or status that public decision-makers give to the belief. However, I should perhaps re-emphasise the limited context in which I mean to present that issue. The ill-foundedness of a belief does not affect the believer's right merely to hold or articulate his belief; nor is it relevant to every manifestation of his belief. Even if the belief that Islam forbids the mere handling of alcohol or pork is mistaken, Muslims who hold that belief should be free to manifest it by avoiding forms of employment or other activities which would involve their handling alcohol or pork. Even if Mr Saggers was mistaken in believing that his religion proscribed trade union membership, he should remain free to manifest his belief by avoiding forms of employment that would require him to join a trade union. The issue of a belief's well-foundedness becomes a practical issue only when an individual's freedom to manifest his belief competes with the (legitimate) interests of others.

We can think of a decision on a religious exemption as a two-stage process. At the first stage, we consider whether the claimant's belief-based practice should be a candidate for an exemption and, if it should, how strong its candidacy is. For example, a court's assessment of whether a claimant sincerely holds the belief he professes belongs to that first stage. If the court adjudges the claimant to be insincere, his claim falls at that hurdle. At the second stage, we take account of the considerations with which the claim for an exemption competes and consider whether the claimant should receive an exemption all things considered. The issue of well-foundedness belongs to the first part of that two-stage process. If a belief is ill-founded, we might hold that it has no claim to be accommodated. Or, less severely, we might hold that it retains some claim to accommodation but one that is diminished by its ill-foundedness. If we allow an ill-founded claim to go forward to the second stage, it may of course be outweighed by competing considerations at that stage. But there is no reason to suppose that ill-founded beliefs, merely because they are ill-founded, are more likely than well-founded beliefs to be outweighed by stage 2 considerations. We cannot therefore rely on the second stage to do the dirty work for us. If a religious claim's ill-foundedness is a legitimate and relevant consideration, it is a consideration that we must confront and resolve at the first stage.

The question of well- or ill-foundedness should be distinguished from another sort of assessment: the screening of belief-based practices for moral acceptability. We might also adopt a stage 1 approach to that assessment. We may hold that a religious practice that involves, for example, injuring or killing children, or subjecting them to psychological trauma, should be ruled out of consideration at stage 1 simply because it is morally unacceptable. Alternatively, we might opt to keep that sort of issue out of the first stage and reposition it as a consideration that should come into play at stage 2. My preference is to follow Cécile Laborde and locate the issue of moral accept-ability at the first stage,[25] in part because we then more clearly distinguish between (a) belief-based practices that we exclude because they are morally unacceptable from (b) those that are intrinsically unobjectionable but which fail to qualify for accommodation simply because they are outweighed at stage 2 by the competing interests of others, public or private. My only concern here is to observe that, if we do locate the question of moral accept-ability at stage 1, we should not elide it with that of well- or ill-foundedness. It is no part of the thesis I mean to examine that the practices spawned by ill-founded beliefs are morally objectionable and should count for less, or for nothing, because they are morally objectionable. In some cases ill-founded beliefs may be morally objectionable, but so too may be some beliefs that are theologically well-founded. We have no reason to suppose, optimistically, that the issue of well-foundedness is co-extensive with that of moral accept-ability.

Article 9 of the ECHR does not make, but is consistent with, the two-stage distinction I have used above. Judges have sometimes commented on the issue of moral acceptability in a way that suggests a 'stage 1' approach. Lord Nicholls, for example, in commenting in *Williamson* on the 'modest, objective requirements' a belief needs to satisfy to receive the protection of Article 9, observed: 'The belief must be consistent with basic standards of human dignity or integrity. Manifestation of a religious belief, for instance, which involved subjecting others to torture or inhuman punishment would not qualify for protection.'[26] Lord Nicholls made equally clear in a much-cited comment that what I have presented as the issue of well-foundedness should be no concern of a court.

> Emphatically, it is not for the court to embark on an inquiry into the asserted belief and judge its 'validity' by some objective standard such as the source material upon which the claimant founds his belief or the orthodox teaching of the religion in question or the extent to which the claimant's belief conforms to or differs from the views of others professing the same religion. Freedom of religion protects the subjective belief of an individual. . . . Each individual is at

liberty to hold his own religious beliefs, however irrational or inconsistent they
may seem to some, however surprising.[27]

Lord Nicholls's words state a judicial orthodoxy that is widely shared, even
if not without exception, in liberal democratic jurisdictions. He did go on to
specify a number of 'threshold requirements' that a belief must satisfy if its
manifestation is to be protected, one of which I cited above: the belief must
be consistent with basic standards of human dignity or integrity. A belief had
also to relate to more than trivial matters and to possess 'an adequate degree
of seriousness and importance'.[28] It had to be belief 'on a fundamental problem'. The belief had to be 'coherent', a quality that may seem to open the
door to the issue of well-foundedness. However, Lord Nicholls set the bar for
coherence deliberately low: the belief had to be coherent 'in the sense of
being intelligible and capable of being understood'; though 'too much should
not be demanded in this regard' since belief in the supernatural 'is not always
susceptible to lucid exposition or, still less, rational justification'.[29] Lord
Nicholls's 'threshold requirements' therefore do little to qualify his general
affirmation that courts should make no attempt to assess the 'validity' of the
belief professed by a claimant.

THE MORAL RIGHT TO RELIGIOUS FREEDOM AND
THE RELEVANCE OF WELL-FOUNDEDNESS

Why then should we be so diffident about claims people make in respect of
their religious beliefs? Is this a matter of principle? Do we wrong someone if
we find their beliefs ill-founded and allow that finding to influence the decision on whether they should receive an exemption? Or is it simply a matter of
practicalities? Is it possible to assess the well-foundedness of someone's
religious belief and, if it is, would an assessment be so fraught with difficulty
that it is an exercise we should not undertake? Even if it is not wrong in
principle to subject someone's belief to critical scrutiny, it may be prudent to
handle religious claims *as if* such scrutiny were wrong. I consider principled
objection in this section and practical objection in the next.

The most obvious 'in principle' argument, in favour of allowing each
individual to be the arbiter of what his religion or belief requires, appeals to
freedom of religion or freedom of conscience. These freedoms, we might
insist, are rightly comprehensive in scope. They properly encompass not
merely the fundamentals of belief but every matter of detail as well. If B
embraces faith X and goes on to assert that X requires y and abstinence from
z, the religious liberty to which B has a right applies as much to his beliefs
about y and z as it does to his belief in X. Thus, if we judge B's belief about y
and z and find it wanting and then allow our judgement to weigh against B's

claim to an exemption, we violate B's moral right to freedom of religion or, more generally, to freedom of conscience. [30]

What is it about religious practices that makes them candidates for exemption? The answer that I and many others find most compelling is that those practices are the subjects of normative imperatives. Religious practices are candidates for exemption if and because they are 'ethically salient'. [31] But if ethical salience is the feature of religious practices that makes them *pro tanto* candidates for exemption, it follows that ethically salient non-religious practices can also be *pro tanto* candidates for exemption. We might then subsume freedom of religion, insofar as it pertains to exemptions, within freedom of conscience.

Subsuming religion under conscience is, however, hazardous in that the morality associated with 'conscience' is commonly subjective in ways that the morality encompassed by religious belief is not. I want to develop my response to the freedom of religion objection by commenting on that contrast between conscience and religious belief.

A morality focused on conscience is often subjective in two respects. First, for any particular individual, that individual's conscience is the wellspring and authoritative source of morality for that individual. The morality of conscience is 'subjective' in that the subject of that morality is also its source. Secondly, for any particular individual, right conduct consists in compliance with the dictates of his or her conscience. It could be that those dictates turn out to be the same for everyone, but then we shall be hard put to explain how it is that different individuals have different moral beliefs. The existence of moral disagreement frequently pushes thought on conscience in a different direction: the voice of conscience can speak differently to different individuals, but even so each individual should be governed by his or her own conscience. Thus right conduct for one individual will not always be identical with right conduct for another. The morality of conscience issues in a form of relativism. It is 'subjective' in that the morality governing people's conduct will vary, rightly, according to the subject of the morality.

If we think in those terms, it will always be wrong to sit in judgement on an individual's moral beliefs and find them wanting, since each individual will be, of necessity, the best authority on what is right for him or her. However, there is much that is implausible and unattractive about the subjectivism of conscience, even as a non-religious morality, and it is not easy to assimilate religious belief and its prescriptions to the model of conscientious subjectivism.

First, for most religious believers, their beliefs, including the moral dimensions of their beliefs, are not sourced entirely within themselves. Most commonly, their beliefs are grounded in external sources such as sacred texts, religious teachings, the doctrines of an organised religion, the shared faith of a religious community, and so on. Individual inspiration can figure importantly in some faiths alongside shared external sources of belief, but for the most part the individuals who register legal claims with courts do so as 'ordinary believers' rather than as self-professed prophets or visionaries claiming direct inspiration from God.

Secondly, religious belief does not normally share in the subjective relativism that can be associated with the idea of conscience. It does not suppose there are different 'truths' for different individuals or that different moral imperatives rightly govern the conduct of different individuals. It usually takes its truth-claims seriously as truth-claims and its prescriptions seriously as prescriptions which are general in application. Again that requires qualification. Not all faiths are, like Christianity and Islam, universalist in nature. The distinction between Jew and gentile is fundamental to Judaism, for instance, although Judaism still conceives its laws as objective givens. There are deep waters here which I shall not enter since I mean to observe only that, by and large, religious belief and its imperatives are conceived, neither by religions themselves nor by their individual adherents, as exercises in individual self-legislation. If courts are right not to subject claimants' religious beliefs to critical appraisal, the justification cannot be that correct religious belief for an individual consists only in what that individual supposes it to be. That cannot be the justification because it is at odds with the reality of religious belief as we know it. Moreover, if a court were to rely on that justification, it would take a stance on the nature of religious truth of precisely the sort that courts generally believe they should not.

Within established religions, there is manifestly scope for knowledge, expertise, informed judgement, interpretive acumen, and so on. Given the wealth of learning and scholarship to be found within the world's major religions, that point does not need labouring. By the same token, there is plenty of scope within established religions for ignorance, error, misconception, unwarranted inference, and the like. So we cannot dispose of the relevance of error or poor judgement simply by supposing that no religious judgement is or can be better than any other.

We should also notice what sort of 'judgement' is at stake here. Because it relates to religious practice and what believers believe they ought (not) to do, we might easily suppose that the relevant judgement must be a moral judgement. That, in turn, can bolster the sense that we should allow believers to comply with their beliefs, for to do otherwise would be to compel them to violate their religious consciences or moral integrity. But the judgement at issue is not a first-order moral judgement comparable to a decree of conscience. The matter to be judged is whether faith X requires or enjoins its adherents to do y or not to do z, and that is a judgement of fact or interpretation. Given that it is a judgement of that sort, it is not at all obvious why we should defer, routinely and equally, to the judgement of each individual. If we can assess the soundness of an individual's judgement, surely its soundness should matter. Indeed, it should matter to believers as conscientious adherents of their faith that they should be governed not by their own judgement, merely because it is their own, but by the best judgement. [32]

A possible riposte to this line of argument is that the badness of the bad of having to act contrary to one's beliefs is independent of whether one's beliefs are well- or ill-founded. That may be true of the painful psychological experience or disagreeable mental condition one is caused to undergo as a consequence of being unfree or less free to comply with one's beliefs, but we should be reluctant to psychologise the bad of being made to act contrary to one's beliefs so that it becomes no more than a disutile mental state. However, the more decisive answer to the alleged irrelevance of a belief's well- or ill-founded character is readily apparent when we recall that the claim at issue here is the believer's claim to be accommodated by *others*. Even if it were true that, for the believer, the quality of her beliefs made no difference to the badness of her lack of freedom to comply with them, it would not follow that the obligation of others to accommodate her beliefs should be similarly unaffected by their quality.

A second possible riposte is that we fail to treat believers with the respect to which they are entitled if we do other than take their beliefs at face value. Kantian thinking of that sort is frequently deployed on behalf of religious freedom, but its force for the kind of case I am considering is questionable. Recall that the issue here is not whether someone should be free to hold or manifest a belief. It is whether they should be able to manifest a belief in circumstances where the manifestation requires an exemption. It is implausible to hold that the respect we owe believers must extend routinely to enduring the costs of their error.

Do we disrespect an individual in merely assessing that individual's judgement on what her faith requires? Obviously not. It is part of the religious liberty to which we are entitled that we should be free to assess the religious beliefs of anyone and everyone. But, if it is not disrespectful merely to assess, it may still be disrespectful to allow our assessment of an individual's belief to affect our treatment of that individual.

Even that is doubtful. Consider the parallel case of culture. Religion and culture are overlapping and interconnected. Often a religious claim can be represented as a cultural claim, and accordingly the literature on exemptions flip-flops between the language of religion and that of culture. Kantian principles are also as commonly deployed in the context of cultural difference as they are in the context of religious difference. Yet the subjectivism so commonly invoked in relation to religion has little plausibility in the case of culture.

Suppose I claim a practice is a constituent of my culture. Whether it is indeed a part of my culture is a matter for objective assessment. If, for example, I register a claim of indirect racial discrimination because an employer's rule conflicts with a practice (e.g. a dress code) that is part of my ethnicity, a court has to establish whether the practice is indeed part of my ethnicity. That requires an objective judgement: is the practice a practice of an ethnic group of which I am a member? Ethnicities and cultures are of course internally diverse and not always easily defined, but that does not justify substituting the beliefs of the claimant for an objective judgement of what is the case. I cannot make a practice part of my culture merely by declaring it to be so. If, having investigated the matter, a court concludes that the practice does not belong to my ethnicity and for that reason dismisses my claim of indirect discrimination, it is hard to accept that the court's judgement constitutes an intolerable act of disrespect merely because it conflicts with and overrides my own claim about my culture. But, if that is true, it is hard to see why it should not be equally true in the case of religion. If a court were to make an objective judgement on whether my faith (e.g. my Roman Catholicism) requires that I should do *y* or not do *z* and reaches a conclusion different from mine and so dismisses my claim to exemption, why should that constitute an intolerable act of disrespect?

The sum of all this is that I am unpersuaded that, in laying claim to a religious exemption, people have a moral right that others should take at face value their own conception of what their faith demands. In principle, a court considering a claim to exemption would not behave wrongly (morally if not legally) if it assessed the well-foundedness of a religious claim and factored its assessment into the calculus of considerations that yielded its verdict.

COMPETENCE AND PRAGMATISM

If it would not be wrong in principle for courts to assess the well-foundedness of an individual's belief, why else should they refrain from that assessment? Judges often protest that they are not 'competent' to evaluate religious beliefs, but what is the competence they lack?

The term 'competence' is ambiguous. In one sense, to have competence is to have authority or jurisdiction. A court has competence over those matters that fall within the limits of its jurisdiction; if it exceeds those limits, it acts *ultra vires*. In a second and more prosaic sense, competence means possessing the knowledge and ability required to deal adequately with a matter. A court may lack competence on religious questions simply in that it lacks the requisite knowledge and ability.

If we take competence in the first sense, my concern is not with how far courts have, or do not have, competence to deal with religious questions, which is a complex matter. Rather, my question is, insofar as courts should not have jurisdiction over religious matters, why should they not? The answer might be that that jurisdiction would be inconsistent with individuals' moral right to religious liberty, but I have already cast doubt on the force of that claim for the limited type of case that is my concern.

Why else then might courts be rightly denied competence, in the first sense, over religious beliefs? The obvious answer is because they lack competence in the second sense. Courts do frequently protest that they are not equipped to rule on theological matters. In remarks that seemed to suggest that even Lord Nicholls's threshold requirements were too demanding, Lord Walker declared that a court is 'not equipped to weigh the cogency, seriousness and coherence of theological doctrines'.[33]

I want to consider quite how it is that a court's lack of competence provides reason for its refraining from judging the well-foundedness of particular religious beliefs. However, I want first to set aside an answer that might seem to be yielded by liberal political theory.

John Rawls famously distinguished between public and non-public reason, a distinction that has been used widely in liberal political theory.[34] Public reason is the reason that the citizens of a society can share and which they and public officials should draw upon in deliberating on and making public decisions. Rawls supposes they will do so in a society that is plural, that is, a society whose citizens subscribe to different and conflicting 'comprehensive doctrines', religious, philosophical or moral. Reason grounded in a comprehensive doctrine he describes as 'non-public' reason. It is non-public because it can function as reason only for those individuals who subscribe to the relevant comprehensive doctrine. That is why it is a form of reason inappropriate to individuals in their public role as citizens and officials. Citizens should justify the use of political power to one another by way of reasons they can share, which will not be reasons drawn from, for example, a religious faith possessed only by some.

Non-public reason is often said to be 'inaccessible' to those who do not subscribe to the comprehensive doctrine upon which it depends. However, the term 'inaccessible' is misleading. A non-public reason is inaccessible to citizens who reject the associated comprehensive doctrine only in that it cannot function as a reason for them. It need not be inaccessible epistemically; it need not, that is, be unintelligible or beyond the individuals' comprehension simply because they do not subscribe to its associated comprehensive doctrine. We do not have to believe *in* a religious faith to be able to understand it and what it requires or permits of its adherents. There are copious instances of people who are experts on a religious faith to which they do not themselves subscribe and whose competence far exceeds that of the faith's 'ordinary' adherents. So Rawls's distinction between public and non-public reason is not obviously relevant here. If judges are not competent to rule on religious beliefs, it is not because those beliefs belong to a realm of non-public reason which, in most instances, judges will not themselves inhabit and which, for that reason, will lie beyond their comprehension.

The simple point remains that judges are equipped to staff courts because of their legal knowledge and judicial skill, not because of their expertise in theology. Yet courts frequently have to deal with cases, such as complex financial or medical cases, to which an expertise is relevant that judges themselves do not have. They do not respond by simply washing their hands of such cases; rather, they call upon the advice of those who have the relevant expertise. So why should they not do so in religious cases? Of course, they frequently do.[35] That sometimes provokes the objection that, in relying upon experts, courts will privilege the views of elites over those of ordinary believers. But that complaint can be merely tautologous: if we want the best judgements, we must turn to those best qualified to make them, and the best qualified, simply in virtue of being so, will be an 'elite'.

That, however, is less than the full story. Those who complain about privileging elites often describe them as 'conservative'. They object to an elite not merely as a body of people distinguished by their expertise, but as one that is likely to be biased towards a particular version of the religion. If experts are drawn from an organised religion and are authorised to speak on behalf of the religion in its organised form, their expertise is especially likely to favour an established version of the religion. That has to be a concern. It is no part of my argument that courts should favour orthodoxy and discourage heresy. The cases with which I am concerned are not those in which some of a religion's adherents set out, deliberately and earnestly, to challenge their religion's orthodoxies but cases in which 'ordinary punters' get things wrong, either because of innocent error or misplaced zealotry. But it may not always be easy to distinguish the error of the ordinary punter from the 'error' of the heretic.

There is another way in which the advice of experts must be less than decisive. My interest is in someone, B, who is an adherent of religious faith X and who believes that X requires him to do y or not do z. The issue is not whether he rightly subscribes to X but whether he rightly believes that X requires him to do y or to refrain from z. Given the nature of that question, a court would naturally turn to the organised version of religion X, supposing one exists, for an answer. But what matters about the question is whether B is justified in his belief about y or z, such that he has a *pro tanto* claim to exemption. The question therefore is not whether an organised religion deems B justified, but whether B *is* justified. If a court allowed itself to be governed by the view of an organised religion merely as the view of that organised religion, it would substitute one subjectivity for another. The view of an organised religion, or of anyone else, can be no more than evidence. Ultimately, the court itself would have to answer the question, *is* the believer justified?

It could not therefore avoid that directly religious question. Is it incapable of answering it? It is not obvious that it is. With sufficient time, effort and expert advice, it could come up with a defensible answer. The advice of experts is likely to be crucial, but judges are used to receiving the assistance of experts without sacrificing their independence of judgement. Of course, religious faiths are internally diverse so that no one view may be identifiable as the single correct view, but the judgement required of a court could easily be adjusted to accommodate that fact. All the court need establish in order to find in B's favour is that B has reasonable ground for believing that X requires y or not-z, not that X's requiring y or not-z is the only conclusion at which a well-informed adherent of X could arrive.

That said, a court still has reason to shun the task of assessing a belief's well-foundedness. The task could be very demanding in time and effort. It could also be difficult to execute with confidence, given that religious faiths are so internally diverse and that religious belief is not subject to ordinary rules of evidence or even logic. Due account would also have to be taken of heterodox as well as orthodox belief. Perhaps above all, it would frequently be difficult for a court to come up with decisions that escaped the sort of contention and controversy that it would not want to attract. So, even if the sorts of case I cited earlier are not entirely beyond the competence of a court to resolve, it may be reasonable that judges, or the society upon whose behalf they act, should take the view that, all things considered, the cake is not worth the candle.[36]

Ultimately therefore, we may conclude that there is reason, all things considered, for courts to abstain from assessing the well-foundedness of the religious beliefs that claimants present as warrants for exemptions, but that reason is to be found not amongst the glistening peaks of high moral principle but in the humble foothills of pragmatism and prudence.[37]

A GROUP TEST OF WELL-FOUNDEDNESS?
THE CASE OF INDIRECT DISCRIMINATION

If courts are justifiably reluctant to assess the well- or ill-foundedness of people's religious beliefs, is there a more indirect device they might use which could act as a proxy test of well- or ill-foundedness? The most likely candidate is a form of group test: do most, or a significant number, of a faith's adherents subscribe to the belief at issue? If they do, that may serve as a rough indicator of the belief's well-foundedness; if they do not, we might set aside the belief as of questionable validity. That test may deliver rough justice, but perhaps rough justice is better than none.

Group tests figure in UK discrimination law, and we might turn to that law for assistance. The Equality Act 2010 exempts organised religions from law prohibiting discrimination in employment on grounds of gender, sexual orientation, gender reassignment, and marital status, but only insofar as that discrimination engages either the 'compliance principle' or the 'non-conflict principle'.[38] The compliance principle allows the discrimination insofar as it is necessary to comply with the religion's doctrines. The non-conflict principle allows the discrimination insofar as it is necessary to avoid conflict with 'the strongly held religious convictions of a significant number of the religion's followers'. The compliance principle is in harmony with the idea of well-foundedness. The non-conflict principle, by contrast, sets a group test but one designed to tap what we might describe as 'the living faith' of the religion's adherents. It might therefore model the sort of proxy test I have in mind.

Another group test that figures in discrimination law, and much more prominently, is that incorporated in the general definition of indirect discrimination. According to that definition, A (an employer or provider of goods or services) discriminates against B if A applies to B 'a provision, criterion or practice' (a PCP) that 'puts, or would put, persons with whom B shares the characteristic at a particular disadvantage when compared with persons with whom B does not share it' and which A cannot show to be 'a proportionate means of achieving a legitimate aim' (the PMLA test).[39] Thus, for B to have a *prima facie* claim to have suffered indirect religious discrimination, it is not enough that B himself is or would be disadvantaged by A's PCP; it has also to be the case that 'persons with whom B shares the characteristic [in this case, his religion or belief]' are or would be disadvantaged by it. That requirement is often described as a test of 'group disadvantage'.

Indirect discrimination law requires a form of exemption. If A's PCP disadvantages or would disadvantage B and those who share the relevant characteristic with B, and A's PCP does not pass the PMLA test, she is required not to apply the PCP to B. She is not required to abandon her PCP; she is required only to exempt B from it. Thus the group test incorporated in indirect discrimination law is a (partial) test of who is entitled to receive an exemption.

That exemption is of just the sort to which a belief's well- or ill-foundedness might be deemed relevant and for which a test of well- or ill-foundedness would be a desideratum. No group test figures in direct discrimination law, but well- or ill-foundedness is not normally relevant to direct discrimination. B may adhere to a manifestly ill-founded belief, but that does not justify A's discriminating directly against him in deciding whether she should employ or promote him (unless the belief was genuinely relevant to B's suitability for the post, in which case it would be relevant irrespective of whether it were well- or ill-founded). But the well- or ill-foundedness of B's belief is not similarly irrelevant to the justifiability of indirect discrimination. Suppose that A has to exempt B from her PCP in order to accommodate B's belief-based practice and incurs costs and inconvenience in so doing. If we discover that the belief upon which B's practice is based is ill-founded, that discovery would seem to undermine the case for imposing upon A the costs and inconvenience of accommodating B.

How far then might we look to a group test similar to that which figures in the definition of indirect discrimination to deal with the issue I have raised in this chapter? That test figures in the definition of indirect discrimination as it applies to all characteristics protected by the Equality Act 2010, not only to 'religion or belief'. Equivalent tests which figured in earlier discrimination legislation were also not limited to religious discrimination. Thus, the test was not put in place to deal with issues specific to religion or belief. Even so, we might ask how well a test of that sort serves the religious case.

An issue the test raises in the case of religion or belief is who constitutes the relevant group. Who are 'the persons with whom B shares the characteristic'? Are they, for example, those who share with B (i) the general faith to which he subscribes (e.g. Christianity or Islam), or (ii) the particular variant of that faith (e.g. Roman Catholicism or Sufism), or (iii) the specific belief that is at issue in B's case (e.g. Sabbatarianism or a belief relating to forms of dress)? The best-known UK discrimination case to have turned on that issue is *Eweida*.[40] Nadia Eweida was a Coptic Christian employed by British Airways (BA) who wanted to wear a silver cross visibly, contrary to BA's uniform policy. The issue that became central to her case was whether BA's PCP (its uniform policy) disadvantaged not only her but also persons with whom she shared her religion or belief. Those hearing her case deemed the relevant group to be Christians at large, which made it difficult for Eweida to claim convincingly that she had suffered indirect discrimination, since Christians in general did not share her belief that they should wear a cross visibly. Had the relevant group been defined more narrowly, the outcome could have been very different.[41] The relevant point illustrated by *Eweida* is that, if we use a group test as a proxy for well-foundedness, the result it yields could be merely an artefact of the particular group we use.

That potential for arbitrariness is exacerbated by a further consideration. The definition of the group relevant to indirect discrimination can affect the burden of justification required to establish the proportionality of the PCP at issue. That possibility is illustrated by *Mba*. Celestina Mba was a Christian Sabbatarian who claimed indirect religious discrimination in respect of her employer's requirement that she should sometimes work on Sundays.[42] In reaching its judgement on her case, the EAT observed,

> the weight to be given to the degree of interference with religious belief of a certain kind will inevitably differ depending upon the numbers of believers who will be affected by the particular PCP concerned. . . . To illustrate, if a PCP affected virtually every Christian to a given extent, it would have a greater discriminatory impact than if the same measure affected only a much smaller number of Christians to that extent. The greater the discriminatory

impact on the group as a whole, the more that has objectively to be shown by the employer to demonstrate that the PCP is necessary, and proportionate. [43]

Thus a PCP that disadvantaged only Sabbatarians required less justification than one that disadvantaged Christians in general. But that inference was entirely an artefact of identifying Christianity rather than Christian Sabbatarianism as the 'religion or belief' that Mrs Mba shared with others and as definitive of the group that was the potential object of disadvantage. Hence, if we follow the model of discrimination law, the make-up of the group that we adopt for our group test can affect not only whether we find a claim to be well-founded but also how much the claim should count for if it is well-founded.

Aside from the issue of which group is the right group for a group test, the most pressing question is how well a group test is likely to perform as a proxy test of well- or ill-foundedness. The answer has to be, very imperfectly. A sizeable group of individuals may believe that a practice is required by their faith and yet still have poor reason for doing so. Perhaps more commonly, a practice may be limited to a small minority within a faith but still have a plausible claim to be well-founded. Arguably that was true of Eweida's practice. As I noted above, the requirement that 'persons with whom B shares the characteristic' should be disadvantaged along with B himself is general to the characteristics protected by the Equality Act 2010 rather than particular to religion or belief. It aims to test the group character of the disadvantage at issue. It is therefore little more than a happy accident if, in the case of religion or belief, it serves as a proxy test of a belief's well-foundedness.

In *Eweida* attention was drawn to the fact that visibly wearing a cross was not a *mandatory requirement* of Christianity; Eweida wore the cross as a personal expression of her faith, as she herself accepted. [44] In *Mba*, the Employment Tribunal observed that Mrs Mba's 'belief that Sunday should be a day of rest and worship upon which no paid employment was undertaken, whilst deeply held, is not a *core component* of the Christian faith'. [45] In neither case, however, was comment on that alleged feature of the claimant's practice intended to cast doubt on its doctrinal soundness; nor could any such doubt have been justifiably inferred from the practice's minority status. The practice's non-mandatory or non-core character was relevant simply as an indicator of the limited extent of group-disadvantage that could be ascribed to the employer's PCP. [46]

CONCLUSION

It is highly unlikely therefore that a group test will serve as a satisfactory proxy for a test of well-foundedness. If we are to test for well-foundedness, we have to do so directly. I have argued that it is not in principle wrong to make a belief's well- or ill-foundedness a consideration in assessing the believer's claim to exemption. A belief has less of a claim, and arguably no claim, to exemption if it is ill-founded. It would be strange if that were untrue. It would also be strange if a defender of the claims of religious belief protested that the issue could not arise because no religious belief could ever be more or less well-founded than any other. If there is reason to abstain from screening beliefs for their well-foundedness, it is neither moral nor epistemic but pragmatic in nature. That conclusion implies that religious belief will sometimes receive more than its due; beliefs will sometimes enjoy exemptions to which in principle their ill-foundedness gives them no right, but that will be a moral loophole that pragmatism requires us to tolerate.

NOTES

I am very grateful to John Adenitire for his helpful comment and advice on earlier drafts of this chapter.

1. Camilla Turner, 'Catholic School Prompts Uniform Row by Banning Muslim Girl from Wearing a Headscarf' (*The Telegraph*, 23 January 2017) at www.telegraph.co.uk/education/2017/01/23/catholic-school-prompts-uniform-row-banning-muslim-girl-wearing (accessed 13 December 2019).

2. *Saggers v. British Railways Board* [1977] IRLR 266.

3. *Saggers v. British Railways Board* [1978] IRLR 436.

4. Ibid., para. 6.

5. *Syndicat Northcrest v. Amselem* [2004] 2 SCR 551, 2004 SCC 47.

6. I put 'dwell' in scare quotes because, in view of the climate of Montreal, the extent to which practising Jews were required to live in a succah throughout the nine-day festival was limited; ibid., para. 113.

7. Ibid., quoted para. 21.

8. Ibid., paras 22–24, 118.

9. Ibid., paras 28–30, 125.

10. Ibid., paras 40–42.

11. Ibid., para. 43.

12. Ibid., para. 56. For Iacobucci J's expansive comment on the 'intensely personal' nature of religious belief, see paras 38–56, 67–69.

13. A fourth judge also dissented but from the majority's view on justification, not from their interpretation of freedom of religion.

14. Ibid., para. 135.

15. Ibid., paras 135, 162.

16. *Arrowsmith v. United Kingdom* (1978) 3 EHRR 218.

17. *R (Williamson) v. Secretary of State for Education and Employment* [2005] UKHL 15, paras 30–35, 62–64, 78.

18. *R (Playfoot) (A Minor) v. Governing Body of Millais School* [2007] EWHC 1698, paras 20–23.

19. In a case of this sort, a court may be more inclined to invoke the 'specific situation' rule: the employees freely chose to accept employment at the supermarket and they retained the option of resigning from it; for that reason their Article 9 rights had not been interfered with. Use of that rule has, however, recently been called into question: *Eweida and Ors v. United Kingdom* (2013) 57 EHRR 8, para. 83.

20. Rex Ahdar and Ian Leigh, *Religious Freedom in the Liberal State*, 2nd edition (Oxford: Oxford University Press, 2013), 166–69; Carolyn Evans, *Freedom of Religion under the European Convention on Human Rights* (Oxford: Oxford University Press, 2001), 120–27. Russell Sandberg argues that, in determining whether a belief should receive protection, use of the manifestation/motivation filter, along with other sorts of filter, should be minimised and the focus should shift to the question of justification under Article 9 (2); in Russell Sandberg, *Law and Religion* (Cambridge: Cambridge University Press, 2011), 83–87, 94, 98–99.

21. I adopt the terms 'severe' and 'direct' from Cécile Laborde, *Liberalism's Religion* (Cambridge, MA: Harvard University Press), 221–25.

22. See, for example, the remarks of Iacobucci J. in *Syndicat Northcrest v. Amselem* [2004] 2 SCR 551, paras 47–50, 67–68.

23. Abner S. Greene, 'Three Theories of Religious Equality . . . and of Exemptions', *Texas Law Review* 87 (2009): 963–1007, at 999–1000.

24. For analysis and discussion of the distinctions, see P. Billingham, 'How Should Claims for Religious Exemptions be Weighed?' *Oxford Journal of Law and Religion* 6 (2017): 1–23. Billingham argues for a subjective use of the distinctions: the relevant consideration should be how obligatory or how central a religious practice is to the individual claimant, not how it ranks within the official faith to which the claimant subscribes, although he allows that a court may draw on a practice's importance within an official faith for evidence of its being similarly important for an individual claimant; ibid., 9–13. For related discussions, see Kent Greenawalt, *Religion and the Constitution, Vol. I: Free Exercise and Fairness* (Princeton, NJ: Princeton University Press, 2006), 202–14; Laborde, *Liberalism's Religion*, 222–25; and Ernest Lim, 'Religious Exemptions in England', *Oxford Journal of Law and Religion* 3 (2014): 440–61, at 449–57.

25. Laborde, *Liberalism's Religion*, 207–9.

26. *R (Williamson) v. Secretary of State for Education and Employment* [2005] UKHL 15, para. 23. Understood according to a 'stage 1' approach, beliefs that were morally unacceptable in ways that Lord Nicholls describes would not be protected by Article 9 (1) from interference. Understood according to a 'stage 2' approach, they would be protected by Article 9 (1), but interference would be justified by considerations itemised in Article 9 (2), especially 'protection of the rights and freedoms of others'.

27. Ibid., para. 22.

28. The ECtHR had previously observed that the terms 'conviction' and 'belief' as they occurred in the ECHR denoted 'views that attain a certain level of cogency, seriousness, cohesion and importance'; *Campbell and Cosans v. the UK* (1982) 4 EHRR 293, para. 36.

29. Ibid., para. 23. For argument that, even so, Lord Nicholls's criteria risk filtering out too much, see Ahdar and Leigh, *Religious Freedom*, 154–55.

30. It is fair to say, I think, that this 'subjectivism' is the prevalent position amongst contemporary moral and political philosophers. For examples, see Billingham, 'How Should Claims for Religious Exemptions be Weighed?'; Paul Bou-Habib, 'A Theory of Religious Accommodation', *Journal of Applied Philosophy* 23 (2006): 109–23; Laborde, *Liberalism's Religion*, 203–7, 222–25; Jocelyn MacLure and Charles Taylor, *Secularism and Freedom of Conscience* (Cambridge, MA: Harvard University Press, 2011); and Martha Nussbaum, *Liberty of Conscience: In Defense of America's Tradition of Religious Liberty* (New York: Basic Books, 2008). For a notable exception to the subjectivist orthodoxy, see Avigail Eisenberg, 'What Is Wrong with a Liberal Assessment of Religious Authenticity?', in *Authenticity, Autonomy and Multiculturalism*, ed. G. B. Levey, 145–62 (New York: Routledge, 2015).

31. Laborde, *Liberalism's Religion*, 197–203. See also Brian Leiter, *Why Tolerate Religion?* (Princeton, NJ: Princeton University Press, 2013); MacLure and Taylor, *Secularism and Freedom of Conscience*; and Chapter 7 of this volume.

32. Cf. Richard J Arneson, 'Against Freedom of Conscience', *San Diego Law Review* 47 (2010): 1015–40, at 1036.

33. *R (Williamson) v. Secretary of State for Education and Employment* [2005] UKHL 15, para. 60.

34. John Rawls, *Justice as Fairness: A Restatement* (Cambridge, MA: Harvard University Press, 2001), 89–94.

35. A good example is *R (Ghai) v. Newcastle City Council* [2009] EWHC 978 (Admin)—a case concerning Mr Ghai's wish, as a Hindu, to be cremated by open pyre; see paras 21–45, 54–60. Having heard at length from two expert witnesses, Mr Justice Cranston commented, 'Notwithstanding all this, the starting point for me is the claimant's genuine belief, held in good faith, that he must be cremated on an open air pyre and the fact . . . that this is a manifestation of his religious belief' (para. 100). Later in the judgment he added, 'It is beside the point that typically Hindus in this country do not share that belief' (para. 160).

36. David Golemboski argues in a similarly practical mode that, even if judges were epistemically capable of assessing religious beliefs, they should refrain from doing so (i) because their judgments would be likely to reflect cognitive and political biases and (ii) because the controversial nature of their decisions would be liable to undermine public confidence in the judiciary. See D. Golemboski, 'Judicial Evaluation of Religious Belief and the Accessibility Requirement in Public Reason', *Law and Philosophy* 35 (2016): 435–60, at 451–55.

37. Administrative ease does not always argue for conceiving religious belief subjectively rather than objectively. In *Saggers*, for example, the British Railways Board suggested that, in deciding who should be exempt from obligatory trade union membership, 'simplification would be achieved if their review of the matter could be confined to an examination of the accepted creed of the body to which the employee belongs, so that they would have to do no more than consider whether the rejection of trade union membership was an integral part of that creed or not'; [1977] IRLR 268, para. 10.

38. Equality Act 2010, schedule 9, Pt 1, para. 2. 'Organisations relating to religion or belief' are also permitted to discriminate on grounds of sexual orientation in relation to their membership and some of their activities but, again, only insofar as that discrimination meets the compliance principle or the non-conflict principle; schedule 23, para. 2.

39. Ibid., Pt 2, Ch. 1, para. 19.

40. *Eweida v. British Airways* [2008] UKEAT/0123/08/LA; [2010] EWCA Civ 80.

41. There was also, however, a question of whether her strong desire to wear the cross was a manifestation of religious belief rather than only a belief-based preference; *Eweida v. British Airways* [2008] UKEAT/0123/08/LA, paras 35, 47–49. The ECtHR subsequently ruled that Eweida's wearing the cross was a manifestation of her religious belief, which was therefore protected by Article 9 of the ECHR; *Eweida and Ors v. United Kingdom* (2013) 57 EHRR 8, para. 89.

42. *Mba v. The Mayor and Burgesses of the London Borough of Merton* [2012] UKEAT/0332/12/SM; [2013] EWCA Civ 1562.

43. [2012] UKEAT/0332/12/SM, para. 46. The Court of Appeal took a more complex view of this issue; [2013] EWCA Civ 1562, especially paras 17–19, 30–42. The problem of taking account of 'discriminatory impact' arises from adopting a weighing or balancing approach to proportionality. I question that approach in Chapter 6.

44. [2008] UKEAT/0123/08/LA, paras 1, 15; [2010] EWCA Civ 80, paras 8, 9, 34, 37.

45. [2013] EWCA Civ 1562, para. 8 (my emphasis).

46. For *Eweida*, see [2008] UKEAT/0123/08/LA, paras 14–16; [2010] EWCA Civ 80, paras 28–29. For *Mba*, see [2012] UKEAT/0332/12/SM, paras 42–49; [2013] EWCA Civ 1562, paras 14–24, 30–33, 39. For further comment on these cases, see Lucy Vickers, 'Conscientious Exemptions in Employment: Is a Duty of Reasonable Accommodation the Answer?', in *Religious Beliefs and Conscientious Exemptions in a Liberal State*, ed. John Adenitire, 185–204 (Oxford: Hart, 2019).

Chapter Ten

Blasphemy, Offensiveness and Law

Of all the freedoms cherished by liberals, perhaps none is more cherished than freedom of expression. Most would accept that some limits should be placed upon that freedom, but what sort of limits those should be and how far they should extend are matters of controversy. That controversy is all the greater when the purpose for which free expression is limited is itself one that is as potentially compromising to liberalism as the prevention of offence to people's feelings. In this chapter I shall examine the relative claims of free expression and offended feelings by focusing on a subject that juxtaposes the two particularly clearly: blasphemy.

By the second half of the twentieth century one might reasonably have supposed that blasphemy, as a legal offence, was of interest to no one but historians. The Blasphemy Act, dating from the reign of William III, was declared obsolete and repealed by the Criminal Law Act of 1967. Blasphemy remained an offence at common law, but no prosecution for blasphemy had been brought for half a century, and for all practical purposes the offence seemed dead. Indeed, during the 1940s Lord Denning described the law of blasphemy as a 'dead letter'.[1] However, two subsequent cases exposed the danger of declaring common law offences moribund before they had been abolished by Parliament, and reopened the issue of whether blasphemy should be a legal offence.

In 1976 a Danish film director, Jens Thorsen, planned to come to Britain to make a film entitled *The Love Life of Jesus Christ*. By all accounts, including those of Mr Thorsen, the film was to be more than mildly porno-graphic. The venture provoked a public outcry, and some people, including the Archbishop of Canterbury, suggested that, if the film were made, the law of blasphemy should be used to prevent its screening.[2] Thorsen's film was never put to the test since, after many months of legal argument about the rights of EEC nationals, he was refused entry into Britain 'on the grounds that his exclusion was conducive to the public good'.[3] Production of his film was banned or otherwise impeded in a number of other countries, including France, Sweden, Italy, Israel and Thorsen's native Denmark.

A few months later *Gay News* and its editor, Denis Lemon, found themselves charged with having 'unlawfully and wickedly published . . . a blasphemous libel concerning the Christian religion, namely an obscene poem and illustration vilifying Christ in His life and in His crucifixion'.[4] The offending poem, entitled 'The Love that Dares to Speak Its Name', was by James Kirkup. It recounted the homosexual fantasies of a Roman centurion as he removed the body of Christ from the cross and 'purported to describe in explicit detail acts of sodomy and fellatio with the body of Christ immediately after His death and ascribed to Him during His lifetime promiscuous homosexual practices with the Apostles and other men'.[5] The prosecution and the defence differed in their appraisals of the poem. To the prosecution it seemed 'so vile that it would be hard for even the most perverted imagination to conjure up anything worse'. The defence, however, insisted that the poem was essentially an account of how one man, an outcast and a homosexual, found Christian love and salvation. By a majority of ten to two the jury found the defendants guilty. Both defendants appealed against their conviction, chiefly on the ground that the judge had ruled that the prosecution had to prove only that the defendants had intended to publish and not that they had intended to blaspheme. Their appeal was dismissed by both the Court of Appeal[6] and the House of Lords.[7]

Reaction to the case was predictably divided. Some thought the conviction an intolerable restriction upon the freedom of expression and protested that a law of blasphemy was utterly anachronistic in contemporary, largely secular, Britain. Shortly after the trial, Lord Willis tried (unsuccessfully) to secure the enactment of a bill abolishing the offence of blasphemy. Others such as Mrs Mary Whitehouse, who had brought the prosecution, rejoiced that a limit had been set. Judge King-Hamilton, who presided at the trial, found Kirkup's poem 'quite appalling' and expressed the hope that the jury's verdict indicated that public opinion was moving back 'to a healthier climate'. The whole question of whether blasphemy should remain a legal offence was subsequently reviewed by the Law Commission; it recommended abolition.[8] Successive governments opted to ignore that recommendation, and blasphemy remained a common law offence until 2008.

Not all of those who accepted that law should place some limits on blasphemy were happy with the law as it stood. The law protected Christianity only. Indeed, there was some authority for holding that it protected only the faith of the established church and that other varieties of Christianity were protected only insofar as they shared doctrines in common with Anglicanism.[9] In view of the diversity of religious beliefs present in British society, it seemed inequitable that the state should give a privileged position to one of them. Consequently, for many people blasphemy law would become acceptable only if the protection it gave to Christianity was extended to other religions.[10] Such a reform would have brought its own problems. How would we decide what was to count as a religion? Should all religions receive legal protection irrespective of the size of their world or British followings? Those questions begged a more fundamental question: should *any* religion receive protection?

JUSTIFYING A LAW OF BLASPHEMY

Why might blasphemy be considered a fit subject for law? The answer which I shall examine in some detail is that law should protect people from that which offends their religious sensibilities. However, a number of other answers have been given, and I shall begin by reviewing them briefly.

In ordinary usage a blasphemy is a contemptuous or irreverent utterance concerning the Deity. In the past, the simple fact that such utterances wronged God or Christ was often regarded as sufficient reason for their criminality. Sometimes people were less concerned with the wrongs themselves than with their possible divine consequences; a community which harboured blasphemers might suffer the wrath of God.[11] As an offence at common law, blasphemy has had a wider meaning than in ordinary usage and for long remained undifferentiated from expressions of unorthodox religious opinion in general.[12] Consequently, the object of legal protection has sometimes been the doctrines and institutions of the established faith rather than the persons of God or Christ. Nowadays, neither protection of the Deity nor the maintenance of the established faith is likely to be urged in defence of a law of blasphemy, and so there would be little point in subjecting either to criticism. However, even in the past, the common law's concern with blasphemy was not primarily religious.

Blasphemy was first declared an offence at common law in 1676 when John Taylor was tried at the Court of King's Bench for saying, amongst other things, that Christ was a 'bastard' and a 'whoremaster' and that 'religion was a cheat'.[13] In sentencing Taylor, Sir Matthew Hale explained that 'such kind of wicked blasphemous words were not only an offence to God and religion, but a crime against the laws, State and government' and therefore punishable in a temporal court. 'For to say religion is a cheat, is to dissolve all those obligations whereby the civil societies are preserved, and that Christianity is parcel of the laws of England; and therefore to reproach the Christian religion is to speak in subversion of the law.'[14] Hale's reasoning appears to have been that without religion there could be no foundation for any obligation including the obligation to obey the state and its laws; consequently the state, in protecting religion, was simply protecting its own foundation. This view of blasphemy as a form of sedition—a view which was regularly reaffirmed by judges throughout the eighteenth and the early nineteenth centuries [15] —is again unlikely to seem plausible nowadays. However, two related arguments about the way blasphemy impinges upon the fabric of society, which were often voiced in the past, would still find support today. One points to the deleterious effect of blasphemy on morality in general. The other is concerned with the immediate threat that blasphemy might pose to public order.

It has often been suggested that a society's religion is the essential basis of its morality and that the law should protect its religion because it should protect its morality; that is why English law protects Christianity. [16] This argument is closely akin to Lord Devlin's justification for the enforcement of morals. Indeed, Devlin himself states that 'without the support of the Churches the moral order, which has its origin in and takes its strength from Christian beliefs, would collapse', that 'no society has yet solved the problem of how to teach morality without religion', and that 'without the help of Christian teaching the law will fail'. [17] In the debate on Lord Willis's bill seeking to abolish the offence of blasphemy, several speakers defended the existing law in these terms. It was said that the law of blasphemy protected 'deeply rooted values in society' and that its removal would endanger 'Christian standards of conduct', 'erode the values which support and enhance our society' and 'reduce our civilization to becoming the "heir of nebulosity," where just anything goes'. [18]

Whether the law should act as the custodian of public morals is, of course, a deeply controversial issue. However, the justification of a blasphemy law in these terms involves much more than the argument about the enforcement of morals. It has to defend legal restrictions upon expression in religious matters such that religious faith, and therefore moral beliefs, will be sustained. Considerable doubts may be raised about the alleged necessity of religion to morality, whether that necessity is conceived either logically or empirically. But, even if we overlook these, such a defence would still be very difficult to maintain. First, it would provide no rationale for restricting criminality to abusive and offensive attacks upon religion. Such attacks are much less likely to shake the beliefs of the faithful than sober and well-reasoned critiques. Yet the suppression of the latter would generally be regarded as an intolerable restriction upon freedom of inquiry. Secondly, short of Draconian measures, it seems unlikely that the law could have much impact one way or the other upon the level of religiosity in Britain. Thirdly, the protection of religion for moral purposes ceases to be feasible in a multi-religious society. We have already touched upon the inequity involved in the state's giving a privileged position to one religion. Yet, if it tried to avoid that inequity by protecting all religions, it would be supporting contradictory beliefs and beliefs which had different moral consequences. It might be suggested that, for moral purposes, any religion is better than none, that differences in religious ethics are too slight to be troublesome, and that therefore the state could and should support all religions indifferently. However, since, at most, only one religion can be true, this would require the state knowingly to foster falsehoods because they were socially useful. Few friends of religion would be likely to embrace so Machiavellian an argument. (This objection requires qualification to the extent that different religions may share common beliefs, e.g. Christianity and Judaism. However, if the state's protection is to be extended to all religions, it would be difficult to find a common core of belief of sufficient substance to be worth protecting, even if one took a fairly strict view of what constituted a 'religion'.) The defence of blasphemy law in terms of its moral utility therefore confronts large difficulties, and it is perhaps symptomatic of these that, while Lord Devlin accepts the importance of religion to morality and the importance of both to law, he himself shows no sign of drawing the conclusion that law should be used to maintain religious belief.

The argument that the law should concern itself with blasphemy because it may provoke a breach of the peace is likely to receive much wider appeal. The maintenance of public order is one of the most widely accepted reasons for limiting freedom of expression; it is accepted, for example, by J. S. Mill[19] and by John Rawls.[20] However, if the law should concern itself with utterances concerning religion only because and to the extent that they may provoke breaches of the peace, there would seem little justification for a law concerning itself especially with blasphemy. Indeed, those who sought to abolish the law of blasphemy were no less concerned about threats to public order than their opponents, but argued that such threats were adequately provided for by the law of public order.[21] Thus, while the defence of a blasphemy law in terms of its moral utility claims too much, appeals to public order prove too little.

Much the most plausible defence of a blasphemy law nowadays is that it is necessary to protect religious believers from suffering offence to their feelings. Indeed, the common law of blasphemy evolved very much in terms of this objective. Prosecutions for blasphemy were brought generally, though not invariably, for attacks upon Christianity that contained an element of contumely or ridicule. However, before the middle of the nineteenth century this was not because the primary concern of the law was to protect Christians from what they found offensive. While judges often made a distinction between reasoned argument and scurrilous attack, they also insisted that Christianity was part of the law of the land and that the law prevented attempts to undermine it. Given this conception of the law, it is hard to see why the distinction between reasoned argument and scurrilous attack should have been thought relevant; indeed, judges often had difficulty in maintaining the two simultaneously.[22] No doubt they made the distinction partly because they were loath to be seen suppressing *bona fide* argument and inquiry and partly because they were primarily concerned with the social consequences of attacks upon Christianity, and popularized attacks which reached 'the lower orders' were thought more serious threats to the morality and stability of society than academic treatises. [23]

The orientation of the law was gradually changed until, in 1883, Lord Coleridge ruled that, 'If the decencies of controversy are observed, even the fundamentals of religion may be attacked without the writer being guilty of blasphemy.' [24] What was novel in Coleridge's judgement was not his willing-ness to take account of the character of an attack upon Christianity, but his willingness to do so in such a way that the object of the legal protection became Christian believers rather than Christian belief. Writings which as-persed Christian doctrine were not to be held blasphemous for that reason alone; the relevant question according to Coleridge was 'whether they are not calculated and intended to insult the feelings and the deepest religious con-victions of the great majority of the persons amongst whom we live; and if so they are not to be tolerated any more than any other nuisance is tolerated. We must not do things that are outrages to the general feeling of propriety among the persons amongst whom we live.' [25] Some, including James Fitzjames Stephen, questioned whether this was a correct statement of the law. [26] How-ever, Coleridge's interpretation of the law was followed in subsequent blas-phemy cases, and in 1917 it received the approval of the House of Lords. [27]

Thus it became clearly established that attacks upon God, Christ or Chris-tianity were blasphemous only if they insulted, offended or vilified and that it was the publication of something of an offensive nature or in terms offensive to Christianity that constituted the crime of blasphemous libel. [28] Most propo-nents of a blasphemy law, including Mrs Whitehouse, [29] seemed content to rest their case upon the offence that blasphemy caused the faithful. More-over, a law thus conceived could easily extend its protection to religions other than Christianity since, in protecting religious believers from offence, it was not implicitly committed to the truth of their beliefs and could therefore protect more than one kind of believer without inconsistency. Indeed, if the purpose of the law is to prevent offence to feelings, it is slightly misleading to describe it as a law of 'blasphemy', although, for ease of expression, I shall continue to do so.

OFFENDED SENSIBILITIES AND LEGAL PROHIBITIONS

Should law protect people from suffering offence [30] to their religious feel-ings? There is no simple way of answering that question. In part it resolves into the wider question of whether law should protect people from suffering offence of any kind, and again there is no easy or obvious way of settling this issue. This may seem the sort of question in which one should invoke Mill's principle that coercion should be used 'only to prevent harm to others'.[31] Yet the ambiguities and vagueness of 'harm' render the principle of little service. In ordinary usage, 'harm' implies some enduring injury to one's person or damage to one's property and would therefore normally stop short of offence. Yet if, with Feinberg, we define harm as 'the invasion of an interest'[32] or, with Lucas, as 'something that most people do not want, and which we think they are right not to want',[33] then being offended would constitute being harmed.

For a utilitarian such as Mill, the relevant consideration would seem to be that being offended involves enduring an experience that one would choose not to endure.[34] Offence is not always painful in the ordinary sense. As Feinberg has noted, being offended encompasses 'a large miscellany of mental states that have little in common except that they are unpleasant, uncomfortable or disliked'.[35] Sometimes being offended is akin to being physically hurt; indeed, offence is often characterized as an 'assault' upon the feelings.[36] Sometimes, however, it is less a matter of experiencing pain than of experiencing revulsion or embarrassment. However, the fact that such states are unpleasant and disliked is sufficient to make them matters of disutility. (Consider the analogous case of being humiliated.) Bentham, who invariably had the courage of his utilitarian convictions, was certainly willing to take account of such 'mental injuries' even when they arose in connection with religious belief.[37]

Whether legal account should be taken of the offence caused by sexual conduct or by racial or religious remarks is clearly a matter of controversy. Yet there are some types of offence which are subject to relatively little controversy. Consider the offence caused by noises, smells or (non-human) sights. Most of us would accept that people are understandably offended by and reasonably take exception to the noise generated by low-flying aircraft or sulphurous smells emanating from a chemical factory. Sights perhaps allow more room for argument, but that people can feel no less strongly about them is demonstrated by the antipathy to 'litterbugs' and by the furore that occurs each time there is a proposal to develop an open cast mine in a beautiful valley. Such noises, smells and sights might be accompanied by other ill-effects. Aircraft noise might impair people's capacity to work, the gases given off by a chemical factory might damage health, and the development of a mine might cause a drop in house prices. But even if these additional harms were absent, we would still feel it right to take account of the simple annoyance caused by these unwanted intrusions into people's lives. To say that they are unwanted is not, of course, to say that they are unwarranted. People are often required to put up with such annoyances because of the social value of the activities of which they are by-products. I am suggesting only that, when making social policy or drafting legislation, we would not feel justified in totally neglecting these nuisances on the ground that they were 'merely offensive'.

It might be objected that offence of this kind is of a quite different order from that caused by indecency, insult or blasphemy, and clearly there are differences between the two sorts of offence. Yet it is difficult to see how any of these differences could provide one with a principled ground for taking cognizance of one sort of offence and ignoring the other. It might be suggested that there is likely to be greater agreement on what constitutes an offensive noise or odour than on what constitutes offensive conduct. But, if unanimity is our concern, there may be many instances in which conduct or speech is also unanimously considered offensive; indeed, in a society with a shared culture and a shared language, this is almost bound to be true. Claims that the offence caused by noises and smells is more intense or less avoidable than other sorts of offence are also claims of a purely contingent kind and therefore may or may not hold true in particular cases. Another difference, it might be alleged, is that noises and smells make direct assault upon the senses, whereas offence arising from conduct or speech usually involves an element of reflection even though that reflection may have become encapsulated in an habitual response. Accordingly, it might also be suggested that disagreeable noises or obnoxious smells, unlike indecencies or obscenities, do not depend upon the acceptance of cultural norms for their unpleasant effect. Whether noises or smells are always found disagreeable in an unreflective or non-cultural manner is certainly open to question. However, even if we ignore doubts of this kind, it is not clear why reflectiveness or cultural relativity should be thought material to whether one should take account of offence. Bentham once wrote that 'it matters not through what sense the wound passes to the mind, if the mind is wounded'.[38] The judgemental or non-judgemental character of offence seems just as irrelevant. Cultural relativity might be thought to raise more thorny issues. However, given that we are concerned here not with enforcing what is, as a matter of morality, right but with preventing what is, as a matter of fact, offensive, there is no reason why the dependence of offence upon cultural norms should be thought especially significant or problematic. Offence is no less real for its dependence upon values and tastes peculiar to a particular culture or system of belief.

In fact, many of the leading voices of liberalism have advocated the legal proscription of offensive conduct. Thus the Wolfenden Report on the law relating to homosexuality and prostitution declared it a quite proper function of the law 'to protect the citizen from what is offensive'.[39] Lord Devlin's foremost opponent, H. L. A. Hart, shares this view.[40] Indeed, Hart goes so far as to advance the unlikely argument that 'the law against bigamy should be accepted as an attempt to protect religious feelings from offence by a public act desecrating the [marriage] ceremony'.[41] Mill too, despite the general thrust of *On Liberty*, thought that public violations of 'good manners', including acts of indecency, fell within the category of 'offences against others' and might therefore be prohibited.[42] Even the libertarian Robert Nozick declares himself undecided on this issue.[43]

There is much greater reluctance to place legal limits upon offensive speech (oral or written). This cannot be because speech is thought less capable of causing offence than action; paradoxically, the ease with which the written and spoken word can cause offence may be one reason why people are chary of accepting offence as a sufficient reason for limiting speech. Rather it is because of the strong presumption in favour of freedom of expression. I shall not rehearse the many well-argued and highly persuasive reasons that have been offered in support of that presumption. Fortunately, they are sufficiently familiar to make such a rehearsal as unnecessary as it would be lengthy. Many people may feel, and may rightly feel, that those reasons are so strong that no limitation upon freedom of expression could ever be justified on grounds of offence alone. Given this strong predisposition in favour of free expression (which I share), I shall confine myself to making two rather peremptory remarks which weigh in the opposite direction.

First, insofar as the presumption in favour of freedom of speech rests upon the contention that speech, unlike action, cannot injure others, it has no bearing upon the present issue since, as we have said, speech seems no less capable of causing offence than action. Secondly, insofar as it rests upon more positive considerations such as the social utility of free expression or its importance to the democratic process or its necessity for individual autonomy,[44] these imply that special protection should be given to certain sorts of speech rather than to speech indifferently. Consequently, there may still be a case for limiting offensive speech if the area of prohibited offence can be delimited such that it does not impinge upon freedom of expression in an objectionable (or sufficiently objectionable) way. However, before considering how one should set the limits of a law proscribing offensive speech such as blasphemy, there is one more general issue that needs consideration.

Why should people be protected from the offence that arises in connection with their *religious* beliefs? If we proscribe utterances that cause this sort of offence, does not consistency require that we silence remarks which offend people's political convictions? Such an extension of the law would be unacceptably restrictive and dangerous; indeed, one might try to justify the distinction between offensive religious utterances and offensive political utterances simply on the ground that more is at stake in suppressing the latter. However, a more convincing reason for the distinction centres upon the sacred in religious belief; it is the special reverence felt for what is deemed sacred that makes people more susceptible to offence in relation to their religious beliefs than in relation to their political beliefs even though their political convictions may be no less strong. Ribald, obscene or abusive attacks upon God or Christ are the verbal equivalents of acts of desecration. That is why the atheist's riposte that his beliefs should receive the same protection as the theist's seems rather weak.

It might be objected that the argument here is merely circular since the sacred *is* simply what people revere. But, for the religious adherent, the sacred is identified primarily as the divine or what is especially associated with the divine and only incidentally in terms of his feelings towards it. What is true, however, is that it is not the sacred *qua* sacred that is relevant to the prevention of offence but only people's feelings towards the sacred. There could be no justification, on grounds of offence, for giving less consideration to feelings about objects which were 'sacred' only in a figurative sense (e.g. national flags) but whose 'desecration' affected people no less deeply. The sacred therefore provides some rationale for singling out religious feelings but, at best, that rationale is one of degree. Moreover, insofar as people's religious beliefs do not contain sacred elements, they have little claim to special protection. It is essential that legal intervention of the kind we are considering should attend closely to the distinction between, on the one hand, what people disagree with or disapprove of and, on the other, what causes them offence. It is certainly not the case that people are offended by all that they disagree with or disapprove of. Nor is it always the case that people disapprove of what they find offensive for reasons other than its causing offence.[45] Very often, however, the capacity of conduct to offend is integrally connected with beliefs about its wrongness. Even then a law devised to prevent offence must take account only of offence and has no concern, except incidentally, with people's beliefs about the inherent rightness or wrongness of the conduct of others.

This may sometimes have the rather odd consequence that the preoccupation of the law is different from that of the person it protects. For example, people offended by obscene or abusive remarks about Christ may be more concerned that Christ should cease to be defamed than that they should be relieved of their offended condition.[46] However, a blasphemy law of the kind we are considering should concern itself only with the latter. The distinction between disapproval and offence is often obscured as, for example, when people speak of 'conduct which outrages community standards', but it is crucial for those who, like Hart and Feinberg, reject the enforcement of morals but accept legal control of offensive conduct. That the enforcement of morals and the prevention of offence may sometimes issue in the same legal consequence is no reason for dismissing the distinction as pointless. On the other hand, it must also be said that, in practice, the disentanglement of offended feelings from censorious beliefs will often be extremely difficult, and that is one more reason why legislators should hesitate before intervening on behalf of the offended.

THE LIMITS OF PROTECTION

In order to explore the issues raised by a blasphemy law still further, let us assume that the offence caused by attacks upon people's religious convictions is sufficient to warrant legal intervention. How are we to determine what offence should be legally prevented and what must be endured? The establishment of clear principles delimiting its scope is crucial to the case for a blasphemy law since many people believe that laws preventing offence can have no rational boundaries and therefore threaten creeping repression. I shall consider five principles which relate to the appropriate legal limits of offensive conduct in general as well as to those of blasphemy in particular. If acceptable, these principles would provide important guidelines for legislation. However, I make no attempt to grapple with the precise definition that a law of blasphemy should have. I say nothing, for example (except implicitly), about the issue of intent that figured so prominently in the *Gay News* case.[47]

Public and Private

One distinction which is widely used in discussions of indecency and offensiveness is that between public and private conduct. The distinction can bear a variety of meanings. It may refer to conduct performed in public rather than in private (behind closed doors), or to conduct which does or does not affect others, or to conduct which is properly the concern of others as opposed to what is thought to be an individual's own business. Thus something done in public may not be, in another sense, a public matter (e.g. the clothes one wears). In discussions of offensiveness the distinction usually refers to the *locus* of conduct. Proponents of the 'public/private principle' hold that actions performed in public which others find offensive may be prohibited but not those performed in private. Interpreted in this way, private conduct does not mean conduct that others are unaware of (and therefore unable to be offended by), but only conduct that others do not or need not actually confront.

What is the rationale of the public/private principle in this form? One possibility is that conduct which one actually witnesses is more offensive than that which one merely knows about. But if that is all the principle amounts to, it reduces to a simple quantitative test and the *locus* of conduct is, in itself, irrelevant. Another possible rationale is that acts become objectionable, and offensive because objectionable, only when performed in public. This is clearly true of some acts which cause offence—for example, sexual relations between husband and wife. But, equally clearly, there are other acts which offend because they are thought to be wrong or objectionable wherever they are performed.

The most persuasive rationale of the principle is that acts performed in public are forced upon the attention of others whereas private acts are not. Hence, it is argued, the law may save people from being the unwilling witnesses of publicly offensive acts but not from offending acts performed in private since these can be avoided. Even this rationale is not without problems. If the central concern is unwillingness, what is special about being an unwilling observer rather than an unwilling knower?[48] However, rather than pursue these problems, I want to examine how the principle might apply in cases such as blasphemy.

The principle has occasionally been invoked in blasphemy trials. In *R. v. Boulter* (1908), for example, Mr Justice Phillimore stated that a man was not free to ridicule sacred subjects 'in a public place, where passers-by, who might not willingly go to listen to him knowing what he was going to say, might accidentally hear his words'.[49] However, in general, the law of blasphemy paid little or no attention to the public/private principle, and there is good reason why this should have been so. The principle is most acceptable where performing an act in private is a real alternative to public performance. In such cases, a law prohibiting public conduct entails a minimal loss of freedom. Thus requiring people not to engage in sexual acts in public is not the same as requiring them not to engage in sexual acts at all, nor does it (usually?) impair the enjoyment of those acts. However, there are other cases where requiring that something be not done in public is tantamount to requiring that it be not done at all. This is particularly true of religious and of most other kinds of argument. If the purpose of argument is to win over those who hold opposing views, it is essential that one should be able to expose one's opponents to ideas and information that they may find disagreeable. Requiring that people confine their expression of offensive views to private audiences of like-minded persons would remove most of the point from expressing those views. Certainly, there is such a thing as preaching to the converted which may have a therapeutic effect upon all concerned, but no one of a remotely liberal persuasion would be satisfied with that.

To the extent that someone's purpose is not to communicate ideas, information or argument but to entertain or to titillate, there is certainly scope for applying the public/private principle. Provided we exclude offence caused by mere knowledge and provided he were careful about advertising, Thorsen could make and show his film without causing public offence (in the relevant sense of 'public'). Moreover, the principle may admit of degree. In the *Gay News* case, the prosecution spoke of Kirkup's poem having been 'inflicted upon the public at large', but that was simply the hyperbole of an advocate. If our concern is with offence, then it would seem at least relevant that the poem appeared in *Gay News* since one may presume that that meant that there were fewer unwitting and unwilling readers of the poem than there would have been had it appeared in *The Times* or the *Daily Mirror*. However, even in those cases in which the public/private principle is applicable, it is less complete than many of its proponents seem to suppose. Unless we are to prohibit all public acts which anyone finds offensive to any degree, we still need to know what sort of public offence must be tolerated and what need not.

Matter and Manner

Some writers who are willing to see the law used to proscribe offence have nevertheless held that no opinion should be outlawed simply because others find the substance of that opinion offensive. Its expression may be curbed, they argue, only to the extent that offence is caused by the manner in which it is expressed.[50] The distinction between matter and manner became extremely important in the law of blasphemy. Some argued that it was always an implicit element of the law;[51] certainly the importance of the distinction between 'calm, serious, dispassionate inquiry' and that which 'reviles and calumniates' was made explicit throughout the nineteenth century. It is not the case, of course, that a distinction between acceptable inquiry and unacceptable attack need coincide with the matter/manner distinction, and it is doubtful whether judges in the early nineteenth century would have made such an equivalence. However, Lord Denman's insistence upon the relevance of 'tone and style and spirit'[52] certainly suggested a distinction between manner and matter, and it is clear that Lord Coleridge intended his ruling in 1883 to imply this distinction.[53] Indeed if 'the decencies of controversy' did not coincide with some such distinction, it would provide very little guidance.

The intention behind the distinction is plain. Granted that it is possible to distinguish manner from matter, a law restricting only forms of expression need not prevent the assertion of any substantive point of view. The usual conflict between freedom of opinion and prevention of offence is therefore largely avoided. Certainly a law controlling forms of expression is still a restriction upon freedom of speech but, if it restricts only manner and not matter, it will not impede one of the major justifying objectives of free speech: the pursuit of truth. Nor need it interfere with people's ability to form their own judgements on religious matters. Equally, the freedom to give gratuitous offence hardly seems a freedom worth fighting for. Thus the distinction between manner and matter offers an attractive middle position for those who wish to give value both to freedom of opinion and to the avoidance of offence.

The main difficulty of this position lies in whether the distinction itself can be maintained. There is certainly some scope for a distinction between offensive opinions and offensive language. If David Hume offended by his *Dialogues*, it was because of the opinions he expressed; if someone offends by hurling obscenities at the name of God, it would be largely because of the language he uses. But contested cases are unlikely to be as clear as these. Take, for example, a passage that figured prominently in the trial at which Lord Coleridge gave his famous ruling about 'the decencies of controversy':

> The God whom Christians love and adore is depicted in the Bible with a character more bloodthirsty than a Bengal tiger or a Bashi-Bazouk. He is credited with all the vices and scarcely any of the virtues of a painted savage. Wanton cruelty and heartless barbarity are his essential characteristics. If any despot at the present time tried to emulate, at the expense of his subjects, the misdeeds of Jehovah, the great majority of Christian men would denounce his conduct in terms of indignation. [54]

The message of this passage may well have been communicable in less striking imagery. But the offence it gave Christians must surely have arisen from the character attributed to God rather than from any peculiarities of the language in which that character was drawn. Yet Coleridge was firmly of the opinion that, having regard to 'the decencies of controversy', this passage constituted a blasphemous libel. Similarly anyone who reads Kirkup's poem and reports of the trial of Lemon and *Gay News* will find that it was the character and deeds attributed to Christ that gave offence and not any special features of the language used in the poem.

The failing of the matter/manner distinction is that it supposes that statements are capable of more or less offensive formulations which are nevertheless identical in meaning. The manner of an assertion is treated as though it were so much verbal wrapping paper whose features had no bearing upon the content of the parcel. In certain cases this assumption may not be unjustified. By the insertion of a few obscenities, a sentence can be rendered more offensive while remaining virtually unchanged in meaning. More often, however, manner and matter are so integrally related that it is impossible to distinguish the offensive manner from the offensive matter of a statement. How, for example, would one apply the distinction to the following sentences for whose publication Henry Hetherington was found guilty of blasphemous libel?

> What wretched stuff this Bible is to be sure! What a random idiot its author must have been! I would advise the human race to burn every Bible they have got. Such a book is actually a disgrace to ourang outangs, much less to men. I would advise them to burn it, in order that posterity may never know we believed in such abominable trash. [55]

Even if the distinction could be maintained, restrictions upon forms of expression may be of greater consequence than we have so far allowed. Insofar as opinions are asserted to persuade others, a restriction upon the manner of their assertion may constitute a serious impediment. It might be better if all argument were conducted in a temperate manner, but, given that this is not the way of the world, one party might feel unfairly handicapped if, unlike its opponents, it is deprived of the normal tools of rhetoric. Moreover, when the expression of a view occurs in a literary work—as in the *Gay News* case—the mode of expression is essential to the enterprise. To say that Kirkup should have produced an academic speculation on Christ's attitude to homosexuality after the manner of Bishop Montefiore would be to say that he should not have written a poem.

In spite of the problems involved in distinguishing manner from matter, it is difficult to see how some such distinction can be avoided by those who wish to give weight both to freedom of opinion and to prevention of offence. Moreover, given that in religious matters offence is most likely to be occasioned by what vilifies the sacred, the tone and spirit of assertions is peculiarly relevant to blasphemy. Ribald or abusive remarks about Christ are likely to cause much greater offence than a serious critique, even though the critique may be a much more damaging 'attack' upon Christianity. The moral of what I have said is simply that the matter/manner distinction will not always provide the clear clinical test that it promises. Given that the main aim of the distinction is to avoid prohibiting serious and acceptable endeavours along with prohibiting offence, it might be better to confront that issue directly. That is, it might be more satisfactory simply to ask whether an author or a publisher had some purpose in communicating the offending words other than that of causing upset and distress to his readers, and whether that purpose is such as to compensate for the offence it occasioned or was likely to occasion.

Consequent Harm

Many people are prepared to accept legal restrictions upon offensive material only if some harm is likely to be consequent upon the offence given. For purposes of this view, being offended does not itself constitute being harmed. As we have seen, fears of the consequences of blasphemy have figured prominently in its legal history. Whatever we may think of those fears, the allegedly harmful effects of blasphemy upon religious belief, government or morality are irrelevant in the present context since we are concerned not with harm caused by attacks upon religion but only with harm consequent upon offending religious believers. The only serious harm likely to be consequent upon such offence is breach of the peace.

The effect of making 'tendency to cause a breach of the peace' an element of the crime of blasphemy may be to transform the purpose of the law. If the law should intervene only because and to the extent that public order is threatened, then it has no concern with the prevention of offence as such. Maintenance of the public peace becomes an end in itself rather than a standard to be used in discriminating between types of offence. If, on the other hand, prevention of offence remains the purpose of the law, it is difficult to see why tendency to cause a breach of the peace should figure as either a sufficient or a necessary condition of the crime. If it were accepted as a sufficient condition for silencing people, the extent of their freedom of expression would be entirely dependent upon the readiness of others to react violently. In effect, people could determine for themselves how much legal protection they received from offence simply by causing a public disturbance. That would be both absurd and unfair. If a breach of the peace occurs or is likely to occur, some attempt must be made to assess whether such a breach is justifiable or excusable and therefore how much of the blame attaches to the offender and how much to the offended. Such an assessment must take account of the degree and reasonableness of the offence; that is, a standard must be employed in assessing an offence additional to its tendency to cause a breach of the peace. It is true that, in exceptional circumstances, the normal rights of the individual may be justifiably overridden in the interests of public order and safety, and the individual may be required to remain silent rather than say something that would cause a riot even though the rioters would be responding 'unreasonably'. But what is acceptable in extraordinary circumstances does not have to be accepted in ordinary circumstances.

The same train of reasoning may lead one to question whether a threat to public order should be a necessary condition for the prohibition of offence. If such a condition has to be satisfied, the sensitive intemperate sect will receive at least some protection, while the sect which is guaranteed to remain passive no matter how great the provocation will receive none. Again this seems anomalous and unfair.

In fact, what place, if any, 'tendency to cause a breach of the peace' occupied in the law of blasphemy is far from clear. Undoubtedly, that law was often regarded as an instrument for dealing with immediate as well as with more distant threats to public order. But 'tendency to cause a breach of the peace' was only proposed as an element of the crime itself in the twentieth century.[56] Even then, what little judicial comment there was on this phrase in the context of blasphemy suggests that it was not taken at face value. The concern seems to have been less with whether a breach of the peace was or might have been a real likelihood than with whether a remark was sufficiently offensive to make a Christian sympathizer reasonably feel like giving the blasphemer 'a thrashing'.[57] It would certainly be hard to take seriously the suggestion that Kirkup's poem represented a threat to public order. Lord Scarman declared that the true test of blasphemy is 'whether the words are calculated to outrage and insult the Christian's religious feelings: and in the modern law the phrase "a tendency to cause a breach of the peace" is really a reference to that test'.[58] It would seem then, not only that there is little justification for making tendency to cause a breach of the peace a standard of criminality in a law whose primary purpose is to prevent offence, but also that the standard figured in the law of blasphemy only as a rough test of what were really quite distinct considerations: the degree and reasonableness of the offence felt.

Quantity

Considerations of quantity are so obviously important that they are in danger of simply being taken for granted. Purely quantitative considerations will not yield a principle to be accepted or rejected, but a range of alternatives from which one can select in accordance with the importance one gives to saving people from offence. However, account has to be taken of two quite distinct quantitative criteria: the intensity of offence and the number of people offended.

In most cases we are likely to feel that conduct or speech has to offend fairly severely before there is any case for legal intervention. Indeed, some people oppose the legal proscription of offensive conduct simply because they believe that the pain or distress it occasions is never sufficient by itself to justify the use of law. There is no way in which different degrees of offence can be stated with precision; the best that one can do is to intimate the requisite level of offence by adjectives or phrases such as 'grossly offensive', 'outrageous', 'deeply distressing' and so on. As we have already mentioned, readiness to breach the peace is often proposed as an appropriate measure of intensity.

What account the law should take of the number of people offended is a more complicated matter. Within any particular religion the relevant group can be defined more or less inclusively. Thus the standard of reference may be what offends virtually all members of a particular faith, or its average adherents, or its devout believers. In law, persons merely 'sympathizing' with Christian ideals was proposed as the appropriate group.[59] At first sight a law which extends its protection to such pallid individuals may seem unduly generous, but its actual effect is the opposite since it takes more to offend the mere sympathizer than the devout believer. The same considerations will bear upon one's view of the appropriate offended group as bear upon one's view of the required intensity of offence; indeed, the criteria of number and intensity will tend to be conflated in stereotypes such as the 'strong' or the 'lukewarm' believer.

The real problems arise when a religious group is considered in relation to an entire society. It is often suggested that offensive conduct should be eligible for prohibition only if it offends the great majority or virtually everyone in a society. However, in cases of religious offence, it is no longer possible to speak of 'the feelings of the general body of the community' or 'the deepest religious convictions of the great majority of the persons amongst whom we live' as judges once did.[60] Such standards would have been even more obviously inapplicable if the law had been reformed so that it included religions other than Christianity. How small then can we allow a minority to be and yet still afford it protection?

It is possible of course to deny the relevance of numbers. This would be implied if one were bold enough to claim a 'right' not to be offended in respect of one's religious feelings.[61] On the other hand, it is difficult to accept that offence is sufficiently important to a person's well-being to warrant the special status and overriding respect that a right (in its strong sense)[62] entails. At the other extreme, it might be held that numbers are everything and that a majority cannot be required to sacrifice its freedom for the feelings of a minority. It is certainly correct to say that a law protecting a minority from blasphemy restricts the freedom of everyone. It is equally legitimate in assessing the significance of that restriction to take account of the extent to which it frustrates people's actual wants. It may well be that potential blasphemers constitute an even smaller minority than the potentially offended. Moreover, a law which protects minorities may not be a minority law. A law prohibiting racial insults protects everyone even if any particular insult applies only to a minority. Not everyone adheres to a religion as they necessarily belong to a race, but it is also possible that the religious minorities protected by a law of blasphemy would, together, constitute a majority. Anyhow, I for one would not exclude minorities from protection simply because they are minorities. Other things being equal, my own inclination would be to have a high intensity requirement but a low numbers requirement on the ground that, if something is important enough to warrant legal intervention, it matters not that only a few are being protected.

Reasonableness

The requirement that offence should be 'reasonably' taken may seem oddly misplaced. Offence, it might be thought, is merely a feeling, an emotional response, and to ask if that response is reasonable is no more sensible than to ask whether a taste or distaste for black pudding is reasonable or whether it is reasonable to feel pain when kicked in the shins. No doubt this is true of some sorts of offence, but not, I think, when offence arises in the context of religious belief. It would clearly be unacceptable to require the law to assess the reasonableness of religious beliefs themselves. However, if, for legal purposes, we can simply accept that people have those beliefs, we can intelligibly ask whether someone adhering to a particular religion would be reasonably offended by certain types of remark. Indeed, it is difficult to see how this question could be avoided by any attempt to assess the reality and intensity of offence. An offended person has no visible wounds to present as evidence, so how are we to judge that he is a genuine victim? We could hardly rely upon his own protestations. Nor, as I have argued, is his willingness to breach the peace a reliable test of strength of feeling. Rather such an assessment would require the judge or jury to take note of what beliefs were central, what objects sacred, etc., to the religion concerned and then to ask themselves whether adherents of that religion would have reason to be offended (or to be offended to the requisite degree) by what the alleged offender had said or written.

The point of reference then in assessing cases of religious offence will be, in large part, the religion itself rather than the simply general community standards of decent behaviour, insulting language, etc. However, some concern with the relative and changing matter of community standards would seem unavoidable even in blasphemy cases. In part this is because the content and strength of belief of stereotypes such as 'the average Christian' are liable to change with time. But it is also because the capacity of something to offend religious believers may depend upon more than their religious beliefs. Thus the ascription of certain sexual proclivities to Christ may be offensive not merely because they are ascribed to Christ but because prevailing opinion disapproves of those proclivities.

So far I have suggested that the test of reasonableness is necessary in assessing the reality and degree of offence. However, it might be thought a desirable test for other, qualitative, reasons. Thus to find someone's claimed offence unreasonable may not be to deny that they really are that offended but simply to deny that they have good reason to be so offended. Much of the intuitive appeal of apparently quantitative tests, such as what the great majority or the generality of citizens find offensive, may stem not from the thought that offence is significant only if everyone is liable to get hurt, but from the sense that abnormally sensitive souls should not receive special protection.

CONCLUSION

An examination of these five principles does not suggest that legislation upon religious offence can be an easy matter or that a law of blasphemy could easily be rendered precise. The public/private principle is of only limited relevance; the matter/manner distinction is much more central but would not preclude difficult choices; concern with breaches of the peace is out of place in a law designed to prevent offence, although the maintenance of public order may constitute a distinct and proper legal purpose; quantity and reasonableness are clearly important but do not provide precise criteria. Imprecision is not at all unusual in law and often has to be accepted as inevitable if substantial harms are to be prevented. However, where the case for a law is finely balanced, the inability to state clearly what that law requires can be allowed to weigh against it.

My own view is that the balance of considerations is against a law of blasphemy. I would not regard offence to religious feelings as trivial, and I have tried to show that one could not rule out legal consideration of such offence in principle without also, in consistency, excluding much that is generally regarded as properly subject to legal control. Nor do the usual arguments in favour of freedom of expression provide a defence for those who seek to give purely gratuitous offence to others. The problem is, of course, that more than gratuitous offence is usually at stake, as is well illustrated by the *Gay News* case, and the boundaries of a law of blasphemy are so difficult to draw clearly that one could not be confident that they would not be overstepped. Moreover, in order to show that something should be prohibited by law it is not enough to show merely that it ought not to be said or done. If a wrong is to be outlawed, it must be of sufficient moment to outweigh the *prima facie* case against legal intervention in terms of the undesirability of coercion and punishment, the cost to society of legal actions, and so on. Consequently, even when it is clear that offence is needlessly, and therefore wrongfully, given, this may still be insufficient to justify legal intervention on behalf of the offended. However, I have not tried to present a conclusive argument either for or against a law of blasphemy; indeed, I doubt if it is possible to present a case which both parties to the argument would regard as conclusive. I have attempted only to set out and explore the issue raised by a subject which has not always attracted the dispassionate and measured discussion that both sides are so keen to protect.

NOTES

I am grateful to Hugh Berrington, Tom Gibbons, Tim Gray and Albert Weale for their comments on earlier drafts of this chapter.

1. Sir Alfred Denning, *Freedom under the Law* (London: Stevens and Sons, 1949), 46.
2. *The Times*, 3 September 1976, 2. *The Times* itself suggested that if Thorsen made his film, he should be confronted by 'the ancient, but comprehensive and still capable of pouncing, common law offence of blasphemy'; 4 September 1976, 13.
3. *Hansard*, 5th series, House of Commons, vol. 925, col. 1438.
4. *R. v. Lemon* [1979] 2 W.L.R. 281 at 283.
5. [1979] 2 W.L.R. 281.
6. [1978] 3 W.L.R. 404.
7. [1979] 2 W.L.R. 281.
8. *Criminal Law: Offences against Religion and Public Worship* (Law Com., No. 145) (London: HMSO, 1985).
9. *R. v. Gathercole* (1838) 2 Lewin 237 at 254.
10. In giving his judgment on the *Gay News* appeal, Lord Scarman proposed that the law of blasphemy should be made more comprehensive; *R. v. Lemon* [1979] 2 W.L.R. 281 at 308–9. An attempt was made to reform the law in this way as long ago as 1885; see Courtney Kenny, 'The Evolution of the Law of Blasphemy', *Cambridge Law Journal* 1 (1922): 127–42, at 138.

11. In 1787 a 'Proclamation for the Encouragement of Piety and Virtue' was issued calling for the suppression of impiety, licentiousness, profaneness and other evils, 'fearing lest that they should provoke God's wrath and indignation against us'. Reprinted in Louis Blom-Cooper and Gavin Drewry, *Law and Morality* (London: Duckworth, 1976), 239–41.

12. See G. D. Nokes, *A History of the Crime of Blasphemy* (London: Sweet and Maxwell, 1928), 64–65.

13. Although Taylor's case was the first in which blasphemy was named as an offence, it has been argued that it represented an extension of the existing law rather than a genuine innovation. See Nokes, *A History of the Crime of Blasphemy*, 52–61.

14. *R. v. Taylor* (1676) I Ventris 293; also reported in 3 Keble 607, 621. It is unclear from either report whether Hale thought his famous dictum that 'Christianity is parcel of the laws of England' simply followed from his argument about the relation between religion and obligation or whether he asserted it upon other grounds.

15. See, for example, the remarks of Raymond C.J. in *R. v. Woolston* (1729) Fitz-G. 64 at 65, of Ashhurst J. in *R. v. Williams* (1798) 26 St. Tr. 653 at 715–19, and of Abbott C. J. in *R. v. Carlile (Richard)* (1819) 4 St. Tr. N.S. 1423 at 1423–24. Even Locke was sufficiently persuaded by this argument to exclude atheists from toleration. John Locke, *A Letter on Toleration*, ed. Raymond Klibansky (Oxford: Clarendon Press, 1968), 135.

16. See, for example, the remarks of Best J. in *R. v. Carlile (Richard)* (1819) 3 B. and Ald. 161 at 167, and in *R. v. Carlile (Mary)* (1821) 1 St. Tr. N.S. 1033 at 1045–46, and the argument of the Attorney General (Sir John Campbell) in *R. v. Hetherington* (1840) 4 St. Tr. N.S. 563 at 568.

17. Patrick Devlin, *The Enforcement of Morals* (London: Oxford University Press, 1965), 23, 25.

18. *Hansard*, 5th series, House of Lords, vol. 389, cols. 302, 316, 321, 335.

19. John Stuart Mill, *On Liberty*, ed. G. Himmelfarb (London: Penguin, 1974), 119.

20. John Rawls, *A Theory of Justice* (London: Oxford University Press, 1971), 212–13.

21. See, for example, the remarks of Lord Gardiner in the debate on Lord Willis's bill; *Hansard*, vol. 389, cols. 313–15.

22. In *R. v. Carlile (Richard)* (1819), Abbott C. J. told Carlile, 'You are not here called in question for having published any work containing a calm, serious, and dispassionate inquiry into the truth, or the evidence of the truth, of our religion; you are called in question for the publication of a work which reviles and calumniates it'. Yet he also stated categorically that 'the law says no man shall deny the truth of the Christian religion, or deny that the scriptures of the Old and New Testament are of Divine authority' (4 St. Tr. N.S. 1423–24).

23. See, for example, the concern expressed for the poor and ignorant in *R. v. Williams* (1797), 26 St. Tr. 653 at 664, and in *R. v. Carlile (Mary)* (1821), 1 St. Tr. N.S. 1033 at 1048, 1054.

24. *R. v. Ramsey and Foote* (1883), 15 Cox C.C. 231 at 238.

25. *R. v. Bradlaugh* (1883), 15 Cox C.C. 217 at 230–31. Lord Denman had already moved the law very much in this direction in his summing up in *R. v. Hetherington* (1840), 4 St. Tr. N.S. 563 at 590. In *R. v. Moxon* (1840), he put the question to the jury, 'Are the lines in question calculated to shock the feelings of any Christian reader?', 4 St. Tr. N.S. 693 at 721.

26. J. F. Stephen, 'Blasphemy and Blasphemous Libel', *The Fortnightly Review*, n.s., 35 (1884): 289–318. See also *Pankhurst v. Thompson* (1886), 3 T.L.R. 199. To those who know Stephen only as the opponent of Mill, it may be a surprise to learn that he opposed a blasphemy law of any kind and drafted a bill abolishing the offence of blasphemy. See Hypatia Bradlaugh Bonner, *Penalties upon Opinion* (London: Watts, 1934), 141.

27. *Bowman v. Secular Society* [1917], A.C. 406.

28. *R. v. Lemon* [1978], 3 W.L.R. 404; [1979] 2 W.L.R. 282.

29. See 'Who the Hell Does She Think She Is?' (an interview with Mrs Whitehouse), *Poly Law Review* 111 (1978): 13–18, at 13.

30. Hereafter, to avoid confusion, I shall use the word 'offence' to refer only to the condition of being offended and not to that which is unlawful.

31. Mill, *On Liberty*, 68.

32. Joel Feinberg, *Social Philosophy* (Englewood Cliffs, NJ: Prentice-Hall, 1973), 26.

33. J. R. Lucas, *The Principles of Politics* (Oxford: Clarendon Press, 1966), 172.

34. For an attempt to restructure Mill's utilitarianism so that no account need be taken of offence caused to people in virtue of their beliefs, see Richard Wollheim, 'John Stuart Mill and the Limits of State Action', *Social Research* 40 (1973): 1–30. Wollheim's argument is criticized by C. L. Ten, 'Self-Regarding Conduct and Utilitarianism', *Australasian Journal of Philosophy* 55 (1977): 105–13.

35. Feinberg, *Social Philosophy*, 29.

36. 'The purpose of blasphemy is to wound and hurt other people in areas of the mind which are, to them, sacred. This is violence, likely to prove more painful to many than physical violence. Therefore, while violence remains a crime, so should blasphemy.' Richard Adams, letter to *The Times*, 23 July 1977, 13.

37. 'All exhibitions, which, being to the minds of individuals taken in any considerable number, productive of uneasiness on a religious account, are offered to their senses in such manner as that the unpleasant sensation produced by them, whatever it be, is unavoidable—all such acts are, in my view of the matter, objects calling for prevention by means of punishment.' Jeremy Bentham, 'Letters to Toreno'; see *The Works of Jeremy Bentham*, ed. John Bowring, Vol. VIII (New York: Russell and Russell, 1962), 546. On 'simple mental injuries' in relation to law, see Vol. III ('Principles of Morals and Legislation'), 225 and note.

38. Bentham, *Works*, Vol. VIII, 547.

39. Cmnd. 247 (1957), para. 13.

40. H. L. A. Hart, *Law, Liberty and Morality* (London: Oxford University Press, 1963), 38–48.

41. Ibid., 41.

42. Mill, *On Liberty*, 168. This passage has often been regarded as a momentary aberration, but it may reveal just how much Mill was taking for granted. See Shirley Robin Letwin, 'Law and Morality', *Encounter* 43 (November 1974): 35–43, at 38.

43. Robert Nozick, *Anarchy, State and Utopia* (Oxford: Basil Blackwell, 1974), 323.

44. T. Scanlon, 'A Theory of Freedom of Expression', *Philosophy and Public Affairs* 1 (1972): 204–26.

45. E.g. people may object to public nudity or to public sexual acts only because these cause them embarrassment.

46. Mrs Mary Whitehouse would seem to have been a case in point. While she accepted that the law of blasphemy was and ought to have been concerned with the prevention of offence, her own reason for taking action against *Gay News* was rather different: 'I simply had to protect Our Lord'. *New Statesman*, 15 July 1977, 74. See also 'Who the Hell Does She Think She Is?', 15.

47. For a discussion of that issue, see Richard Buxton, 'The Case of Blasphemous Libel', *Criminal Law Review* 1978: 673–82.

48. For an answer to this question, see Hart, *Law, Liberty and Morality*, 45–48, and for a critique of that answer and of the public/private principle in general, see David A. Conway, 'Law, Liberty and Indecency', *Philosophy* 49 (1974): 135–47.

49. *R. v. Boulter* (1908) 72 J.P. 188 at 189.

50. E.g. Joel Feinberg, '"Harmless Immoralities" and Offensive Nuisances: Reply', in *Issues in Law and Morality*, ed. Norman S. Care and Thomas K. Trelogan (Cleveland and London: Case Western Reserve University Press, 1973), 131–33.

51. E.g. Lord Sumner in *Bowman v. Secular Society* [1917], A.C. 406 at 466.

52. *R. v. Hetherington* (1840), 4 St. Tr. N.S. 563 at 590.

53. *R. v. Ramsey and Foote* (1883), 15 Cox C.C. 231 at 238. Coleridge made explicit use of the matter/manner distinction.

54. *R. v. Bradlaugh* (1883), 15 Cox C.C. 217 at 219.

55. *R. v. Hetherington* (1840), 4 St. Tr. N.S. 563 at 565–66.

56. In *R. v. Boulter* (1908), Phillimore J. remarked that Boulter's words might have led to a breach of the peace, but it is unclear whether he thought that tendency to cause a breach of the peace could affect the question of law as to whether words constituted a blasphemous libel (72 J.P. 188 at 189). In *Bowman v. Secular Society*, Lord Parker offered the opinion that 'to constitute a blasphemy at common law there must be such an element of vilification, ridicule or

irreverence as would be likely to exasperate the feelings of others and so lead to a breach of the peace' ([1917] A.C. 406 at 446). This view of the law was clearly followed in *R. v. Gott* (1922) 16 Cr. App. R. 87.

57. *R. v. Gott* (1922), 16 Cr. App. R. 87 at 89.

58. *R. v. Lemon* [1979] 2 W.L.R. 281 at 312. Lord Edmund-Davis (at 307) simply rejected the suggestion that 'in order to justify a conviction for blasphemous libel, the publication, when objectively considered, must tend to lead to a breach of the peace'.

59. *R. v. Gott* (1922), 16 Cr. App. R. 87 at 90.

60. *R. v. Gott* (1922), 16 Cr. App. R. 89; *R. v. Bradlaugh* (1883) 15 Cox C.C. 217 at 230.

61. Mrs Whitehouse claimed this as a 'basic human right', *Daily Telegraph*, 22 February 1979, 3.

62. On the strong and weak senses of a 'right', see Ronald Dworkin, *Taking Rights Seriously* (London: Duckworth, 1977), 188–89.

Chapter Eleven

Respecting Beliefs and Rebuking Rushdie

Freedom of expression and freedom of religion are two freedoms securely embedded in the culture of modern Western societies. Their conjunction in the right of people to express themselves freely on religious matters for long seemed a particularly secure and widely held conviction. So true had that been that, for decades and with few exceptions, that freedom passed virtually unchallenged both in the politics of Western societies and in Western political thought. The Rushdie Affair put an end to that easy consensus.

The publication of Salman Rushdie's *The Satanic Verses* led to worldwide protests that it constituted a gross insult to Muhammad and to other important figures in the Islamic faith as well as to Muslims themselves.[1] That in turn led to calls for the book to be withdrawn from circulation by the publishers and for all existing copies to be pulped. There were also calls for governments to ban the book. Indeed, the book was banned in India and in Pakistan, Indonesia and very many other Muslim countries, but also in some non-Muslim countries, such as South Africa and Venezuela. Nor were the complaints confined to Muslims. Prominent leaders from other religions— including the Archbishops of Canterbury and York, spokesmen for the Vatican; the American evangelist Billy Graham; and leading rabbis in Britain and Israel—expressed their sympathy with the protests of Muslims and suggested a variety of measures to prevent a recurrence of this sort of episode. In Britain, although some members of the government expressed sympathy for the hurt caused to Muslims, the government officially refused to contemplate a ban and protested that, anyway, it had no power to impose one. However, some Muslim groups claimed that Rushdie could have been, and should have been, prosecuted under the Public Order and Race Relations Acts. Others sought to mobilize the English common law of blasphemy against Rushdie, but those efforts came to nought since blasphemy law protected only Christianity. That, in turn, led to vigorous calls for reform of the law so that its protection was extended to other religions and so that books such as *The Satanic Verses* would, in future, be subject to its full rigours.

The whole issue was further intensified and complicated by Ayatollah Khomeini's notorious *fatwa* sentencing Rushdie to death and calling upon 'all zealous Muslims' to ensure that the sentence was carried out, adding that whoever was killed in the attempt would be deemed a martyr. Various financial rewards were offered to those who successfully assumed the role of executioner. Rushdie himself was forced into hiding. His subsequent qualified apology for the distress he had caused Muslims was judged by his would-be executors to be insufficient to rectify his wrong, and it seemed that Rushdie's life would remain under threat for the foreseeable future and very possibly for the rest of his days.

In this chapter, I want to consider the general issues raised by the Rushdie Affair for a plural society. By a 'plural society', I mean one characterized by a diversity of fundamental beliefs and, more especially, one characterized by a diversity of religious beliefs. I shall assume that all parties to the argument accept the legitimacy of a plural society. The issue, therefore, as I shall examine it, is not one of which, if any, of a number of competing religions should be adopted by a society as the 'correct' one to the exclusion of all other (false) beliefs. It is not about whether a society should be committed to Christianity or to Islam or, indeed, to atheism. Rather all parties to the argument are assumed to accept that members of the society should be able to hold and to live according to their own beliefs; so the issue amongst them is simply about the way in which the society should accommodate the diversity of beliefs that they hold. In examining this issue I shall make use of the arguments and claims thrown up by the Rushdie Affair, but my ultimate concern will not be to deliver a verdict on the rights and wrongs of the affair in its every detail. Instead, my interest will be in the general question of what should be required of the members of a plural society by way of deference to beliefs that they themselves do not share. In particular, I shall consider the plausibility and the implications of the claim that we should show 'respect' for the beliefs of others.

In examining the principle of 'respect for beliefs', I shall argue that, although it has some affinity with the idea of not offending people's sensibilities, it is actually a distinct idea with a different moral foundation and some different practical implications. I shall examine the principle both in its strong form, in which it would limit substantive criticism of people's beliefs, and in its weaker form, in which it would constrain only the manner in which others' beliefs are treated. Finally, I shall consider whether the difficulties that we confront when we invoke the offence principle or the principle of respect for beliefs can be by-passed by focusing instead upon the requirements of public order.

COPING WITH CONFLICT

It should not be taken for granted that there *must* be some set of rules that is acceptable to all members of a plural society in spite of their different beliefs. Different groups of believers may accept the legitimacy of a plural society but still disagree about the rules that should govern that society. For example, if Christians, Muslims, Buddhists and humanists each draw upon their own bodies of belief in deciding what the common rules should be, there is no guarantee that they will come up with identical sets of proposals. If no such 'overlapping consensus'[2] is forthcoming, we may have a virtual state of war among different groups of believers. There are certainly elements of the Rushdie Affair which fit that description. Ayatollah Khomeini was not interested in providing for a plural society, and he did not command the allegiance of all Muslims. But many Muslims in Britain and in other Western societies accepted Khomeini's *fatwa* sentencing Rushdie to death and affirmed their willingness either to carry out that sentence or to collude in its being carried out by others. In addition, bookshops were bombed and a campaign of civil disobedience was threatened. Other Muslims rejected Khomeini's *fatwa* and were unwilling to resort to illegal tactics to achieve their aims but, even amongst them, there seems to have been a general conviction that they could never give up their protests and simply accept that others had a right to subject their religion to the sort of treatment it had received at the hands of Rushdie.[3]

How might we get beyond this state of conflict? One possibility is peace based upon mere compromise. For example, Muslims might come to endure attacks upon Muhammad and the Koran, not because they believe that they are obliged to do so by some principle that supersedes their religion, but only because, in practice, that is all that they can do short of leaving the society. Alternatively, the non-Muslim section of the population might agree to the prohibition of severe attacks upon Muslim beliefs, not because it believes that there is really anything wrong with those attacks, but only to assuage those who would be outraged by them and who might react violently. I describe each of these as 'mere compromise' because neither is an arrangement that both sides regard as truly right or fair. Each is no more than a *modus vivendi*, a truce, in which force of circumstances has induced one side to concede something that, it believes, it should not have to concede. That may be preferable to open conflict but it is still an unhappy state of affairs, for it does not represent a genuine consensus on what the rules of the society should be. Is there no more principled basis upon which people might defer to one another's beliefs?

What has become the standard liberal position may be regarded as a minimum starting point. All would at least agree that people should be free to hold and live according to their own beliefs, subject to the usual qualification that their doing so did not involve harming or infringing the rights of others. People can, of course, believe that this sort of liberal position is wrong in principle and that they are duty-bound to attempt to make everyone conform to their own uniquely right beliefs. However, I am contemplating a population whose members accept the legitimacy of a plural society, and it is hard to see how, if they accept that, they cannot also accept, as a minimum, that people should be allowed to hold and to pursue their own beliefs.

The question is whether more than that minimum can be required. My right to hold and to pursue my own beliefs does not, of itself, impose any limit upon what others may say about, or do with, the beliefs that I hold. Rushdie's *Satanic Verses* could not be said to interfere with Muslims' right to conduct their lives as Muslims, nor could Scorsese's *The Last Temptation of Christ* be said to impede the freedom of Christians to live as Christians. Yet there is a widely shared sentiment that some limit should be placed upon the treatment that may be meted out to other people's most cherished beliefs, particularly if they are religious beliefs. What can justify that sentiment? What reason can there be for a society's throwing a protective cordon around people's beliefs? If I am a Christian, I have reason to object to the vilification of Christ because, as far as I am concerned, he is the Son of God. But what reason can I give a non-Christian, which will count as a reason for a non-Christian, for refraining from what I regard as a sin? And why should I myself refrain from vilifying Muhammad, since, as far as I am concerned, he is a figure who has no divine status and who was indeed a false prophet? Clearly, whatever reason there might be for limiting freedom of expression out of concern for people's beliefs, it cannot be a reason that presupposes the truth of those beliefs, for that would disqualify it as a reason for all except those who already hold those beliefs.

OFFENDING SENSIBILITIES

That goes some way towards explaining why 'offensiveness' has become such a prominent concern both in relation to the general question of whether people's religious beliefs should receive legal protection and in relation to the specific controversy over Rushdie's book. People can acknowledge the offence caused by attacks upon others' beliefs even though they themselves do not share those beliefs. The non-believer, because he is a non-believer, cannot share the Christian's or the Muslim's conception of the essential wrongness of blasphemy. However, he can recognize that blasphemies cause distress and offence to the devout, that the distress and offence is undesirable, and that that provides a (*prima facie*) case for prohibiting blasphemies. He must still regard these offended reactions as, in a sense, 'mistaken', for they depend upon beliefs which are (for him) false; but he may regard that as a matter of no consequence since the reality of offended sensibilities is unaffected by the truth or falsity of the beliefs upon which they depend. Nor is this reasoning relevant only for atheists. Insofar as different religions do not have overlapping beliefs, they will have different conceptions of what is blasphemous. As far as the Christian is concerned, an attack upon Muhammad cannot be truly blasphemous; in relation to Islam, he too is a nonbeliever. Thus he too must find reason for not attacking the Muslim's beliefs in something which does not imply his own acceptance of the beliefs at issue—such as the avoidance of offence.[4]

As for believers themselves, the offence caused by blasphemy is not likely to be their major preoccupation. For the Christian, impugning the character of Christ and, for the Muslim, impugning the character of Muhammad is wrong as such. Each may be offended by the blasphemy, but that offence is merely a by-product of the wrongful act; it is not the offensiveness of the act which explains its wrongness but the wrongness of the act that explains its offensiveness. If the Christian or the Muslim characterizes the blasphemy as a wrong *to* anyone, she will regard it as principally a wrong to Christ (and to God) or to Muhammad (and to Allah) rather than to herself. It would be a derogation from her faith to do otherwise.[5] Even so, she has to recognize that she is in a society many of whose members do not share these beliefs and for whom these cannot provide reason for refraining from blasphemy. But she can present the distress and the offence caused to her by blasphemy as a concern that others ought to recognize whatever their own beliefs and, insofar as blasphemy is wrong because it is offensive, she can present herself as the person who is wronged by it.

Although being offended is a disagreeable experience, it is often a fairly slight one which does not bear comparison with harms such as physical injury. Consequently, when it is weighed against values such as freedom of expression, it is often found wanting. However, the potential for offence related to religious belief is very great. The conception of certain figures and symbols as 'sacred' in Christianity and in Islam makes them special objects of reverence, and acts which treat those figures and symbols irreverently are therefore especially offensive. That is why, of all belief-related offence, that occasioned by religious belief seems the most intense.

The English common law of blasphemy developed in a way that was closely related to the prevention of offence. At one time the purpose of that law was to uphold the truth of Christianity, for it was upon that truth that the social and political institutions of England were said to be founded. Blasphemy, either against Christianity in general or against the Church of England in particular, was viewed as a form of sedition. However, during the nineteenth century, the character of the law was gradually modified so that its prime purpose became protecting Christians from offensive treatment of their beliefs rather than asserting and upholding the truth of Christianity itself. Provided they observed the 'decencies of controversy', people could attack the very foundations of Christian belief without being guilty of the legal offence of blasphemy.[6]

Given that revised understanding of blasphemy law, its protection could have been extended to other religions without anomaly, for, as we have seen, preventing belief-dependent offence does not presuppose the truth of the beliefs at issue. Indeed, it came to be seen as anomalous that its protection was limited to Christians. If the law's purpose was to protect people from what they found offensive, why should that protection be extended to some citizens but not to others? Thus the very character of the law intimated its own reform. That reform would have brought certain complications in its train, such as what exactly was to count as a religion for legal purposes, and those difficulties played some part in persuading successive British governments not to extend the law's scope, although they also fought shy of abolishing blasphemy as a legal offence until 2008.[7]

I examine how far a case can be made for the prohibition of blasphemy on grounds of offence in Chapter 10 and I shall not repeat that exercise here. That earlier study was prompted by the *Gay News* case, which was pursued in the English courts from 1977 to 1979. My conclusion then was that, while the offence caused by blasphemy deserved to be taken seriously, it was insufficient, when weighed against rival concerns, to justify blasphemy's remaining a crime. The Rushdie Affair did not induce me to revise my earlier argument or its conclusion. Moreover, even if the law of blasphemy had been extended to include Islam, it should not be taken for granted that a court would have found *The Satanic Verses* to have contravened it.

RESPECTING BELIEFS

Offensiveness is, however, not the only ground upon which different religious groups in a multi-faith society may call for legal protection for their beliefs. The Rushdie case served to highlight a distinct, if related, form of argument. That argument appeals to what I shall call the principle of 'respect for beliefs'. This principle holds that people should behave in ways that are consistent with their respecting the beliefs of others. As with the offence principle, respect for beliefs is a principle that is especially relevant to a plural society in which different groups of people hold fundamentally different beliefs. It holds that, in such a society, not only should people be allowed to conduct their lives in accordance with their most deeply held beliefs, but they should also not have to endure attacks upon those beliefs. An attack upon the beliefs of others is a violation of one of the understandings that should underpin a society in which people are expected to live together in spite of their different beliefs.

Like the argument from offence, the appeal to respect for beliefs does not presuppose the truth of the beliefs at issue. For example, it would require people to refrain from vilifying Christ or Muhammad not because it presumes that Christ really was the Son of God or that Muhammad really was God's Prophet, but out of respect for those who hold Christian or Muslim beliefs. As with the offence principle, therefore, the ultimate objects of concern in the principle of respect for beliefs are not beliefs as such but the people who hold them.

The demand that we respect the beliefs of others is, as I shall argue in a moment, fraught with difficulties, particularly for liberal political philosophy. Even so, it is a principle that liberals should at least find intelligible. The idea of individuals as objects of respect has figured prominently in liberal thinking. The arrangements required for a liberal society have been worked out as those appropriate to persons capable of forming and acting upon their own views of the ends to which they should devote their lives.[8] A liberal society is one whose members are allowed to form and to pursue their own beliefs. It stands opposed to a society in which people are compelled to live in accordance with beliefs that they themselves do not share or which, in other ways, pays no heed to the conscientious convictions of those who make up its citizens. The principle of respect for beliefs, as I have described it, can be seen as an extension of this way of thinking. It holds that the mutual respect which is required of citizens who form a plural society should be taken to include their not acting in ways which affront one another's beliefs. That, it asserts, is one of the minimum guarantees that people should be able to demand as a condition of their accepting the obligations of citizenship.[9]

Before seeing how well this principle stands up to scrutiny, let me say a little about how it differs from an injunction not to offend people's sensibilities. These two will often be closely allied, for it is likely that people will be offended when they find their beliefs being treated disrespectfully.[10] We should not therefore expect to find the distinction between these two sorts of complaint being closely observed when people register their protests. Yet, despite their close association, neither is reducible to the other. My person or my beliefs may be treated disrespectfully even though I experience little or no offence and, equally, my offended reaction does not, of itself, establish that either I or my beliefs are being treated without due respect.

The ethical substructures from which each of these notions derives its appeal are also quite different. The notion of 'being offended' encompasses a variety of mental states which share little in common except that they are unpleasant, perhaps sometimes painful, mental responses.[11] It is the disagreeable character of the experience that makes offence a ground for complaint and that, in turn, indicates that underlying objections, which appeal to offence, are considerations of an essentially utilitarian character. By contrast the principle of 'respect for beliefs' is an altogether more rights-based notion.[12] Its appeal derives not from the disutility that people suffer when their beliefs are attacked, but from the premise that people are 'self-originating sources of claims',[13] who are entitled to a certain minimum of respect from their fellows. To subject beliefs to attack, ridicule or contempt is simultaneously to subject the people who hold those beliefs to attack, ridicule or contempt, and that is to accord them less than the respect to which they are entitled.

As I have already indicated, the language of offence and the language of respect will not always indicate clearly which form of concern someone is intending to avow. Each thought might find expression in the language of the other. Thus, someone who asserts that we should treat the beliefs of others 'with respect' may turn out to believe, not that that respect is of intrinsic value, but only that it is of instrumental importance. They may believe, for example, that disrespect will cause offence or social conflict and that that is the main or the only reason why it should be avoided. Similarly, people may be offended by something and may declare that they are offended, without intending to suggest that their offence is their reason for objecting to what they find offensive. People are offended and upset by the existence of genocidal concentration camps, but it would be a very odd person who cited their upset and offence as their reason for objecting to genocidal concentration camps. Analogously, people may find attacks upon their religious beliefs offensive but may hold that those attacks are wrong, not because they cause offence, but because they are intrinsically 'sinful' or because they do not accord others the respect to which they are entitled. However, despite these 'semiotic confusions', the distinction between these two ways of condemning attacks upon beliefs remains and, in what follows, I shall give the terms 'offence' and 'respect' the specific interpretations that I have described.

Once this notion of respect for beliefs is brought to bear upon the Rushdie controversy, certain of its features become more intelligible. One reply frequently given to protesting Muslims was that, if they believed that they would find *The Satanic Verses* offensive, they need not read the book. Indeed, that reply was given by Rushdie himself.[14] Yet Muslims seemed to have been singularly unimpressed by this riposte. What is more, their own protests and demonstrations would have been oddly counter-productive if their primary concern was with the offensiveness of Rushdie's writings, for by their actions they greatly increased the number of people who became aware of the alleged blasphemies and who therefore were offended by them. Mosques displayed samples of Rushdie's blasphemies, and organizers were reported to have handed out photocopies of the offending passages during demonstrations. This would indeed have been strange behaviour if the ground of their complaint was the offence, the 'mental pain', caused to the Muslim population. If, however, the essence of their complaint was not the offensive character of Rushdie's words but the disrespect that they manifested for the beliefs of Muslims, their conduct was altogether more intelligible and condonable. Spreading the word about Rushdie did not then amount to compounding the evil.

Another reason that Muslims have given for their being unimpressed by the invitation not to read the book is that they did not need to read Rushdie's actual words in order to be aware of what he had said and to be offended by it.[15] Mere knowledge of Rushdie's themes was enough to cause them anguish. Yet this too creates a puzzle. If Muslims were offended by their mere awareness of what Rushdie said, what would be the point of banning *The Satanic Verses*? Virtually all Muslims in Britain must have known about it, and banning the book would not have erased Rushdie's remarks from their consciousness. It is difficult therefore to see how a case could have been made, merely on grounds of preventing offence, for banning the book. (It is, of course, easy to see how a case might have been made for banning *future* books of this sort on grounds of offence.) However, more sense can be made of calls for the book to be suppressed if we introduce the idea of respect for beliefs. The suppression of the book might have been demanded by Muslims as a gesture of respect for themselves and their faith and as acknowledgement of the respect that should be shown for their beliefs by members of the majority society who do not share them.

There is one further way in which respecting beliefs might be held to score over preventing offence. Offence can be a highly idiosyncratic reaction. What offends some people does not offend others, and some people seem generally more easily offended than others. Should the freedom enjoyed by the members of a society be at the mercy of such a subjective and erratic phenomenon?[16] Might not the fault sometimes lie with those who take offence rather than with those who purportedly give it? The dangers of idiosyncratic or unreasonable reactions may seem to disappear when we are concerned with large groups of people, as in the case of offence felt by the adherents of a religious faith, yet groups may also be very uneven in their propensity to feel offence. Imagine a society characterised by two religions. One of these has roots deep in the society's past but, with the development of secularity, its adherents have had to become accustomed to attacks upon their fundamental beliefs and have, in consequence, developed a degree of 'mental resistance' to them. The other religion is relatively new to the society. Its adherents are not similarly used to secular assaults upon their beliefs and consequently react with much greater hurt and indignation when their beliefs are questioned or attacked. Should the law give greater protection to the new than to the old religion? If our only concern is to prevent offence, it should. Yet it seems unjust that the adherents of the old religion should have to put up with a greater amount of ridicule and contumely merely because they have become more resigned to it. If people's most cherished beliefs are to receive legal protection, should not that protection be extended to all believers equally—as would be required by the principle of respect for beliefs— rather than be dependent upon the contingencies of their mental states?

One final point should be made about the different implications of preventing offence and respecting beliefs: if our purpose is to prevent offence, that provides some justification for singling out religious beliefs as of special concern. As I explained earlier, the sacral element in religious beliefs makes people particularly susceptible to offence in relation to them. That is why there seems something disingenuous about the atheist's riposte that he is just as liable to be offended as the theist and therefore should receive the same protection. However, if our guiding concern is securing respect for beliefs rather than preventing offence *per se*, it is not at all clear that religious beliefs can claim a unique status. If the rules are to remain neutral between the different contents of people's beliefs, should non-religious or irreligious beliefs receive any less respect than religious beliefs? Might not identical claims to respect be made for moral or political beliefs?

Clearly, we do not think that all of a person's beliefs are equal candidates for respect. We would not ordinarily suppose that my beliefs about whether it will rain tomorrow, or about the likelihood of a team's winning a football match, impose strong obligations of respect upon others. It is not easy to specify what it is that makes some of a person's beliefs more demanding of respect than others, beyond the general observation that it has something to do with the centrality of a belief to a person's life and being. But, however one makes the distinction, it is quite implausible to suppose that the principle of respecting beliefs should issue in an injunction to respect religious beliefs only. Thus I shall continue to focus on religious beliefs for the remainder of this chapter, not because I suppose that they have a unique claim to respect, but only because they were central to the Rushdie Affair and because conflicts of religious belief have proved particularly difficult for plural societies to handle.

How strong a case is there, then, for embracing the principle of respect for beliefs? One thing I have not done so far is to specify the precise scope of the principle, and that might seem to be an essential preliminary to subjecting it to examination. Just how demanding is it? What precisely does it forbid? Rather than simply stipulate an answer to these questions in a more or less arbitrary fashion, I would prefer to let one emerge from an examination of the general idea of the principle. However, I shall begin by assuming that the principle takes a fairly strong form—strong enough to forbid challenges and criticisms designed to undermine the beliefs of others. Is that a principle we should accept?

Little progress can be made in answering that question by invoking distributive values such as justice or equality, even though it is those values that have dominated recent liberal political philosophy. Justice and equality are concerned with how freedom and protection should be distributed amongst people rather than with what freedoms and protections there should be, and, *prima facie*, a system of laws which extends the kind of protection at issue here to *everyone's* beliefs seems neither more nor less just than one which gives that protection to *no one's* beliefs. Where then are we to look for an answer?

First, there is the entire phalanx of arguments that may be invoked in defence of freedom of expression. I cannot review all of those here, so I shall confine myself to a few brief comments.[17] Much was made of the rights of Rushdie as an author in a way which implied that creators of literature, because they were creators of literature, had some special claim to freedom. That is not perhaps the most persuasive of defences since it has the appearance of a mere prejudice which elevates the interests of a small group of literati above those of many millions of Muslims. Much was also made of the requirements of a democratic society. Now the phrase 'democratic society' can be variously interpreted but, if it refers to the prerequisites of a democratic political process, it is not immediately obvious that restrictions upon blasphemy would seriously impede the operation of that process. However, I concede that it is difficult and perhaps impossible to state, *a priori*, which opinions will be relevant to a political process and which will not, so that some headway may be made in defending Rushdie by reference to democracy.

For my money, the most persuasive defence of freedom of expression in religious matters is the kind of argument developed by J. S. Mill in the second chapter of *On Liberty*.[18] If we are serious about wanting to possess true beliefs, and presumably anyone who professes a 'belief' must be concerned that it is a true belief, we must be willing to live in the kind of society that allows the truth of beliefs to be examined. That is a society in which all beliefs are open to question and none is immune from scrutiny. It is unnecessary for me to restate the arguments for freedom of expression and discussion so ably marshalled by Mill. His is the kind of non-distributive concern for liberty that has been unduly neglected in recent liberal thinking and which is of first importance for episodes such as the Rushdie Affair. It serves to show how we each have an interest, not only in our own freedom of expression, but also in one another's freedom of expression. Of course the concern here is not quite the same as Mill's. He feared the imposition of a uniformity of belief either by governments or by the pressure of social opinion; we are contemplating a society of diverse beliefs in which each body of belief is insulated from criticism and challenge by the rivals that exist alongside it. But the ideal of a society in which 'mutual respect' requires rival bodies of belief not to speak to one another is as vulnerable to Mill's criticisms as a society in which only one body of belief is respected.

I concede that Mill's argument about the need to test beliefs may not persuade someone whose beliefs depend entirely upon claims of revelation.[19] Such a person may hold both that the truth of his beliefs is utterly beyond question and that ordinary standards of argument and evidence are entirely irrelevant in matters of religious belief. However, the fact that some people take that view does not entail that they take it *rightly*. Actually, belief in revealed truths is rarely based upon what has been revealed directly to the believer. Nor should we overlook the central places occupied by argument and scholarship in both the Islamic and the Christian traditions. Some of those who spoke up on behalf of Muslims in the Rushdie Affair did so by suggesting that truth was not really at issue in religious belief and that it was misplaced to allow our response to the diversity of religious beliefs to be guided by a concern for the pursuit of truth. But that sort of argument is unlikely to be welcomed by Muslims themselves, who would regard their own beliefs (rightly) as beliefs about what is supremely true. Rather than rushing to sever any connection between religious belief and truth, Muslims are more likely to regard the sceptical relativism implicit in that proposal as itself part of the unfortunate fallout of secular liberalism.

However, a strong version of the principle of respect for beliefs is open to a second objection that is even more decisive than the strictures set out by Mill. In its strong form the principle would seem to require us to treat an individual's beliefs as a well-defined territory over which he has a sovereign right. Just as he may be said to possess an inviolable right over his person and his property, so too he may be said to possess an inviolable right over his beliefs. Indeed, on this view, his beliefs are virtually a part of his 'property', and that is why it is incumbent upon a society to ensure that they are protected.

There are two reasons why this way of viewing and valuing people's beliefs must collapse into incoherence. The first is that the contents of people's beliefs overlap and conflict. That observation is as important as it is pedestrian, and it is especially important in relation to religious beliefs. The very existence of different religious faiths, and of differences within religious faiths, must mean the existence of conflicting bodies of belief. Christianity impugns the truth of Islam, and Islam impugns the truth of Christianity. Likewise Protestantism and Catholicism stand in contradiction to one another (although not of course in every detail). How are we to decide whose beliefs are to be privileged and therefore protected? Who should we regard as the victim and who as the assailant in this conflict of beliefs? Clearly those questions are incapable of receiving neutral answers. The only way of honouring the principle that no one's beliefs should be subjected to attack, either explicitly or implicitly, would be to require, absurdly, that no one should ever give voice to a belief.

This strong version of respect for beliefs is also at odds with itself in a second way. It may have some intuitive appeal as long as a person's beliefs are purely self-directed, that is, as long as they are beliefs only about the believer himself and how he ought to live. But as soon as those beliefs become beliefs about others as well, it becomes nonsensical for him to insist that the content of those beliefs is properly of concern to none but himself. Yet it would be a very odd set of fundamental beliefs that had relevance to no one but the believer. Typically, fundamental beliefs are about what is true of the world or humanity at large and about the right or the good way for people generally to conduct their lives. Christianity and Islam, for example, are comprehensive bodies of belief about the nature of existence, about man's place in it and about the proper conduct of human life. It would therefore be singularly perverse for those who hold Christian or Muslim beliefs to insist that what their beliefs are beliefs *in* is a matter which is somehow private to Christians or Muslims and properly of concern to none but themselves. On the contrary, they must, and do, insist that the content of their beliefs is of importance to everyone.

The distinction that is in danger of being overlooked in respect for beliefs is that between (i) a belief's being mine in the trivial sense that it is what *I believe* and (ii) a belief's being mine such that *what I believe in* comes to belong exclusively to me. My beliefs are obviously 'mine' in the first sense, but that does not make them 'mine' in the second sense. Propositions, ideas, theories, theologies and the like cannot be appropriated and removed from the public domain simply by some individuals coming to believe they are true. The 'marketplace of ideas' is a happy metaphor, but it should not mislead us into supposing that adopting ideas, like buying goods, amounts to acquiring a right of private ownership over their content.

Finally, although what constitutes treating another's beliefs 'with respect' is a contestable matter, it is not infinitely malleable. On almost any view of what constitutes respecting a person, it is hard to take seriously the complaint that conducting a sober examination of the truth of another's beliefs amounts to not treating him, or his beliefs, with respect. Arguably, it is more insulting to have one's beliefs treated as though their truth or falsity were of no consequence; for that is to have one's beliefs not taken seriously as *beliefs*. That is a trap into which some varieties of multiculturalism seem to fall. There are many reasons for both tolerating and promoting cultural diversity, and there is nothing illogical about supporting and encouraging diverse forms of music, dance, literature and lifestyle, each of which has its roots in a particular culture. Now, cultures are often caught up with beliefs, particularly with religious beliefs. Again there are many reasons for tolerating all of those beliefs. However, it would be odd to find amongst them the claim that a world characterized by different religious beliefs is the best of all possible worlds and that nothing should be allowed to diminish that diversity. Different religious beliefs are rival religious beliefs. They represent rival claims to truth. 'Beliefs aim at truth', as Bernard Williams puts it.[20] For that very reason, to treat the truth of someone's beliefs as a matter of no consequence is already to have ceased to take them seriously as beliefs. But to seek to immure people's beliefs so that they will never be threatened or changed is effectively to do just that. It is to treat the continuance of those beliefs as of greater moment than their truth. It is to hold that it matters less that people should live lives grounded in falsehoods than that their existing beliefs, and the ways of life grounded in them, should remain undisturbed. At least those who challenge beliefs signal in so doing that they take them seriously as claims to truth. By contrast, those who seek to 'protect' beliefs so that they become, in effect, exhibits frozen in a social museum run the risk of reducing them to mere objects of curiosity which make no demands for serious consideration upon those who do not already hold them. No doubt those who wish to extend this protection to others' beliefs are generously motivated, but their efforts may ultimately be more patronizing than the attempts of others to refute them in the ordinary rough and tumble of argument.

Earlier I connected respect for beliefs with the liberal idea of respect for persons. If a strong version of respect for beliefs is untenable, and if indeed some of the reasons for rejecting it are reasons traditionally associated with liberalism, what is amiss in making that connection? After all, liberalism's propensity to treat beliefs, particularly religious beliefs, as essentially 'private' matters may itself have encouraged people to embrace the principle of respect for beliefs. The logic that I previously suggested ran from (i) respecting persons to (ii) the right of individuals to form and to pursue their own beliefs and then to (iii) their having the right not to have those beliefs attacked. The step from the first to the second notion—that is, from respect for persons to the right to form and pursue one's own beliefs—is not without complications, but I shall not examine those here.[21] More to the point is the step from the second to the third—from the right to form and pursue one's own beliefs to the right not to have those beliefs criticized. Of course, in strict logic one does not entail the other—my being free to form and pursue my own beliefs does not require that others abstain from questioning and criticizing those beliefs. Even so, there might still seem to be some affinity between these two notions. If my beliefs are reckoned to be of sufficient moment to be the subjects of guaranteed freedom, does that not imply that they constitute a territory which others should 'keep off'? Lord Scarman, for example, argued, in the context of the law of blasphemy, that Article 9 of the European Convention on Human Rights, which provides for freedom of religion, also 'by necessary implication . . . imposes a duty on all of us to refrain from insulting or outraging the religious feelings of others.'[22]

The apparent affinity between these two notions is, however, misleading. Why should people be free to form and pursue their own beliefs? That question can be answered in many ways, but the answer which seems fundamental to the deontological liberalism at issue here is that individuals' lives are their *own*; they should therefore be free to conduct *their* lives as they see fit. Thus the reason why I should be free to live in accordance with my beliefs is not that those beliefs come to acquire a peculiar sanctity merely because I adopt them. Rather I should be entitled to shape my life according to my beliefs because it is *my life*. In other words, insofar as there is something like a notion of ownership at work here, it is ownership over my life rather than ownership over certain propositions that I have come to believe in. That is why my right to live according to my beliefs entails that others are duty-bound not to prevent my so living but does not entail that they are duty-bound not to challenge the beliefs to which I devote my life.[23]

RESPECT, DECENCY AND MANNER

Are we then to conclude that the principle of respect for beliefs is entirely without merit? Are people to be free to speak, write and behave without having any regard for the beliefs of others? My previous arguments have shown that a strong version of the principle of respect for beliefs is untenable. Can the principle receive a less demanding and more plausible interpretation? Both sides in the Rushdie Affair were to be heard espousing the value of freedom of expression, and both also exhorted us to treat the beliefs of others with respect, albeit with varying degrees of enthusiasm.[24] That implied an understanding of 'respect' which was not seriously at odds with, or which was at least in some way reconcilable with, freedom of expression. What might that understanding have been?

Some of Rushdie's defenders may have meant by 'respecting another's beliefs' no more than the liberal idea of allowing people to live according to their beliefs. If that is all that respect for beliefs requires, it provides no reason for limiting free expression. Indeed, it is sometimes suggested that exceeding that minimal liberal position would entail 'imposing' others' beliefs upon people.[25] However, others who spoke in defence of Rushdie clearly did intend their injunction to respect others' beliefs to imply something more than the minimal liberal position, even though that 'something more' would leave substantial room for freedom of expression. Likewise, many of Rushdie's critics declared their acceptance of the right of freedom of expression and complained only that Rushdie had abused, or exceeded the limits of, that right.[26]

How then might we set a limit to the demands of respect for beliefs so that these fall short of prohibiting all serious challenges to people's beliefs? There are a number of possibilities.

Some of the antagonists in the Rushdie Affair seemed to want to place some subjects 'off-limits' altogether. Some matters, which religious believers regard with special reverence, should simply not be open to challenge. There are two difficulties with that view.

Even though it is only some aspects of a person's beliefs, rather than all of a person's beliefs, that are placed beyond the pale of criticism, that would still run into the objections that I have already outlined. Should any matter be placed beyond challenge and inquiry? If some aspects of people's beliefs are of especial importance to them, is it not also especially important that the truth of those aspects be open to scrutiny? And can it really be an act of disrespect merely to question what another asserts, however tenaciously they hold their belief?

Secondly, how are we to decide which matters are off-limits and which are not? It is not easy to see how there could be a single criterion that could be applied across all religions, and it would clearly be unacceptable to let each religion, or each sect of each religion, determine for itself the schedule of subjects which should be excluded from public discussion. Moreover, even the faithful may regard this approach as unnecessarily severe. Their own understanding of the demands of 'respect' is often less one of what should, and what should not, be open to challenge and criticism and more one of *how* that challenge and criticism should be conducted.

That takes us on to a second possibility. Every subject, it might be said, should be open to challenge and critical scrutiny, provided that that challenge and criticism respects the 'decencies of controversy'. It is not criticism or questioning that is objectionable; it is the conduct of criticism and challenge in a way which exceeds the bounds of 'decent' or 'civilized' or 'respectful' discussion.[27] A standard of that sort was long part of the English law of blasphemy.[28]

Once again, however, that proposal presents us with two difficulties: one technical, the other political. The technical problem is that of drafting a law that will indicate to people, with reasonable precision, what they may say and what they may not. Phrases like 'decent' or 'civilized' leave everything to interpretation. A law stated in those terms would make it almost impossible for people to know in advance whether their statements were permitted or prohibited; they could be sure only after the court had decided. Nor would it be easy to infer from a court's past decisions what its future decisions would be.

The political problem is how we are ever to achieve a reasonable degree of consensus on what it is acceptable and what it is unacceptable for people to say, remembering that we are legislating for a society of people with different sets of beliefs. The problem here is not merely that different individuals may have different views on what decency requires. It is also that different faiths, and different variants of the same faith, may have different conceptions of the limits imposed by 'decency'. In other words, rather than 'decency' providing a criterion that people can recognize and embrace independently of whatever beliefs they hold on religious matters, it may itself be a belief-dependent notion and so vary according to belief. Fundamentalists, for example, be they Muslim or Christian, are likely to possess a more severe view of what decency requires than those who are, in religious terms, 'liberals' or 'modernists'.

All of this may seem to make the attempt to exclude certain matters of substance from criticism seem hopeless as well as undesirable. However, there is a third possibility which might seem more promising. That option turns upon a distinction between the matter and the manner of what is said. Broadly, it holds that people should not be prevented from saying things merely because others dislike the 'matter' of what they say, but that they may be prevented from saying things in an objectionable 'manner'. Thus, your taking exception to the substance of my opinions is not an acceptable reason for my being silenced; but I may be prevented from expressing those opinions in an unnecessarily disrespectful way.

This is another distinction that was frequently invoked in relation to the English law of blasphemy. James Fitzjames Stephen, for example, characterized the law as follows:

> Every publication is said to be blasphemous which contains any contemptuous, reviling, scurrilous or ludicrous matter relating to God, Jesus Christ, or the Bible, or the formularies of the Church of England as by law established. It is not blasphemous to speak or publish opinions hostile to the Christian religion, or to deny the existence of God, if the publication is couched in decent and temperate language. The test to be applied is as to the manner in which the doctrines are advocated and not as to the substance of the doctrines themselves.[29]

There is much that is attractive about dealing with this issue in terms of the distinction between matter and manner. For one thing, it seems to offer a more workable distinction than appeals to 'decent' or 'civilized' discussion. Secondly, it would appear to offer us the best of both worlds. Freedom of expression would be limited, but in a quite unobjectionable way. No opinion would have to remain unstated, no subject would be excluded from open discussion and none would be exempt from critical scrutiny. All that would be proscribed would be attacks upon beliefs that were formulated in an unnecessarily abusive manner, and there would seem little reason to champion unnecessary abuse. Thirdly, the very phenomenon of treating other people's beliefs 'disrespectfully' often seems to be a question of manner rather than matter. As I argued above, subjecting another's beliefs to sober and serious examination can hardly be represented as treating those beliefs, or their holders, disrespectfully. It is when matters of special reverence are subjected to ridicule, contempt, vilification and the like that people are most likely to object. If the demands of respect concern the manner rather than the matter of one's treatment of another's beliefs, the principle of respect for beliefs will provide a secure normative underpinning for that distinction.

Does, then, this distinction between matter and manner provide an acceptable and workable standard for setting the boundary between freedom of expression and respect for beliefs? The distinction clearly has some merit. A sceptical academic treatise and an abusive vulgar lampoon may both deny the existence of God, but, although they agree in their matter, there would be a clear difference in their manner and a difference that is likely to be significant for those whose beliefs are under attack. The problem is that applying the distinction between matter and manner is rarely as straightforward as that. More often form and substance are so interrelated that it is not possible to treat one as a dispensable feature of the other. Manner and meaning are not wholly separable. Nor need a forceful and contemptuous manner be without justification. If strong and colourful prose enables an argument to hit its target more effectively, and if we believe that a religion or cult deserves to be targeted, then we are likely to feel that this more effective medium is justified. Religions are many and various and have been responsible for many of the worst, as well as some of the best, episodes in human history. Moreover, the exponents of religion have themselves not always been notable for the temperateness of their language. Those who possess a religious faith may be amongst the most reluctant to forsake the full armoury of language in opposing doctrines that they believe to be bogus and harmful or in condemning conduct that they regard as evil.[30]

Nor is it clear that this distinction was actually followed in English law or that it would have been acceptable to those who wanted some legal restriction placed upon blasphemy. It is quite obvious that it was the matter, and not merely the manner, of James Kirkup's poem that led to the successful prosecution of *Gay News* and its editor in 1977. The same is true of many earlier cases of blasphemous libel, even though judges who presided over those cases claimed to be applying the distinction between matter and manner.[31] It is also difficult to apply the distinction to Rushdie's work. For one thing, it is hard to know quite what should count as matter, and what as manner, in a novel. For another, it is quite clear that it is *what* Rushdie was understood to have suggested about Muhammad, the Koran and other important aspects of Islam, and not merely *how* he stated those thoughts, that Muslims and others found objectionable.

PUBLIC ORDER

Finally a word is needed about public order. The maintenance of public order is typically considered an uncontroversial obligation of governments; it is also widely regarded as an acceptable reason for curtailing freedom of expression. Even Mill was prepared to concede that the urgent need to prevent a riot should take precedence over free expression. A government might claim that it is obliged to proscribe what members of its population find offensive or disrespectful simply to prevent disorder, violence and social conflict. That seems to have been part of the motivation for banning *The Satanic Verses* in India and Pakistan, where people died in demonstrations against the book. In Britain there were suggestions that the sort of issue raised by the Rushdie Affair might be most satisfactorily handled in terms of the maintenance of public order and the avoidance of social conflict. In his response to the Rushdie Affair, the Chief Rabbi of Britain, for example, proposed that law should prohibit 'the publication of anything likely to inflame, through obscene defamation, the feelings or beliefs of any section of society, or liable to provoke public disorder and violence'.[32]

Yet there is reason to be deeply unhappy with this sort of proposal. If the prospect of violent and disorderly reactions is sufficient reason to curtail a freedom, that freedom is placed at the mercy of others' willingness to react in violent and disorderly ways. The readier they are to respond violently, the more they can curtail the freedoms they find objectionable. The more aggressive and intemperate a group, the more protection it will receive; the more stoical and pacific a group, the less protection it will receive. That cannot be right.

If we are to distinguish between justified indignation and mere bully-boy tactics, we have to have some way of distinguishing between justifiable and unjustifiable (or excusable and inexcusable) disorder. If disorder occurs, or is likely to occur, we need some way of determining whether the responsibility for that lies with the speaker or writer (was he being unreasonably provocative?) or whether it lies with those who have resorted to disorder and violence (were they responding in an unreasonable way?).[33] That, in turn, requires us to return to questions of what, all things considered, constitutes unjustified offence or what, all things considered, constitutes intolerable disrespect for people's beliefs. We cannot therefore satisfactorily evade the issues that I have raised in this chapter by making public order our concern.

It may be, of course, that a violent reaction is likely to occur, even though it would be unjustified, and that a government may feel unable to prevent or contain it except by disallowing what the reactors find objectionable. That government may then judge that it is duty-bound to maintain the public peace even though that entails preventing people saying what they ought to be free to say. However, it is still important to distinguish between (i) cases in which the fault lies with the speaker and in which a government merely prevents him from saying what he has no right to say, from (ii) cases in which the fault lies with the reactors and in which a government feels compelled to override people's rights of free expression only as the lesser of two evils. Clearly, more is required to justify government action in the second case than in the first.

CONCLUSION

What, then, are we to conclude? In spite of the difficulties that the notion of respect for beliefs encounters, it is not a principle that is wholly without appeal. I have shown that, in any very strong form, the principle is unsustainable. If we interpret the principle less demandingly, so that it is concerned with the manner rather than the matter of statements, it is still not without its problems and difficulties. However, the objections that it encounters in this weaker form are, perhaps, less imposing and less conclusive. If the principle is concerned more with the way something is said than with the substance of what is said, it does not run into the simple contradictions that characterize its stronger version, nor does it collide so readily with the concerns that underlie freedom of expression. Moreover, there is reason to object to remarks which are intentionally or gratuitously disrespectful, whether they concern religion or any other subject, and, of course, a whole range of terms and phrases exist in our language whose very purpose is to insult, humiliate, belittle or wound.

There can then be cases in which someone's disrespectful treatment of another's beliefs is properly condemned. Whether we should translate that moral condemnation into legal condemnation is another question. Suppose that we do encounter a case in which people's complaints of disrespect are well-founded and in which the author of the disrespectful remarks can claim no countervailing justification for them. Are these 'wrongs' really of sufficient moment to warrant bringing in the engine of law? If we draw only upon the idea of respect for beliefs, and do not allow that to be supplemented by claims about the *religious* wrongness of the author's words, is he guilty of very much more than bad manners or gross discourtesy? And, given the problems of definition that a law on this matter would face, and given the risk of serious and justified criticism being suppressed along with scurrilous and gratuitous insult, do we really want to have these matters decided upon by judges and courts? The conflicting interpretations that have been offered of Rushdie's *Satanic Verses* serve notice that these are likely to be 'hard cases' and ones which judges and lawyers will be poorly equipped to handle. My worries about translating the more modest version of the principle of respect for beliefs into law are of this more practical kind. They indicate that the safest course, as far as law is concerned, is to err on the side of freedom of expression.

However, if we do abjure resort to law, we can still insist that those who avail themselves of the right of free expression are under a moral obligation to exercise it responsibly. That does not mean that it must never be exercised in a way which people will judge disrespectful. Clearly, if people are wrong, it is usually desirable, as well as justifiable, for others to tell them so, even if they themselves find that exceptionable. Even if people are not wrong, it may be no bad thing, as Mill argued, that from time to time they should have to confront challenges to their most cherished beliefs. But to recognize that is not to endorse indiscriminate abuse. Strong, derisive, colourful, hurtful language may, on occasion, all things considered, be justified. But it may also, on occasion, all things considered, be unjustified.

The position that I am arguing for here then is that, legally, people should be entitled to do what, morally, they may be unjustified in doing. People ought not gratuitously to vilify the most cherished beliefs of others even though, legally, they should be unprevented from treating beliefs in that way—just as people should not call for the banning of books whose content they dislike, even though legally that is a call that they should be free to make. I would therefore be loath to see law, in the wake of the Rushdie Affair, used to limit freedom of expression in the name of respect for beliefs. I would also want public bodies to withstand the use of other sorts of coercive tactics such as attempts to prevent books being held by public libraries. However, if we can demand a certain minimum of robustness from readers, we can also demand it of authors. That does not mean, of course, that they should have to endure threats of assassination or other forms of physical assault. But they cannot expect to be spared the vigorous protests of those who strongly object to their works; for example, provided it does not form the prelude to something more sinister, I can see nothing wrong with people burning their own privately purchased copies of books to manifest their disgust at their content. Whatever the moral and practical limitations of the principle of respect for beliefs, it is a notion that should not be wholly dispensed with, and those who wield the pen should not feel themselves wholly free to disregard it.

NOTES

I am indebted to many people for discussions on the subject of this chapter. I am particularly grateful for their comments to Kay Black, David George, Robert Goodin, Tim Gray, Barbara McGuinness, Susan Mendus, Andrew Reeve, Albert Weale and two anonymous referees.

1. Salman Rushdie, *The Satanic Verses* (London: Viking, 1988). For a useful collection of documents on the Rushdie Affair, see Lisa Appignanesi and Sara Maitland, eds., *The Rushdie File* (London: Fourth Estate, 1989). Timothy Brennan, *Salman Rushdie and the Third World*

(London: Macmillan, 1989), examines *The Satanic Verses* in the context of Rushdie's other writings. Two general accounts of the Rushdie Affair and its background, one written from a Muslim and the other from a non-Muslim stance, are Shabbir Akhtar, *Be Careful with Muhammad! The Salman Rushdie Affair* (London: Bellew, 1989), and Malise Ruthven, *A Satanic Affair: Salman Rushdie and the Rage of Islam* (London: Chatto and Windus, 1990). At the height of the affair, Rushdie gave two main defences of his position: 'In Good Faith', published in *The Independent on Sunday*, 4 February 1990, 18–20, and 'Is Nothing Sacred?', Herbert Read Memorial Lecture, 6 February 1990 (London: Granta, 1990).

2. On 'overlapping consensus', see John Rawls, 'The Idea of an Overlapping Consensus', *Oxford Journal of Legal Studies* 7 (1987): 1–25.

3. Cf. 'Many writers often condescendingly imply that Muslims should become as tolerant as modern Christians. After all, the Christian faith has not been undermined. But the truth is, of course, too obviously the other way. The continual blasphemies against the Christian faith have totally undermined it. Any faith which compromises its internal temper of militant wrath is destined for the dustbin of history, for it can no longer preserve its faithful heritage in the face of the corrosive influences.

The fact that post-Enlightenment Christians tolerate blasphemy is a matter for shame, not for pride . . .

Those Muslims who find it intolerable to live in a United Kingdom contaminated with the Rushdie virus need to seriously consider the Islamic alternatives of emigration (*hijrah*) to the House of Islam or a declaration of holy war (*jehad*) on the House of Rejection. The latter may well seem a kind of hasty militancy that is out of the question, though, with God on one's side, one is never in the minority. And England, like all else, belongs to God.' Shabbir Akhtar, *The Guardian*, 27 February 1989 (Appignanesi and Maitland, eds., *The Rushdie File*, 240–41).

4. Whether the truth or falsity of beliefs is really of no consequence here is a nice question. It is arguable that, if my offence is misplaced because it stems from false beliefs, it cannot provide adequate reason for limiting your freedom. However, even if we take that view in principle, we may still regard it as of little consequence in practice, since, in religious matters, there is such radical and unresolvable disagreement about which beliefs are true.

5. Cf. 'The Rushdie affair is, in the last analysis, admittedly about fanaticism on behalf of God'; Akhtar, *Be Careful with Muhammad!*, 61, 'It is true of course that God is above human insult in one sense; but there is another equally valid sense in which the believer is morally obliged to vindicate the reputation of God and his spokesman against the militant calumnies of evil. Only then can he or she truly confess the faith. For faith is as faith does.' Ibid., 103. In taking action against *Gay News* for blasphemous libel in 1977, Mrs Mary Whitehouse explained, 'I simply had to protect Our Lord'; *New Statesman*, 15 July 1977, 74.

6. For the history of the English law of blasphemy, see G. D. Nokes, *A History of the Crime of Blasphemy* (London: Sweet and Maxwell, 1928).

7. The British government's considered position on the issues raised by the Rushdie Affair was set out in a letter sent by John Patten, Minister of State at the Home Office, to a number of leading British Muslims, 4 July 1989. The full text of the letter was published in *The Times*, 5 July 1989, 13, and is reprinted in *Law, Blasphemy and the Multi-Faith Society*, ed. Bhikhu Parekh (London: Commission for Racial Equality, 1990), 84–87. Following the *Gay News* case, the Law Commission recommended that the common law offences of blasphemy and blasphemous libel should be abolished; see Law Commission, *Working Paper No. 79: Offences against Religion and Public Worship* (London: HMSO, 1981), and the Commission's subsequent Report to Parliament, *Criminal Law: Offences against Religion and Public Worship* (Law Com., No. 145) (London: HMSO, 1985). For other discussions of the English law of blasphemy, see Richard Buxton, 'The Case of Blasphemous Libel', *Criminal Law Review*, November 1978, 673–82; J. R. Spencer, 'Blasphemy: The Law Commission's Working Paper', *Criminal Law Review*, December 1981, 810–20; St John A. Robilliard, *Religion and the Law* (Manchester: Manchester University Press, 1984), 25–45; David Edwards, 'Toleration and the English Blasphemy Law', in *Aspects of Toleration*, ed. John Horton and Susan Mendus (London: Methuen, 1985), 75–98; and Parekh, ed., *Law, Blasphemy and the Multi-Faith Society*.

8. E.g. John Rawls, *A Theory of Justice* (Oxford: Oxford University Press, 1971); 'Kantian Constructivism in Moral Theory', *Journal of Philosophy* 77 (1980): 515–72; Ronald Dworkin,

Taking Rights Seriously (London: Duckworth, 1978); *A Matter of Principle* (Oxford: Claren-don Press, 1986), pt. 3; Bruce A. Ackerman, *Social Justice in the Liberal State* (New Haven, CT: Yale University Press, 1980).

9. The following statements, prompted by the Rushdie Affair, provide examples of opin-ions which imply a commitment to something like the principle of respect for beliefs.

'In our view, it [*The Satanic Verses*] is a mere collection of insults, sacrilege, blasphemy and obscenity against Islam. No individual with the slightest grain of self-respect can accept being insulted and it is a more serious matter when a whole world community is subject to outrageous abuse of its inviolable sanctities.' (Dr Mughram Ali Al-Ghamdi, chairman of the UK Action Committee on Islamic Affairs; quoted in Appignanesi and Maitland, eds., *The Rushdie File*, p. 113.)

'The right to freedom of thought, opinion and expression should not be practised at the expense of the rights of others. Islam should not be degraded under the banner of freedom of thought. Cursing any divine religion (Islam, Christianity and Judaism) could not be excused on the basis of freedom of thought, expression and opinion; it is a low act which deserves to be condemned by the whole world.' (Declaration of the Islamic Conference Organization, *The Times*, 18 March 1989.)

'The Labour Party is a secular political party in a secular state. Britain, however, is a multi-racial, multi-faith society. There must be respect and understanding for everybody from every-body. This must impose constraints and restraints on freedom of speech.' (Max Madden, *Tribune*, 7 April 1989, 1.)

'When a prophet is treated in a supercilious, dismissive or crude manner, what is at stake is not his honour—for he is dead and too big a person to be affected by insults. What is really at stake is the sense of self-respect and integrity of those living men and women who define their identity in terms of their allegiance to the prophet. Their pride, good opinion of themselves, dignity and self-esteem deserve to be protected and nurtured, especially when these are sub-jected to daily assaults by a hostile society.' (Bhikhu Parekh, *New Statesman and Society*, 24 March 1989, 33.)

'The laws of this country [Britain] were made before the Muslim peoples arrived. . . . Now they must adapt to us. Others must respect our faith.' (Pir Mahroof Hussain, quoted in *New Statesman and Society*, 2 June 1989, 14.)

'Faith is something to be respected and revered: not to be used as an opportunity to humiliate.' (Keith Vaz, *The Independent*, 29 July 1989, 11.)

'One would think that, in a plural democracy, we should all generate respect rather than hatred for opposed yet conscientiously held convictions. . . . It can never be right to defend, in the name of liberalism, works that demean and humiliate human nature and tradition in any of their established forms.' (Akhtar, *Be Careful with Muhammad!*, 7.)

10. Note, however, that my offended reaction may be caused not by the fact that what you say amounts to disrespect for my beliefs, but simply by my taking exception to the substance of your remarks; for example, if you make abusive remarks about Christ, I may be offended, not because that constitutes disrespect for *me* as a Christian, but simply because you are abusing the Son of God.

11. For a catalogue of offended conditions, see Joel Feinberg, *The Moral Limits of the Criminal Law; Vol. 2: Offense to Others* (New York: Oxford University Press, 1985), 10–13.

12. On 'rights-based' moralities, see Dworkin, *Taking Rights Seriously*, 169–73; J. L. Mack-ie, 'Can There Be a Rights-Based Moral Theory?', in *Theories of Rights*, ed. Jeremy Waldron (Oxford: Oxford University Press, 1984), 168–81.

13. Rawls, 'Kantian Constructivism in Moral Theory', 543.

14. Appignanesi and Maitland, eds., *The Rushdie File*, 28.

15. For example, 'You are aggrieved that some of us have condemned you without a hearing and asked for the ban without reading the book. Yes, I have not read it, nor do I intend to. I do not have to wade through a filthy drain to know what filth is. My first inadvertent step would tell me what I have stepped into.' (Syed Shahabuddin, in Appignanesi and Maitland, eds., *The Rushdie File*, 47.)

16. In some measure this difficulty might be handled by subjecting offence to a test of reasonableness; see Chapter 10, this volume, and *Report of the Committee on Obscenity and*

Film Censorship (the 'Williams Report'), Cmnd 7772 (London: HMSO, 1979), 122–25. However, not everyone would accept that 'reasonableness' is an appropriate test to apply to offence; see, for example, Feinberg, *Offense to Others*, 35–37.

17. The grounds for freedom of expression are examined in relation to the Rushdie Affair in Jeremy Waldron, 'Too Important for Tact', *Times Literary Supplement*, 10–16 March 1989, 248, 260; and Albert Weale, 'Freedom of Speech vs Freedom of Religion?', in *Free Speech*, ed. Bhikhu Parekh (London: Commission for Racial Equality, 1990), 49–58.

18. For a contrary view, see Susan Mendus, 'The Tigers of Wrath and the Horses of Instruction', in *Free Speech*, ed. Parekh, 3–17.

19. For an examination of the significance of revelation for the Rushdie Affair, see Preston King, 'Rushdie and Revelation', in *Free Speech*, ed. Parekh, 28–48.

20. Bernard Williams, *Problems of the Self* (Cambridge: Cambridge University Press, 1973), 136.

21. I have examined some aspects of this relation in 'Liberalism, Belief and Doubt', in *Liberalism and Recent Legal and Social Philosophy*, ed. Richard Bellamy (ARSP, Beiheft 36) (Stuttgart: Steiner, 1989), 51–69; republished in my *Essays on Toleration* (London: ECPR/Rowman & Littlefield, 2018), 153–76.

22. *R. v. Lemon* [1979] 2 WLR 281 at 315. See also Weale, 'Freedom of Speech vs Freedom of Religion?', 55–58. For criticism of Lord Scarman's view, see the Law Commission, *Working Paper No. 79: Offences against Religion and Public Worship*, 78–80.

23. This may also explain why liberalism tends to concern itself much more with some sorts of belief than with others, an unevenness of concern which would seem odd if what mattered were beliefs as such. Why all the angst about moral and religious beliefs? Why not an equal concern with people's beliefs about the natural world or about art? Part of the answer would seem to be that moral and religious beliefs are 'life shaping' and are therefore more directly relevant to the kind of rights that the deontological liberal wants to assert.

24. For example, 'For Unesco, as a world-wide forum for dialogue and understanding, freedom of creation, of opinion and of expression, with respect for convictions, beliefs and religions, is essential. . . . It is every person's duty to respect other people's religions; it is also every person's duty to respect other people's freedom of expression.' (Frederico Mayor, Director-General of UNESCO, in Appignanesi and Maitland, eds., *The Rushdie File*, 125). 'Western emphasis on freedom of speech and tolerance is essential to civilisation. But reverence towards the traditions and ideals which other peoples hold dear is also an essential part of a healthy and happy society.' (H. B. Dehqani-Tafti, Bishop of Iran, Letter, *The Times*, 1 March 1989.)

25. For example, 'censorship is wrong and any calls for censorship by any fundamentalist religious leaders should be resisted. Not because of any lack of respect for anyone's sincerely held personal faith. But because it cannot be right to have one set of views imposed on everyone else by force, punishment and the censor.' (Diane Abbott, Letter, *The Guardian*, 16 February 1989, in Appignanesi and Maitland, eds., *The Rushdie File*, 111.) 'It is important that their [British Muslims'] spiritual values should be respected. . . . They, in turn, however, must not seek to impose their values either on their fellow Britons of other faiths or on the majority who acknowledge no faith at all.' (Editorial, *The Independent*, 16 January 1989.)

26. For example, 'It is not civilised to insult the religious sanctities of any people. We do not object to anyone writing critically about Islam—there are hundreds of such books in our libraries—but as you see these *Satanic Verses* belong to an entirely different genre.' (Spokesman for the Islamic Council, in Appignanesi and Maitland, eds., *The Rushdie File*, 78.) 'That Rushdie has insulted us is evident. . . . Of course, the rights of the individual, notably to free expression, are inalienable. Those of the community, notably the respect of its beliefs, are no less so.' (Moncef Marzouki, in Appignanesi and Maitland, eds., *The Rushdie File*, 182.) 'Islam and Muslims are not against freedom of expression but they are against freedom to insult and injure the religious beliefs and sentiments of any community.' (Drs S. M. Khalil, I. Mojahid, and M. S. Khan, Letter, *The Independent*, 3 March 1989.) 'The Muslims did not object to anybody disagreeing with Islam but only to somebody insulting it. Whether this right to insult exists, is the issue.' (Shoaib Qureshi and Javed Khan, *The Politics of Satanic Verses* [Leicester: Muslim Community Studies Institute, 1989], 27.)

27. 'No freedom can be absolute and, in a democratic society, the individual, whether a writer, an artist or an ordinary man in the street, must voluntarily restrain his freedom to stay within the universally accepted bounds of civilised conduct. If he does not, then he is asking for restriction to be imposed upon him. Some argue that writers and artists are a special category and must enjoy unrestricted freedom of expression. This notion must be challenged. No one who has read the book can deny that Mr Rushdie has transgressed all boundaries of decency and propriety in *The Satanic Verses* and for that he must be condemned.' (M. Akbar Ali, Letter, *Daily Telegraph*, 9 March 1989, in Appignanesi and Maitland, eds., *The Rushdie File*, 217.) 'This book is not a threat to Muslims. It is a threat to decency. One cannot and should not malign or publish libellous statements against leaders of any faith. Islam can withstand any controversy and criticism. No religion should tolerate blasphemy.' (Shaikh Mohommad, Letter, *The Independent*, 20 January 1989.) 'Freedom to criticise one religion from the basis of another is not under threat. . . . Muslims accept criticism but they will not tolerate vilification of the Prophet Mohamed. They in turn may criticise the beliefs of Christians but would never insult Jesus. . . . Criticism will be met, as it has been in the past, by "the ink of the scholars." But why should vilification be allowed? Surely it is not beyond the capability of intelligent people to distinguish between useful religious debate and deliberate distortion and insult.' (M. Hossain, Letter, *The Independent*, 1 June 1989.)

28. In *R. v. Ramsay and Foote* [1883], Lord Coleridge declared, 'I now lay it down as law, that, if the decencies of controversy are observed, even the fundamentals of religion may be attacked without the writer being guilty of blasphemy' (15 Cox C. C. 231 at 238). He was not, however, the first to interpret the law in that way.

29. *Stephen's Digest of the Criminal Law*, 9th edition (1950), article 214. This formulation of the law was endorsed by Lord Scarman in *R. v. Lemon* [1979], 2 WLR 281 at 315.

30. Cf. 'Religion is a luxuriant growth. Alongside major historical traditions is a tangled mass of lesser and newer ones, not always easily identifiable, fiercely competitive, some of them much given to litigation, and with beliefs that range from the profoundly impressive to the suspiciously barmy. Where does one draw the line? Is Ron Hubbard, for instance, a candidate for posthumous inviolability? And if not, why not? And what might be the consequences of protecting the reputation of religious founders who, in any sane and tolerant society, would deserve to be ridiculed?' (Archbishop of York [commenting on a proposal to extend the law of libel to the founders of religious faiths], Letter, *The Times*, 1 March 1989.)

31. See further, Chapter 10.

32. Letter, *The Times*, 9 March 1989 (in Appignanesi and Maitland, eds., *The Rushdie File*, 215–16). Similarly, though rather more opaquely, the Archbishop of York suggested dealing with the issues raised by the Rushdie Affair by developing 'that aspect of the present law of blasphemy which focuses on the shaking of the fabric of society when widespread sensibilities are offended. Implicit in this is the belief that stable societies contain a sacral element, and that it is unwise to allow this sense of sacredness to be undermined by scurrilous attack.' (Letter, *The Times*, 1 March 1989.)

33. Note that, even if we judge that the speaker was speaking improperly, that need not suffice to condone a violent or disorderly reaction.

Chapter Twelve

Religious Belief and Freedom of Expression

Is Offensiveness Really the Issue?

My interest in this chapter is in the offence that people feel, or claim to feel, when their beliefs are criticised or ridiculed and which they present as reason for others to desist from criticism and ridicule. My main interest is not so much in the large question of whether, all things considered, we should or should not criticise or ridicule others' beliefs. Rather my concern is more specific: if there is good reason for not attacking, or for curbing the way in which we attack, a belief, does that 'good reason' consist in not causing offence to those who hold the belief?

The issue is well illustrated by the furore over a series of cartoons, carica-turing Muhammad, that came to a climax during February 2006. The car-toons were originally published by the Danish newspaper *Jyllands-Posten* on 30 September 2005, but it was only some months later that the controversy sparked by their publication became global in scope. The general features of that controversy are well known and I shall not recount them here.[1] That affair was only one of a number of controversies that have raised much the same issues. Other prominent examples have been the controversies sur-rounding *Jerry Springer: The Opera*, *Behzti* (the play by a young Sikh wom-an, Gurpreet Kaur Bhatti, staged in Birmingham that upset other Sikhs), Martin Scorsese's *The Last Temptation of Christ*, and, of course, casting its long shadow over all of these, Salman Rushdie's *The Satanic Verses*. Pope Benedict XVI was the unlikely cause of a further episode when, during a lecture delivered at the University of Regensburg in September 2006, he quoted a fourteenth-century Byzantine emperor, Manual II Paleologus, saying that the new things that Muhammad had brought to the world were 'only evil and inhuman, such as his command to spread by the sword the faith he preached'. Shortly afterwards, the Berlin Opera cancelled its production of Mozart's *Idomeneo*, fearing the reaction of Muslims to a scene in which the King of Crete severed and held aloft the head of Muhammad along with those of Jesus, Buddha and Poseidon.

One issue raised by these cases is how they bear upon the proper content of law. Should law protect people from offence to which they are susceptible because of their beliefs? However, the larger question they raise is what constitutes acceptable conduct in the public domain. Public conduct that the law permits is still conduct that is open to critical appraisal and, nowadays, social norms governing acceptable expression are likely to be at least as significant as the letter of law.

I shall question the relevance of offence for cases such as the Danish cartoons, but my doing so does not imply that those who complained had nothing to complain about. Rather, it casts doubt on whether offence constitutes the proper ground of their complaint.

OFFENCE AND BELIEF

Why is offensiveness so readily cited as an objection to assaults upon people's beliefs? The obvious answer is that people evidently dislike and object to attacks upon their beliefs. If we take the cases I have just cited, that is all too evident in the reactions they evoked. But the invocation of 'offence' in relation to beliefs is explained by more than just that. Consider the Danish cartoons again. If I am a Christian or an atheist, how can I recognise that the authors of the cartoons were wrong to draw them and that others were wrong to publish them? That cannot be because I agree with Muslims that the artists and the publishers wronged God's Prophet, because I do not accept that Muhammad was God's Prophet. If I am a Christian, I must regard Muhammad as a false prophet and, if I am an atheist, I must reject the very idea that anyone is, or has been, or might be, God's prophet.

What I can recognise, however, is the offence caused to Muslims by the cartoons. I can also recognise that offence as a negative experience that, other things being equal, it is undesirable that anyone should suffer. Thus, even though I do not myself subscribe to Islam, I can still recognise the badness of the impact of the cartoons upon Muslims. Muslims can, in the same fashion, recognise and regret the offence caused to Christians, Jews or Hindus by assaults upon sacred aspects of their faiths. Thus, offensiveness can function as a common denominator amongst people who hold different and conflicting beliefs. Each group may reject the beliefs of others, but each can nevertheless recognise and deprecate the offence that another group suffers when its false but cherished beliefs are attacked. Each group can also recognise that the badness of causing offence gives it reason not to attack the beliefs of others, and gives others reason not to attack its beliefs.

The readiness with which people now register complaints of offence may be impelled by more than the logic I have just described. Sometimes it may be explained by embarrassment. In a context of diverse beliefs and cultures, people are often reluctant to insist upon the rightness and superior wisdom of their own beliefs. Such insistence, they fear, might seem arrogant and at odds with the equal status that they should accord others who think differently. One way in which they can avoid the embarrassment of seeming arrogant and disrespectful is to subjectivise their complaint. If they complain only that others' conduct has offended them, they avoid asserting that their uniquely right beliefs should count for more than the benighted beliefs of others. They simply make a statement about themselves. They report only that the conduct of others has caused them to undergo a disagreeable experience. They are then able to offer the authors of the objectionable conduct a reason to desist from it while avoiding questions concerning the status of the beliefs at issue. To that extent, there is an association between the relativism that people often feel impelled to concede in a context of diversity, and their readiness to formulate their complaints in the subjectively oriented language of offence.

Use of the language of offence in relation to religious beliefs therefore depends for much of its appeal upon a distinction between the experience of offence and the beliefs upon which that experience depends. Generally, in a society characterised by different and conflicting beliefs, especially different and conflicting religious beliefs, people will find it unacceptable that beliefs should be imposed upon them that they do not share. Moreover, insofar as they regard others' beliefs as false, they will lack reason to give weight to those beliefs. But the reality and unpleasantness of offence can be distinguished from the truth of the beliefs upon which it depends. We therefore have reason to take account of belief-based offence, even though we reject the beliefs upon which it is based. Muslims may complain about the wrongness of the cartoons rather than about the offence that the cartoons cause them to feel. But non-Muslims can and should take account of the offence that Muslims feel rather than the wrongness of which Muslims complain.

FOUR PATHS NOT TAKEN

My main purpose in this chapter is to challenge the position I have just described. However, there are a number of ways in which the relevance or significance of offence can be challenged upon which my own argument will not rely.

(1) Perhaps the most common reason given for setting aside complaints of offence is that offence is too slight and trivial an experience to ground a claim that it should be taken seriously. Thus, for example, those who embrace the harm principle often exclude offence from its ambit because it is too slight an injury to count as harm. That is not an objection upon which I shall rely. There is clearly an element of arbitrariness about the tightness or generosity with which we define 'harm', and the issue of whether offence should figure in our moral and legal calculations should not be settled by mere definition. Offence is, by its very nature, disutile, and that seems to provide good *prima facie* reason for its figuring in our assessment of what we should and should not do. It is true, of course, that the slightness of offence means that it will frequently be outweighed by competing considerations, especially in the area of speech and expression. But to say that offence will be frequently outweighed is not to say that it has or should have no weight at all.

(2) A second possible objection to giving weight to offence is that, although we may be able to separate offence from beliefs, the practical effect of responding to offence will be just the same as imposing beliefs. Christians will be offended by Islam, and Muslims will be offended by Christianity. If we respond to the offence of each, we shall find ourselves vetoing Christianity for the sake of Muslims, and Islam for the sake of Christians. So, while we may be able to distinguish offended sensibilities from the beliefs upon which they are based, the practical effect of preventing offence is likely to be no different from privileging and imposing the beliefs of the offended. On this issue, I would bet with J. S. Mill: 'there is no parity between the feeling of a person for his own opinion and the feeling of another who is offended at his holding it, no more than between the desire of a thief to take a purse, and the desire of the right owner to keep it' (1974: 151). The interest that Christians and Muslims have in being free to pursue their own faiths outweighs any interest they have in vetoing one another's faith. It is unlikely to be true therefore that, if we take account of offence, we shall find ourselves instituting exactly the same measures as if we were imposing beliefs.

(3) But there is another, more fundamental, way in which the attempt to separate offence from belief might be challenged. Are the offended feelings that we experience when we witness wrongful conduct separable from the belief that generates those feelings? Is not our propensity to experience those feelings integral to our believing that the relevant conduct is wrong? Can we believe a particular act to be wrong and yet remain utterly unmoved by it, utterly bereft of any feeling of distress, anger or indignation? If not, it might be suggested that a belief and the feelings of offence associated with it are really parts of a single whole. We cannot treat them as separable phenomena

such that we can take account of one but not the other. To recognise and to give weight to belief-based offence is to recognise and give weight to the belief that is integral to that offence (Ellis 1984).

Contrary to these claims, it does seem both possible and reasonable to distinguish the disagreeable experience caused by the contravention of a belief from the belief itself. The thinking behind giving significance to offence seems to be essentially utilitarian in character. Putting it crudely, offence is bad because it is unpleasant, and the more unpleasant it feels the worse it is. That is not to say that only comprehensive utilitarians can give significance to offence. It is to say only that, insofar as we take account of offence in the sorts of context that are my concern, we do so because of its disutile character. If, when people's beliefs are attacked or contravened, they experience hurt or pain or distress, it is the disutility, the painfulness, the disagreeable nature, of that experience that makes offence a relevant consideration. We can therefore give weight to the disutility people experience because of the beliefs they hold, even though we give no weight to their beliefs as truth-claims.

(4) A more compelling claim is that we should subject claims of offence to a test of reasonableness. People *take* offence as well as give it, and we can ask therefore whether they *reasonably* take offence—which is to ask whether they have good or adequate reason to be offended. If someone takes offence unreasonably, we may think their offence has no claim to be taken seriously, even though we do not doubt the reality and the unpleasantness of the offence they feel.

Two tests of reasonableness are potentially relevant to belief-based offence:

1. Given that I believe x, is it reasonable for me to be offended by y, and reasonable that I should be offended by y to the extent that I am or claim to be?
2. Is my belief in x reasonable? If it is not, do others have reason to take my offence seriously? Arguably, belief-based offence should not count if the belief upon which it depends is unreasonable.

Since one person's offence is not readily accessible to another, we may often need to use test (a) to gauge the reality and degree of offence that we can suppose a person actually feels, rather than merely as a test of the offence they have good reason to feel. In other words, we may need to use it as an empirical, or a presumptively empirical, test as well as an evaluative one. The appeal of test (b) is tempered by its obviously problematic character: where people have different and conflicting beliefs, they are likely to have different and conflicting views on what constitutes a reasonable belief. Use of the test may therefore mean that offence ceases to be a common denominator for those who hold different and conflicting beliefs.

The appeal to reasonableness gets closer to my concerns since it begins to shift the focus towards the reason for the claimed offence. Nevertheless, an appeal to the idea of reasonable offence still supposes that offence provides the burden of the argument. It is still offence that lends weight to the claim, even though that will be only offence that passes a test of reasonableness.

TWO BASIC FEATURES OF OFFENCE

For my purposes, two elementary features of offence are particularly significant. First, it constitutes a *negative* experience. To experience offence is to suffer a disutility. It is only because and insofar as offence is a 'bad' that it has any claim to be factored into our moral and legal thinking. That is not to say that offence need always be bad all things considered. If I challenge your beliefs robustly, I may cause you offence, but I may also cause you to rethink your beliefs and to develop different, more soundly based, beliefs. In that case, both of us might accept that the offence was a price worth paying. But that is consistent with holding that offence itself should rank as a negative and, other things being equal, ought to be avoided.

Secondly, offence describes a mental state. To be offended is to undergo not just a *negative* experience but also a negative *experience*. In that sense, offence is a subjective phenomenon. Typically, we say that it is a person's feelings or sensibilities that are offended. We sometimes speak as though the offensive character of an act has a more objective quality. For example, rather than saying that x 'offends me', I might say that x 'is offensive', which may suggest that 'offensiveness' describes a property of x itself rather than the effect x has on me. That is a natural phraseology to use given that the members of a community are likely to be offended by the same things. Because they have shared reactions, any particular member of the community can say, 'x is offensive' rather than 'x offends me'. Indeed, the fact that the generality of people are offended by x may enable me to say, 'x is offensive', even though I myself do not actually experience x as offensive. But there is still here an essential reference to a mental state—the mental state that x induces in most people or in the typical person.

Of course, people are not always precise in their use of language, and they may, on occasion, use 'offensive' simply to mean 'wrong'. If, for example, I describe a colleague's Machiavellian conduct as 'offensive', I might mean only that it is wrong and unacceptable—and wrong and unacceptable not because it causes me or others offence but wrong and unacceptable as such. As the language of offence has become more ubiquitous, so it seems people have become more inclined to use 'offensive' to mean 'wrong'. I want to resist that extended usage because it confuses two quite different sorts of claim. In particular, offence cannot function as a common denominator amongst people who have different and conflicting beliefs if it comes to mean precisely the kind of thing over which they differ and disagree.

TYPES OF OFFENCE

'Offence', then, describes a negative mental state, and the 'badness' of being offended consists in the disutile nature of that mental state. I now want to consider how well that conception of offence maps onto the various cases to which the noun 'offence' and the adjective 'offensive' are commonly applied. In fact, those terms are used in conjunction with a wide variety of conditions.[2] Rather than review all of those here, I shall consider only three broad types: sensory offence, convention-based offence, and belief-based offence.

Sensory Offence

The most uncomplicated instances of offence are those in which our senses are assaulted. Some odours are foul, some sights are unpleasant, and some sounds set our teeth on edge. Often the offence that we experience in these sorts of case seems to be the direct product of a stimulus to our senses that we experience immediately as unpleasant. It is these instances of direct sensory offence that conform most straightforwardly to the conception of offence as a negative experience.

There are, however, instances of sensory offence in which belief plays a mediating role. Joel Feinberg notes that 'the smell of freshly baked macaroni and cheese smells very little different from that of much human vomit' (1985: 15). Clearly how offensive we find that smell, and perhaps whether we find it offensive at all, is likely to be affected by which of these— macaroni cheese or vomit—we believe ourselves to be smelling. We are likely to find the smell of rotting flesh of any sort unpleasant, but we are likely to find it even more unpleasant if we believe it to be, or know it to be, the odour of rotting human flesh rather than the rotting flesh of some other animal.

Even so, the role of belief in sensory offence is different from its role in what I describe as belief-based offence. In the case of sensory offence, the belief that makes a difference is a belief about what we are experiencing. In the case of belief-based offence, the belief has its effect not merely by making us think that, as matter of fact, something is taking place, but by identifying an act or a state of affairs as wrong. We might mark this difference by distinguishing between 'belief-informed' offence and 'belief-based' offence. In belief-based cases, it is the perceived wrongness of the conduct that the belief identifies as wrong that is critical to the experience of offence. That is not true of offence that is merely belief-informed, and sensory offence, even when it is belief-informed, continues to map fairly straightforwardly onto the general conception of offence as a negative mental state.

Of course, issues of right and wrong can arise in relation to sensory offence. If I identify your pig farm as the source of the disgusting smell I have to endure, I may complain that you are wrong to engage in a form of farming that imposes a negative externality upon me which significantly diminishes my quality of life. But that alleged wrong is external to the offensiveness of the smell itself: the alleged wrong plays no part in causing me to experience the smell as offensive. Rather it concerns where responsibility lies for the unpleasant experience I undergo. So, for example, whether I can really claim to be a victim of the farmer is likely to be affected by whether I chose to buy a house next to an already-existing pig farm or whether the farmer chose to establish his pig farm next to my already-existing home. But, even if I acknowledge that the farmer is blameless, that will not transform the odour of his pigs' dung into the smell of sweet violets.

Convention-Based Offence

I use this term to encompass the sorts of offensive conduct normally associated with indecency. The paradigm cases are public nudity, public sex and public defecation. Whether this sort of offence is genuinely distinct from belief-based offence is rather less clear than in cases of sensory offence. First, there is considerable disagreement over whether indecent conduct is objectionable only because it is offensive or because it is thought wrong in a way that is not wholly reducible to its offensiveness. Those who take the latter view usually go on to claim that the capacity of indecent conduct to offend depends upon its being found wrongful (e.g. Simester and von Hirsch 2002). If we adopt that view, we have scope for a further disagreement: is the 'wrong' of indecency a wrong of a sort that is the same as, or different from, the wrong that figures in cases of belief-based offence?

Here I shall not attempt to resolve either issue. But it may be that there is no issue to resolve in that different people will object to conventionally indecent acts for different reasons. For some, public sex and public nudity may be objectionable only because they are distasteful or embarrassing. In other words, they are objectionable only because they cause awkward and undesirable mental states in those who, unwillingly, observe them.

Amongst those who object to indecent acts as 'wrong', some may use that term only in a weak moral sense or perhaps in no moral sense at all. That is, they might concede that indecent conduct contravenes social norms that define conduct that is conventionally 'proper' but deny that the relevant 'right conduct' is 'right' in a more profound sense. They would accept that, if another society has different conventions according to which public nudity and public sex are unexceptionable, there is nothing fundamentally wrong with that society. On that view, the capacity of conventionally indecent conduct to cause awkwardness, embarrassment or other unpleasant reactions—in other words, its capacity to cause offence—can still play a significant part in explaining why people should refrain from indecent conduct.

For others, however, indecent conduct might be thought wrong in a more profound sense. Take, for example, the injunction shared by many Muslims that one should present oneself modestly. That has the character of a more deeply based obligation, and it does imply that a society is in error if its members see nothing wrong in freely displaying their genitalia. For people who have this deeply moral conception of decency, indecent conduct—if it is characterised in the language of offence—will fall within the category of belief-based offence rather than mere convention-based offence.

Belief-Based Offence

By belief-based offence I mean offence that presupposes and stems from the holding of a belief. In this sort of offence, the fact that an act is perceived as wrongful by the offendees is crucial to their finding it offensive. That was obviously so in the case of the Danish cartoons. Clearly, in the eyes of Muslims, the artists who drew the cartoons of Muhammad, and the newspaper editors who published them, were guilty of a wrong. It was that wrong that was the source of the offence they experienced. If what the cartoonists had done had been morally innocent in the eyes of Muslims, their protests would have been unintelligible. The same applies to Christians who objected to the way in which Jesus Christ, the Son of God, was portrayed in *Jerry Springer: The Opera*.

In the case of this putative form of offence, the principal question I want to ask is whether our focus should really be upon offence. What were Muslims and Christians complaining about? It was not the mental state that they were caused to have by the cartoons; rather it was the wrongful treatment of a figure sacred to their faith. That might be acknowledged but thought irrelevant. It may be that their offended condition did not matter most, or at all, to Muslims in the case of the cartoons or to Christians in the case of *Jerry Springer*; but, for reasons I explained earlier, the offence experienced by each might still be others' proper concern, and properly their only concern. Yet, there is something decidedly odd about that. When a group complains, there is something odd about sidelining what they actually complain about and attending to something that they do not complain about. But I shall pass over that for the moment.

I want to dig further into the nature of the offence that Muslims and Christians were supposed to have suffered. What kind of mental state were they caused to undergo?

That is not easy to answer, and the answer might have been different for different believers. One set of emotions might have been hurt and distress, and those sorts of emotions stay closest to the disutile experience that is crucial to the idea of offence. But another set of emotions that seem to have been even more evident were anger, indignation and outrage. Let's think of it in those terms. Suppose I feel anger at your conduct. Should your conduct be constrained because it causes me to experience anger?

The first thing to be said about these emotional responses is that anger, indignation and outrage do not fit the simple model of a disutile experience. Is anger painful? Does indignation hurt? Is the experience of outrage like the experience of an unpleasant smell or a disagreeable sight? None of these equivalences seems persuasive. Yet the appeal of offence as a ground of complaint relies on its being disutile, painful, or hurtful. Thus, once we start unpacking the different responses that 'offence' or 'offended' is used to encompass, we shall find that it is not all of a piece and we might want to say very different things about its different variants.

A second point is that the mere fact of my anger is not normally adequate reason for my preventing, or for others preventing, the conduct that makes me angry. At the very least, we would want to distinguish between justified and unjustified anger and to discount the claims of unjustified anger. But that may seem to do little to damage the claims of belief-based offence, since we previously saw that we can distinguish between reasonable and unreasonable offence and give weight only to offence that is reasonable. So, let's stick with a case of justified anger.

Even in that case, it is not my anger itself that is likely to be the focus of my objection but the act that causes the anger. Suppose I am angry with you because you keep stealing plants from my garden. What matters is not the anger I am caused to feel by your wrongful act but the wrongfulness of the act that causes me to feel anger. Your wrong consists in what you do, rather than in how your act makes me feel. That applies both for myself as victim and for any third party I might expect to intervene on my behalf. In a similar fashion, if we look to the emotional experience of Muslims and Christians as the proper focus of our concern—their anger, outrage and indignation—we are likely to be looking in the wrong place. We ought to be looking at what they are angry about, rather than at some negative mental state they are allegedly caused to undergo.

My claims here are partly empirical. When people describe irreverent and disrespectful treatments of sacred aspects of their faith as 'offensive', they need not be understood as meaning that the wrongness of those irreverent and disrespectful acts consists in their causing an offended mental state.

Rather, the description 'offensive' can be merely a way of marking an act as wrongful, just as phrases such as 'it makes me angry' and 'it makes me sick' mark an objection without articulating what that objection is. Indeed, as I noted earlier, the language of offence has become so fashionable and so ubiquitous that people now sometimes use 'offensive' merely as a synonym for 'wrong', so that the focus shifts entirely from their mental state to the quality of the act they condemn. But, if we make that shift, 'offensiveness' ceases to contribute anything to an explanation of why the act is wrong.

The issue here is, however, not only empirical. It also concerns what constitutes a good reason or any reason at all. If 'offensive' retains its meaning of inducing a negative mental state, reporting that I find something offensive is not very different from reporting that I do not like it or that I find it objectionable. In the case of a sensory offence, such as a foul smell, my not liking it or my finding it objectionable may count as a reason against it; indeed, there may be little else that I can say. But in the more complex cases that arise from the interface of belief, action and expression, we are unlikely to accept 'I don't like it' or 'I find it objectionable' as a self-sufficient reason. We shall want to know *why* the objector does not like it or objects to it, and we shall think we have reason to take account of the objector's complaint only if he gives us a reasonable explanation. If the objector can say no more than 'I just don't like it' or 'I *experience* it as objectionable', that provides us with little or no reason to defer to the objector and to curb our conduct.

TWO FURTHER CONSIDERATIONS

That is the primary way in which I want to question the relevance of offence in cases like the Danish cartoons and *Jerry Springer*, but, before proposing an alternative, I want to mention two rather different points concerning offence that push in the same direction.

Stoicism and Sensitivity

Suppose there are two different religious faiths, A and B. The adherents of faith A have had to get used to living in secular contexts and have become accustomed to criticisms of, and attacks upon, their beliefs, including attacks that take a mocking and satirical form. Because they have had to experience those attacks over a long period of time, they have become in some measure inured to them. The adherents of faith B are not, in the same measure, used to that form of criticism and attack. Thus, when the two faiths are attacked in similar fashions, the adherents of faith B become much more upset and protest much more loudly than those of faith A. Does that provide good reason for giving the adherents of faith B greater protection than those of faith A? If our concern is with the offence people experience, with the disutility of the mental state they undergo, it would certainly seem to. Yet surely, if two faiths are attacked in equivalent ways, the adherents of each faith have equal ground for complaint and, if they have equal ground for complaint, that ground must consist in something other than their respective mental states.

'Bare-Knowledge' Offence and Reasonable Avoidability

Amongst those who take the claims of offence seriously, there is one sort of offence to which even they are reluctant to give much, if any, significance. That is offence caused by 'bare knowledge'. If, for example, a couple has sex in public such that it is forced on the attention of unwilling observers, we may think that the offence of those observers is both real and reasonable and that it provides good reason for prohibition. Similarly, if someone were to decide to become a latter-day Diogenes of Sinope and to masturbate and defecate in public, we may think that those who have these activities forced upon their attention have reasonable ground for complaint. But suppose now that someone says they are offended by the bare knowledge, or the bare belief, that people are having sex or masturbating or defecating in private; we are likely to regard their claimed offence very differently.

Indeed, there seems to be a widely shared consensus amongst people who write on this subject that bare-knowledge offence should be disregarded. Different sorts of reason can be, and have been, given for discounting this sort of offence.

(i) Sometimes the reason is that an act's being performed in public or in front of unwilling observers is essential to its being offensive, as in the case of public sex and public defecation.

(ii) Sometimes it is because those who claim bare-knowledge offence are thought to possess abnormal sensibilities, and the abnormality of their sensibilities provides reason to discount them.

(iii) Sometimes the empirical conjecture is made that, even when bare-knowledge offence is real, it will be too slight, too lacking in intensity, to have any significant claim to our consideration.

(iv) And sometimes this sort of offence is discounted out of concern for individual liberty. In a well-known passage, H. L. A. Hart insisted, 'To punish people for causing this form of distress [distress occasioned by bare knowledge] would be tantamount to punishing them simply because others object to what they do; and the only liberty that could coexist with this extension of the utilitarian principle is liberty to do those things to which no one seriously objects. Such liberty plainly is quite nugatory' (1963: 47).

But consider now the offence that was at issue in the cartoons case. For the vast majority of the millions of Muslims who protested against the cartoons, that offence was occasioned by 'bare knowledge'. Certainly, the cartoons were published initially in a Danish newspaper and subsequently in newspapers in other European countries. But Muslims in the Middle East, Pakistan and Indonesia were at no risk of confronting the images in those European newspapers. Even in countries in which the cartoons were published, Muslims could easily avoid them by not buying or not reading the newspapers in which they appeared. The cartoons were made available on the internet but, again, they were easily avoided by anyone who wished not to see them. Similarly, Christians who objected to *Jerry Springer: The Opera* could, without difficulty, have refrained from attending performances of the opera and could easily have avoided it when the opera was screened by the BBC.

So in both of these cases the vast majority of believers either had never seen the source of their offence or, if they had seen it, had sought it out and seen what they could easily have avoided. If they had not seen the cartoons or the opera, their offence was bare-knowledge offence, which, if it were to be regarded as bare-knowledge offence is normally regarded, would have no claim to be taken seriously. If they had sought out and seen the cartoons or the opera, they had done so wilfully and willingly and, to that extent, were the authors of their own offence and so had no reasonable ground for complaint.

Does that mean that Muslims had no reason to protest about the cartoons—or no reason that could count as a reason for non-Muslims? Were Christian complaints about *Jerry Springer* so completely lacking in substance? If the yardstick of offence enables us to dismiss their complaints quite so peremptorily, we have reason to reconsider whether it is offence that is only or primarily at stake.

RESPECTING BELIEFS

If offence should not be our primary concern in the treatment we mete out to others' beliefs, what should? Can we have any other sort of concern for beliefs we do not share? There are, of course, considerations such as incitement to hatred, social cohesion and public order, but I want to conclude by commenting briefly on the alternative that I propose in Chapter 11, which is both close in concern to, but categorically distinct from, offended sensibilities: the principle of 'respect for beliefs'. The phrase 'respect for beliefs' is really a shorthand way of expressing what is really respect for people as holders of beliefs. It draws upon the general idea of persons as proper objects of respect. That general idea of respecting persons is closely allied to the principle that we should accord them the right to embrace whatever beliefs seem most compelling to them and the right to live their lives in accordance with the beliefs they embrace. The idea of respect for beliefs is, in turn, an extension of that idea. If we take seriously the idea of respecting people as the bearers of beliefs, we have reason, *ceteris paribus*, not to subject their most cherished beliefs to vilification and ridicule.

Now, even if we accept this idea of respect for beliefs, there is reason to interpret its demands parsimoniously, and I shall say something in a moment about how far we should allow it to limit free expression. But, before taking up that issue, I shall indicate how respecting beliefs differs from abstaining from causing offence.

The principal difference is that respecting beliefs is not about causing or avoiding certain mental states in others. It is about treating people in a right or wrong way, and the rightness or wrongness of that treatment turns upon the character of the treatment itself rather than upon the mental state it induces in people. Consider the case of insult. An insult is likely to cause offence to the insulted person, and we are likely to accept that it is both reasonable and appropriate for the victim to be offended by the insult. But neither the idea of an insult nor its wrongfulness is reducible to the idea of offence. The insult consists in the negative characterisation it presents of the insulted person, and its wrongfulness (if it is wrongful) resides in that negative characterisation. Offended feelings are epiphenomena of the insult rather than essential to its being either an insult or wrongful. In the same way, disrespecting someone's beliefs may cause offence, but we can distinguish the disrespectful character of the act from its capacity to offend and we can locate the wrongness of the act in its disrespectful character rather than in any offence it may or may not occasion.

If we operate with the idea of respect for beliefs, rather than with that of offended sensibilities, we no longer have to suppose that the wrong of treating people's beliefs disrespectfully consists in their being caused to 'feel funny inside' or to undergo some other unpleasant mental state. We do not have to assimilate it to noisome smells or grating sounds, nor even to the embarrassment or distaste caused by public nudity or public sex, or the revulsion caused by public defecation.

In addition, we do not have to worry about the inaccessibility of the offended feelings of others and how we are to determine how offended their feelings really are. Nor do we have to worry about giving people an incentive to pretend to be deeply offended in order to put a stop to something that they actually object to on other grounds.

Respect for beliefs also gives us reason to treat different groups of believers in an even-handed fashion, rather than give greater consideration to some groups simply because they are more susceptible to offence or more readily take offence.

We can appreciate too the irrelevance of whether offence is occasioned by direct witnessing or by 'bare knowledge' of the offending conduct. In general, the wrongfulness of an act is unaffected by whether or not we witness its commission. We have no less reason to deprecate acts of murder, rape or fraud simply because we were not present at the scene when they were committed. If Muslims conceive the caricaturing of Muhammad as wrongful and if Christians conceive the lampooning of Jesus as wrongful, there is no reason why that should weigh with us only if they have directly witnessed, or cannot avoid directly witnessing, those wrongs.

I previously suggested that, when people complain of a wrong rather than of offence stimulated by the wrong, it is odd to ignore what they complain of and to focus on something else. The same observation might be made in relation to respect for beliefs. What concerned Muslims about the Danish cartoons was the wrong done to the Prophet rather than the disrespect for Muslim beliefs manifested by the cartoonists. What concerned Christians about *Jerry Springer* was the opera's disrespectful treatment of Jesus rather than of themselves. So, if we focus on respect for beliefs, are we just as removed from the real concerns of believers as if we focus on their offended sensibilities?

In fact, respect for beliefs does seem to have been an immediate concern in the cartoons affair, in that many Muslims saw the cartoons as a calculated act of disrespect, a calculated insult, directed at Muslims themselves (Laegaard 2007b). But let's put that to one side and suppose that the primary concern of Muslims was the disrespect shown to Muhammad rather than themselves. Respect for beliefs is still arguably closer than offended sensibilities to that concern. People's beliefs about what is wrong matter to them because it matters to them that wrong should not be done. We recognise that when we accept that there is something peculiarly bad about compelling people to commit acts that they conscientiously believe to be wrong. Think, for example, of making conscientious objectors fight in wartime, or requiring Christians to denounce Christ, or compelling Muslims to defile the Koran. But it matters to people not merely that *they* should not do wrong but also that *wrong should not be done*.

There are, of course, instances of people who seem concerned only that their own hands should be clean. But that exclusive concern with personal purity is narcissistically self-obsessed, deeply unattractive and, for most moralities, thoroughly reprehensible. It is hard to understand how anyone can take the idea of wrongful conduct seriously and be morally oblivious to anything but their own purity. One of the imperatives behind respect for beliefs is recognition that it matters to people not merely that they should not do wrong, but also that there should not be wrong in the world. In that way, respect for beliefs stays close to the concerns of believers themselves.

This turn in my argument will no doubt set off alarm bells, and so it should. If we allow people's beliefs, particularly their religious beliefs, to dictate not only their own conduct but also the conduct of others, we seem to have a recipe for repression. So let me now make clear that I think we can give only limited weight and scope to the idea of respect for beliefs. The very circumstances that make that idea relevant—a society, or a world, in which there is a plurality of different and conflicting beliefs, religious and irreligious—severely limit what it might justify.

First, in a plural society and a plural world, people's beliefs are conflicting as well as different. The Christian's belief is, of necessity, critical of the Muslim's belief, and the Muslim's belief is, of necessity, critical of the Christian's belief. And that will be true across the whole range of beliefs, including atheism and agnosticism. So it would make no sense, in these circumstances, to say that respect for beliefs demands that no one should criticise or attack anyone else's belief.

Secondly, there are limits to what we can reasonably describe as disrespectful treatment. If I give serious critical attention to a belief, it is hard to see how that could count as disrespectful to those who hold the belief, even though they may not welcome my critical attention and even though my critique will do much more to undermine their belief than any exercise in ridicule or irreverence.

Thirdly, the panoply of well-known arguments for freedom of expression must weigh very heavily in the balance and against the propensity of 'respect' to curtail that freedom. Thus, the scope of the principle of respect for beliefs will be set by considerations external to the principle as well as by those implicit in the principle itself.

Fourthly, even if we concede that there is some force in the idea of respect for beliefs, we might still insist that there are some beliefs that have no claim to be respected. Some beliefs may be so absurd, so depraved, so evil, so outrageous, that they do not deserve our respect; indeed, they may deserve our disrespect. And it is worth noting that those who insist most vehemently on this possibility are likely to include those who hold the strongest and most uncompromising religious beliefs.

The sum of all this is that respect for beliefs is likely to count for most when assaults on people's beliefs are merely gratuitous, that is, when they have no serious purpose or no purpose that justifies their not giving countervailing weight to what matters to others. The difficulty is, of course, that whether an act is merely gratuitous is often disputed between its perpetrators and objectors. Consider the case of the Danish cartoons again. For protesting Muslims, the cartoons did have the character of a gratuitous assault. But for the cartoonists and their publishers, the cartoons were a rejection of self-censorship, a studied assertion that they would not allow themselves to be bullied or intimidated into treating Islam with greater reserve than other systems of belief. In some measure, the reaction to the cartoons made their point for them. However, my concern in this chapter has been not to arrive at a verdict on the Danish cartoons or any of the other episodes I have mentioned, but rather to tease out what is and what is not relevant to reaching a verdict in cases of that sort.

The idea of respect for beliefs deserves to be taken seriously, but it is an idea that has to compete with many other important concerns, particularly in the spheres of speech and expression. In practical terms, there is good reason to fight shy of mobilising law on behalf of respect for beliefs. There is too great a risk that that clumsy instrument will silence what ought not to be silenced and that it will be used for the underhand purposes of opportunist politicians. But I began by saying that our public concerns relate not only to law but also to how we should treat one another as citizens within the law. It is within the law that the idea of respect for beliefs should figure in our calculus of what constitutes acceptable conduct.

NOTES

1. For critical discussions of the issues raised by the Danish cartoons that relate to the concerns of this chapter, see Cram (2009), Keane (2008), Laegaard (2007a, 2007b), and Rostbøll (2009). See also the following special journal issues: 'The Danish Cartoon Affair: Free Speech, Racism, Islamism and Integration', *International Migration* 44(5) (2006); 'The Mohammed Cartoons Controversy in Comparative Perspective', *Ethnicities* 9(3) (2009).

2. For a lengthy catalogue, see Feinberg 1985: 10–13.

REFERENCES

Cram, Ian. 2009. 'The Danish Cartoons, Offensive Expression, and Democratic Legitimacy'. In *Extreme Speech and Democracy*, ed. Ivan Hare and James Weinstein, 311–30. Oxford: Oxford University Press.

Ellis, Anthony. 1984. 'Offense and the Liberal Conception of the Law'. *Philosophy and Public Affairs* 13(1): 3–23.

Feinberg, Joel. 1985. *Offense to Others*. New York: Oxford University Press.

Hart, H. L. A. 1963. *Law, Liberty and Morality*. London: Oxford University Press.

Keane, David. 2008. 'Cartoon Violence and Freedom of Expression'. *Human Rights Quarterly* 30(4): 845–75.

Laegaard, Sune. 2007a. 'The Cartoon Controversy: Offence, Identity, Oppression?' *Political Studies* 55(3): 481–98.

Laegaard, Sune. 2007b. 'The Cartoon Controversy as a Case of Multicultural Recognition'. *Contemporary Politics* 13(2): 147–64.

Mill, J. S. 1974. *On Liberty*, ed. Gertrude Himmelfarb. Harmondsworth: Penguin.

Rostbøll, Christian F. 2009. 'Autonomy, Respect and Arrogance in the Danish Cartoon Controversy'. *Political Theory* 37(5): 623–48.

Simester, A. P., and Andrew von Hirsch. 2002. 'Rethinking the Offense Principle'. *Legal Theory* 8(3): 269–95.

Index

Abdul-Aziz, Faruq, 186
abortion, 48–49, 51n12, 51n13, 51n14, 74.
  See also exemptions and abortion
accommodation, xxiv–xxv, 33, 37,
  151–152, 176; cultures, of, xv–xvi, 1, 4,
  167–168; equality and, 154–161, 170;
  obligations and, 163–167, 168–170;
  religions, of, xv, 131–132, 141–142.
  See also exemptions
Ackerman, Bruce A., 122
Ahmad, Mr, xxvii, xxviii, 109–111,
  120–121, 125, 126n2, 126n6
Amish, xxvi
An-Na'im, Abdullahi A., 50n7
authenticity, 84, 101, 133, 136
autonomy, 133, 134, 135, 136

Barry, Brian, xxix–xxx, 9, 26n4, 107n18,
  107n20, 135, 153–154, 160, 164, 165,
  169, 170n2, 171n16, 195
Behzti, 279
Beitz, Charles, 54, 78
beliefs: burdens versus consequences of,
  121; choice, and, xxvii–xxviii,
  113–117, 127n10, 132–136, 147n11,
  168; diversity of, promoting, 118–120;
  manifestation versus motivation,
  211–212, 227n20, 228n41; objective
  and subjective tests, xxxi–xxxii, 138,
  147n15, 147n16, 205–225;
  responsibility for, xxvii, xxix, 112–113,

118, 133, 135–136, 139, 200n6;
  responsibility for the consequences of,
  xxvii–xxix, 109–125, 132–133,
  137–144, 160, 165; sincerity of,
  xxxi–xxxii, 138, 205, 208, 209, 210,
  213; truth, and, 263–264, 265–266, 268,
  274n4. *See also* freedom of belief; ill-
  founded religious belief; respect for
  beliefs
Bentham, Jeremy, 235, 236, 250n37
Bhatti, Gurpreet Kaur, 279
blasphemy, xxxiv–xxxv, 229–248, 253,
  256, 257–258, 263, 266, 268, 269, 270,
  274n7
Buchanan, Allen, 55, 78
Buddhism, xviii

Canadian Charter of Rights and Freedoms,
  xxvi, 210
Christianity, xiii, xviii, 217, 230, 231–234,
  243, 257–258, 264, 265
Christians, xxxiv, 197, 256, 257–258, 287,
  291; corporal punishment, 211;
  crucifix, and, xxvi, 181, 224, 228n41;
  purity ring, and, 157, 181, 211; same-
  sex relations, and, xxvi, 181; Sundays,
  and, xxvi, 111, 139, 147n18, 157, 181,
  184–185, 201n33–202n34, 224–225
circumcision, ritual, 179–180
Cohen, G. A., 133, 139–140, 146n8

297

Coleridge, Lord, xxxixn8, 234, 241, 242, 250n53, 277n28
compromise, 255
conscience, morality of, 216
Cruft, Rowan, 81n49
cultural determinism, 161–162
cultural relativism. *See* relativism
culturalism, xix, 2, 5, 8, 12, 14–15, 19, 25, 26n1
cultures: beliefs, and, 11–12, 14–15, 19, 27n5, 114–115, 218–219; community constraints, and, 162–163; concept of, xvi–xvii, 2; contexts of choice, as, 27n6; shared goods, as, xviii–xix, 5–7. *See also* diversity, cultural; human rights and cultural diversity; human rights, ethno-cultural; identity; recognition of cultures

Danish cartoons of Muhammad, xxxvi, 279, 280, 281, 287, 289, 290, 291, 293, 294
'decencies of controversy', xxxiv, xxxvi, 234, 241, 242, 258, 268, 277n28
deliberation, 21, 25
democracy, 263; justice, and, 21–25
Denman, Lord, 241, 249n25
Denning, Lord, 110, 229
Desrosiers, Sarah, 130–131, 143, 145, 146n6
Devlin, Lord, 232, 233, 236
difference. *See* diversity
difference-blindess, difference-sensitivity, xv, 97, 103–104, 152
Diogenes of Sinope, 290
discrimination, 109, 110–111, 116, 127n15; direct religious, xxvii, 130, 132, 144, 148n22, 158; indirect religious, xxvii, xxviii–xxix, 130–132, 141–145, 158–160, 168–169, 190–193, 199, 200n2; group test for, 222–223; law on, xxvii, xxviii–xxix, xxx, xxxi, xxxixn6, 126n6, 129, 130, 132, 138, 142, 144, 146n1, 146n2, 147n15, 147n16, 151, 158–160, 166, 168–169, 177, 178–179, 191; organised religions, and, 143–144, 165, 171n20, 177, 189, 222–223; proportionality, and, 130, 131, 141–144, 147n18, 147n19,

159–160, 192–193, 228n43
diversity, xiii–xvi; cultural, xv–xvi, 1–26, 31–50; religious, xiv–xv, xxxiii, 254, 255–256, 258–259, 265–266, 294; value of, 152
Donnelly, Jack, 58, 60
Dworkin, Ronald, 50n5, 133, 135, 140, 146n8

Eisgruber, Christopher, 183–188
equality, 83, 152, 154; deontic, 154–156, 158, 170; freedom, of, xxi, 47, 179–180; fulfilment, of, 119–120, 127n18; merit, of, xxiii–xxiv, 4, 14; opportunity, of, xix, xxix–xxxi, 152–154, 169–170, 177, 192; respect, of, 8, 9, 14; rights, of, xxi, 41, 74–75; status, of, xxi, xxiii–xxiv, 38, 41, 44, 62, 72, 74; telic, 154–155, 158. *See also* recognition, equal
essentialism, 101
esteem: self-, 86, 87, 102–103; social, 87, 98–101, 106n11, 106n13
European Court of Human Rights, xvi, xxvii, 110, 148n21
Eweida, Nadia, 224, 225
exemptions, xxv–xxxii, 129, 151, 155–157; abortion, and, xxvi, 177, 178; adhockery, exercises in, xxxi, 196, 199; distributive justice, and, xxx–xxxi, 175–199; dress codes, and, xxvii, xxx; equality and, xxix–xxxi, 154–158, 175, 182–189, 198–199; ill-founded belief, and, 205–226; justification of, xxix–xxxi, 160–161, 163–167, 168–170, 179; military service, and, xxvi, 188, 190; on-balance judgment, and, 156–158, 160, 166, 182–183, 195, 200n15, 212; passport photographs, and, 178, 198; rights to, xxvi–xxvii, 181–183; statutory, xxv, xxxi, 131–132, 176, 177–178, 189–190, 194–197. *See also* accommodation
expensive preferences, 139–140, 160–161

fairness among cultures, xv–xvi, xix–xx, 7–26, 154–155
Feinberg, Joel, 235, 238, 275n11, 285
Fraser, Nancy, 105n1, 106n7, 107n19

free exercise, US constitutional right of,, xvii, xxvi, xxxviiin5, 183–189, 200n17

freedom: association, of, 64; belief, of, xv, xvii, xxvii, 41, 42, 47, 109, 110, 117–118, 136–138; conscience, of, xvii, xxx, 111–112, 165, 166, 170, 176, 190, 215, 216; expression, of, xxxii–xxxviii, 76, 229, 230, 232, 237, 240, 241, 244, 248, 253, 257, 263–267, 271, 272–273, 276n17, 282, 294, 295; obligation and, 163–164, 171n19

religion, of, xiv–xv, xvii, xxvi, xxx–xxxi, xxxii–xxxiii, 63–64, 68, 110–111, 116, 124, 129, 132–133, 134, 136–139, 145, 177, 178, 179–181, 215–219, 253

Galeotti, Anna Elisabetta, 85–86, 97–98, 102, 106n10

Gay News, xxxiv, xxxvi, 230, 239, 240, 242, 243, 248, 258, 270

gays, 86, 97, 102, 107n18

Gilabert, Pablo, 54

Golemboski, David, 228n36

Green, Abner, 212

Griffin, James, 54, 73, 74, 76, 81n50

Habertal, Moshe, 27n8

Hale, Sir Matthew, 231, 249n14

harm and the harm principle, 234–235, 243–244, 282

Hart, H. L. A., 164, 236, 238, 290

hate speech law, xxxiii–xxxiv

Hegel, G. W. F., 83–84, 93

Hetherington, Henry, 242

Hinduism, xiii

Hindus: cremation by open pyre, and, 147n16, 157, 181–182, 228n35; diet, and, 153

Hobbes, Thomas, 44

homosexuality. *See* gays

Honneth, Axel, 14, 86–87, 98–101, 103, 105n3, 106n11–107n17

human rights, 31–50, 53–78; children's, xxii, 73, 76, 81n45; collective, 45–47, 53, 57–65, 77–78, 79n16, 79n17, 80n20; collective goods, and, 45, 51n8, 53, 61–64; conditional, 75, 76–77; continuous and discontinuous

conceptions of, xxi, 37–43; cultural diversity, and, xx–xxi, 31–50; derivative, 76; dignity, and, 71; ethno-cultural, xxi–xxiii, 53–78; group-specific, 53–54, 66–78; human nature, and, 72–73; human status, and, 71–72, 73–75, 77–78, 93; humanist conception of, 54, 55–56, 72, 78; individualism, and, 44–47; legal conception of, 55–56, 78; political conception of, 54–56, 72, 78; scepticism about, 50n2; second-level conception of, 40–43, 51n11; universal, xx, 31–33, 53–54, 66, 69, 72–77; women's, xxii, 74, 76; worth, and, 71. *See also* human rights, collective

human rights law, xxx, xxxi, 55, 56, 78, 138, 144, 147n16, 157–158, 177, 178–179, 181–183

Hume, David, 241

Hutterites, xxvi

Iacobucci, J, 210

Iceland, xiv

identity, xxiii–xxiv, 8, 14, 169. *See also* recognition of identities

identity politics, xxxiii–xxxiv, 100–101

Idomeneo, 280

ill-founded religious belief: examples of, 207–210; group test for, 222–225; judicial agnosticism and, 213–215; judicial competence on, 219–222; moral acceptability and, 214; pragmatic approach to, 222; right to religious freedom, and, 205–206, 209–210, 214, 215–219. *See also* beliefs, objective and subjective tests

immigration. *See* migrants

impartiality: cultures, among, xix, xx, xxi, 1, 9–26, 26n3, 26n4, 27n6, 28n16; first-and second-order, 26n4; human rights and, 42, 49, 74; liberal, 97; religions, among, 125, 178

incitement: hatred, of, xxxiii, 291; violence, of, xxxiii

indecency, 236–237, 239, 286–287

indigenous peoples, xiii, xx, 20, 57–58, 64, 66–67, 75, 77, 78

insult, 292, 293

Iran, xiv
Islam, xiii, xviii, 207–208, 217, 264, 265

Jehovah's Witness: blood transfusion, and,
    121, 128n20; trade union membership,
    and, 128n26, 208–209, 213, 228n37
Jerry Springer: The Opera, xxxvi, 279,
    287, 289, 290, 291, 293
Jesus Christ, xxxvi, 238, 242, 243, 247,
    257, 259, 287, 292–293
Jews, xxvi; discrimination law, and,
    147n15, 172n25; ritual slaughter, xxv,
    152, 155, 156, 165, 178, 194, 195, 198;
    Sabbath, and, 111, 201n33; Succot,
    festival of, 209–210; yarmulke, 153
Jovanović, Miodrag A., 80n29
Judaism, 217, 233
justice, 21–22; beliefs, and, 112–113, 131;
    comparative and non-comparative, 176,
    180, 186; distributive, 26, 177–179,
    263; fulfilment, and, 119–120;
    legitimacy and, 22; luck, and, 133;
    procedural, perfect and imperfect,
    23–24; procedural, pure, 22–23. *See
    also* exemptions and distributive
    justice; Rawls, theory of justice
Jyllands-Posten, 279

Kant, Immanuel, 50n6, 84
Kantianism, 8, 91, 100, 218
Khomeini, Ayatollah, xxxv, 254, 255
King-Hamilton, J, 230
Kirkup, James, xxxiv, xxxvi, 230, 240,
    242, 243, 244, 270
Koran, xxxvi
Kukathas, Chandran, 13, 27n10
Kymlicka, Will, xx, 13, 27n6, 27n10, 66,
    75, 80n27, 170n3

Laborde, Cécile, 200n15, 214, 227n21
Larmore, Charles, 35, 50n4
Last Temptation of Christ, The, 256, 279
law and freedom of expression, 268,
    272–273, 280, 295
law of blasphemy. *See* blasphemy
Lemon, Denis, xxxiv, 230, 242
liberal democratic societies, xiii, xiv–xv,
    xxvi, 85, 86, 129, 135

liberalism, 10, 27n6, 27n12, 51n14, 97,
    109, 112, 256, 259, 266, 267, 276n23
Locke, John, 63, 249n15
Lucas, J. R., 235
luck egalitarianism, 133, 139–140, 146n8,
    146n9, 168, 172n24

Macklem, Patrick, 55
Margalit, Avishai, 27n8
matter and manner, xxxvi, 241–243,
    250n53, 269–270, 272
Mba, Celestina, 224, 225
Mead, G. H., 98
migrants, xiii, xix–xx, xxiv–xxv, xxvi, 20,
    70, 80n40
Mill, John Stuart, xxxvi, 7, 162, 233, 234,
    235, 236, 250n34, 250n42, 263, 264,
    271, 273, 282
Miller, David, 162, 163
Milne, Alan, 38, 50n6
minorities, xiv; cultural, 17, 46; language,
    20, 62, 64, 68–70, 74–75, 80n36;
    majorities, and, 111, 155–156,
    197–198; national, xiii–xiv, xx; 'old'
    and 'new', 70, 80n40. *See also* migrants
modus vivendi, 25, 28n17, 255
Montefiore, Bishop, 243
moral standing, 41, 47, 49; individual
    versus group, 16–19, 27n10, 27n12,
    44–47, 59–60, 65, 105n4
morals, enforcement of, 232–233, 238
Mozart, 280
Muhammad, xxxv, xxxvi, 253, 256, 257,
    259, 280, 293. *See also* Danish cartoons
    of Muhammad
multiculturalism, xiii, xvii, xix–xx, xxix,
    16, 21, 84, 151–153, 167–168, 169,
    170, 265
Muslims, xxxv, 85–86, 89–90, 97,
    253–254, 255, 256, 260–261, 264, 280,
    287, 290–291; beards, 186, 188–189,
    192; dress, forms of, 153, 157, 160,
    165, 181, 193, 198; Friday prayers,
    xxvii, 109–111, 120, 121, 126n2,
    126n6, 157, 181; handling alcohol and
    pork, 207, 211, 213; headscarfs,
    xxviii–xxix, 85, 86, 103, 130–131,
    207–208; ritual slaughter, xxv,
    151–152, 155, 156, 165, 166, 178, 194,

195, 198, 202n34
Mustafa, Shakoor, 186

Nagel, Thomas, 27n12
neutrality. *See* impartiality
Nicholls, Lord, 138, 214–215, 220, 227n29
Nickel, James, 76
Noah, Bushra, 130–131
Nozick, Robert, 237

offensiveness, xxxiv–xxxv, xxxvi–xxxviii, 229, 231, 233–248, 254, 256–258, 259–262, 275n10, 279–291, 292–293; bare-knowedge, 290–291, 292–293; belief-based, 281, 282–283, 287–289; breach of the peace, tendency to cause, 243–245, 250n56, 251n58; convention-based, 286–287; intensity of, 245; numbers, and, 245–246; reasonableness, and, 246–247, 261–262, 275n16, 283–284, 288; religious sensibilities, and, 237, 238, 241–243, 257, 262, 288–289; sensory, 285–286; susceptibility to, 289–290, 292. *See also* matter and manner
Opportunity. *See* equality of opportunity
overlapping consensus, 37–40, 43, 50n6, 50n7, 255

Parekh, Bhikhu, xxix, xxx, xxxviiin3, 26n2, 151–155, 156–157, 161–162, 163, 165, 167, 169, 170, 170n1, 171n17, 171n18
Patten, Alan, xxxviiin4, 80n40
Pentassuglia, Gaetano, 79n16
personhood, 48, 51n12
Phillimore, J, 240
Pope Benedict XVI, 279
plural society. *See* diversity
public order, 233, 243–245, 271, 291
public/private, xv–xvi, 111–112, 239–241

Quebec Charter of Human Rights and Freedoms, 209, 210
Quong, Jonathan, 193, 201n33–202n34

Rawls, John, 9, 22, 23, 27n12, 35, 36, 37–38, 41, 43, 50n3, 50n4, 50n6, 50n7, 54, 78, 81n56, 233; public and non-

public reason, 220; theory of justice, 112, 113, 122, 141
Raz, Joseph, 16, 51n9, 54, 78, 80n19
reasonable disagreement, 35–36
recognition, 83–104; cultures, of, xxiii–xxiv, 14–15, 84–85, 90, 95–97, 100; equal, xix, xxiii, 14–15, 83–84, 85, 92–93, 95–96, 99–100, 104, 107n16; difference, of, 84, 87, 91–92, 103–104; identities, of, 84–86, 89–92, 94–98, 100–101, 103–104, 104; meaning of, 88–89; mediated and unmediated, 90–92, 94–95, 104–105; merit, 92–101, 102, 104–105, 106n6, 106n8; mutual, 83–84; persons, of, 87, 91, 104, 106n7; redistribution, and, 83, 105n1; status, 92–101, 102, 104, 106n7, 106n8; struggles for, 14, 84, 86, 87, 88, 94; universalism and, 84, 87, 91–92. *See also* toleration as recognition
relativism, 264, 281; cultural, xviii, 3–5, 12, 236; conscience, of, 216, 217
religion: definition of, xvii; established, xv, 69, 230, 231. *See also* diversity, religious; freedom of religion; 'religion or belief'; religious practices
'religion or belief', meaning in law, xvii, 146n2, 167, 214–215, 227n28
religious practices: central versus peripheral, 212–213, 225, 227n24; moral acceptability of, 214; obligatory versus discretionary, 212–213, 225, 227n24
Renteln, Alison Dundes, 38, 50n6
respect: beliefs, for, xxxv–xxxvi, xxxvii, 133, 136, 162, 254, 258–270, 272, 275n9, 291–295; cultures, for, xix, 5, 7–9, 14; people/persons, for, 7–9, 291; self-, 86, 87, 102–103, 162; social, 87, 98. *See also* recognition
right versus the good, 9, 166–167
rights: animal, 49; cultural, xx, 46, 53–78; group, xix, xxi–xxii, 16–17, 45–47, 51n9, 51n10, 53, 57–65, 79n15; group-specific, xxi–xxii, xxii, 13, 27n8, 53–54; language, xxii, 53, 60, 62, 64, 68–70, 74–75, 76, 104; minority, 53, 68–70, 80n36; natural, 72; peoples', 57–58, 67; welfare, 74, 76, 77. *See also*

equality; freedom; human rights; rights, group; rights, group-specific
ritual slaughter, xv, xxv, 156, 165, 166. *See also* Jews, Muslims
Rorty, Richard, 19, 114
Rushdie, Salman, xxxv, xxxvi, 253–254, 255, 260–261, 263, 267, 270
Rushdie Affair, xxxv, 47, 253–254, 255, 256, 258, 260, 262, 263, 264, 267, 271, 274n7

sabbatarianism, 123, 139, 147n18, 193. *See also* Christians; Jews; Seventh Day Adventists
Sager, Lawrence, 183–188
Saggers, Mr, 128n26, 208–209, 213
same-sex marriage, 86, 102
Sandel, Michael, 51n14
Satanic Verses, The, xxxv, 253, 256, 260–261, 270, 271, 272, 279
Saudi Arabia, xiv
Scanlon, T. M., 9, 135
Scarman Lord, 110–111, 244, 248n10, 266
Scorsese, Martin, 256, 279
Seglow, Jonathan, 107n20
self-determination, right to: collective, 60, 62–63, 64, 80n21; individual, 63; national, 18; peoples', 66
self-government, xiii–xiv
Seventh Day Adventists, xxxviiin5, 184–185, 192
Sherbert, Adell, 184
Sikhism, xiii
Sikhs: discrimination law, and,5n6 5n10 6n15 7n25 8n31: dress code of, xxvii, 162; facial hair, 158–159; kirpans, and, xxv, 66, 155, 156, 166, 171n8, 180, 195–196, 198; nagar kirtan, 63; turbans, and, xxv, xxx, xxxi, 66, 103–104, 123–124, 127n16, 153, 156, 162, 165, 166, 171n9, 177–178, 191–192,

194–195, 198
slavery, 32, 51n14
social cohesion, 20, 145, 152, 169, 291
social contract, 63–64
Stephen, James Fitzjames, 234, 249n26, 269

Tasioulas, John, 54, 73
Taylor, Charles, xxiii, xxiv, 14, 27n9, 84–85, 95–97, 102, 103, 105n2, 106n8–106n9
Taylor, John, 231
Thorsen, Jens, 229, 240, 248n2
toleration, xiv–xv, xxiv, 4–5, 104, 109, 111, 249n15, 274n3; toleration as recognition, 85–86, 97–98, 106n10
Tully, James, 84

UN Charter, 71
US Constitution, xvii
US Supreme Court, xvii
utilitarianism, 120, 123, 235, 265, 283

value pluralism, 99–100

Waldron, Jeremy, 163
Walker, Lord, 220
well-being, 8
Wellman, Carl, 54, 74, 76–77, 79n9, 81n50
Whitehouse, Mary, xxxiv, 230, 234, 250n46, 251n61
Williams, Bernard, 266
Willis, Lord, 230, 232
Wolfenden Report, 236
Working Group on Minorities of the Sub-Commission on the Promotion and Protection of Human Rights, 70

Young, Iris, 104, 106n7

Zaffar, Waseem, 208

Index of Legal Cases

Ahmad v. ILEA, 1976, 1977, 1978,
109–111, 125n1, 126n4–126n6, 157,
171n11, 181, 200n11
Ahmad v. UK, 1981, 110, 126n3
Ansonia Board of Education v. Philbrook,
1986, 126n6
Arrowsmith v. UK, 1978, 211, 226n16
Azmi v. Kirklees Metropolitan Borough
Council, 2007, 201n32

Baggs v. Fudge, 2005, 146n2
Bowman v. Secular Society, 1917, 234,
241, 249n27, 250n51, 250n56

Campbell and Cosans v. UK, 1982, 227n28
Copsey v. WWB Devon Clays Ltd, 2004,
2005, 157, 171n10, 181, 200n11

Dawkins v. Crown Suppliers (PSA), 1991,
1993, 126n6

Employment Division v. Smith, 1990, xxvii,
xxxviiin5, 185, 201n25
Esson v. London Transport Executive,
1975, 126n6
Eweida v. British Airways, 2008, 2010,
142, 147n16, 147n19, 172n23, 224,
225, 228n40, 228n41, 228n46
Eweida and Others v. UK, 2013, 148n21,
181, 200n9, 200n10, 226n19, 228n41

*Fluss v. Grant Thornton Chartered
Accountants*, 1987, 126n6
*Fraternal Order of Police Newark Lodge
No. 12 v. City of Newark*, 1999,
186–187, 188, 192, 201n26

Grainger PLC & Others v. Nicholson,
2009, 146n2

*Hussain v. London Country Bus Services
Ltd*, 1984, 126n6

*London Borough of Tower Hamlets v.
Rabin*, 1989, 126n6

Mandla v. Dowell Lee, 1982, 1983, 126n6,
127n10, 147n15, 162, 172n25,
191–192, 201n31
*Mba v. The Mayor and Burgesses of the
London Borough of Merton*, 2012,
2013, 147n18, 201n32, 201n33,
224–225, 228n42, 228n43, 228n46

Naiz v. Ryman Ltd, 1988, 126n6
Noah v. Desrosiers, 2008, 130–131,
142–143, 145, 146n5, 147n17

*Oestreicher v. Secretary of State for the
Environment*, 1978, 126n6

Panesar v. The Nestle Company Ltd, 1980, 171n15

Pankhurst v. Thompson, 1886, 234, 249n26

Post Office v. Mayers, 1989, 126n6

Prais v. EC Council, 1977, 126n6

R v. Aylesbuy Crown Court ex parte Chalal, 1976, 124, 128n23

R v. Bradlaugh, 1883, 234, 241–242, 245–246, 249n25, 250n54, 251n60

R v Boulter, 1908, 240, 244, 250n49, 250n56

R v. Carlile (Mary), 1821, 232, 233–234, 249n16, 249n23

R v. Carlile (Richard), 1819, 231, 232, 233, 249n15, 249n16, 249n22

R v. Gathercole, 1938, 230, 248n9

R v. Gott, 1922, 244, 245–246, 250n56, 251n57, 251n59, 251n60

R v. Hetherington, 1840, 232, 241, 242, 249n16, 249n25, 250n52, 250n55

R v. Lemon, 1978, 1979, 230, 234, 244, 248n4–248n7, 248n10, 249n28, 251n58, 266–267, 276n22, 277n29

R v. Moxon, 1840, 249n25

R v. Ramsey and Foote, 1883, xxxixn8, 234, 241, 249n24, 250n53, 277n28

R v. Taylor, 1676, 231, 249n13, 249n14

R v. Williams, 1798, 231, 233–234, 249n15, 249n23

R v. Woolston, 1729, 231, 249n15

R (Begum) v. Denbigh High School, 2004, 2005, 2006, 157, 171n12, 181, 200n8, 200n16

R (Ghai) v. Newcastle City Council, 2009, 2010, 147n16, 157, 171n14, 181, 200n12, 228n35

R (Playfoot) (A Minor) v. Governing Body of Millais School, 2007, 157, 171n13, 181, 200n8, 200n14, 211, 226n18

R (Watkins-Singh) v. The Governing Body of Aberdare Girls' High School, 2008, 172n25

R (Williamson) v. Secretary of State for Education and Employment, 2005, 138, 147n13, 147n14, 200n14, 211, 214–215, 220, 226n17, 227n26, 227n29, 227n33

Saggers v. British Railways Board, 1977, 1978, 128n26, 208–209, 226n2–226n4, 228n37

Seide v. Gillette Industries Ltd, 1980, 147n15, 172n25

Sherbert v. Verner, 1963, xxvii, xxxviiin5, 184–185, 192, 200n19–201n24

Singh v. British Rail Engineering Ltd, 1986, 127n16

Syndicat Northcrest v. Amselem, 2004, 209–211, 226n5–226n15, 227n22

TWA v. Hardison, 1977, 126n6

United States v. Seeger, 1965, xxxviiin2

Welsh v. United States, 1970, xxxviiin2

Index of Statutes and International Instruments

Abortion Act 1967, 177

Blasphemy Act 1697, 229

Criminal Justice Act 1988, 155, 171n6, 171n8, 196
Criminal Law Act 1967, 229

Education Act 1944, 110
Employment Act 1989, 155, 171n5, 171n9, 177, 200n5
Employment Equality (Religion or Belief) Regulations 2003, xxxixn6, 146n2, 146n4, 172n25, 177
Equality Act 2006, xxxixn6, 172n25, 177
Equality Act 2010, xxvii, xxxixn6, 130, 141, 143, 146n2, 146n3, 146n4, 147n16, 148n20, 158, 160, 165, 168, 169, 177, 191, 200n3, 222, 223, 224, 228n38, 228n39
European Charter for Regional or Minority Languages (1992), 80n40
European Convention on Human Rights (1950), xvii, xxvi, 68, 80n23, 200n2; Article 9, xvii, 63, 138, 144, 157–158, 166, 167, 177, 181, 182, 211, 214, 227n26, 266
European Framework Convention for the Protection of National Minorities

(1995), 60–61, 65, 68–70, 80n24, 80n36
EU: Council Directive 2000/78/EC, xxvii, xxxixn6, 146n1, 177

Fair Employment and Treatments (Northern Ireland) Order 1998, 146n7
Fair Employment (Northern Ireland) Act 1976, xxxixn6, 132, 146n7
Freedom Restoration Act (US) 1993, 185

Human Fertilisation and Embryology Act 1990, 177
Human Rights Act 1998, 147n12

Industrial Relations Act 1971, 208

Motor-Cycle Crash Helmets (Religious Exemption) Act 1976, 124, 155, 171n4, 177, 200n4

Race Relations Act 1976, 126n6, 172n25, 201n31
Religious Land Use and Institutionalized Persons Act (US) 2000, 185–186
Road Traffic Act 1988, 155, 171n4, 177, 200n4

UN Beijing Declaration and Platform for Action, Fourth World Conference on Women: Action for Equality, Development and Peace (1995), 81n46

UN Convention on the Rights of the Child (1989), 73

UN Declaration on the Rights of Indigenous Peoples (2007), 57–58, 60, 65, 66–67, 76, 77

UN Declaration on the Rights of Persons Belonging to National or Ethnic, Religious, and Linguistic Minorities (1992), 60–61, 65, 68–70, 80n35, 80n38

UN International Covenant on Civil and Political Rights (1966), xvi, xxii, 63, 66, 68, 69, 71, 79n18, 80n23, 80n32, 80n33, 81n45

UN International Covenant on Economic, Social and Cultural Rights (1966), xvi, 66, 71, 80n33, 81n45

UN Universal Declaration of Human Rights (1948), xvi, 63, 68, 71, 72–73, 80n32, 80n33, 81n45

UN Vienna Declaration and Programme of Action (1993), 71

Welfare of Animals (Slaughter and Killing) Regulations 1995, 155, 171n7

www.ingramcontent.com/pod-product-compliance
Lightning Source LLC
Chambersburg PA
CBHW021849020426
42334CB00013B/247